BLACK NATIONALISM IN THE NEW WORLD

D1521978

*A book in the series*

*Latin America Otherwise: Languages, Empires, Nations*

*Series editors:*

*Walter D. Mignolo, Duke University*

*Irene Silverblatt, Duke University*

*Sonia Saldívar-Hull,*

*University of California at Los Angeles*

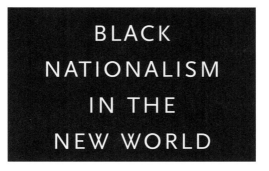

# BLACK NATIONALISM IN THE NEW WORLD

Reading the African-American and West Indian Experience

## Robert Carr

Duke University Press    Durham and London 2002

Printed in the United States of America on acid-free paper ∞

Typeset in Scala by Keystone Typetting, Inc.

Library of Congress Cataloging-in-Publication Data

appear on the last printed page of this book.

Chapter 4 originally appeared in *Callaloo* 18:1 (winter 1995).

Portions of chapter 6 originally appeared in *Scattered Hegemonies:*
*Postmodernity and Transnational Feminist Practices*
(University of Minnesota Press, 1994); and
*Dispositio/n* 19:46 (1994).

Robert Carr's *Black Nationalism in the New World: Reading the African-American and West Indian Experience* adds a new dimension to the goals we established for the *Latin America Otherwise* series. First, our emphasis on languages, nations, and empires is fully realized in this study. Second, the narrative and the argument of the study evolve around the gray zone of the *Anglo* Caribbean with respect to *Latin* America. Third, the book underlines the fact that the Caribbean is a *connected unit*, not because each island repeats itself but because of the region's colonial history of slavery and the crucial African components in the New World. Finally, Caribbean history, in spite of the variety of colonial languages spoken in the islands, is part of the history of the Americas, that is, the colonial history of the New World and of the Atlantic commercial circuits established during the Spanish and Portuguese empires in the sixteenth century and the Dutch, French, and British empires in the seventeenth century.

Carr's book is exemplary of the goals of the series in other respects as well. He recovers the notion of the New World, which, although of the same colonial origin as the term Americas, has the advantage of reminding us of the colonial history that the term America, with its hegemonic connotation, has erased. Carr gives a new dimension to the concept of subalternity by linking, on the one hand, the history of colonial India to the colonial history of slavery in the Caribbean and in the United States, and on the other, by showing that colonial subalternity, as it has been defined by the South Asian Subaltern Studies collective, always has a "color." In this volume, Carr has shown the color of subalternity by showing the inextricable links between subalternity and coloniality. Moreover, he teaches us how to read literature in tandem with political economy and with colonialism, and, last but not least, he has brought the New World back again into the global imaginary.

*for those who insist on loving in the face of hardship*

*for Ileana, who always leads*

*for Peter and for June*

*for all those in danger of being thrown away*

*So injustices may not be perceived as injustices,*

*even by those who suffer them,*

*until somebody invents a previously unplayed role.*

*Only if somebody has a dream,*

*and a voice to describe that dream,*

*does what looked like nature begin to look like culture,*

*what looked like fate begin to look like a moral abomination.*

RICHARD RORTY

*We have been beaten for a hundred years,*

*but I tell you, girl, we have courage for a thousand.*

SIMONE SCHWARTZ-BART

# CONTENTS

# ACKNOWLEDGMENTS

As has become a truism in many projects of this kind, this study would never have been written without the help of many people. First, I need to thank my *compañera,* Ileana Rodríguez, who listened to me wrestle with the issues of this book before anything was written and then continued to listen all the way to its completion. Thanks are also due to Gordon Rohlehr and the late Martin Carter for taking time out of their very busy schedules to discuss the conditional issues of this project. Rudy and Carol Collins also graciously invited me into their home under sensitive circumstances to talk with me about the history of Guyana's transition to Independence. Throughout the writing of this study, Brian Carr and the late Dr. Thomas Carr also gave me the benefit of their insights into Trinidadian society and politics, and Dean Innerarity helped keep me abreast of developments in Jamaica. This project would not have been the same without these conversations.

Special thanks are also due to June and Peter Carr, who lived many of the experiences described in the three chapters exploring issues in the West Indies and who gave me the benefit of their insights into what it was like to live through such critical transitions. Thanks also to Susan Lanser, Carla Peterson, Sangeeta Ray, Lynn Bolles, the late Rhonda Williams, and Sharon Groves who read, commented on, and helped to shape the manuscript, and to Melvin Lewis who brought his own political negotiations to bear in reading my critique of the Black Panthers. Thanks are due, too, to my students Nitin Govil, Jane Williams, Mark Williams, and Crystal Philcox whose work in a graduate seminar on the postcolonial condition also contributed to the final shape of the ideas presented in this book.

An earlier draft of chapter 4 appeared in *Callaloo* 18.1 (1995): 133–56, and short portions of chapter 6 appeared in *Dispositio/n* 19.46 (1996): 127–45, and in *Scattered Hegemonies: Postmodernism and Transnational Feminisms*, ed. Inderpal Grewal and Caren Kaplan (Minneapolis: University of Minnesota Press, 1994). I am grateful for permission to include this work here.

Special thanks are due as well to Lee Hartman, Richard Macksey, John Howard, and Ralph Heyndels for their kindness and mentoring that opened new worlds and laid the foundations on which a project such as this could be built.

I would also like to thank the team at Duke University Press for their expertise and commitment in bringing this book into print. I am especially thankful to Reynolds Smith for his commitment to this project and his dedication to seeing it in print.

Thanks, in the end, to a community of committed scholars for slugging along with me through the issues and the stylistics of critical analyses conducted as an act of conscience and love, rather than of war, which unfortunately is still the paradigm under which we are taught to speak to each other.

# INTRODUCTION

How you come to think of where you are, and how you come to think of your relation to where you are: this is very dependent on the character and the location of power as it exists where you are. You yourself do not, at a certain stage, decide who you are, and what your relationship to where you are should be. A certain prevailing power determines that.—George Lamming

In fall 1986 I began teaching a course on Caribbean literature in the English Department at the University of Maryland. For the most part, the Caribbean was barely known to these students anxious for a new kind of literary experience, but they drank in the region's history, politics, and economics, and in doing so thought about this other world in terms of their own possibilities and their own lives. For each of them, the question of difference—in ethnic heritage, in personal history, in family history, and beyond to national history—gained a new complexity.

The African-American students in the class came into the experience with a feeling already of connectedness. Their reading took on the same joy of recognition and the same sensibility that emerges in African-American studies, but with a certain cautiousness and, to varying degrees, an anger toward sharing the experience with their Anglo-American classmates. Pressed, they would lose sight of the difference between African-American issues and the problems of Caribbean life, opting for a protonationalist response of solidarity that had less to do with the Caribbean than with African-American relationships to Anglo-America. In the heat of the moment, race and nation would supersede geography. And, true to the nationalist impulse, the African-American students always sat together.

The Anglo-American students reacted very differently toward each other, with varying senses of problems within their own culture, but they tended, as well, to want to understand from a distance their black class-mates' reactions. At the same time, it was clear that their prior concep-tions of the Caribbean—beautiful beaches, smiling black women, land-scapes seen in soaring camera angles—were under a severe, if desired, transition. They struggled to understand some of the issues at stake in the international division of labor and the Caribbean predicament: for example, the exportation of low-paying jobs to export processing zones that forbid unionization; the struggle to transform economies developed over five hundred years for export of raw materials and profits to benefit Europe and the United States that also disregard the development of a self-sufficient local economy; and the growing debt burdens faced by such countries as they try to balance their needs with their budgets. Most, however, could never allow themselves to think too deeply about the personal and macropolitical issues that divided them from their black counterparts; that is, the difference race makes in the United States. Knowing beforehand that they were to read a foreign black literature, most had suspended their resistance to discussing institutional preju-dices and issues of race and class, a resistance that dominates much of the U.S. debate.

The Caribbean students watched this drama unfold around them with varying degrees of comprehension. For them, it was a return to their own culture and history, which they had never experienced in a classroom. Suddenly the expressions they exchanged among their Caribbean friends were embedded in stories of cultures, writing their lived experiences of another world. The people, places, and experiences of that other world, intimately perceived for them, were being discussed by students from the United States through the lens of U.S. social norms and the tradi-tions of liberalism or conservatism the American students had gleaned from their parents and from political debates endemic to superpower surroundings. Most of the time the Caribbean students were silent, and communication between them as Caribbean folks was felt at the level of significant smiles and looks of mutual recognition. For traversing and marking the frontiers of understanding among all of us were the differ-ences of worlds and the locations of our developed or developing economies in the international division of labor, the differences of the nature of the social pacts we felt with our home countries, and the differences in the choices we were making about our personal lives and what it meant for us to be living in the United States.

This project began in thinking about some of the issues that are at stake in this triangle of African-Americans, West Indians, and Anglo-Americans and about the struggles for civil rights and decolonization, as well as the transnationalization of Caribbean culture, that brought all of us together in that classroom. Although African-America and the West Indies are the main focus of this study, the position of Anglo-Americans as the ethnic group holding power in the United States makes their presence—political, social, economic—inextricable to the power dynamics of both groups. For among the differences separating the Anglo-American students from the African-Americans and the West Indians was the fact of global political representation; that is, the fact that the United States demands world hegemony in Anglo-America's name.

As this small example suggests, to undertake a study of African-American and West Indian nationalist texts is thus to unpack worlds differentiated in politics, ethnicity, economics, history, and positions in relation to government. Not surprisingly, the analyses of instances in the literary African-American and West Indian nationalist traditions presented in this book cross disciplinary boundaries. Each of the seven chapters that follow takes a different and deliberately innovative approach to the task of cultural critique, to studies of nationalism and nationalist thought, and to methods for undertaking cultural studies and interdisciplinary work to uncover what is possible to ask of national texts and what the connections are between literature and other disciplines in the humanities and the social sciences (history, economic history, development economics, government and politics, and so on). In the cases of both African-America and the West Indies the experiences of these pressures, splintered into disparate disciplines, combine to constitute a collective experience, and this is what creates the nationalist impulse in these two groups. The studies in this volume look at new strategies of textual analysis that suggest, more broadly, new kinds of combinations for cultural studies interventions as well as analyses of the concepts of nations, nationalism, governance, and citizenship in African-American and West Indian studies.

This task necessarily invokes the questions of natural communities and created (or imagined) communities. For the communities I discuss, "nationalism" means a deep, critical perspective on the core issues pertaining to the daily lives of the groups involved. As Ralph Premdas writes of the strongly related concept of ethnicity, "group membership is not a theory to the ordinary person, but a practical map that defines the environment with built-in expectations and rules for survival" (*Ethnic Conflict* 2). In the seven chapters that follow, then, I ask certain questions of this nationalist impulse: how it works to construct the world, how it shapes cross-cultural and intranational exchange and perception, and how it determines the spectrum of human interrelationships.

In the analyses that follow I address the interplay of seven concepts: the state, gender, citizenship, the "New Man," the "New Woman," nation, and the ideological effects of the international division of labor. Each of the works studied here takes up contemporary political debates in various ways. As a rule, I have read the work of each author for what its highly charged scenarios and statements subtend, realizing that the author's intentions can only be gleaned in terms of what their openly political scenarios enable, diverge from, and overlap with. Given, in each tradition, a desire to address issues of political transformation, it is this address and the acumen behind it that orders each writer's projected conceptual universe, and thus the projected national plots.

Revealingly, most of the major, ambitious, and most esteemed theoretical literature on nationalism entirely ignores the experiences of the two Caribbean groups studied here, with Latin America receiving the lion's share of the small space allotted to the developing countries of the New World.[1] And while the English-speaking Caribbean only rarely appears on these analysts' world maps, African-American nationalism is dismissed to the point of invisibility. When Caribbean or African-American nationalisms are mentioned at all in the dominant literature, they are represented as mininationalisms that are dubious and cannot compare to the more serious and interesting issues at stake in nationalism in Western or Eastern Europe or the United States. Western Europe and the Middle East dominate the liberal debate, supplemented by a growing body of analyses of what used to be the Eastern bloc in the wake of nationalist splintering and the accompanying atrocities. As the new global paradigms emerged in the 1990s, as a result of the strategic alliance between Israel and the United States and in anticipation of the battles of the new world order after the collapse of the Soviet Union, focus shifted to the politics of a radius centered on Israel and the Middle East. This has become even stronger in the wake of the suicide bombing of the World Trade Center and the Pentagon on September 11, 2001. As such, within the field of studies of nationalism, African-American and West Indian nationalisms recede from the brink of recognition.

The standard literature on nationalism can be organized around three cultural-political situations: liberal, marxist, and postmodernist. The first group is by far the most hegemonic. Relying on the authority of John Locke, these writers assume the appropriateness of a social contract that can only be provided by the power of the laissez-faire state. Nationalism becomes variations on the protean capitalist nation creating a state as its supreme representation and in its own image. Marxism is international. As an organizational concept, class solidarity supercedes nations and workers replace citizens. Plotting class, nations, and nationalism, Europe is again the model, even in the sophisticated work of historians like E. P. Thompson and Eric Hobsbawm.

Postmodern postcolonialism sees the concept of "nation" as a hoax—a lesson learned perhaps too well from the marxists. Rather than replace the citizen with the worker, the postmodernists replace the citizens with the "margin" in the "centers" of the developed metropolises, with hybridity and fluid identities of denationalized subjectivities. Paul Gilroy's advocacy of *The Black Atlantic* "as one single, complex unit of analysis . . . to produce an explicitly transnational and intercultural perspective" falls within the purview of this group (15). Critiquing Homi Bhabha—postcolonial postmodernism's celebrated critic in the contemporary macrotheoretical debate—both Abdul JanMohammed and Henry Louis Gates Jr. point out that Bhabha's project empties history of it dead bodies. Gates is correct in that Bhabha's (and postcolonial postmodernism's) project is ultimately a psychoanalytical one, because subject identity formation takes center stage and so colonialism is a psychological agenda. Moving to the left of the debate among postcolonial commentators, for marxist-inspired postcolonial critics like Partha Chatterjee in his *Nationalist Thought and the Colonial World* nationalism is inexorably an Enlightenment discourse produced by the liberal-rationalist state.[2] Here Benedict Anderson's *Imagined Communities,* a seminal moment in the elaboration of the postmodernist school, is rescued from Bhabha's cultural semiotic play in that it poses, for the diehards, "the ideological creation of the nation as a central problem in the study of national movements" (Chatterjee, *Nationalist Thought* 21). This formulation of "nation" and "national" is also central to the analyses in this volume.

My work differs from traditional macroanalytical ventures in that, following an argument touched on by Wahneema Lubiano, I consider black New World "nationalism" to be a tradition of "registered opposition to the historical and on-going [prejudice] of the . . . state and its various institutions and apparatuses . . . deployed to articulate strategies of resistance" (5). As Premdas, Balibar, and Wallerstein point out, such racism has become endemic to nation-states around the globe as we forge into the twenty-first century.[3] New World black nationalism thus emerges from and circulates in direct opposition to the racism of existing states. By emphasizing counter-macrological sentiment, then, this volume necessarily stands in direct opposition to the Euro-centered macrotheoretical literature discussed above. Differing from Lubiano, however, my argument is that Eric Hobsbawm's recent study *Nations and Nationalisms since 1780* consolidates a useful and suggestive model.[4]

Acknowledging the seminal work of Miroslav Hroch, Hobsbawm begins with the tenet that "nationalism" per se is a cultural invention of a bourgeois elite, and that in this small circle lies its first moment; that it becomes protonationalism when it finds pioneers and militant advocates, its second moment; and that it only becomes full-blown nationalism once the state has been founded and made it its business to foster an ahistorical but ideologically useful allegiance to the state and a lying, ahistorical relationship to a "national" history among the people; its third moment, a history promoted by the primary and secondary public educational system and elsewhere. In his insights on the role of the belief systems and agendas of the "national" elite, Hobsbawm's arguments share tenets with African-American and Caribbean nationalist traditions. His is a model with which New World black nationalisms can productively enter into a dialectic. (I come back to this in the course of the analyses that follow.) Still, there is a critical reservation: almost all of Hobsbawm's historical material comes from the traditional Western European bloc, and the levels and points of African-American and Caribbean convergence with his paradigms remain a point of debate. Following Chatterjee, but with a difference, I use the agenda of liberal state representation as critical to defining "nationalism" in a way that distinguishes it from other collective social movements (politicized evangelism, Jeffersonian agrarianism, tribalism, and so on), although to define nationalism as not these social movements does not mean the two don't appear together.

Within both the celebrated and decried literature it has become a notorious truism that the concepts of "nation" and "nationalism" are exceedingly difficult to define. These epistemological and ontological problems stem mostly from the fact that many groups rising up and declaring their battle to free their "nation" almost never pause to define the term, and that when each group eventually does, its claim to a national identity may be based on a range of terms, logics, and events.[5] From the perspective of the critic, "nation" and "national" become catch-all terms for defining an "us" whose difference from "them" is chaotically described. From the perspective of people mobilized by the call of "the nation" to win a place for themselves in the world community of "nations," to genuinely not know what the "nation" is in the midst of the struggle is to define oneself as the paradigmatic outsider, against representation and empowerment. "Nation" and "nationalism" here are thus inextricably phenomena—that is, processes—and the macrotheoretical literature of nationalism is thus a series of attempts, from differing ideological perspectives, to make sense of the diverse historical records left in speeches, in writings, and above all in the dead bodies that nationalist struggles inevitably leave in their wake every day.

Like Lubiano and Hobsbawm, I find two basic points critical to analyzing "nation" and "nationalism." First, I believe that the historical materialist approach has the strongest explanatory power in addressing the diverse material describing, even as it constitutes, the phenomenon of "nation" and nationalism. Although marxism carries its own tyrannical ideological baggage, to my mind it remains the most revealing inroad into the arguments *against* chronic structural oppression, and *for* representation and dignity, that provide the backdrop against which the nationalist impulse arises in African-America and the West Indies. Second, my discussions of nationalism are framed in dialogue with those who call themselves nationalists, or who have since been called nationalists by those who call themselves nationalists, or who begin thinking from the center of nationalist debates to further the interests of a nationally defined group; that is, a community defined by its peculiar historical experience. For example, Wilson Harris, known for his postnational sentiments, is concerned in *The Guyana Quartet* and elsewhere in his work with what it means to be Guyanese in Guyana. Thus if common denominators gleaned from analysts of the European experience include a separate language, print culture, a history peculiar to the sociopolitical group, and so on, these criteria are not necessarily met in the New

World experience, as Benedict Anderson reminds us. Language, he points out as an example, was not a structuring difference at the root of the "American" Revolution of 1776; print culture, I would point out, has not structured the pervasive sense of difference—in state and dominant-community sanctioned oppression, a common history and common cultural traits—that binds the African-American community together. In fact, the written literature analyzed in the following pages finds the liberal/marxist nationalist impulse a generative ally and an interlocutor, but, against Anderson's and Hobsbawm's arguments, the written literature does not here create "nationalism" as a monster written for (oppressed/black) people to reckon with.

This refutes, then, the conceptualizations of "nation" and "nationalism" that dominate Homi Bhabha's *Nation and Narration* where the nation is a narrative imposed on the population.[6] In the West Indian and African-American traditions, nationalism begins as an impulse moving definitionally from the bottom of the social scale to the top. In the black New World experience the question posed by the "nation" is not whether or not black people in the different territories constitute distinct groups of people sharing the required traits.[7] This becomes a prime example of the question that, within the context of a quotidian racism and an imperialist disregard for those still suffering from the onslaught of colonialism, has served to exile African-Americans and West Indians from the macro-national debate over "nationalism" for as long as the term "nation" carries constructive political weight. This is done by developing criteria from the Western experience under rapid industrialization and expecting developing and transitional communities to comply. It remains as true in the United States and the Caribbean today as it was under British colonialism that the state is the carrier of a "dominant cultural core" whose existence "as an exclusive unit of loyalty is challenged" in a redefinition of the state itself through the demands of "ethno-national" populations and, we might add, of women, a phenomenon circling the globe (Premdas, "Public Policy" 1, 3). The more pressing question is whether the representatives of these nations who emerge as representatives in fact represent the "people"—or "black folks," as poor and angry African-Americans and West Indians refer to their oppressed social body—or whether they merely represent themselves and consolidate their elite status on the backs of the threat of grassroots violence.

The power and heft of black nationalist thought ought not to be underestimated. As Lubiano remarks, black nationalism's clout comes from its ability to retrieve a past shattered by violence; its ability to hail, in the Gramscian sense, an otherwise disarticulated politicized group sensibility, the call to new nations. As an unavoidable popular force, black nationalism "functions as a historical and political genealogy," "an articulation," "an aesthetic," "a utopian . . . rallying cry," and a "critical analysis" (Lubiano 2). The new black subject so created stands poised in the lag between the objective and subjective conditions for the constitution of the black community, as what Lubiano calls "blacks as a *political* class" (12)—"racial solidarity across class lines" (8)—a precondition for "a black Left intellectual practice" (8).

This book begins in the mid-nineteenth century with African-American Martin R. Delany's militant revolutionary novel *Blake; or The Huts of America* (1859–62), which was serialized as Civil War broke out in the Union. The second chapter offers a reading of African-American Pauline Hopkins's fin de siècle *Contending Forces: A Romance Illustrative of Negro Life North and South* (1899), written in urgent response to the catastrophic rise in lynching, to black American political disarray, and to the withdrawal of the federal troops that had stood between a bitter, white politicized sector and a struggling black economic base. Chapter 3 begins the exploration of West Indian nationalism with Ralph de Boissière's *Crown Jewel* (1952), a social realist novel about the historic riots in colonial Trinidad that eventually forced the legal and bureaucratic recognition of workers' rights throughout the West Indies. The fourth chapter analyzes West Indian author Wilson Harris's *The Secret Ladder* (1963), a novel about Guyana on the eve of transition from colony to "co-operative socialist" nation-state in the 1960s; a transition, Harris argues prophetically, that contained the seeds of chaos and the reproduction of authoritarian repression within it.

Chapter 5 moves back to African-America to look at the testimonials, interviews, and essays of three of the most charismatic members of the Black Panthers—Huey Newton, Bobby Seale, and Eldridge Cleaver—as representatives of radical black leftists who dramatically helped to change the face of global racial politics in the late 1960s and the 1970s. I focus, in particular, on Huey Newton's testimonial *Revolutionary Suicide* (1973), Bobby Seale's extraordinary political autobiography *Seize the Time: The Story of the Black Panther Party and Huey P. Newton* (1970), and Eldridge Cleaver's collection of autobiographical political essays *Soul on Ice* (1968).

Chapter 6 returns to the Caribbean to read the Sistren Collective's *Lion-heart Gal: Life Stories of Jamaican Women* (1986) against the backdrop of 1970s Jamaica.

As a women's empowerment organization, Sistren has also come to represent a transition in both the political and women rights' movements in the region. The policies of Prime Minister Michael Manley's two terms in office (1972–76 and 1976–80) have gone down in history as a significant political experiment in a Caribbean transition from capitalism to socialism and will form a critical interlocutor in my reading of *Lionheart Gal*. For this reason my reading is intended as a dialogue between Manley's and Sistren's analyses and evaluations of the national predicament on the basis of a series of common agendas: the institutionalization of democracy and social justice as a critical developmental target and the incorporation of women into developmental paradigms. In looking to our own era, I examine three recent (post?)nationalist texts—Cornel West's *Race Matters* and gay novelist Julian's *Just Being Guys Together* from African-America; and Ileana Rodríguez's *Women, Guerrillas, and Love: Understanding War in Central America* from the Caribbean—in light of the issues raised by the historical studies and novels given above, and especially in light of our ongoing transitions under globalization.

It is immediately noticeable that I have not chosen the canonical authors from either tradition—for example, Frederick Douglass or Harriet Jacobs, Richard Wright or Ralph Ellison, C. L. R. James, George Lamming, Samuel Selvon, or Roger Mais. In thinking about how to cut across temporal and spatial differences, it seemed to me to be more revealing of the nationalist consciousnesses to engage with thought-provoking texts that have not been analyzed to the point of familiarity and near canonization. I have taken, then, a stance in favor of openly strategic readings of texts offering deep structural critiques of New World societies. Such texts revisited as we enter a new geopolitical and geocultural era, I argue, yield different perspectives from the ones embedded in utero in the two tradition's respective canons. In fact, most of the texts studied here have only recently felt the stirrings of interest they deserve.

From the perspective of the macrological theories of (white) nationalism, as the relatively moderate writer Wilson Jeremiah Moses points out in his *The Golden Age of Black Nationalism,* in one respect black nationalism begins in the liberal European paradigm because it starts as a counterreaction to European domination and vilification, thus embedding itself in the conceptual structures of the West. This, of course, is a deconstruction of pre–new world order black nationalism's constitution of itself on the basis of difference. To find Europe at the root of the black nationalist response asserts national concepts of mulatto culture and the hybridity of black New World culture rather than separateness and distinctiveness, an assertion that complicates much contemporary thinking. This notion is at the heart of Paul Gilroy's agenda in *The Black Atlantic*, from the left of the political spectrum, which is seen as a corrective to the studied myopia that has created, for example, "the purified appeal of either Africentrism or the Eurocentrisms it struggles to answer" (190).

As the following studies of nationalism reveal, there is much validity to Gilroy's perspective. In this sense, Martin R. Delany's strategy is to insert another race into the central Subject of the nation-state as it was constituted in the mid-nineteenth century, complete with the patriarchal imperialism that was part and parcel of the century generally accepted as the heyday of European nationalism, a century that closed, revealingly given Delany's insights, with the invasion and partitioning of Africa. Similarly, Pauline Hopkins looks for strategies of representation and national integration—citizenship—through the U.S. state structure. Following suit, we could say that the Black Panther Party, as the grassroots U.S. political movement studied here, begins with a rethinking of epistemes that begins in white fixations on blacks and obsessive relationships with the black penis; with who has access to black and white women's vaginas; and with guns in racialist hands as critical symbols of (an always inevitably phallic) power. And on the other side of the international division of labor, granted control of the state in the 1960s, we could argue that West Indian nationalism becomes the tool of the elite that Hobsbawm claims for it, although there is always the fact that national control of the state reasserts the nagging question of mass representation; that is, government representation of the community monitored somewhat through an open-ended voting process. F. S. J. Ledgister makes the argument that it is the mutually dependent coalition of a middle-class elite with a politicized mass base that gives Caribbean nationalist movements their character, and the same can be said for African-Americans as contemporary judgments of the past and present heroes of the African-American pantheon show. The bond between the leadership and the people in the name of political and cultural representation thus becomes central to New World black nationalist debates.

Behind this issue of representation and definitions of "nation" and "nationalism" lies the concept of the state. If the definition of the "nation" can be nebulous, the concept of the state most certainly is not, especially in regard to New World black nationalisms. Simply put, the state can be defined as the bureaucracy subtending a set of social relations, whose form and purpose are defined and controlled by those whose interests it serves, reserving the right to open and public coercion for itself. For Premdas, as for nationalists, it is the state as bearer of a dominant cultural core that is at the root of "ethno-national" and "migrant-minority" conflict around the globe in the fallout of empire; for Caribbean nationalist and other struggles it is also the classed control over the state that is the center of conflict; for feminist women and men, it is additionally gender biased. In all cases, however, the state is a body that enforces its right to police the community, organizing, as a result, the process of arbitration or lack of arbitration between itself and the social body and within the social body in the interests of those it serves.

As political geographer Roy Mellor describes it, the "state is a sovereign legal entity, internationally recognized, whose responsibility is to organize and guarantee the welfare and security of its citizens within its territory, where it is the supreme authority, tolerating no competitor or challenge to its sovereignty and demanding obedience from the inhabitants" (32). The state, then, defines itself through its network of social relationships but backs up its authority with the threat of force: armed troops with whom it maintains a series of special judicial relationships. Granting itself forces armed with weapons of destruction (from local police to national guards to full-blown international armies, given sufficient capital), states have also come to claim for themselves the power to discipline, to punish, to kill as it deems fit anyone or any group within or extending beyond the confines of its territory through extradition treaties or military invasions.[8] Within Mellor's definition, it is the state that determines what is "legal," and it is what the state "internationally recognizes" that defines "authority," "security," and so on throughout the definition's key terms, but allegedly in the name of the citizenry from whom it "tolerat[es] no competitor or challenge to its sovereignty and demand[s] obedience" in the name of representation and its allegiance to "the nation." Because democracy is at stake, in both traditions studied here this allegiance is proven tenuous.

The role of masculinism and masculine virtues has become a central topic in analyses of such allegiances. "Nation-states," writes Hilary Beckles in reference to the Caribbean, "as hegemonic civic enterprises, functioned [at the moment of Independence] essentially as 'boys only clubs'—the odd woman was admitted but on terms set out by her brethren" ("Historicising Slavery" 49). At the same time, many feminist critics who have tackled the intersections of gender and nation have discovered a central function that the concept of "woman"—and from there women and the feminine/feminization[9]—is made to play in nation building and the national cause. For Jean Franco, woman represents nation; for Ileana Rodríguez and Doris Sommer the family house represents nation; for Rodríguez, *de*nationalization is further gendered, as the loss of the state is metaphorized as men's loss of their "balls," or as Samir Amin has it, weakened states in the periphery occupying the "fag end" of the world system (73).

Under the masculinization of nationalism and state confrontation or state-building, the national project, in which the nation's men rule, extends into the domestic sphere and the performance of gender, into proper hierarchies within the household as much as the national struggle and state formation and representation. For Catherine MacKinnon, a patriarchy of the dominant cultural core of the state is built into the U.S. Constitution and jurisprudence. Endine Barriteau argues from the Caribbean that "the philosophical contradictions of [the Enlightenment discourses of] liberal ideologies predispose [West Indian postcolonial] states to institute unjust gender systems" and that "colonialism and Western expansion were themselves part of the Enlightenment project of Modernity" (186). Emmanuel Eze's collection of the writings of Enlightenment philosophers on race, from von Linné to Hegel, bears her out on the question of race and expansion. As feminist critics throughout the New World have pointed out repeatedly, these projects of race, gender, nation, and territory converge and are reproduced in both liberal and radical nationalist movements.[10] In Rodríguez's example of Venezuelan President Romulo Gallegos's *Doña Bárbara*, a text that circulated in 1930s Trinidad, the independent woman landowner, Doña Bárbara, must be contained, just as the forest/jungle and the peons on the territory must be contained and disciplined (in the Foucauldian sense). The linking of a series of key concerns and tropes (woman, jungle, people, chaos) all in the name of male-dominated development becomes an issue in the chapters at the center of this volume. In each of these cases, the nation is phallocratic and order is signaled by transparency, just as chaos is signaled by opacity and disobedience.

The massive black presence in the Americas starts with slavery, and it is there that the crises of black inclusion in national representation—crises of black citizenship—begin.[11] New World black history thus develops in a state-sanctioned and irreversible violence, in Africans forcibly transported and sold as captive labor and incorporated into the bottom of social structures of European design. Initially the narratives justifying such administrative policy were religious, at a historical moment in which European political economic agendas were generally justified in religious terms. Thus slavery was good for Africans because it exposed them to a culture and civilization that would Christianize them, saving their souls from eternal damnation in the fires of hell. With the decline in the authority of religious narratives and the rise of science, slavery was defined on the basis of a genetic racial inferiority, doing away with the discursive dangers of acknowledging black humanity at some level, a danger at the heart of the narrative of white nations saving black souls. In the case of either "religion" or "science"—and these narratives summarize some four hundred years of history—the power of the Crown and then the modern state was invested in the maintenance of this physically, psychologically, and from there culturally violent exclusion.[12]

If African-American and West Indian black nationalism start as mass movements, differing from Hobsbawm's paradigm, it is because the states and federal government of the United States in the cases of African-Americans and West Indians, as well as England in the case of the latter, make it clear that they have reserved a special pocket of brutality and dehumanization for peoples of color in the New World, that they cannot be of the people/nation represented. Rather, in the West's elite national political imaginaries, people of color are deliberately constituted as potential threats to those whom surviving states represent. This alienation by and from states is constitutive of the shared history of black citizenship, of blackness as a sociopolitical category in the New World. For both African-Americans and West Indians, on the horizon behind sits the desolate specter of slavery and underdevelopment; on the horizon ahead sits the promise of a nation-state: security, economic development, protection—that is, somehow national representation and citizenship.

Despite these kinds of clear historical points of connection, instances of dialogue or comparison between African-American and West Indian sociopolitical and economic traditions are only slightly less rare than their inclusion in the West/East-dominated macrotheoretical literature. Most of this comparative work has been done in the social sciences, and then it typically documents the alienation of West Indians from the African-Americans and vice versa.[13] In fictional and social scientific writings, and in popular culture as well, there are all the examples of West Indians accusing African-Americans of laziness, of self-defeatism, of an annoying and disruptive anger. Similarly, African-Americans denounce West Indian arrogance, their capitulation to the cultural norms of white American culture, their selling out anything remotely akin to a community interest for the sake of their own petit bourgeois aspirations. In its simplest formulation, a study wanting to shift the terms of what connects and disconnects the two groups could begin with a story of nineteenth-century collaboration, crescendo with an elegy for Marcus Garvey, and then end with a joint celebration of the mid-twentieth-century Black Power movements in the West Indies and African-America that shook the place of blacks in New World politics.

By foregrounding the distinctive relationships between the state, gender, the New Man, the New Woman, the nation, the citizen, and the difference made by the international division of labor this study takes a very different route from such a study. I differ from Gilroy's project of offering a black Atlantic paradigm that encompasses thinkers of the African diaspora. Before we can begin to talk about our commonalities we first have to understand the nature of our differences, differences that have everything to do with the locations of power—worlded, gendered, sexed, classed, and so on.

By offering an interweaving of textual readings I hope to provide a basis for understanding who we say we are in our literature through the lens of history and politics, reading the world into the texts. The differences are clearly established in my first two chapters on nineteenth-century African-American nationalism and in chapters 3 and 4 on West Indian nationalism. In chapters 5 and 6 I tackle a common issue: the integration of socialist insights on class struggle and the history of antiracist work on the colonization of black culture and black minds toward a collective liberation. The Black Panther Party is thus part of an implicit black New World dialogue whose promise of internal democracy is superceded, to my mind, by the work of Sistren. Gilroy's call finds an interlocutor in my assertion of the need for understanding the differences between blacks in the diaspora in order to pave the way for real dialogue. This also explains why Gilroy's choices of W. E. B. Du Bois and Richard Wright as the two anchors for his argument—with apologies for barely mentioning C. L. R.

James and Franz Fanon—could not hold here. In Gilroy's dialogue with Eurocentric and Afrocentric proponents of the ties that bind them, the differences of the diaspora can only barely be grappled with, or only through the lens of African-America. This exemplifies what I believe is a critical determinant for Gilroy's project: the place of national thinking in the new world order. For it is globalization that pushes us toward larger and larger territorializations both in terms of resources (the African diaspora, European modernity) and markets ("all those interested in cultural studies, in African-American studies, in popular culture, in the African diaspora in the New World and in Britain, and in debates about modernity and postmodernity; and the explorations of gender that . . . engage with central questions in current feminist theorizing" as Anthony Appiah puts it in advertising Gilroy's book). At the same time, the slippage between "African-American studies" and "the African diaspora" or "the Black Atlantic" is a telling one, for it suggests that the experiences of the over-developed countries continue to take preeminence in reterritorialization projects, thus overriding the realities of the international division of labor.

As a backdrop to my discussion, the present study attempts to put the knowledge technology of the West Indian and African-American traditions into dialogue, interwoven with some lessons gleaned from Latin American studies.[14] "Knowledge technologies"—the tools (epistemes, paradigms, ontologies) that allow the production and reproduction of knowledges—explicitly become part of the critique of the status quo in both traditions. The critical divergences from Eurocentric macrotheoretical models, divergences we reencounter in reading black nationalist literature from the United States and the West Indies, is one way of invoking the problem for both African-Americans and West Indians of knowledge technology and knowledge production, a dilemma that recurs throughout the history of the two traditions. It has been argued that literature becomes the frontier of such a project.[15] At the macrological level, and in the beginning, the inter/intranational division of labor and the question of group income, technology, and resources into which knowledges and strategies for development are embedded become frontiers of the debate for both groups. In addressing questions of gender, class, sexuality, and relationships to power within the national body, looking back from the perspective of the beginning of the twenty-first century, the issues that recur in the Latin American traditions of cultural criticism, as much as those of the West Indies and African-America, form primary interlocutors. Thus the much-debated concepts of mulatto culture and hybridity, of the inter/intraethnic politics permeating personal life, the lessons of collective cultural thinking, and the persistence of a historical violence personalized in and through the body are integral to these analyses.

Using one marginalized culture's terms and concepts to analyze another's is not, however, without its difficulties. The concepts of "mulatto" and "mulatto culture," concepts central to Latin American studies, are everywhere in circulation in my analyses of the African-American texts, for example. The pervasive rejection of "mulatto" as inevitably degrading by black Americans is nevertheless an important political/cultural point that carries over into the more elite ruminations of African-American academics. In Hortense Spillers's words, the concept of the "mulatto" as it has been used in the racial struggles of the United States "designates a disguise, covers up, in the century of Emancipation and beyond, the social and political reality of the dreaded African presence" ("Notes" 166). Nevertheless, one of the arguments that runs throughout the studies that follow, in profound agreement with Wilson Jeremiah Moses's and Gilroy's arguments, is the inextricable influence of white sociopolitical realities on the worldviews of blacks in the Americas. I incorporate the terms "mulatto" and "mulatto culture" in recognition of this, and in recognition of the tradition of useful work already extant in Latin American cultural criticism. To incorporate these concepts into my analyses is thus to push at the warp and woof of the very identities posited and reflected by the literature analyzed. This is in part a response to the attempts by these texts to look deeply into the problems and resources of the African-American and West Indian communities, and in part to engage the meanings of the terms of blackness. I want to experiment in utilizing applicable knowledge technology across New World (black) national borders as an experiment in advancing the debate on culture and politics. The concepts of "mulatto," "mulatta," and "mulatto culture" are thus used in my analyses of African-American issues in response to the socially conscious revisionary mandate that is at the heart of the two traditions, and not in response to white desires to see themselves always and everywhere reflected as progenitors. Unlike Gilroy, I want to engage with syncretism as both a biological and a cultural process. The democratic impulse behind the First World gay, lesbian, and feminist movements are similary omnipresent in my analyses of the Caribbean.

Because I have chosen three responses to perilous transitional moments from the history of nationalist literature in the two traditions, my study is also one of flux, of radical revisions. Each of my readings is itself an experiment in reading the social text, toward what Anna Deavere Smith calls "an open conversation" (272), delineating strategies at key historical crossroads for reading our own and each other's history.[16] These analyses are connected not as a historical overview but as snapshots of national strategizing and self-interrogation at moments of crisis and transition in which the world is turned upside down, and these thinkers are grasping to put their insights and their strategies into language. Each chapter in this book takes its methodological cue from the interdisciplinary issues raised by the texts, always in a dialectic with our current concerns. In this sense, the narrative formed here of each tradition is a narrative of the need for order in the face of chaos, of the imperative to action and renewal in the face of overwhelming odds. At the same time, the narratives analyzed here are also narratives of a growing history of political learning, of a profound understanding of all that is at stake and that needs to be resaid. In this light, each of the texts studied represents an attempt at a radical break from the earlier national tradition, a willful disconnect for the sake of rescuing the social body from the quagmire of its history that constitutes the writer's national tradition. This project is thus part of that ongoing tradition, although it takes up the drive toward a common agenda across the national borders adopted by these traditions. These studies turn, too, on the lessons learned in the record of the 1960s from the West Indian recognition of the role of African-American enfranchisement in shifting U.S. foreign and domestic policy, as much as from African-American interest in what new knowledges and technologies of knowledge could be and are produced in the many black-majority social laboratories of the West Indies.[17]

Each of the essays in this volume marks a dialectical relationship to history and the lenses that produce it, and in conceiving the project I have written with a view to a network of interconnections between chapters. Chapter 1, on Delany's conceptualization of a black nation-state, and chapter 6, on Sistren and the struggle to rethink the social pact between Jamaica's government and Jamaica's impoverished majority, employ political economic history in particular as the text against which the literature might be read. In the first case, the study of mid-nineteenth-century political economics is the base on which Delany analyzes the position of blacks in the New World and plots his construction of a black nation-state. In my reading I have brought his underlying logic to the surface and read it back into U.S. political economic history, in search of, among other things, Delany's implicit concept of "white nationalism" and therefore black political exile. Chapter 6 follows this road but in the opposite direction. The women of Sistren are overwhelmingly from the underclass, but it is the quotidian problems of political economics that structure their life stories. Thus if Delany moved from the macrological heights of political economics to the daily events of black lives, Sistren moves from testimonial to political economics to government and the (dis)function of the social pact.

In chapter 2 on Pauline Hopkins's woman-centered nationalist romance and chapter 4 on Wilson Harris's novel of the jungle I confront logical vortexes. Here, at pivotal moments, the nationalist paradigms inherited from each author's tradition (patriarchal capitalism for Hopkins and multicultural marxist anticolonialism for Harris) are turned inside out. Both of these chapters examine attempts to remap the world from new paradigms of social health. Interestingly, the central terms of "woman" in Hopkins and "jungle" in Harris (two tropes signifying chaos in the imperial, masculinist European tradition) meet; crossing borders, Hopkins's narrative begins in a West Indies marked by multilayered transitions from jungle to garden for her own purposes, and Harris writes woman as exiled for his. Also, both of these novels occupy contested and contestory spaces in the traditions of nationalist literature. Although they are and have consistently been met with applause by nationalist critics, Hopkins's focus on the mulatta and Harris's on the inadequacy and folly of monocultural nationalism have raised questions as to the appropriateness of their inclusion here.[18] In fact, as I will argue in the chapters devoted to them, they operate from within a central paradigm of nation, but are concerned to question its logical and "realpolitical" parameters. Hopkins will question the central organizing concept of racial purity and the relegation of women, hence the mulatta; Harris will question the limits of inclusion in the nation and the difference of the protosocialist postcolonial nation from the colonial regime, and hence representation of marginalized peoples, including women. They both, then, function squarely within their respective nationalist traditions—these novels' powerful insights are copula to those traditions—even as they work to turn the nationalist paradigms inside out for the benefit of progress and national development, African-American and Guyanese respectively.

Chapter 3, on the birth of Trinidad as a nation through the vehicle of the 1937 riots, and chapter 5, on the Black Panthers' "revolutionary" epistemology of U.S. social relations and the black nation in particular, grapple with narratives of revolutionary organizations that take to the streets. For each the social body is trapped in the midst of a brutal regime that targets them because of race as an epistemological crisis, and each finds that collective bargaining leading to a redistribution of wealth and a radical restructuring of political representation is the only way out. Both argue that nation formation is inextricably tied to a marxist-inspired transformation of the community into an army, and in both cases it is only a shortage of weapons that is seen to stand in the way of revolution and seizing control of the state.

To read these studies in this way, of course, is to read against history as an unfolding event, although in fact the novels that form the focus of the chapters are organized in historical succession for each group. As a narrative of two histories, each has its own path to follow. The work of Martin R. Delany, as "the father of black nationalism," marks an official beginning for most of the post–1960s generation of African-Americanists studying nineteenth-century nationalism. Most historical studies of black nationalism published in the United States take the 1960s ideology of Black Power as a defining framework, reading this framework back into history.[19] Seen through the militant lens of black revolutionary fervor, inspired by the guerrilla and anticolonial writings of Latin America and the Caribbean, the difference of the nineteenth-century conceptual universe has exiled much of black nineteenth-century strategy. Moses's *The Golden Age of Black Nationalism, The Wings of Ethiopia*, and his introductory essay to *Classical Black Nationalism*, as well as Gilroy's *The Black Atlantic* and Wahneema Lubiano's work, are among the notable exceptions, and I have benefited tremendously from their eloquent and complex arguments.

The second half of the nineteenth century is considered the "women's era" by nineteenth-century specialists in black feminism. Among the group of activist black women, as Hazel Carby has amply demonstrated, Pauline Hopkins stands out as one of the most radical voices, one anchored in a highly politicized diasporan conception of the black community. As with Carby, the work of Carla Peterson and Hortense Spillers has sought to explore issues revolving around nineteenth-century political black women's dialectics and the problems of culture and empowerment. Caribbean feminist Ileana Rodríguez's study of Caribbean women's novels of national transition raises similar issues in relation to the transitions in state policy toward the Caribbean and Latin American multiethnic social bodies and the national territories. The works of these four critics provide starting points for the explorations undertaken in chapter 2, as well as in the rest of the book.

Predictably from the economic history of West Indian underdevelopment that determines its political history, the literary narratives of black nationalism (as opposed to Pan-African sentiments) start, to my mind, not with the nineteenth century—when West Indian nationalism blossomed and withered as white nationalism—but with a group of local writers who published a literary political magazine in 1930s Trinidad.[20] From the handful of novels produced by writers in this group, I have chosen de Boissière's history/story of the riots of 1937. Unlike the novels produced by other members of the group, de Boissière's *Crown Jewel* was not published until the 1950s when the real political move toward Independence was reflected in what has come to be called the West Indian Literary Boom. The literary process of nation formation in the West Indies, as eminent West Indian critics like Reinhard Sander have noted, is revealing for its attempts to grapple with the problems of political representation in multiethnic societies. De Boissière's novel, called Trinidad's "most important political novel . . . [and] the fundamental work of fiction in [Trinidadian] society" (Sealy 3), stands out for its depiction of the islands as home to the descendants of many immigrant groups: Africans, Indians, Chinese, Syrians, as well as a diverse smattering of Europeans. It is against the rule of this last group that the creole de Boissière exemplifies Trinidadian nationalism as a coalition of mass and intellectual movements among people of color.

From another conceptual horizon—after Gandhi, World War II, Castro's revolution, and the emergence of the mid-century Civil Rights movement in the United States—West Indian literature of the 1960s comes to question the certainties of the region's traditions. Writers from Trinidad and Guyana in particular come to the table to ask about the realities of West Indian national cultures and the politics of each of the elements now finding themselves constituted collectively as a new nation on the eve of Independence: the leadership elite, the black men who now stand a chance for upward mobility in the national bureaucracy, the aspiring Indian agro-industrialists, the workers who suddenly are promised a country, and the exiles—women and agrarian black and indigenous peoples. Wilson Harris's epic *The Guyana Quartet* traverses

Guyanese history and geography with a keen eye to the socialist promises of the political parties standing in the wings. Guyana is remarkable in the English-speaking Caribbean not only for its jungle terrain but for the fact that there Independence and self-rule were always inextricably tied to some form of explicitly institutionalized socialism, for both the impoverished masses and the emerging political elite. Politician and pioneering West Indian critic Kenneth Ramchand is my interlocutor for a political reading of Harris's novel.[21]

In the shift from literature to testimonial in chapter 5 we move from the fictional universe toward the "real," for Black Panther writing moves from fiction to testimonial as a political act and as an act of remembrance and historiography. If the bibliography on the other authors studied here is brief, the work done on the Panthers is exhaustive. To some extent, I have noted the sense of regret in Michelle Wallace's 1990 introduction to *Black Macho and the Myth of the Superwoman*. Her critique of her book as naively misguided, extending to a certain desire to withdraw it from circulation, has led me to try to retrace her critical journey, but with the benefit of the growing body of work on the FBI's "Counter Intelligence" Program and the work by African-American women and gay men on African-American women and gay men as people, as citizens, and as conceptual categories.

Ten years after Independence was achieved in Jamaica, the social subject at the center of nationalist Caribbean narratives began to shift. Women from impoverished communities came to speak their own stories as testimonials, and so the women who permeate the configurations of West Indian nationalism in the 1930s and 1960s horizons found a mediated voice in the 1970s. The Sistren Collective represents a turning point in West Indian conceptualizations of nation: as sistren they change the debate over the nature of the men cast as heroes who populate the center of the literature of the 1960s generation, narratives in which, as Rhonda Cobham has pointed out, poor women like themselves hover at the margins. Although I have read against the grain of what we can call Harris's inability to see women as women, his *Quartet* is typical in that women are almost inevitably adjuncts. At best they cope with marginalization, at worst they are stick figures and metaphors for abstract macro-concepts—time, history, nature, emotion, truth; in short, they act as mirrors for the men posited at the center of the national plot to resolve their own confusions. Because, as Cobham also points out, women are predominantly the metonym of the nation in the narratives of the 1930s, Sistren's *Lionheart Gal* represents coming full circle. The participation of women in nation formation and institution building was erased in writing the overall West Indian transition to political power, in both the fictional and the social scientific literature that came to constitute the official national history and culture.[22] But in the climate of Jamaica's 1970s socialist transition, through the vehicle of a collective testimonial, the impoverished women who persevered just off center in the national literary landscape have their own priorities and their own stories to tell.

In the 1990s we began to confront a growing crisis of transition from multinationalism to globalism. Burgeoning new paradigms of relations began to transform the roles of governments, people, and industry, and even threaten the role of the nation-state as the primary form of geopolitical organization. These issues are still our current dilemmas and are the ultimate backdrop that underwrites this book, and the arguments expressed here are as much a product of their historical moment as the novels, testimonials, and essays I analyze. In closing this volume, I intertwine my concluding remarks with an interweaving of supplementary texts documenting the emerging global paradigms: Ileana Rodríguez's *Understanding War in Central America*, Julian's *Just Being Guys Together*, and Cornel West's *Race Matters*. Read through the lens of the strategies and witness of the texts that precede them, West's political essays, Julian's fictional black gay utopia, and Rodríguez's literary criticism represent three texts grappling with global transitions from within the remnants of national horizons.

In the tradition of the politically committed African-American and Caribbean writers who precede them, each of these three writers works to find new prospects for democratic change as the concepts of nation and nationalism increasingly, if unevenly, come to signify chaos, backwardness, barbarianism, and the antithesis of the progress and development for which nationalism was once an indispensable vehicle. Problems and crises of managing ethnic governance dominate our time. As we enter the twenty-first century, in challenging the nation-state we find the rising hegemony of the World Trade Organization and the corporate state, home to globalized and globalizing postnational "corporate families" of multiethnic, multiracial "corporate citizens." Gathering increasing power and strength, they loom on the horizon with the overhauling and restructuring of the routes for centralizing value in the new global metropolises. These transitions also mean the restructuring of geopoliti-cal patterns of power and intervention, patterns from which the majority of African-American and Caribbean peoples have been excluded. With the nation-state as the cushion between big business interests and the people in decline, danger now lies in finding ourselves in what seems like political economic limbo, a danger we confronted, in fact, at the beginning of both the African-American and West Indian traditions as I have constituted them here. Rodríguez's book opens with despair in the face of the mounting toll of dead bodies at the bottom of the world's oceans, in the cities, in the increasingly abandoned nonindustrialized zones. The lessons of history often prove instrumental, however. So, to begin. . . .

# 1

## F(o)unding Black Capital:
## Money, Power, Culture, and Revolution
## in Martin R. Delany's *Blake;*
## or *The Huts of America*

■

Geography, teaches a knowledge of the world, and Political Economy, a knowledge of the wealth of nations. . . . These are not abstruse sciences, or learning not
easily acquired or understood; but simply, common School primer learning, that
every schoolboy may get. And, although it is the very Key to prosperity and
success in common life, but few know anything about it.—Martin R. Delany

Often described in radical histories written in the wake of the Civil
Rights movement as the father of U.S. black nationalism, if not U.S. Pan-
Africanism, Martin R. Delany, born a free man of color to a free mother
and an enslaved father, lectured throughout the United States, addressing the ways and means for the social, political, and economic empowerment of black Americans (Painter 150; Ulman ix; Miller, *Search* 272;
Moses, *Golden* 149). Through his leadership in National Conventions on
Emigration in 1854, 1856, and 1858, Delany's impassioned arguments
for black liberation through emigration to Africa or the Caribbean became sufficiently important to garner him national prominence among
the Northern black abolitionists and the Anglo-American ruling elite. In
the rising heat of the debate on slave labor in the South, Delany presented a national plan for emigration that was the logical outcome of his
political economic analyses of the United States and his unrelenting
commitment to black enfranchisement. Frederick Douglass remarked of
him, "I always thank God for making me a man simply, but Delany
always thanks Him for making him a black man" (qtd. in Quarles n.p.).
    During the 1830s, Delany advocated "moral suasion" as a solution to

the atrocities against U.S. blacks that had gone on for centuries since the founding state charters. Along with William Whipper, Lewis Woodson (Delany's mentor), William Lloyd Garrison, and Benjamin Lundy, Delany argued that "hard work, thrift and temperance" on the part of African-Americans was the solution to racial problems in the United States (Adeleke, "Race" 23). As Tunde Adeleke points out, implicit in the strategy of moral suasion "was the assumption that situational deficiency (i.e. condition), not racial intolerance (racism), was the more critical reason blacks were disadvantaged" (23). In the late 1840s, however, with the rise in attacks on black businesses, the lack of recourse in the legal system, and the passing of the Fugitive Slave Law of 1850, Delany became convinced that emigration was the only means to the ends of black political representation. African-Americans were trapped in a national agenda in which they were—explicitly again in the 1857 Dred Scott Decision—excluded from the rights of citizenship and superdisenfranchised by birth, by culture, and by blood even as the terms of U.S. citizenship were being more and more defined.

Like many other African-American emigrationists, Delany's relation to the federal state changed dramatically with the upheavals of the election of Abraham Lincoln and the secession of South Carolina from the Union (Ullman 247). With the advent of the Civil War, Delany found new hope for a "unity of interests" between black and white peoples in the United States, leading him to propose a black division led by black officers to fight alongside Union forces. After four years of persistent application, President Lincoln and Secretary of War Stanton finally endorsed the plan and Delany became a major, the first black field officer in the Union. In support of his military aspirations, Lincoln described him to Secretary Stanton as a "most extraordinary and intelligent black man" (qtd. in Quarles n.p.).

During Reconstruction, Delany played a prominent role in southern politics, becoming increasingly alienated from freedmen and freeborn alike and retreating into what Nell Painter calls an "apolitical, elitist, Southernizing/New South position [attractive] to many respectable blacks in the [postwar] South" (168).[1] At the end of his life he turned again to the emigrationist mandates of his youth, in support of Liberia. In the history of the antebellum struggle, however, Delany was tireless in his efforts to theorize the liberation and empowerment of blacks in the New World. With enormous energy and determination to fashion and promote a black nationalist agenda, Delany produced a treatise in 1852 titled *The Condition, Elevation, and Destiny of the Colored People of the United States;* helped to organize national conventions, which he also attended; and scouted Africa for territory and Europe for capital in 1859. On his tours of England and the United States, he sought to prove to those prepared to listen that the United States of America had declared war on black Americans politically, economically, and morally. For Delany the only end to this war was the creation of a modern black diasporan nation-state that could compete within an industrializing world. Black labor had built the southern U.S. economy,[2] and Delany argued that this same labor could bring black revolution on a global scale by establishing a homeland.

In his only novel, *Blake; or The Huts of America,* written during the 1850s and serialized between 1859 and 1862 in the *Anglo-African Magazine* and the *Weekly Anglo-African,* Delany presents us with his blueprint for black revolution in the United States and the Caribbean basin. His tour through the South to gather the information for his plan was a dangerous undertaking and could have quietly cost him his freedom or his life (Moses, *Wings* 48). As it stands, *Blake* is a testament to the scope of his vision; the work of writing his blueprint forced him to textualize the myriad relationships between the political and economic situation of blacks internationally, the means by which a plan for international black revolution could be achieved, and the nature of the new black man who could bring this about. Delany's novel is most often heralded for its creation of the hero to save the nation and for its "affirmation of the intercultural and transnational" (Gilroy 29). As Painter points out, Delany's reputation as the father of black nationalism in the United States has rested on eliding the split in class interests that became so apparent in Delany's postbellum political activity (149).[3] Eric Sundquist in his 1993 *To Wake the Nations* sees *Blake* as a paradigm of revolutionary insight, with both Delany and his title character as the heroic representation of the people. In Sundquist's analysis, Delany emerges as a champion of democracy, outstripping his more famous antebellum peers through his political and aesthetic representation of black Americans and the democratic ideal. Sterling Stuckey argues that in Delany's hands the culture of Africa gains a new level of acceptance in nineteenth-century black nationalism and that he in fact "broke with the view of African barbarism in modern history by arguing for the existence of

luminous aspects of Africanity from which Americans were already benefiting" (*Slave Culture* 229). "The names of his children, ideally," Stuckey
writes, "reflected a progression beyond ethnicity and reinforced a sense
of oneness in their consciousness and in the consciousness of those
blacks who called their names" (226). Gilroy makes the same point (29).

In fact, glimmers of the split in class interests Painter identifies are
apparent even in Delaney's antebellum work.[4] What emerges coterminously with his black nationalism is the tangled issue of ethnicity in
nation formation, an issue that bears directly on the question of class
interest in black national representation. Grappling with this issue will
take us further into the problems inherent in forging a new national
culture; that is, the problem of the role of a national culture in serving the
political interests of the men and women designated slaves or freedmen
and freedwomen, versus the political interests of the black petit bourgeoisie. For at the heart of Delany's strategies there is a split in the
conceptualization of the role of ethnicity in culture, a split that points
directly to the problem in Delany's work: that is, that the role of ethnicity
underscored by class in black culture leads to a rift between the people
and the leadership.[5]

In much of the northern black leadership's perception of the slaves we
confront the problem of industrial versus agrarian identities, as well as
the implications of this problem for political representation of the black
majority by the black national leadership. It is here we confront the split
in class interests (to use modernism's terminology) played out through
debates on ethnicity and barbarian culture. "For all the strength of the
Pan-African environment of the day," Stuckey writes, "so effective was
anti-African propaganda—so convinced were educated blacks that there
was nothing of value in the ceremonies and customs of the mass of
slaves in America—that consciousness of African cultural formation
was no advantage to one seeking a leadership role outside the slave community" (*Slave Culture* 145). Modernism in black antebellum America
comes to signify the internalization of industrialization and the personal
and political projects of European Enlightenment as norms. "Agrarianism" comes to signify, in the instance of slave culture, an agriculturally
based, subsistence-oriented economy and the internalization of magi-
cal/mystical/religious epistemologies and ontologies that circulate outside the paradigms of Reason.

The difference from European thought in slave culture, a culture that I refer to here as "agrarian," is a profound one. As Stuckey writes, folktales, songs, the ring shout, the cross, baptism, and many other aspects commonly recognized as constituting slave culture are in fact infused with complex transformations of African cultural norms into new terms and new processes. White Americans—and, as Stuckey argues, free black Americans—could not recognize this deep cultural mesh without a process of acculturation. Here, then, class divisions and ethnic divergences intersect at the level of culture in dramatic ways that divide the black nation. As Stuckey goes on to argue, the secrecy surrounding the African holdovers at the heart of slave culture was great:

> The division between the sacred and the secular, so prominent a feature of modern Western culture, did not exist in black Africa in the years of the slave trade, before Christianity made real inroads on the continent. . . . This quality of African religion, its uniting of seeming opposites, was perhaps the principal reason it was considered savage by whites. It was the source of creative genius in the slave community and a main reason that whites and free blacks thought the slaves lacked a meaningful spiritual life. . . . But the possibility that whites might discover the guiding principles of African culture kept blacks on guard and led them, to an astonishing degree, to keep the essentials of their culture from view. (*Slave Culture* 24)[6]

"Modernity" is thus antithetical to black slave culture, the culture of the antebellum black majority. It is here that class and ethnicity converge. The problem is that the trajectory of escape from slavery is through economic self-sufficiency and political representation—that is, development—and is therefore ineluctably modern.

"Modernism" comes to signify the reconceptualization and reorganization of society, labor, and the self. Throughout Delany's writings the notion of nation formation appears as a modern phenomenon, and its terms are states, capital, industry, labor. The new terms of this transformation have already been set by the rise of industrialization and the political takeover by the bourgeoisie of Europe. If nationalism is seen as a mass movement prior to state formation and territorial consolidation—what Hobsbawm, Stuckey, and Moses call "protonationalism"—then questions of whom the (proto)national/political leadership represents become critical for determining both the viability and future of black nationalist movements in the United States. Such a split occurs over a fracture in antebellum politics in which the slave is being represented—spoken for politically.

Given the plantocracy's strategic use of visible aspects of slave culture to develop and refine its modes of oppression and destabilization of the slave community for economic and psychological ends, the fact of this political-*cum*-cultural need to keep one's culture hidden from the view of outsiders leads to two crucial points. First, slaves are structurally linked to the concept of the "subaltern"; that is, those who are strategically unrepresented culturally and politically.[7] Second, it is this combination of secrecy as resistance that comes to constitute the positive aspects of "slave culture" in the minds of the relative elite.[8] At the same time this relative elite holds the opposite argument, namely that slave culture is debased and barbarian. As Moses suggests, this debate is an expression of how black culture can be read through the lens of white culture or, better, how white culture as the only paradigm of logic knows black cultures, which entangles the interrelationships between ethnic groups. For the black intelligentsia to approach slave culture from the side of the comparative elite—those who can write, those who have never been enslaved—is indicative of their critical remove from slave culture, at least in part.[9] These degrees of integration into the dominant ideologies in turn have their effects on cultural identity and conceptualizations of power, of norms of behavior and self-perception.

This difference from the culture of the black intelligentsia is due in large part to the acknowledged persistence of Africanisms in slave culture, of African cultural norms clashing with the antebellum black leadership's agenda of integration into international capitalism.[10] Southern slaves keeping the secrets of their culture is the other side of the northern black leadership's accusations of slave ignorance. Thus slave culture comes to signify black oppositional culture of the oppressed masses and tells of "other suppressed narratives and perspectives" (Pandey 224). Behind this silence is a political struggle over both national culture and the place of Africanness within it.

In the next section of this chapter, I examine Delany's complex rendering of the position of blacks in the New World political economy, given the mid-nineteenth century alignment of nation-states. This rendering lays bare the networks of power, ethnicity, and money regulating the policies of the U.S. elite. At the same time, however, it is important to acknowledge that without the support of a moneyed elite there can be no nation building. From there, in the second section, I raise issues of culture, subalternity, and modernity in nation formation in order to examine the questions of who forms the nation, the constitution of national leadership, and the social pact promised by this national leadership. The concept of class enters the text of the novel through the back door and will be coded through the terms of "intelligence" versus "ignorance," terms bearing the weight of the debates over modernism versus barbarism to which Stuckey alludes. In closing my analysis, I look to Delany's political speeches, reports, and tracts to discern the nature of power and citizenship in his postulated nation-state through the problem of territory as the culmination of his political theory, his hope for a new state reuniting the black diaspora.

### White Power, Political Cadres, and the Dynamics of (Inter)national Administration: The Constitution of the Nation-State

In teasing out the assumptions and dynamics of Delany's racialized political economy, we can begin by grappling with the intersections of race, capital, and geography that Delany embeds in *Blake*'s opening scenarios. Reading closely his first installments (particularly "The Project") within a series of historical contexts, we can recover Delany's understandings of the position of blacks in the complex relationships between industrial and industrializing states.

*Blake* is divided into two parts. The first part introduces the novel's heroic main character, Henry Blake, details the practices of slavery and slave culture in the United States, and describes the hero's work to set the stage for a massive slave revolution that would cover the entire slaveholding South, including the successful escape of several generations of enslaved African-Americans. Part 1 ends with Henry's journey to Cuba. In part 2 Delany extends the plot for black revolution to Cuba. But in order to understand the nature of Henry's heroism and his relationship to the oppressed he is constructed to represent, we need to examine the conditions under which such a hero becomes necessary and from which such a hero emerges. This is the main topic of *Blake*'s first six installments. In these installments we find the forces and paradigms Delany conceives the black nation to be up against, his political-economic analyses of blacks in the United States, his insight on how power works at the level of everyday life, and his illustration of the alliances between the various sectors of the social order that constitute the realities of nations represented by nation-states.

### National cadres of the New World elite

*Blake* begins with six businessmen meeting to discuss the outfitting of the ship the *Merchantman* and the decision to use Baltimore's facilities. Four of the men—Colonel Franks, Major Armstead, Captain Paul, and Captain Royer—are from the United States, while the other two—Captain Garcia and Captain Castello—represent the interests of the Cuban colonial elite. Carefully orchestrating the possibilities and implications of decision making and power brokering among these wealthy investors, and setting them in a dialectical relationship to *Blake*'s opening installment's enigmatic title ("The Project"), Delany outlines a black theory of the political economy of the antebellum United States. Through the assumptions and dynamics of the decision to come to Baltimore, Delany textualizes the quotidian mechanics of the U.S. nation-state operating in an international economic order. Inextricably, in Delany's political-economic analyses of the United States, the logic of the relationship between the state and the nation it defines for itself excludes the possibility of black enfranchisement.

At the outset, the economic order of "the project" is seen in international terms, crossing national borders in the pursuit of profits and national capital accumulation. For the U.S. investors, Baltimore offers the "greatest facilities" and deserves their financial support for its superior "encouragement and protection of the trade" (3), specifying the concrete mechanics of an alliance between political and economic investments. As a liberal racialist wind blows through Washington, D.C. (the advocacy of abolition through "moral suasion" and sentimental and pathetic descriptions of black Americans exemplified by the runaway success of *Uncle Tom's Cabin*), the investor's diversion of capital to Baltimore thus serves the double purpose of ensuring Baltimorean political support for their venture, while economically rewarding and strengthening an ally.

For the Cuban investors, Havana presents itself as an investment in the future because the U.S. political climate had been marked by "the continual increase of liberal principles in the various [U.S.] political parties" (3). In view of the long-term health of their industry, Captain Garcia and Captain Castello argue, Havana's mercantile outfitting businesses warrant their support. Its location in the Spanish colonial backwater makes it a safe haven from such liberal principles as may threaten the onslaught of litigation against them within the United States. At the same time, increased economic ties, deepened by the diversion of U.S. capital to Havana merchants, would encourage Cuban political support for the interests and allies of U.S. investors among the Cuban nationalist factions vying to chart the island's changing relationship to Spain.[11]

The fact that the trade is in black men and women, and that the commodity is their bodies as labor power, immediately underscores the position of blacks in the U.S. and Cuban political economies. The New Economic historians are not alone in reminding us that "many leaders of the independence movement in the Thirteen Colonies were slave-owning agrarian magnates" (Anderson, *Imagined* 75). In Delany's first installment, black Americans have been reduced epistemologically to beasts turned units of captive labor power, and because they are a commodity on whose sale and abuse national capital accumulation is premised in both the United States and Cuba, it stands to reason that, definitionally, they cannot be of the nations to be enriched. To reconceptualize blacks as "Americans" is thus to confront directly a national frontier, a border codified by law, stemming from a religious-*cum*-scientific declaration of difference (Christian versus heathens; moderns versus barbarians; men versus apes) as a critical "us" versus "them" of internal ethnonationalism and nation formation in the United States and Cuba. Hobsbawm argues that in its early stages, except for skin color, modern nationalism avoids the question of ethnicity explicitly, in which case the tendency is to stratify the polity horizontally more so than vertically, according to lighter and darker skins (66). From the perspective of peoples of color, this stratification is as critical as it is unavoidable. In Delany's opening moments, this white (trans)nationalist stratification is built into New World political economies.

The threat of "liberal principles" invoked by the Cuban interests, then, refers us to a range of areas within the U.S. social text. On the one hand, there is the strategy of romantic racialism. Embodied in sentimental abolitionist tactics, it is social pressures stemming from emotional appeals directed at the white population on behalf of enslaved blacks that creates the possibility of shifts in political representation, and thus legislative status.[12] In Delany's writings, these social pressures register in their economic ramifications: they threaten the business interests of sections of the merchant class by attacking a key industry in continued national economic expansions. At the same time, there were various factors implicated in the growing and diversifying abolitionist sentiment. The shifting position of slave labor and the southern plantation lobby in the increasingly industrialized global economy; Emancipation in the English, Dutch, French, and Portuguese New World; black revolution in Haiti; continuous slave revolts in the southern United States; the black press; and the booming northern market for the horrifying narratives of escaped slaves and repentant slave traders were all gaining increased circulation.[13] In combination, these diverse strands inevitably made an impact in the spaces they opened up in the U.S. national consciousness for a successful abolitionist movement. The social text within which *Blake*'s six gentlemen make their economic decision is thus constructed in terms of an interweaving of politics, the law, moral principle, economics, the differential between federal legislation and state cooperation, infighting over national agendas, and the international flows of capital.

The superior economic position of the United States in relation to Cuba is reflected in the decision to outfit the *Merchantman* in Baltimore, a decision helped on the one hand by the presence of the ship in Baltimore, and on the other by the fact that four of the investors are nationals of the powerful United States while only two operate from Cuba. Thus if their discussion involves international financial and social concerns, then the questions of nationalism and colonial center-periphery relations in the Caribbean basin prove inextricable. Lurking behind the debate over the most suitable port is the enrichment of one national economy over another, the primitive accumulation of capital. Given the anticipated role of the United States in the move to change Spain's imperial relations with Cuba (U.S. President Pierce tried to purchase it for $130 million in 1854), it seems inevitable that the superior political economic strength of the U.S. interests wins out over the interests of the Cubans (Dolan and Scariano 29).

At the inauguration of his book, then, Delany exposes the relationships between different cadres of men managing national projects. Garcia and Castello are clearly merchant seamen in the international naval trade, a trade crucial to the industrializing economies of Cuba, the United States, and Spain. The presence of Colonel Franks and Major

Armstead, however, signals a suture in the legal narrative of the official relationships between the merchant class and the U.S. military, pointing to the emergence of the military-industrial complex. According to the U.S. Constitution as it stood in 1804, the military was a federally controlled body whose role was to protect the United States from foreign threats and invasions, open foreign markets, and quell internal upheavals that threatened the social order.[14] However, Delany argues, on the micrological level of everyday life there are socioeconomic and therefore political bonds between the colonel and the major as representatives of the federal armed forces, and the merchant captains of slavery, U.S. and Cuban. Colonel Franks also invests heavily in agro-industry and administers a portfolio of plantations himself. It is a function of this relationship between the military, the managers of agro-industry, and the merchant elite that gave rise to the serious discussions among the southern planter class of incorporating the increasingly prosperous and developing preabolition Cuba into the Union as a strategic move in the debate on slavery and relegalizing the slave trade.[15] In his first installment, then, Delany unveils political economic complicities among the New World merchant class—already transnational "national" bourgeoisies—and the military, complicities thus obscured in the official rhetoric of the Constitution.

### The politics of the law

In the very next installment, Colonel Franks receives a message from a guardian of the law, one Judge Ballard, assuring him that despite the increase in pressures from northern "liberal principles," he will stand by the colonel and the weakening planter lobby, as much as by his own interests. Ballard has just been part of a landmark decision anticipating the Supreme Court's Dred Scott[16] in the attempt to secure federal and military fidelity to the interests of the South, and thus of the national economy, in a manner friendly to the colonel, himself, and his fellow investors. The judge, "so far as an individual might be concerned" we are told, has economic investments not only in the South but in Cuba as well, placing him "beyond suspicion" as a fighter in the national cause (5). The personal interests of the elite horizontally stratifying the polity on the question of ethnicity thus guide the national agenda. For captains Royer, Garcia, Paul, and Castello, together with Colonel Franks and Major Armstead as well as Judge Ballard, their network of connections to capital, the army, and the law will yield, they hope, control over the policies guiding the ship of state, in this case the debate over slavery and decriminalizing the slave trade. Such rewritings of the apparent absorption of the merchant class in "self-interest," "industry," and the "democracy" of a "free market" open up the U.S. social text in order to examine the workings of money, race, and power. Value and international capital accumulation in governance are secured through a complex of socio-economic networks of power. These networks, Delany suggests, ensure that the interests of the agro-industrial magnates remain paramount—hence the invocation and dismissal of the presidential election in the first installment of the book—and it is these networks that constitute the United States as a nation-state and the place of black Americans in it.

### Constituting the Constitution

Historically, the Constitution stands out as the document in which the United States laid down its tenets, charted its agenda, and established its national identity. For the largest investors in the U.S. economy—that is, the new national elites whose later incarnation Delany depicts—the territorial abundance of land and raw materials combined with expanding U.S. industries and a growing population promised untold amounts of potential wealth to be claimed and regulated. Yet political economic relations were highly unstable: the settler economy was running amok with local political and fiscal independence, and with this independence, control over future profits. Many settlers had fought in the 1776 Revolution to dissolve centralized government. The newly independent political and economic elite were now confronted with a series of dilemmas in the new freedoms. There was ever-increasing public debt and fluctuating income from the federation;[17] near-insurmountable difficulties in making centralized foreign policy and therefore regulating the federation's lucrative place in the international economy;[18] an unstable, rapidly depreciating money system; uprisings of the indebted and disenfranchised; and, to the horror of the elite, events such as Rhode Island's adoption of utopian socialism. In the face of such mounting chaos the framers of the Constitution convened in closed sessions in Philadelphia. For these men whose interests were played out in the national and international economic order—via banking and trade laws, manufacturing and shipping interests, real estate speculation in the West and plantations in the South—a strong centralized authority that could monitor the economy of the new nation and direct the growth of capital was essential. Hence the Constitution.

In her essay "The Liberal State," feminist legal scholar Catherine MacKinnon points out that the Constitution's language as a supralegal document, in providing the keys to the new federal government's jurisprudence and its relation to society, contains within its apparent openness the exclusion of all but a few as subjects of law. In the language protecting "free speech" from federal infringement, for example, is the preconditional assumption of the prior existence of "free speech" as a macropolitical concept. Women (particularly women who would later be called lesbians), slaves, Native Americans, men who would now be considered openly gay, Chicanos, and unpropertied Americans, among others, had no such preexisting right.[19] Constitutional amendments would have to be ratified, litigation would have to ensue, a civil war fought, revolts and riots ignited, and people imprisoned and killed before the right of a collective majority living on the territory and under its governmental rule to speech as a macropolitical concept (expressed, for example, not only as the right to vote but more importantly to be elected) could be written into law. Even in the antebellum North where blacks were sometimes allowed to vote, Delany argues, the structural exclusion of African-Americans was built into the constitution of the state. Thus, according to Judge Ballard, man of the law and agro-industrial magnate, slaves "stand in the same relation [to the law] as [northern] Negroes. In some states they are permitted to vote, but can't be voted for, and this leaves them without any political rights at all. Suffrage sir, is one thing, franchisement another" (61).

The Constitution, as the law of laws laying out the critical interrelationships between U.S. jurisprudence, government, religious status, and civil society, remains infused within the conservative and propertied social, political, and economic agendas of such (agro-)industrial magnates. As Frederick Douglass pointed out in an 1849 *North Star* editorial, the Constitution as signed and ratified by the new national bourgeoisie went so far as to condone in four separate places the trade in black Americans as animal labor, from the official acknowledgment of slaves as import commodities to the return of fugitives as security for southern capital to the use of federal armed forces to "safeguard the Southern tyrant against the vengeance of the outraged and plundered slave" (*Life* 265).[20] In deference to the power of the various constituencies of politicized financial magnates represented in Philadelphia, the Constitution draped itself in the mantle of "objectivity" and the "negative state"—the belief that the state should avoid intervention in the social order—designed to stabilize and protect the status quo. As MacKinnon points out, the "negative state" "ensures that the law will most reinforce existing distributions of power when it most closely adheres to its own ideal of fairness" (163).[21]

The framers of the Constitution, representatives of the groups constituting the white national bourgeoisie designing the state, recognized this. In the pages of the *Federalist Papers* three of the new men for the new nation, future Secretary of State Alexander Hamilton, Virginia plantation investor James Madison, and John Jay, coauthor of the New York State Constitution and negotiator of the new federal government's treaty with Britain, hammered out the juridical and structural implications of their economic agenda and how best to organize the distribution of power in the new centralizing apparatus of the federation (Boorstein 338). "The smaller the society of the represented," Madison wrote,

> the fewer probably will be the distinct parties and interests, the more frequently will the majority be found in the same party. . . . Extend the sphere, and you take in a greater variety of parties and interests; you make it less probable that a majority of the whole will have a common motive to invade the rights of other citizens; or if such a common motive exists, it will be more difficult for all who feel it to discover their strength and to act in unison with each other. (Ollmann and Birnbaum 50)

*Power/nation/capital*

If the position of the wealthy southern slaveholding lobby in the U.S. economy, government, and law was slipping in the sectional politics of the 1850s, the role that black labor and expertise had played and was continuing to play was crucial to both building national capital and to the development of the nation-state.[22] "It is notorious," Delany wrote in 1852,

> that in the planting States, the blacks themselves are the only skillful cultivators—the proprietor knowing little or nothing about the art, save that which he learns from the African husbandman. . . . They were, in fact, then, to the whole continent, what they are now, to the whole Southern section of the Union—the bone and sinews of the

country. And even now, the existence of the white man, South, depends entirely on the labor of the black man—the idleness of the one, is sustained by the industry of the other. (*Condition* 64, 66)

The value of capital in slaves in 1860 is estimated at $2.7 billion (Lee and Passell 215). Through the market in slaves alone—although internationally the trade was being driven underground by English and French policing of compliance with antitrade laws—the United States and its allies continued to reap large profits (Marx 199), generating the casual speculation in bodies reported in antebellum black autobiographies.[23] The average price of a slave in the United States increased dramatically from $736 in 1821–25 to $1,252 in 1851–55, then rising to $1,596 in 1856–60, a climb brought to a halt only by the advent of the Civil War (Lee and Passell 169).[24]

The overseas market for southern cotton expanded 5 percent every year from 1830 to 1860, a critical element in Delany's plan for founding an economically powerful black state. Southern production rose to meet this demand, shooting up from 150,000 bales in 1815 to 4,500,000 in 1859 and continuing to expand even after the Civil War (Hacker 285). Such a booming economy put the South well ahead of the farming communities of the northwest region. While the per capita income of northwesterners is estimated at $65 in 1840 and $89 in 1860, southerners averaged $74 and $103 for the same years, with the population of the west-south-central region peaking at $151 per capita in 1840 and $184 per capita in 1860. As strange fruit of national policy, the majority of African-Americans labored to produce the high per capita incomes of the South. To declare slaves men born equal was to attack a crucial industry for the national economy: in Mississippi, which boasted a national high figure of $253 per free person, 55 percent of the population was African-Americans who were constitutionally denied access to the enormous wealth produced by their labor (Lee and Passell 216). Religious and scientific discourse (increasingly "science" by now) established the national necessity of enslavement, or as Delany put it, the subjection of black people as "the meanest underlings, subject to the beck and call of every creature bearing a pale complexion" (*Condition* 46).

The Cuban captain's "liberal principles" had in fact been brewing since the fateful meeting in Philadelphia. Constitutional delegates from Virginia, Maryland, and Delaware had condemned the trade in high moral tones, to the degree that delegates from Georgia and both South and North Carolina had refused to sign the Constitution if the trade were hampered in any way. It was left to Elbridge Gerry of Massachusetts to suggest the inconsistency of condemning the trade while supporting slavery (Du Bois, qtd. in Ollmann and Birnbaum 98).

To make matters worse, the naval power of the United States was great enough in 1858 to prevent the combined imperial antislavery forces of England and France from boarding any vessel in the regions of Africa or the Americas flying the Stars and Stripes (Marx 197). The U.S. flag thus became the slaver's insignia of choice, as Delany employs it in *Blake* (228–30). Delany's novel is then at pains to articulate a black national identity trapped in the *Merchantman* cargo; that is, the codification—in science, religion, the military, and the law—of blacks in the Americas as capital in property. Coming upon the city of Washington, seat of the federal government, the new black man surveys the horizon: "The slave prison conspicuously stood among the edifices; high in the breeze from the flagstaff floated defiantly the National Colors, stars as the pride of the white man, and stripes as the emblem of power over the blacks" (117).

*The project*

In his 1854 speech titled "The Political Destiny of the Colored Race," adopted in its entirety by the membership of the 1854 National Convention on Emigration,[25] we can find what is perhaps Delany's most explicit general statement on his view of "The Project:"

> We regret the necessity of stating the fact, but duty compels us to the task, that, for more than two thousand years, the determined aim of the whites has been to crush the colored races wherever found. With a determined will they have sought and pursued them in every quarter of the globe. The Anglo-Saxon has taken the lead in this work of universal subjugation. But the Anglo-American stands pre-ëminent for deeds of injustice and acts of oppression, unparalleled, perhaps, in the annals of modern history. ("Political" 204)

Invested in the negotiations over the outfitting of the *Merchantman* is, then, the very Constitution of the United States as a nation-state and its processes of nation-state formation through capital accumulation, regulating de facto and de jure: (1) the making of Africans into slaves and the exportation of value from Africa to the United States; (2) the forced extraction of black labor power; (3) the accumulation of capital to build the wealth of the U.S. nation-state and give it increasing international power; (4) the elevation of elements of the local white ruling class to wealth of international proportions; and (5) the centralization of capital in white hands in general and the ruling cadres of the white U.S. elite in particular. The price of this nation-state formation through capital accumulation was the commodification and structural disenfranchisement of blacks in the New World. As he circles back from the city of Washington into the slaveholding South, Delany's hero cannot help but breathe: "How long, O Lord of the oppressed, how long shall this thing continue" (117).

### The New Man, Subalternity, and the Problem of Black Nation Formation

The hero of the novel, the man to build a new nation, is physically absent until the sixth installment, allowing Delany to establish the networks of power and gender relations on the plantation against which his hero is defined. It is a mark of Henry Blake's omnipresence, however, that he is heralded before his entrance and the installment is called not "Henry's Appearance," or "Henry," but "Henry's Return." Prior to this, Henry's wife Maggie is sold to Judge Ballard's wife because both Colonel Franks (owner of Maggie and Henry) and Mrs. Ballard resent Mrs. Franks's inclination to treat Maggie in terms of friendly labor relations rather than the forced conscription of a not-quite-human creature, the latter view of which they both agree national security demands:

> The conduct of Mrs. Franks toward her servant was more like that of an elder sister than a mistress, and the mistress and maid sometimes wore dresses from the same web of cloth. Mrs. Franks would frequently adjust the dress and see that the hair of her maid was properly arranged. This to Mrs. Ballard was as unusual as it was an objectionable sight, especially as she imagined there was an air of hauteur in her demeanor. It was then she determined to subdue her spirit. (6)

Much of the heralding of Henry's return revolves around the wrath that the sale of Maggie will unleash, the birth of a modern revolutionary black spirit.

### The birth of the new man

Delany capitalizes on the difference that isolates Henry from the rest of the slave community—a difference we can term the internalization of modern paradigms—by marking it at every opportunity. Whereas the other slaves speak in black English, Henry always speaks in nineteenth-century literary Anglo-American English. Whereas Maggie's parents, elders in the slave community, invoke God's will, Henry responds with a critique of the function of Christianity in the perpetuation of slavery: " 'Religion!' replied Henry rebukingly. 'That's always the cry with black people. Tell me nothing about religion when the very man who hands you the bread at communion has sold your daughter away from you'!" (20). Henry's remarkable difference is credited to his having been born a free "African" raised and educated in the Caribbean, stolen away as a child and sold into southern U.S. slavery.[26] Our hero gains his heroic attributes based on his Pan-African identity.

At the same time, Henry's Pan-African manhood, and thus his natural leadership, is constituted in comparison to Colonel Franks's masculinity, just as Maggie's femininity, and thus her status as a suitable object of pity, is constituted in relation to Mrs. Franks's femininity. The black couple at the center of the novel, in fact, rival the white couple who buy and sell them: despite Mrs. Franks's acknowledged womanly appeal, "it often had been whispered that in beauty the maid equaled if not excelled the mistress" (6). For his part, Henry is "a black—a pure Negro—handsome, manly, and intelligent, in size comparing well with his master, but neither so fleshy nor heavy built in person. A man of good literary attainments—unknown to Colonel Franks, though he was aware he could read and write—having been educated in the West Indies, and decoyed away when young. His affection for his wife and child was not excelled by Colonel Franks's for his" (16–17). Both Henry and Maggie thus exceed gendered terms of value established by Anglo-American society. And, too, the silence in what Franks knows of Henry will come back to define Henry's relationship to the state and the white nation, a relationship that will structure the first part of the narrative in which Delany plots revolution in the slaves' huts. This greater manliness (embodied by his physical fitness) and all that lies behind what Franks does not know (a modern education in political economics and strategy for war) foreshadows Henry's full-blown emergence as the radical to constitute—and in constituting, save—the black nation. On hearing of the sale of Maggie, as a result of his superior education and his manliness and pure African blood, the new man to free blacks in the Americas is able to actualize his radical potential and see his enslavement in terms of a social contract he was always free to break: "You may do your mightiest, Colonel Franks. I'm not your slave, nor never was and you know it! And but for my wife and her people, I never would have stayed with you till now. I was decoyed away when young, and then became entangled in such domestic relations as to induce me to remain with you; but now the tie is broken!" (19).

*Subalternity as a black nationalist concept*

When the colonel reads this response as a rebellion, "a cloud that's fast gathering around us" (19–20), he predicts precisely the plot of the book. The revolution begins with Henry's refusal to accept the hegemonic constitution of slave subjectivity, as the African-American writer and activist Reverend Pennington put it in 1849, his identity as synoymous with "a being in whom another owns property" (198).

The descriptions of Henry's actions throughout his stay in the United States—before he returns to Cuba and plots to hijack the *Merchantman* in the Middle Passage—constitute his relation to the state in terms reminiscent of what some cultural analysts refer to as "the subaltern." Considering the implications of this in reading the debates surrounding slavery and black leadership will take us into the project of (and the struggle over) reading and writing slave culture and the project of black political identity.

In a discourse initiated by Antonio Gramsci and developed most thoroughly by the Subaltern Studies Group through South Asian historiography, the "subaltern" is defined as the unrepresented, as "a name for the general attribute of subordination in South Asian society whether this is expressed in terms of class, caste, age, gender, and office or in any other way" (Guha and Spivak 35). Most often in the group's work on South Asia, "subaltern" refers to those who operate out of an/other epistemological and ontological sign-system, and who participate in, for example, mass movements, riots, and revolts, but whose agendas are ultimately structurally blocked by the decision-making bodies of the state. Taken from the vocabulary of the British military, in the hands of the South Asian Subaltern Studies Group the "subaltern" comes to imply an agrarian, precapitalist economy and the implications for identity that such an economy implies.

Under the scrutiny of the Subaltern Studies Group, the Indian subaltern as a political subject takes his or her place at the bottom of a social ladder that may include members of a similar ethnicity or sociopolitical hierarchy. The group's editor and most-cited theorist, Ranajit Guha, provides a useful outline of the sociopolitical model of India on which the project is predicated in which the category comes down to us as a historically negativized space. Thinking through the matrix of Delany's political economic analyses, as Guha himself describes it, "peasant"/slave subalternity was materialized by the structure of property, institutionalized by "laws, sanctified by religion and made tolerable—even desirable—by tradition. To rebel was indeed to destroy many of those familiar signs by which [the subaltern] had learned to read and manipulate in order to extract meaning out of the harsh world around him and live with it. The risk in 'turning things upside down' under these conditions was indeed so great that he could hardly afford to engage in such a project [lightly]" (Guha, "Prose" 45).

Given the position of slaves in the New World political economy, separatist black nationalism sees blacks in terms similar to the "subaltern" as elaborated by the South Asian Subaltern Studies Group. The reverberances between slavery in the New World and the status of peasant subalternity in India in separatist black nationalist texts have their place in a history of black nationalist criticism down into the twenty-first century that sees blacks in the United States as constituted into an oppressed caste. Much like the concept of the subaltern developed by the South Asian Subaltern Studies Group, African-Americans had fought on both sides in the War of Independence and, as chattel, were trapped in a national agenda in which they were—again in the Supreme Court's 1857 Dred Scott Decision—explicitly excluded from the rights of citizenship and perceived as threats to national security.

Because slaves were thus super-disenfranchised by birth, by culture, and by blood, those who acted to (re)present a subaltern political agenda meant to represent the slaves as "men" (therefore citizens) were arrested and executed as threats to the state; consider, for example, John Brown and Nat Turner. It is definitional of subalternity for individual, active subaltern political representation to disappear from history except as a problem of law and order—that is, to have their activities criminalized. Although the dehumanization and subjugation of all blacks was part and parcel of the (white) nationalist agenda—and thus codified in the laws of the state and reflected in the common practices of the nation—the place reserved for those classed as "subaltern" is located at the extreme. The investment of black nationalist leaders in the liberation of slaves begins here as a fulcrum from which to liberate African-Americans as a nation, to incorporate blacks as citizens. Entrance into modernity is thus the horizon of the black elite; the political agenda of the subaltern slave class is more difficult to discern.

Northern cultural conceptualizations, prevalent among educated blacks, of southern slave culture as degraded and immoral, throw the questions of political representation back onto the leadership of the (comparative) elite.[27] Given that for slave culture "it was not power that was a content wrapped up in a form external to it called religion [but] a matter of both being inseparably collapsed as the signifier and signified . . . in the language of massive violence," one such question that returns in the historiography of slave rebellions at the primary, secondary, and tertiary levels is this: does the slave rebel have a place in this history "as a subject of rebellion"? (Guha, "Prose" 78, 71).

Writing the new black man into being in the antebellum United States thus turns on the question of the proper Subject of rebellion. For Delany's historical model/heroes—the leaders of slave rebellions—entrance into U.S. history was marketed as an urgent call for public adherence to the agenda of state coalitions categorically excluding blacks from "humanity" in order to facilitate the forced extraction of black labor power for financial and psychological profit. As Thomas Gray, transcriber and publisher of Nat Turner's *Confessions* and self-described "ob't serv't" of "the public" wrote in his preface, the 1831 publication of the "savage's" *Confessions* was "calculated . . . to demonstrate the policy of our laws in restraint of this class of our population, and to induce all those entrusted with their execution, as well as our citizens generally, to see they are strictly and rigidly enforced" (97). Just as the "our" and "citizens" = whites, and the "class of our population" both "laws" and "policy" must restrain = blacks, it is constitutional policy that slaves who are interested in freeing not only themselves but their race as a people—Guha's "turning things upside down"—are written into official history only when they bring governance into a crisis, their story released only as crisis management, written as trial records, crime reports, and published confessions, lessons for the resolve of the citizenry proper.

The movements of slave insurgency, then, of antebellum black subaltern leadership, are written in the negativity suppressed to produce the positivistic progressions of official history: they leave their tracks in the failures of meaning, in catachresis, chaos, and collapse, rather than in the documents on which the understandings of history are traditionally built. At the same time, writing the black subaltern revolutionary hero within a blueprint for revolution requires the writing of the hero into the historical world. In the shifting positionality of the novel's relation to official history, Henry leaves marks the institutions of the state cannot read: "Proceeding on in the direction of the Red River country, he met with no obstruction except in one instance, when he left his assailant quietly upon the earth. A few days after an inquest was held on the body of a deceased overseer—verdict of the jury, 'By hands unknown' " (68).

Thus throughout the novel Henry's manhood and heroism are (or must be, given Delany's understanding of the position of blacks in America) constituted explicitly as outside the control of the state's apparatuses of law and order, the taking back of black consciousness meeting the networks of white power on its own terms. Such a shift, from slave to revolutionary American, places the new black Subject beyond the categories recognizable by the institutions of the white nation-state. The hero, like the novelist, documents the dynamics of a political cold war shrouded in positivistic science and religion and enacted in the legal right to mutilate and trade in black bodies—man, woman, or child.

The recognition of "slaves" as subjugated citizens, as African-Americans, initiates an identity transformation at the personal and national levels and sees black labor as agreed and not forced—a recognition that appears in many slave autobiographies as inextricable from the decision to break the slave social contract and take flight.[28] In Delany's hands, Henry's reconceptualization of the slave social contract and thus the black self leads specifically to a network of white destruction, a determination paralleled less in the narratives of ex-slaves than in the testimony of national military leaders in prison, preserved as records of the trial and judgment of criminals: Turner, Vesey, Gabriel.

### The problem of culture and the new man
Henry steals through the South to Washington, D.C., and then back into slave country, moving from plantation to plantation, identifying community leaders and recruiting them for rebellion.[29] Within the silence necessarily surrounding the project of revolutionary black nation formation,

Henry's strategies of counterintelligence among the slave population and willingness to kill make him a hero constructed on the borders of subalternity and integration. He leaves traces of subaltern insurgency only in moments of negativity, in white presumption of his passing as the invisible agent implied by criminal activity. The interests of sub-alterns, as embodied by Henry at key moments, and the interests of the nation-state, are thus epistemologically at odds: "Antagonism between the two is irreducible," Guha writes, "and there is nothing in this to leave room for neutrality" ("Prose," 59).

Such politicized tactics of reconceptualizing history, culture, sub-alternity, insurrection, and the social text seem at first glance to reiterate the strategies of reading that Delany proposes and seeks to textualize in *Blake,* as for example when Henry is seen as "a force to be conquered and silenced" (Schwarz 187). From the perspective of the state, his tracks are written in the destruction of the South and in the wrath of a God threat-ening to break the silence: "From plantation to plantation did he go, sow-ing the seeds of future ruin to the master and redemption to the slave, an antecedent more terrible in its anticipation than the warning voice of the destroying Angel in commanding the slaughter of the firstborn of Egypt" (83). It is the construction of Blake as a subaltern-avenging hero that makes him the emblem of the new black man who represents the op-pressed slave community.

But there is a crack at the center of the significations of collectivity in Delany's new man, almost invisible in the beginning—we have already seen its first signs—that widens till it yawns. This split, in fact, swallows the new man's definition as simultaneously the apotheosis of the most op-pressed within the black nation and the hero to dissolve the divisiveness and subservience that makes African-Americans weak and oppressable.

On his journey through the South "sowing the seeds of a future crop, only to take root in the thick black waters which cover it, to be grown in devastation and reaped in a whirlwind of ruin" (112), Henry goes deep into the Dismal Swamp. This dense forest gives cover to "the much-dreaded runaways of the woods, a class of outlawed slaves who con-tinually seek the lives of their masters" (110) and who reveal themselves to Henry as remnants of the band of Nat Turner. Among this group of High Conjurers, we are told, "the names of Nat Turner, Denmark Vesey, and General Gabriel were held by them in sacred reverence" (113). Given Delany's pantheon of black national heroes, these rebel communities would seem to be a natural source from which Blake could select his revolutionary cadres as well as recover the history of revolutionary strategy and its points of failure. As black rebels gone back to the bush—maroons—they represent men who have recognized and rejected their place in the dominant sociopolitical and economic order, and so represent black men who "fully understood themselves," to cite Delany's conceptualization of New Revolutionary Men (205). The maroon conjurers also represent the highest group of elders in the interplantation slave society, powerful in a slave culture based on African and Christianized African epistemologies and ontologies. This combination of the old and the new takes up the question of competing paradigms of mulatto culture (modern/agrarian) that we will see again in chapter 2. Therefore, while actualizing their right to own their bodies and culture as a revolutionary insight, they participate in—are the keepers of—precisely the aspects of Pan-African subject constitution that whites in general, and whites in the United States in particular, considered a heathenism signaling subhuman status sanctioning enslavement.

### Modernism/agrarianism/culture

We come here face to face with a clash of paradigms, one black agrarian (the African-centered universe of the conjurers) and the other resolutely industrial (Henry and the paradigms of nation-states). As even a cursory reading of *The Confessions of Nat Turner* makes clear, Turner spoke precisely out of a warrior/priest/king's worldview, constituted in a religious/cultural/political synthesis of ancestor worship as a mark of agrarianism and black syncretism in the U.S. social text:

> And about this time I had a vision—and I saw white spirits and black spirits engaged in battle, and the sun was darkened—the thunder rolled in the Heavens, and blood flowed in the streams. . . . And [a spirit] appeared to me, and reminded me of the things it had already shown me, and that it would then reveal to me the knowledge of the elements, the revolutions of the planets, the operations of tides, and the changes of the seasons. . . . And from the first steps of righteousness until the last, was I made perfect. (102–3)

If for Thomas Gray, his redactor and publisher, a "savage madness" is self-evident from Turner's leadership (96) as from his words (113), politics, and "religion . . . wrapped up . . . in the language of massive violence" (Guha, "Prose" 78), the power of difference in African subject constitution remains catechristical to Delany's Afro-Christianity. Thus in Delany's equally religious worldview, if the "*Physical* Laws" of a "perfect" and "immutable" God were exploited by white men robbing black Americans of their labor—transformed into capital whose accumulation led to world power—it was a confusion of the nature of the Godhead that led black Americans to look to the "Spiritual" medium of prayer for "*Physical*" salvation (*Condition* 38–39). In this critical distinction, agrarianism is assimilatable with spirituality, but the "*Physical* Laws" are resolutely modern, incorporating the new sciences, including political economy.

To allow conjure its place in the world of black thought and knowledge is not necessarily to bow to its hegemony, but to push at the meaning and borders of antebellum black political and cultural (re)presentation. Revolutionary subaltern slave culture does not for Delany count as speech but rather gibberish, and so, following the dictates of modern law, the speakers of gibberish can—in moments of national crisis, must—be silenced by national leadership and the citizenry. Subaltern slave religion is not, then, the black Christianity that sees, in the best-case scenario, Armageddon and Heaven as the final repositories of justice in black/white relations, but what is spoken furtively, defensively, when the empowered are not looking, where modernity cannot see and finds only chaos and barbarianism.

The gap between Henry as king among conjurers and Henry as apotheosis of the people—"pure Negro," "intelligent," "proud," "manly" (16)—yawns further, if we recognize that the concept of true Christianity that serves as the moral touchstone of the United States, elaborated by Douglass in the appendix to his 1849 *Narrative,* is shared by antislavery activists and organizations North and South, raising again the question of cultural and political representation. Hobsbawm argues that the job of establishing the hegemony of modernity and silencing vanquished ethnicities in state consolidation is performed by transforming the people's history and religion into rumor, folklore, and superstition—subaltern cultural norms into eccentricities, into barbarism. Delany's handling of conjure, juxtaposed to Douglass's for example, reveals all the anxiety of the will to power and national politics as the self-fulfillment of an (however relatively) elite group over those beneath it, an anxiety we saw earlier severing the social contract between black and white Americans.

Delany, like Turner, rejects conjuration, but Delany holds his own politically conflictive religious worldviews: lurking behind his concept of "Spiritual laws" is the catechristical division between true "Christianity" and black "heathenism." Slave narratives suggest that such dismissals of Afrocentric beliefs and slave culture by escaped slaves were not unanimous, however. Indeed, even in negotiating a politically vital public capitulation to an Enlightened, modern worldview, nationally influential spokesmen like Douglass and William Wells Brown invoke conjure at the fundamental moment of crisis in new subject formation. In their writings, when they describe their break psychologically from the institution of slavery and see themselves as men and not chattel, the resolution of the dilemma of conjure's epistemology through the paradigms of modernity or Christianity is impossible. The most popular of U.S. slave autobiographies, Douglass's 1849 *Narrative,* can provide an example. At stake is power as democratic or authoritarian.

In the interstices of the now-celebrated passage in which Douglass moves from "slave" to "man," we can find the mechanics of a disruptive univocity, a shifting heuristic difference, marking African-American slave culture:

> I found Sandy an old advisor. He told me, with great solemnity, I must go back to Covey; but that before I went, I must go with him into another part of the woods, where there was a certain *root,* which, if I would take some of it with me, carrying it *always on my right side,* would render it impossible for Mr. Covey, or any other white man, to whip me. . . . [U]pon entering the yard gate, out came Mr. Covey. . . . He spoke to me very kindly, bade me drive the pigs from a lot near by, and passed on toward the church. Now this singular conduct of Mr. Covey really made me think that there was something in the *root* which Sandy had given me. . . . All went well until Monday morning. On this morning the root was fully tested. (81)

Covey, of course, bent on the transformation of black bodies from nature into laboring machines, attacks: "Mr. Covey seemed now to think he had me, and could do what he pleased; but at this moment—from whence came the spirit I don't know—I resolved to fight; and suiting my action to the resolution, I seized Covey hard by the throat" (81). Thus it is on the importance of reading into slave religion a syncretic religious worldview—as cross-culturally African as it is American—that Stuckey bases his groundbreaking reading of slave culture.

In its epistemic secularism, Delany's political economy of "*Physical Laws*" distinct from spirituality—"make your religion serve your interests" Henry declares early on (41)—intersects with the political economics of his contemporary, Karl Marx. For both, the reigning order protects itself through a religion promising salvation that becomes the opiate of the people; the central role of a capitalist economy in the historical progression toward a utopia; and the need for the collapse of the exploitative world system. This collapse had to come through an ultimately international revolution brought about by the recognition, in the most exploited stratum, of the contradictions inherent in their role within industry and the state. At the same time, Delany inherited an investment in individual competition, a continent-wide federal government, and a free local and international marketplace constituted within the terms of a profoundly North American national agenda, even as the three faces of the Judeo-Christian Godhead return as the final/original guarantee of a pure and objective metaphysical justice.

From Delany's perspective, the fact that the group of conjurers makes Henry supreme among High Conjurers is simply another step in his climb to modern national leadership and testifies to the unanimity of his election as a "messenger of light and destruction" from the depths of the black nation to the upper echelons of the white (101). Thus slave culture on the one hand is marked by a radical alterity that Delany uses as threatening to the dominant ethno-ideological social order, while on the other it is a function of "the darkened region of the obscure intellects of the slaves" registering an alienation from the culture of the black majority at the point of slave, free, and rebel political congruity (101). Later, Henry explains to a group of fellow conspirators that the only reason he accepted the honor was for a cynical politics: the power in credibility it would give him among the "ignorant" slaves (126). The rebel maroons' benediction becomes proof of their lies, in that by giving him their blessing and forming a political alliance with him they show their weakness, their failure. Blake makes it a "special part" of his journey among the slave communities "to enlighten them" on this sign of critical weakness among the rebel band secreted in the Dismal Swamp (137). In this Delany may well be taking Turner's alleged *Confession* one step further, where Turner says he "always spoke of [conjuring] with contempt" (103). But where Turner's alienation is from one belief system among others within slave culture. Delany's is from culture compounded by class. This reiterates the classed ethnic fracture within black nationalism at a macropolitical level, a fracture bearing down on Henry's constitution as the embodiment of the black nation.[30] On the one hand he represents the slaves; on the other, his leadership is constructed in terms of his superiority to them, a superiority directly attributed to his pure black blood, his manhood, his free origins in the Caribbean, and his modern Enlightenment.[31]

### Pan-Africanism and the new man

Henry's constitution as Pan-African subaltern collapses, however, once he returns to Cuba. As the good ship *Merchantman* is renamed in Caribbean waters by Delany as the *Vulture*, so Henry is transformed and reveals himself when he travels outside of the United States. To be sure, Delany is careful to have onlookers from Africa and the Caribbean continue to acknowledge Blake's "natural" accession to black (inter)national leadership at every opportunity. A literate black man of superior intellect, coming out of the geopolitical wild space of the Caribbean, Henry could read the slave-master relation as a social contract, initiating a crisis in the forced extraction of black labor and recuperating the crisis for black revolution. The radical potential of such a Pan-African revolutionary subject, however, is lost as Henry revealed in Cuba reflects less the Pan-African subaltern, or the political representative of the subaltern writ large, than a wealthy subject of the Cuban colonial regime: he becomes Henrico Blacus, radical heir to a prosperous manufacturer, son to "one of the wealthiest and most refined black merchants in the West Indies" (199).

The sudden introduction of a storehouse of capital into the silent background from which a Pan-African hero might emerge has its precedent in Delany's modern conceptualization of the elements necessary to the struggle. In the first part of the book, the plan for slave revolt was shrouded in secrecy, but given a broader understanding of Delany's worldview one crucial term escapes: "capital" (40). "Keep this studiously in mind" Henry tells his inner circle of conspiring men,

> and impress it as an important part of the scheme of organization, that [the slaves] must have money, if they want to get free. Money will obtain them everything necessary by which to obtain their liberty. The money is within all of their reach if only they knew it was right to take it. . . . So you must teach them to take all the money

they can get from their masters, to enable them to make the strike without failure. (43)

The coincidence of the eagle as a national emblem of the United States and a metonym for money used to bribe whites along the escape route— passage through "the white gap" (43)—not only proves the efficacy of Henry's plan but reaches its climax when Henry's subjectivity is revealed as the product of an original accumulation of capital. If the incorporation of the black petit bourgeoisie into the nationalist struggle is crucial for the success of the (proto)movement, the emphasis on the slaves as the mass to be liberated and the pressure to fashion a hero rising up from the people create a structural conflict that can only be resolved by deferring the importance of both a storehouse of capital and the modern education necessary for understanding and instituting nation-states. Just as the reader, excluded from the most critical details of the revolutionary war strategy, is often positioned in terms of the enemy for national security, so the shroud of the macropolitical extends into the micropolitical, and the critical importance of capital in Henry's background is hidden from his slave compatriots.

The political problem of the role of ethnicity in black culture, of the gap between a man to consolidate a nation—(re)presentation by proxy as well as by portrait of the (slave) masses—and the superiority of the hero's difference splits the black coalitions further. In a rite of passage on reentering Cuba, Henry disappears into a Cuban High Priest's hut for three days where he learns of the situation of blacks in Cuba and their readiness to revolt, as well as of the secret power of conjuring the notorious attack dogs used by Cuban planters to control the slave population. Barbarian agrarian culture, what in the United States he called the ignorant slaves' "long cherished silly nonsense of conjuration," has lessons the modern hero can use (137). In Cuban territory, where the hero comes from the mulatto bourgeoisie and the black slave masses disappear into the background, rather than where the hero himself is forced to be a member of the enslaved, slave and free ethnicity can merge in a man mastering modern and barbarian knowledges. In book 2 of the novel Henry returns to his history and reveals his true financial/class identity as well as consolidates the conflictive elements of black national culture. In the epigraph that opens book 2, the rebirth of the revolutionary hero is hailed as the return of the new Pan-African savior. Power and religion collapse into each other, thus rewriting the politics of Harriet Beecher Stowe through a black Armageddon, the apotheosis of the new man as a "thief in the night" (111):

> Hear the word!—who fight for freedom!
> Shout it in the battle van!
> Hope! for bleeding human nature!
> Christ the God, is Christ the Man! (161)

The revolutionary hero is thus the highest of conjurers, the master of the modern paradigms, and the black revolutionary incarnation of the Godhead—literally the Second Coming. Nevertheless, to the extent that Delany recognizes difference in the condition of slaves in the Caribbean colonies, he can only constitute his hero in terms of the tenets of class privilege and his expansionist religious identity: capitalism, civilization, and Christianity are at the foundations of the new black utopia and the revolutionary black subject but are alien to the African-based core of slave culture in both Cuba and the United States. In his backyard re-birth, Delany's hero is no longer a slave among slaves—of the "people-nation"—but a modern, wealthy heir, albeit a radical one, within a hostile white plantocracy, a man for the people but not entirely of them.

### Hut/woman/nation

Gender is central to Delany's agenda. The critical role of black men becomes the (re)constitution of black manhood, a reconstitution both inside (Blake as wealthy heir) and outside (Blake as revolutionary fugitive) the law. Black manhood here is defined in terms of its difference from womanhood; that is, by means of the traditional polarities: mind/body, intelligible/sensing, activity/passivity, logos/pathos, culture/nature, and so on (Jardine 72). All the tenets of Enlightenment liberalism are in situ, according to feminist Jane Flax:

1. The belief that rationality is the only means by which individuals achieve autonomy;
2. The notion that an individual and citizen is a male household head;
3. The separation of society into the private and the public: the world of the dependence, the family, and the world of freedom, the state and work;

4. The gendering of that differentiation so that women are posed in opposition to civil society, to civilisation. (Flax 6)

The struggle of black men to police gender constitution (for women's own safety) stands as a sympton of black men's "feminization" under slavery, their relegation to the second term in Jardine's pairs and expulsion from the world of freedom, the state, and the exchange of labor power for capital that Flax describes. General of the revolutionary army Henrico Blacus, as Henry's apotheosis, takes back through military might the terms of blackness and maleness that supercede the "feminization-as-emasculinization" of blacks in the Americas, a condition only conceivable in the absence of a powerful black state to represent the interests of the black people-nation through money and war. Thus Henry's turning point is his outrage that his wife, as his wife, has been sold: like David Walker before him, the state of the nation is here predicated on the ability of its men to regulate the condition of its people—to be "men"—and it is this failure that sparks the revolt. Maggie's sale is a sign of gendered political humiliation.

I have not spoken of the "new woman" in Delany's scheme because vast as his canvas is, he considers access to the privacy of the domestic sphere the revolutionary horizon for black women. Grappling with the macrological problems of nations, states, and political economics, and reflecting his times and his deep roots in patriarchal culture, Delany incorporates gender entirely as defined by the dominant culture. Gender in Delany is thus a matter of power: white negation of black access to the paradigms of manhood and womanhood reserved for white society, and black affirmation of the right to access those paradigms as a model of modernity—thus, for example, the defiant manliness of the hero and the obedient femininity of his wife. Accordingly, in his political strategizing—given the peremptory logic of gender in patriarchy—almost all of his black female characters, slave and free, function as hinges in the plot, as facilitators rather than agents.

Delany's conception of women becomes clear, for example, when it is revealed that Maggie is in dire need of political education. As Madam Blacus, she is in fact politically conservative: "I don't know, husband," she tells the general of the new black national army, "I may be wrong, and I expect you will say so; but I think our people had better not attempt [armed revolt], but be satisfied as we are among the whites, and God, in

His appointed time, will do what is required" (192). In this she is coded with the attributes that Delany elsewhere censures in the black nation.[32] Her subsequent deference to her husband is thus linked to a deference to authority in men, positivistically embodied in Henry as the new man who "fully knows himself." At the same time, Maggie's willingness, even desire, to be corrected by her husband saves her from revealing herself as a traitor. For were she to act on her conservative convictions she would logically be required to betray the revolution, which would mean forging an alliance with the white enemy. Submission to her husband is, then, her salvation.

This is not to say that women have no value in Delany's universe, but rather that a woman's value is directly related to, and a reflection of, the status of her nation's men. Thus the sale of Maggie is the catalyst for the birth of the revolution; but only because she is a battleground across which the black hero and the white oppressor meet. The dynamics of this exchange are revealing, however, in that they display Delany's sensitivity to the patterns of victimization particular to enslaved women. Maggie, it is hinted, is in fact Colonel Franks's daughter, and her sale is expedited by her refusal to submit to Colonel Franks's sexual demands.[33] Nevertheless, it is also true that it is less Maggie's sale per se that unleashes Henry's wrath and Delany's outrage than the fact of her sale as plotting the depths of white infamy (here Colonel Franks's betrayal of a pact, the threat of incest, and the violation of a woman's honor). Woman's victimization, then, directly connects black manhood to the black national agenda in that it stems from a white refusal to acknowledge blacks as human beings, and from black men's inability to protect black women's honor and labor for the black domestic sphere; that is, a failure to be "men."

In Delany's *Blake*, women throughout the black diaspora enter the national scenario almost entirely as metaphors for the old, defeated nation. Thus women exemplify blackness at its most submissive and fearful (from Mammy Judy to Madam Blacus); or, in the mansions and haciendas of the black and mulatto Caribbean elite, as the wives of the wealthy new men, women decry their (nation's) fallen condition at the hands of repressive slave laws, "throwing" themselves "carelessly on a sofa" (312). At best, Delany's women hover on the brink of agency, and Delany is explicit that a woman's duty is to be "devoted as a wife to [her husband's] . . . interests" (213). And if the revolutionary hero is sometimes sympathetic to women, women nevertheless have no head for politics: at the micrological level, women "don't understand political matters" (184) and, thus, at the macrological level "the misses" are "admitted" to the political meetings "by courtesy" (255).

The paradigm plays itself out vertically as well. Below the level of the leadership elite, Delany's black women are shy maidens, kidnapped or long-suffering heroines, portly cooks, or wives of the male leaders; that is, a constitution for women offering little beyond the prison of sex roles developed by and for the international white bourgeoisie Delany rails against. In the southern United States, Blake's encounter with slave women—for instance, a "maiden gang of cotton girls" (180)—amounts to a debriefing and dismissal: "Well, girls, I believe I'm done with you; but before leaving let me ask you, is there among your men, a real clever good trusty man?" (78). If revolution is a national agenda, it is incontestably a problem for men among men, resolutely a masculine domain.[34]

Delany's politics begin working from the masculinist national-global economy and the macrological paradigms of the nation-state; from the modern man-hero who has mastered reading the worlds of oppressor and oppressed (*Blake*) back toward the violated black domestic sphere and those impoverished by slavery and ignorance (*The Huts of America*). Because he never questions the definitions of gender, and because of his alienation from the slave masses, in the slippage from man as a metaphor (= man) to a metonym (man = men + women, the people) Delany's *Blake* shifts from democracy into an authoritarianism that employs repressive tactics to heal the breach between the hero and women, which is mirrored in the breach between the hero (the New World black bourgeoisie) and the nation (women and the enslaved black masses). Delany's domestic sphere, the slave hut signaled in the title, is as crucial as his hero because it presents a premium productive/reproductive space somewhat but not entirely surveillable by white power or its nation-state; a sphere controllable by black men therefore a space from which black men can plot revolution. We have already seen the struggle for dominance and hegemony within the slave populations of the United States and Cuba. There are consistent structural equivalencies, therefore, between the place occupied by women and the place occupied by the enslaved black masses. The roach-infested hut of slavery is not a black home, although women and ignorant slaves try to make it so.

Within the epistemic heterosexuality of Delany's national paradigm, women must nevertheless be represented to populate the nation. Because women's vulnerability to degradation (in a paradigm we will encounter again a century later in the Oakland Black Panthers' philosophy) is a symbol of men's disempowerment, the idea that haunts Delany's text is that the condition of men's rights over women is, in a strong sense, the same as the condition of men's rights to control their nation. According to this ultimately conservative logic, the success of black freedom is marked by black men's property rights over their women, rather than women's and men's rights over themselves.

This tension plays out repeatedly in antebellum black thought and has powerful roots in the horrors of slavery within the gendered discourses of power and brutalization. When the African-American writer and activist Reverend Josiah Henson, like Reverend Pennington and so many other ex-slaves, establishes the horrors of slavery in the fact that the male body is "one in whom another owns property," what is at stake is manliness, masculinity, and the constitution of gender.[35] As Hortense Spillers has argued, in the macronarratives of slavery the black body is ungendered as a commodity itself, although that body's productive capacity is inevitably reengendered on the micropolitical plane: the abuse of women as objects of sexual pleasure and the appropriation of their children—the by-product of their bodies—as a commodity, an asset, a stepping stone in the rise of the white owner in the promise of America.[36]

Such considerations inevitably fall back on the economics of gendering, the making of a man as a man, the rendering of a woman as a woman; that is, considerations, everywhere in antebellum black writing, already disruptive of the macronarrative through the micronarratives. Within the minds of antebellum black men writing in reclaiming their manhood, black women and children reengendered within these narratives become the rightful property of black men. In its broadest economic terms, these writers equate manliness with labor power sold and managed at an ever-increasing profit, the better to maintain women and children in the domestic sphere outside the circulation of capital.

It is in making this claim that Delany's "huts" find their radical political potential, a space before the appropriation of labor power that must be occupied by the invading economics and psychodynamics of an order denying the black man as worker, the black man as individual rather than labor unit. Women come to supplement the power of men, equated with men's ability to reconceptualize and then to actualize a masculinized

African diaspora as workers within a modern capitalist economy, exporting the American Dream in the emergence of the African-American identity. In this light, the Civil War that reversed Delany's political relationship to Anglo-America is a transition of African-Americans from the degradation of Africans to the possibilities of Americans as part of the pool from which labor may be drawn, a resource for investment. Within Delany's socially conservative domestic paradigms, then, the problem of establishing men's right to women is linked to the problem of success in constituting the nation in modernity. Thus the problem of black men's control over black women's destiny is simultaneously the problem of binding the black diaspora internally and of binding the leadership to the people.

*Blake*'s unions and reunions of the diaspora are, toward the novel's conclusion, finally set in place by multiple weddings—sanctioned by the Catholic Church—among the inaugurators of the international revolution and the new state, an organization possible in the wild space of the Caribbean. The implementation of heterosexual marriage as a social contract, at first on the micropolitical level as the tie keeping Henry enslaved to Colonel Franks, returns as the macropolitical contract reuniting the diaspora in asserting the rights of blacks to modern humanity. William Wells Brown argues the same in *Clotel* (1853) that within the nineteenth-century modernist paradigm, marriage "is, indeed, the first and most important institution of human existence—the foundation of all civilization and culture—the root of church and state" (61). The pre-eminence of modern paradigms that can take root within the black New World community is established in opposition to the denial of marriage that constitutes the barbarianism to which the slave masses, modern blacks argue, are reduced for profit.

The problem of ethnicity, again linked to the problem of class and modernity versus barbarism and ignorance, permeates the new national pacts. As we saw in the ethno-cultural problem of conjure, the African man must be dispatched in what is something on the order of an ethno-cultural coup to ensure Henry/Henrico/modernity's leadership.[37] Thus as Henry/Henrico comes to be called "Chief," Mendi, the captured African warrior chief who is the African mirror of Henry and a potential rival as paragon of black manhood, disappears after falling to his knees "in thankfulness to God" when confronted with the poetry of the revolution (251). Mendi's African-agrarian culture disqualifies him from a position in the new leadership, and the best he can achieve is assimilation into the black nation through conversion to Christianity as his first step toward modernity. In the absence of Mendi this conflict is written on the body of "Abyssa," the captured Sudanese trading woman, as the bearer of African culture. The Cuban cutler, lowest in social origin among the revolutionary cadres, marries the "simple," "good-hearted" African trading woman (249). Carrying in her ethnicity the unfortunate conflation of woman/barbarianism/agrarianism, in confronting the Cuban Catholic Church and prostrating herself like a converted savage before it, the already Christian Abyssa gains her entrance into the civilization of the new black nation through awe in the face of Catholicism and modern marriage.

On the other side of the hierarchy, at the heights of the political/military elite of the black New World, the wealthy Cuban Henrico in turn remarries ex-slave Maggie, the violated U.S. mulatta who is herself a product of a personal and historic violation. Since marriages here stand as much for a (re)union of nations in modernity as a cultural necessity for a militarized union of the black diaspora, in wealthy heir General Henrico's marriage to Maggie we thus find the metaphor for the man-leader uplifting and embracing the debased slave masses, which is to say the nation. For women throughout the diaspora, Christian marriage becomes the horizon and the limit of women's sociopolitical contract with the new black nation-state.

The novel's fictional narrative of black woman's salvation parallels, as we will see in closing, Delany's global salvation narratives in public policy. For just as the general's plan to free his wife entails his travels throughout the South and his return to Cuba to then create a massive uprising, Delany's political-economic plan to end southern U.S. slavery (in the service of which he held back *Blake*'s serialization) had come to incorporate geopolitical geography—in this instance, the spread of colonization to Africa.

*(De)territorialization and Black Power:*
*Resolving the Problem of Fiction in Policy*

*Territorialization*
The final installments of *Blake; or The Huts of America* are not yet recovered as the issues of the *Anglo-American*, in which it was serialized, have not been found. This disappearance stands as a mark of the novel's

radical critique of the function of race in U.S. political economy: it took some one hundred years and the Black Power movement for *Blake* to be collected and marketed successfully as a commodity, despite the problems we uncovered as we pushed at the question of nationalist representation and the limits of Delany's founding concepts of revolution. Compare the publication history of *Uncle Tom's Cabin*. The absence of the conclusion, Floyd Miller notes in his introduction, may well provide the best possible ending for Delany's novel; that is, the reunited diaspora on the brink of its salvation through armed and international revolution. In the absence of a fictional conclusion to Delany's blueprint for revolt, we might look elsewhere for the resolution of the national plot. As *Blake* incorporates insights developed in Delany's various policy reports, we can reverse the dialectic and read the novel into his reports and back again, careful to take into account the shifts embedded in the narrative logic that weaves *Blake* together as a blueprint.

Like the plot of his novel, Delany's schemes for emigration were a trans-Atlantic counterattack to the white (trans)national agenda he outlined, detailed, and vilified throughout his many books and speeches and, as throughout his novel, created on a global scale. In his early twenties, Delany advocated African-American settlement on the western coast of Africa. Following in the footsteps of the U.S. Treasury in the 1780s and 1790s, a delegation of black "Representatives of a Broken Nation" was to approach France and England for the capital required to found and fund a state in Africa for the new black nation (*Condition* 212). The result would change the racial politics of the international flows of capital and thus the function of race in the global economy. "The whole Continent is rich in minerals, and the most precious metals" Delany wrote in his *Official Report of the Niger Valley Exploring Party* (1860), "[and] a great rail road could be constructed . . . which would make the GREAT THOROUGH-FARE for all the trade with the East Indies and Eastern Coast of Africa, and the Continent of America. All the world would pass through Africa upon this rail road, which would yield a revenue infinitely greater than any other investment in the world" (212, 213). Further, his new black nation-state would develop a cotton trade with England and mainland Europe to capture those ever-expanding cotton markets from the southern United States, causing a collapse of the southern economy—thus an end to U.S. slavery—and cutting severely into the European markets for the milled cotton of the North (Blackett 8–9).

Through configurations of the world order based on Delany's under-standings of geography and political economy, New World blacks trans-planted to Africa would begin to claim for themselves the capital that flowed into the hands of white America and the European continent. The insistence with which Delany places his novel in the world, the fact that he blocked its publication until his return from Africa, and the consis-tency of his arguments between his return in 1859 and the advent of the Civil War, all suggest that *Blake*'s silent conclusion partakes of the les-sons Delany learned in seeking to resolve dilemmas of black policy given the realities of his antebellum world. The problem of the missing conclu-sion is, then, less what happens than where, because as the novel builds to a climax General Henrico Blacus has already chosen his cadres, raised an army, alerted the slave population, distributed administrative/military posts, and declared war to take territory. The only question is which territory the new black military will take, a dilemma haunting militant separatist U.S. black nationalism down into the present day.

## Deterritorialization

In a twist that traces the shifts in identity marking the erosion of a premodern African/slave cultural context for subject constitution and the emergence of a modern northern/agro-industrial American one, Delany, like most northern blacks concerned with the elevation of "the race," repeatedly expressed the view of Africa as a heathen country in need of "civilization and enlightenment" (*Condition* 160). Delany makes his agenda for these heathens clear in his *Official Report of the Niger Valley:* "Our policy must be . . . *Africa for the African race and black men to rule them*. By black men I mean, men of African descent who claim an identity with the race" (cited in Ullman 225).

Periodically, and this is the plan as it emerges in *Blake*, Delany shifted the site for black empowerment to the Caribbean, favoring Nicaragua and Cuba in particular. There he sought to consolidate what he estimated as the Caribbean's 24,470,000 peoples of color against white U.S. capital and the hegemony of "power" over "right" (*Blake* 308) by contributing the labor and expertise of 600,000 free blacks in the United States to the economies of the newly freed states ("Political" 210). The potential in manpower was great: a mass U.S. slave revolt would have meant the mobilization of 3,500,000 slaves on the plantations of the South (De-lany's estimate, *Condition* 203).

In Delany "nation" is, then, de facto a racial concept, a fact of black blood and thus a natural-scientific concept, following on the debates of the times.[38] Thus, as David Walker had written, blacks and whites in the New World become self-evidently "natural enemies" (11) and "distinct race[s]" of beings" (19). In Delany's political logic, the black "nation" extrapolates into a de jure revolutionary political concept precisely because it can only be resolved by a territorial solution. Failing the necessary capital and cadres for imposing a new national bourgeoisie on Africa (those "who claim an identity with the race"), Delany turned to black inclusion in a criollo Bolívarian struggle for South American parity with the colossus to the North.

Deterritorialized, then, and faced with Spanish-American hegemony, "nation" in the Latin American alternative slips beyond the ties of a common experience of the ravages of slavery or language or religion (the latter two already elided in the Cuba–U.S. national tie) or even culture. But even in the face of cultural assimilation, the problem of claiming rights to territory comes back to haunt the plan. As if to further underscore the extent to which the politics of his concept of a black national pact were defined as opposition to the United States, Delany was deeply concerned that with the proximity of any new black-inclusive state in Latin America to the white nationalist U.S. bourgeoisie, the power and "prejudices of the mother-country and the white colonists alike" would facilitate U.S. and Spanish intervention in the revolutionary mandate for "independent self-government" (*Blake* 289). Again, however, his plan for cooperation inevitably entailed an (African-American) agenda for economic domination modeled on the strategies of ruling-class Anglo-America: the states of South America would be formed into a Union, with the U.S. threat serving strategically to keep the new Union together just as the perceived threat from England had served the United States. The practical problem of the racism of the criollo hegemony and the liberal and conservative reconceptualizations of Latin American administration falls by the wayside in the urgency to find territory and thus a country, although criollo racism emerges near the novel's climax in laws increasingly restricting the movements of the entire black Cuban population, working to spur the final black putsch. Only then, when power puts the colored elite back into the position of the enslaved, do we return to the language of—and a social pact with—subalternity.[39]

*The zero sum of the quid pro quo*

In Delany, then, modern national culture is to be, above all else, mulatto. Accordingly, ethnicity becomes the site of internal conflict between the leadership and the people. Gilroy applauds Delany for his "explicitly anti-ethnic" stance, which Gilroy sees as paving his way for "a truly Pan-African, diasporan sensibility" (27). Yet the relationship between these two forces, as we have seen, is not so easily resolved for democracy or for a black Atlantic understanding of black culture and modernity. African ethnicity in the novel is debased, ignorant, superstititous; the new men-heroes, as a requirement for citizenship, understand the white para-digms of power and political economy and must be able to meet, and beyond that to master, these paradigms in the formation of the new nation. Hobsbawm's aside that national communities ignore ethnic dif-ference except in the case of skin color thus comes back with a ven-geance, and it is here that the split we identified in terms of class and religion found its ethnic realization. Culture becomes a point of political conflict (love for and representation of the people/masses) expressing itself as an ideological conflict (the "ignorance" of the slaves and slave culture).

For Delany, the terms of the nation-state (i.e., Europe) replace the terms of premodern-*cum*-barbarian worldviews and knowledge bases (i.e., Africa): "Whatever liberty is worth to the whites, it is worth to the blacks; therefore, whatever it cost the whites to obtain it, the blacks would be willing and ready to pay, if they desire it" (*Blake* 192). Like a good wife, obedient to her husband, Maggie as metonym of the nation tied to the revolutionary hero, must "work out this question in political arithme-tic . . . and by the time [she gets] through and fully understand[s] the rule, then [she] will be ready to discuss the subject further" with him, the national leadership (192). Until then, she must stand aside and devote herself to his interests. Speech, as a macropolitical concept, is only granted if the speaker accepts the terms established by the hegemony of the paradigm of the nation-state and the instrumentalization of culture in everyday life.

Nation formation—here embodied and achieved in revolt-*cum*-revolution—thus necessitates a transformation of the central subject of the nation at several levels. In the micrological instance, it involves the transformation of those who people the nation. And in the macrological instance, it involves taking the paradigm of the nation-state and putting the black (male) subject in the place historically occupied by white men. Further, the terms of this critical transformation invite a hierarchy of ethnic traits. Europe (nation-state, industrialization, modernism) supersedes Africa (tribalistic, agrarianism, barbarianism). The culture of the new nation is thus something to be brought into being, something embodied in Blake but not, for the most part, in the masses who will people the nation. Hence the complex muddiness of power relations in Delany's concept of culture, and hence the menial strata reserved for Africans in the new African nation-state that is to be the black man's salvation.

Just as the novel opened by invoking white nationalist strategies implemented by cadres of the white/Cuban criollo elite, so it moves to closure on a wave of resistance in the cadres of the black/mulatto Cuban bourgeoisie. In the shift from the United States to the Caribbean, the (con)figurations of Henry/Henrico and his black political allies, as elite, educated New World blacks, are elided in the constitution of the black subaltern population in the United States, Africa, and the Caribbean as ignorant, debased, superstitious, feminized, or disappeared men and politically useless women or slaves. As predictable by the structure of the liberal state, the social pact between the majority and the new state strategically ignores its intrinsic structural inequalities.

Delany's agenda in proposing a Pan-African/American nation-state, we can note in conclusion, would have mimicked the development of the U.S. economy, because the first step in the ex-colony's rise to world power was ending English appropriation of its capital in order for its national bourgeoisie to accumulate its capital for itself. The problem of course is that the United States gained its riches by itself engaging in the exploitative strategies of an imperial power in regard to African labor under slavery. Delany's plan was for African-Americans to go to the source of black gold, "the slave factory" (*Blake* 214), capitalizing not only on African labor power but on capital existing as natural resources, with cadres of black Americans educated in the new industrial paradigms to lead the transformation of African culture, society, and politics, managing and appropriating the wealth of Africa within a bourgeois capitalist paradigm—in short, the taking of Africa.

The assimilationist alliance Delany proposes in South America is in fact a logical extension of his politics, for by the end of the nineteenth century the new elite of the South American countries would develop neoliberal paradigms of sociopolitical hierarchy remarkably similar to

"Africa for the African race *and black men to rule them*" (Ullman 225). Turn-of-the-century Latin American national transformations, in the name of progress, reveal strategies that we have seen Delany articulate: the desire is to civilize, which means to fence, to shoe, to clothe, to regulate "the social behavior of productive beings" (Rodríguez, *House* 25).[40] And in the name of civilization as transition, old hierarchies must be displaced and new ones reconstituted as an organizing principle "to order and educate as conditions of progress" (25). Here "progress is the institutionalization of society through a series of dualities: men's hegemony over women, the master over the peon, whites over other ethnic groups" (25) except that whiteness in Latin America is replaced by blackness in Delany, a blackness paradoxically at once "pure" (as embodied in the man-hero) but nevertheless mulatto in practice (the primacy of European over African macrological paradigms). Barbarianism, the enemy of progress and development, is embodied in ethnic difference: in the case of South America, the mass of ignorant blacks and indigenous Americans in Delany's case, African epistemology embedded like an enervating disease in Delany's enslaved black masses. In Delany, mulatto culture is a liberating force in that it marries black peoples to modernity; that is, to European ontologies and epistemologies in sociocultural relations and political economic principles, if not European racial epistemology.

In the end, the relations between Christianity, capital accumulation, and the conditions for the emergence of a revolutionary hero are crucial, if hidden within the novel. If, as Gilroy points out, "Delany's primary concern was not with Africa as such but rather with the forms of citizenship and belonging that arose from the (re)generation of modern nationality in the form of an autonomous, black nation state" then the place of Africa and African ethnicity, the other side of blackness, is critical to "the inner dialectics of diaspora identification" (23). By entering into a nationalist and Christian capitalist utopia Delany enters into a closed circuit (intellectual/economic) that ultimately participates in, as much as it anticipates, the exploitation of Africans and the disenfranchised black masses along with the reregulation of culture as value (albeit in a fantasy of equal exchange); that is, the exportation of value in the form of capital (economic/intellectual) from oppressed agrarian economies (the black Caribbean, Africa, enslaved blacks of the southern United States) to hegemonic modern economies (a transnational black bourgeoisie) for the enrichment of cadres of a like-minded, educated elite. Indeed, the persistent assaults by ruling-class America on the revolutionary governments in the region—especially Cuba and Nicaragua, precisely as Delany feared would happen—are inevitably attendant on the socioeconomic system that Delany both critiqued and sought to reproduce as he struggled to resolve the dilemmas of black/national territory and sovereignty. As a remedy for the malaise at the heart of his Pan-African/territorial theories, Delany, *pater progenitor* of the new black nation, casts the Gulf of Mexico and the Caribbean Sea (*Blake*) or the Atlantic Ocean (the "Reports") in the perceptual gulf between his reckoning with the Union and the culture of the world's black masses he sought to lead into redemption, even as he grappled to enlist the Pan-American black bourgeoisie in founding, funding, and administering a new global future for black peoples.

# 2

## Of What Use Is History?
## Blood, Race, Nation, and Ethnicity in
## Pauline Hopkins's New Woman

■

Beyond the common duties peculiar to the woman's sphere, the colored woman must have an intimate knowledge of every question that agitates the councils of the world; she must understand the solutions to problems that involve the alteration of the boundaries of countries, and which make and unmake governments.—Pauline Hopkins

The year 1877 saw the collapse of Reconstruction and the rollback of black social, legal, and political advances made at the insistence of a greatly expanded federal civil service. With the withdrawal of federal troops from the southern territories and the rewriting of state constitutions, the wounded slaveholding elite, so untimely ripped from the rich womb of slavery, moved to eliminate black senators, black congressmen, and black voters from the body politic.[1] Lynching and rape were on the rise, as white nationalist attacks—popularly based and federally sanctioned—on the sociopolitical and economic improvements in the condition of U.S. blacks festered, particularly in the South where Jim Crow became law in 1896. In an atmosphere rife with the resurgence of U.S. nationalism in the aftermath of the Spanish-American War and the rhetoric of self-help within the economic possibilities of an imperial capitalist economy—Hawaii and the Philippines had just been conquered— Pauline Hopkins wrote about the individual and the community as a network of "contending forces" in which, on one hand, black successes were undermined by individualist selfishness within the black community, and, on the other, where the state refused to police attacks on black businesses and on civil rights.

Pauline Hopkins worked as an editor for the reformist *Colored Ameri-can Magazine*, where she serialized her novels and wrote a series of articles on famous black women as well as several short stories.[2] When the magazine was moved to New York after it was purchased by Booker T. Washington, Hopkins was ousted, probably for her more radical political ideas.[3] Throughout her tenure at the journal, Hopkins displayed a fascination with the concept of the mulatta, a fascination that has come back to raise questions about the place of her novel in black nationalist culture. Since its republication in 1988, her book *Contending Forces: A Romance Illustrative of Negro Life North and South* (1899) has generated a small flurry of attention, yet nothing like that surrounding the republication of Jacobs's *Incidents in the Life of a Slave Girl*.[4]

At the center of Hopkins's political economy for the liberation of New World blacks stands the figure of woman and the useful possibilities of the sphere of the domestic economy. In this, Hopkins inherited generations of black feminist thinking in the United States that focused on the importance of "useful knowledge" as the "woman's sphere," ranging from the early protofeminism of Jarena Lee's spiritual autobiography (1836) to the work of Anna Julia Cooper, Francis Harper, and Ida B. Wells, Hopkins's contemporaries.[5] In the hegemonic U.S. cultural imaginary, the realities of being black in a white nationalist state and being a woman who needed to work for a living confronted the "cult of true womanhood" that posited fantasies of white bourgeois women at the center of woman's respectability. In their novels, black feminist writers like Hopkins and Frances Harper thus developed the notion of a politicized mulatta culture that struggled to combine the mechanics of what then constituted respectability in women with an astute African-American agenda. Politically, in the attempt to underscore the viability of black contributions to U.S. society, nineteenth-century black feminists also developed a range of strategies for both public and private empowerment linked to the feminist movement, founding their dialogue with the nation on the premise that the contribution of women's work was a crucial component to "help raise the race" (Hopkins, "Literary Workers" 1:278).

The black/nationalist dilemma within which *Contending Forces* takes place is constrained by the promises of a capitalist work ethic integral to U.S. nationalism as well as by questions of communal uplift and the dynamics of social spheres—out of the *oikos* (the domestic sphere) and into the *polis*—within which such strategies of economic and political improvement, as well as the stability of black class structures, could be maintained: "We love this country, we adore the form of government under which we live; we want to feel that it will exist through ages yet to come. We know that it cannot stand if the vile passions which are convulsing the people at the present time are allowed to continue. Let the women then, continue to help raise the race by every means in their power, and at the same time raise our common country from the mire of barbarism" (Hopkins, "Literary Workers" 1:278). Thus, if woman is at the center of Hopkins's worldview, bourgeois rights and moral capital accumulation for blacks within the class structures of the United States function as the utopia toward which her "useful work" strives, and the journey toward this utopia is administered on the premise of upward mobility. In Hopkins's historical/fictive universe, the factor that dislocates the machinery of black power is the violence of a coalition of white power groups among the grass roots, managers, and elites against the new black citizenry. In this, Hopkins shares Delany's conception of the state: "It is the idea of the Negro holding political preferment that is so hard for the North and South to swallow" (*Contending Forces* 251) despite the promises of Civil War, Emancipation, and Reconstruction. She thus raises the question of a lack of political incorporation into the promise of "America": "Let us compare the happenings of one hundred—two hundred years ago with those of today. The difference between then and now, if any there be, is so slight as to be scarcely worth mentioning. The atrocity of acts committed one hundred years ago are duplicated today, when slavery is supposed no longer to exist" (*Contending Forces* 15).

It is a mark of Hopkins's vision that she conceptualized, through the prism of women's work and the domestic economy, her political community "at this crisis in the history of the Negro in the United States" (*Contending Forces* 16) across national borders: the novel, in taking up the traditional African-American issues of political rights and reconstructing families, begins in Bermuda, moves then to Boston, and ends with a journey to England. As a beginning, I want to trace some of the implications of this international trek, but we can note at the outset that two points in contention are immediately apparent: first, that woman has no country[6] and, second, that the search for a liberationist black identity takes black U.S. heroes, as it took the Anglophone Afro-Caribbean leaders of Independence in the 1920s and 1930s, to the notion of mulatto culture; that is, to England and Europe in search of education and enlightenment.

The women at the center of *Contending Forces* are almost all mulattas. Hortense Spillers has already pointed out that "the thematic of the 'tragic mulatto/a'" loses its currency at the end of the nineteenth century, though it lingers well into the twentieth ("Notes" 166).[7] Nevertheless, on the verge of its disappearance from the cross-racial debate, after the ethno-national disasters accruing in the 1890s and at the brink of a new century that Du Bois predicted would be that of the color line, Hopkins sought to reconfigure mulatto culture as "a middle ground of latitude," a balm to heal a divided nation ("Notes" 165). Her last novel, *Of One Blood; or, The Hidden Self* (1902–3), reconstructs in the mulatto a hero for Africa in an African-American returning to the motherland, a drama played out on the historical geography of Egypt, a country whose mulatticity has been embattled since the European Renaissance.[8] In this sense, Hopkins was as concerned to question the cultural value of "African" as of "American," the better to trace the outlines of a figure straddling the hyphen that dissolves once these two poles of cultural reference move, a figure still resonating as a possibility, a shadow in the shift from a noun to two unevenly weighted adjectives. If the position of black identity within the borders of the United States insisted on that hyphen in the second half of the twentieth century, as denoting a whole identity, it is in the space of that bar between two continents, a middle passage in its own right, that the subject must come to rest.

The space of the "mulatto/a" itself positions the subject in the breach, in the shadows of the inescapable effects of gendering lost in the name of the subspecies "mulatto/a." Its horrific attributes, so much decried by both blacks and whites as the monstrous betrayal, the undoing of a nation, were countered in the scientific assertion that mulattos could not reproduce, and in banishing as obscene from polite society the term "miscegenation" whose resonance casts a shadow of the erect white penis. "Mulatto," says the OED, is from "young mule," the animal by-product of a horse and donkey, which is generally sterile; just as Ven Everie assured his readers in 1861, mulattos were declared to be sterile in the fourth generation.

But in the detailing of the figure of the "mulatto/a," a figure Spillers evocatively describes as an "accretion of signs" to voice the "unspeakable," the uses of gender reorder the place of women in the typology of the social sciences ("Notes" 166). For, if in the sign "mulatto/a" the neuter is gendered male (here the sign of woman appended by the indefinite article singular), it is to the hyphenating sign of the mulatta that black woman's illicitness was seen to most profitably accrue.[9] The masculine sign for the incubus was painted black.

This shift in the rubrics of race in the politico-libidinal economy suggests the effects of placing gender at the center of the drama of the nationalist psyche. In *Contending Forces,* woman is equal to a new nation, and the mulatta subject has stolen for itself the space of the hyphen between Africa and America, the middle passage of nation formation figured on her body, in her tragedy and in her sexuality and "mindless fertility," signed by the shadow on the nationalist psyche, a double contradiction in the shape of her features, the shade of her skin (Spillers, "Notes" 172). Cast as a "neither/nor," this by-product of New World socioeconomic and agro-industrial production finds itself too American to be African, too African to be admitted to the social body of Americans. If the split in the national psyche returned most obsessively to the poles of "blackness" and "whiteness," "mulattos" and "mulattas," as configurations of humanity, most often find themselves as the deconstructive locus of national fantasies among both the cultural elite and the disenfranchised. The mulatta stands in as the object of desire, as a site of contamination insisting on the historicity of the international confrontation, and as the national battlefield of property rights on women we saw in Delany and repeatedly will see again. In *Contending Forces* (1899), when the schematics of class and caste come to rest in this series of hyphens, the vessel in which the alchemy of the production of black labor power is performed accrues to herself a new middle passage.

Following the threads of Hopkins's conceptualizations of mulatta culture, I begin by questioning the utopic elements of her construction of 1790s Bermuda as the home of Grace, the (mulatta?) plantation mistress. From there, I discuss the role of mulatta culture in nation formation as Hopkins exemplifies it in her novel through Dora and Sappho, the young women at the center of the novel, and I argue that Sappho becomes an emblem of the nation on the brink of a new era. Next, I focus on the role and nature of power in the women at the height of the political and cultural spheres of the book. Here the two strands of culture (Africanisms in the case of Madam Frances, representing the South, and Enlightenment in the case of Mrs. Willis, representing the North), are configured and debated as models of both nation and mulatta culture with and in power. In the sections on Dora and Sappho and on Madam Frances and Mrs. Willis, I also examine the implications of foregrounding mulatta culture for national strategizing. This will take us to the question of Hopkins's men and the question of the black couple. In conclusion, I look briefly at how woman as nation is reconstituted in constituting the couple, and the grounds on which the new black couple faces the national future.

### The Political Economy of the White Mulatta

In the first chapter of *Contending Forces*, Charles Montfort, a Bermudan plantation owner, travels to North Carolina in search of a profitable economic environment. Hopkins's stated investment in historical truth is perhaps nowhere as dramatic as it is here. Whereas there are political speeches cited in whole or in part at the center of the book, the entire skeleton of the history of the Montforts, she tells us twice, is taken from archives in North Carolina and from the seat of federal government, Washington, D.C. (*Contending Forces* 14, 383–84). Given this investment in historical specificity in crossing territorial borders to assess and strategize public policy for a black ethno-nation, I want to turn Hopkins's famous question, "Of what use is fiction?" on its head, and ask, in the sphere of this wild space reconstructed through official documents of Bermuda and North Carolina in the 1790s: "Of what use is history?"[10]

At the head of the Montfort household is Charles, paterfamilias, who, faced with the triumph of coalition abolitionist and laissez-faire lobbies in England's Parliament, decides to transport his movable capital to the United States, where no such disregard for the protection of his "patrimony" is impending (28). Hopkins makes it clear that Charles is concerned with the profitable management of his property in cattle, equipment, and slaves. But when he decides to move to the United States, a fissure appears in his command over his wife as his property that provides us with the departure point for a reading of Hopkins's investments along the axis of woman in the *oikos* and the domestic sphere of Bermuda's ruling classes: " 'But surely you will not expose your wife to the inconveniences of life in that country,' said another. 'She has had her choice, but she prefers hardships with me to life without me,' proudly returned Montfort" (29).

Within the context of Hopkins's Caribbean household, woman has the right to decide her own destiny, can establish her independence, and break from her husband if she wishes. For Hopkins, this is indicative of the "romantic" Caribbean social text allowing a freedom and harmony among social groups that is nonexistent in the uncivilized territory of the southern United States. We can extrapolate from this a series of interconnected spheres and consider the function of women in each: the domestic economy of the Great House, the ministate of the plantation, the protonationalism of Montfort's response to global nineteenth-century economic transitions, and the constitution of Bermuda as a Caribbean island in an empire in two transitions: the Renaissance and nineteenth-century laissez-faire.

Within the spheres of territories and empires, economic transitions bring violence in their wake. If the history of blacks in the New World has been written in blood, the moment of transformation marked by the abolition of slavery and mercantilist protectionism for the Caribbean colonies represents a heightened crisis. For Hopkins's Montfort, this transition takes him back to the "New Men" of the Renaissance, those who left the civilization of Europe to expand the boundaries of the emerging European nation-states and to establish Bermuda as a British colony: "Why [is the move to North Carolina] dangerous? Is it any more so for me than for those who left England to build a home here in the wilderness?" (25).

The running critique of the United States as a "land of savages" (29) thus takes its place beside the original state of Bermuda before English settlement, pointing to the "progress" of British culture and society against the degeneracy and chaos of the South. Like the harmonious and democratic gender relations proudly reported by Montfort above, British settlement of the Caribbean wilderness represents here the "progress" of civilization, pointing to the inevitability of Amerindian genocide, slavery, and emancipation. Most important for Hopkins, settlement represents "progress" as the economic advancement of the mulatto cultures of the New World. Such understandings of progress and civilization are only possible if we posit ourselves as the center of history and pinnacle of development, the identity endemic to the nationalism of imperial countries and to peoples maintaining the option of determining the future of foreign territories in their own interest.

The history of Bermuda's settlement as recorded in private and public documents, however, complicates such a utopian understanding of England (also the utopia of the novel's conclusion) as the seat of a civilization opposed to U.S. barbarism. In the initial calls for colonists, Silvester

Jourdain described the islands as a paradise teeming with fruits and wildlife, and whose climate had miraculous healing properties: "It is in truth the richest, healthfullest, and pleasing land, (the quantity and bigness thereof considered) and merely natural, as ever man set foot upon: the particular profits and benefits whereof, shall be more especially inserted" (8; transliteration mine). Jourdain's *Plaine Description of the Barmudas* and its anonymous appendices struggle to catalogue the abundance of fine timber, the tameness and sweet meat of the fowl as well as the abundance of their eggs, the abundance of fish, and the richness of the soil for growing European crops.

Already there are the stirrings of a white Bermudan protonationalist consciousness that creeps into Jourdain's description through reconceptualizations of new indigenous species, as sustenance, as capital, a practical delineation hinging on violence and a metaphor of women that transcends national constraints. Jourdain continues:

> Fowles there are of divers sorts, but amongst all there is a bird like unto yours, which you call in England a Crow, which though they talk in the Bermudan language, yet their tongues shall walk as fast as any English womans: we cannot go by into the woods, but they will follow after us with such an outcry, that it would fret a man to hear them; they are very good meat, fat, and as white flesh as a Chicken, we many times make some of them leave their talking with stones or cudgels, for they will sit and face you hard at your hand. (24)

Women here function as the ground across which the old nation and the new national consciousness confront each other: as that which talks back and is in trouble, the ground whose fruits are plundered en route to "progress" that is synonymous with the objective of primitive accumulation in administering the new territory. That women have no place in the new country except as natural resources is further suggested by the record of births where women exist only as children born or as the anonymous bearers of these children, or not at all as in the list of easily obtainable proportions: "Three [birds] for a childe, boy or girl, for a man foure" (29).

The development from such random plunder of the fecund wilderness to a productive territory is initially worked by white labor from England, communally first in this "vnsetled and confused Chaos," as surveyor

Richard Norwood put it in his journal, "to receive a conuenient disposition, forme and order" (lxxvii)[11] that is the transition to private property, and thence to export agro-industry through organized slave labor. Just as in what would come to be called the United States, the conceptualizations of the Caribbean climate, flora, and fauna (including the indigenous people-species) as natural resources for the wealth of the growing empire combined with the reconceptualizations of African apes as workers, providing the basis for administering the exploitation of the wilderness and the progress of civilization. In the lexicon of Bermuda's new administrators—woman = apes = workers = natural resources = indigenous people-species—the administrative problem of this unsettled chaos is marked by the slippages of signs guaranteeing the territory as a paradise.

The people identified in this unsettling series (women, Africans, indigenous peoples), whose transformation into resources for the territory is the first task of the new men, are incorporated or excluded from the new national formations: military rule (no women, no ape-workers) then agro-industry (women and ape-workers mandatory). On the frontiers of the mercantilist British Empire the wilderness becomes a fortress, a zone of Christian men at war, and in the process of development the estate becomes the microunit of the state in the Caribbean territories where the wealthiest planters, with a handful of British officials, constitute the government of the territory as a whole. It is the fall of the plantations as the seats of power and the rise of new industrial and trade interests to governmental power in England—extending their sphere of influence to the economic organization of the empire—that leads to the socioeconomic crisis Montfort is contemplating, and from which the islands are still struggling to recover at the beginning of the twenty-first century, some more successfully than others.

The national interests multiply: the concepts of wilderness and frontier are always the vanishing point of the national project, as we will see in the novels of Wilson Harris. The formation of the state becomes disposable, and once the territory has been transformed in light of another administrative gambit (frontiers internal to the national borders), the old administrative areas revert to wilderness, to chaos. So with abolition, the transformation of ape-workers into freedmen and women, the Great Houses of the Caribbean, once the seats of government, become the junk of history or decrepit figures of the old forms of organizations, and are abandoned, haunted by white ghosts (figured in Jean Rhys's *Wide Sargasso Sea* or H. G. De Lisser's *The White Witch of Roschall*) or transformed into tourist attractions, the locus of international nostalgia for an era safely past.

The "ferocious acts of brutality" under slavery to which Hopkins alludes (*Contending Forces* 22) stem from the cooperation of the planter classes and the imperial government in the exploitation of slave labor as a natural resource for the islands, the violence crucial to the transformation of the African people-species into British agro-industrial workers, the transformation of flesh into machine. This violence within which such ministates were managed for profit disappears, however, from Hopkins's rendering of the slaves on the island, even as the Afro-Caribbean people-species are collapsed into the balmy, languid, profitable landscape on a Sunday, the day "the slave forgot his bonds" (24):

> In the direction of the square a crowd of slaves were enjoying the time of idleness. Men were dancing with men and women with women, to the strange monotonous music of drums without tune, relics of the tom-tom in the wild African life which haunted them in dreamland. Still, there was pleasure for even a cultivated musical ear in the peculiar variation of the rhythm. The scanty raiment of gay-colored cotton stuffs set off the varied complexions,—yellow, bronze, white,—the flashing eyes, the gleaming teeth, and gave infinite variety to the scene. Over there, waterfalls fell in the sunlight in silvery waves; parti-colored butterflies of vivid coloring, and humming-birds flashed through the air with electrical radiance; gay parakeets swung and chattered from the branches of the trees.
>
> "Where, my son," said the clergyman, indicating the landscape with a wave of his hand, "will you find a scene more beautiful than this?" (26)

The horrors of slavery dissolve in the narration of the islands as an exotic paradise, predicting the administrative structures of tourism (your pleasure is our only business) already in place, Hopkins tells us, "at the beginning of a new century" as "Bermuda presents itself, outside of its importance as a military power for a great nation, as a vast sanitorium for the benefits of invalids" (21). For Hopkins, the historical and geographical description climaxes in the apotheosis of English cultural nationalism as Shakespeare, as the administration of nature and the local worker-species as resources for the benefit of international travelers: "The island of Prospero and Miranda . . . become . . . to the traveler 'The spot of earth uncurst, / To show how all things were created first" (22).

The seeming incongruity of the novel's abrupt shift to the definition of Charles Montfort as "the owner of about seven hundred slaves" and exporter of several tropical crops resolves itself in the harmonious depiction of the African New World peoples as a part of the riches of the natural landscape. What is blocked in this schematic is a black New World alliance, in favor of the charm of the exotic setting, and the proclivity of Hopkins's readership for romantic images of the savage noble African. If the progress of black peoples is predicated on the transformation of flesh into machine, these workers are seen to revert to a state of nature, and it is this that distinguishes them from slaves in the United States who are only seen working, while always decrying the violence of the transformation wrought on their bodies.

For Hopkins, then, the proximity of Afro-Caribbean slave culture to African culture excludes them from her political alliance. In her romanticization of life in the British Caribbean islands, she focuses, like Delany, on the phenomenal wealth extracted from the territories as a source of primitive accumulation to found and fund a nation. In the shift from unproductive to productive social subjects, from the chaos of the African people-species who still carry the old African worldviews and forms of social administration, we sound the depths of a psychological and sociopolitical middle passage, the transformation from the old forms of social organization to the new agro-industrial worker to the managerial class of the new century. Unlike Delany, Hopkins recognizes her alienation from African ethnicity in a hyphenated space that marks the creation of her own culture of the black intelligentsia, and opts, instead of slave alliances, for the shadow darkening the value of the mulatto through the possibilities of the (mixed?) blood of the creole Caribbean plantation owners, although always only as an indeterminate possibility. Hopkins's mark of the superior development of English/Bermudan society is its ability to accept the facts of "amalgamation" (which means people administered the developmental processes of transition, whitewashing in the process of distilling the citizen from the worker from the unsettled chaos of African apes):

> In many cases African blood had become diluted from amalgamation with the higher race, and many of these "colored" people them-

selves became rich planters or business men (themselves owning slaves) through the favors heaped upon them by their white parents. This being the case, there might even have been a strain of African blood polluting the fair stream of Montfort's vitality, or even his wife's, which fact would not have caused him one instant's uneasiness. (23)

The myth of the ascension of the Caribbean mulatta to wealth, power, and social acceptance is greatly exaggerated, although in the crisis societies of the British Caribbean islands of the late 1700s, the coincidence of blood, skin color, and hard labor was indeed carefully controlled. In a 1788 letter from Antigua, John Luffman describes the dynamics of race, gender, value, capital, and work in the British Caribbean islands, resolutely the province of men:

The general idea of Europeans, that blacks only are slaves, is very erroneous, for slavery extends to every descendant of negroes (slaves) by white men, such as mulattoes, mestees and quarteroons, and the latter two mentioned, are frequently as fair as Englishmen, at least such of them as have been habituated to a sea-faring life, or to tropical countries. I have seen persons sold here, having blue eyes and flaxen-hair, and complexioned equal to almost any on your side the water, but such people fetch a lower price than blacks, unless they are tradesmen, because the purchasers cannot employ them in the drudgeries to which negroes are put to; the colored men, are therefore mostly brought up to trades or employed as house slaves, and the women of this discription are generally prostitutes. . . . There are persons in this island who let out their female slaves for the particular purpose of fornication. . . . These women are much more subservient to the will of their enamorators, from a dread of punishment than a white would be, or even the laws of the country suffer, for it is not uncommon for some men to beat, and otherwise severely correct their colored mistresses. This connexion strikes at the root of honorable engagements with the fair, prevents marriages, and is, thereby, detrimental to the increase of the legitimate population. (qtd. in Abrahams and Szwed 334–35)

The results of this violent miscegenation are embedded in Hopkins's description of the dancers' skin ("yellow, bronze, white") but point to an exaggeration of African ethnicity: physiologically in the "flashing eyes" and "gleaming teeth," just as the "tom-toms" and "monotonous music" on the other side of a cultivated ear suggest an alien culture. Hopkins thus shrouds the violence against women at the birth of mulatto Caribbean societies in the exotica of collapsing imperial conceptualizations of Afrocentric ethnicity and in the marks of poverty and enslavement in their "scanty raiment of gay-colored cotton stuffs" considered so complimentary to their skin tones. No one is whipped in Hopkins's version of British Bermuda. This peculiar conceptualization supercedes even the romantic racialists, unacceptable to Hopkins in depicting the black community of the United States, but rendered beautiful and historically grounded for blacks of the Caribbean. What Hopkins seeks is the coexistence of strains of black blood, social acceptability, wealth, and harmonizing social relations in the paradise of Bermuda, and so her descriptions are careful in their alliances to the idea of the mulatto/a and to harmonious social structures.

Historically, then, intersections of race and gender in political economy play a crucial role, as the limits of humanity in the celebration of Bermuda's fecundity, as sites of violent gestation for the mulatto country and as metaphors for nations. The one Caribbean slave seen working on Sundays, as Caribbean slaves actually did from necessity, is a woman on the threshold of the plantation: "A Negro woman was weeding her little garden; her pickaninny was astride her back, spurring his mother as a rider his horse. The woman and the child looked up and smiled at the master and his guest, and the woman put the child on the ground and stood upright to bob a queer little courtesy" (27).

More developed, for Hopkins, than the dancers in her smiling "queer" imitations of civilized ethnicity, the Afro-Caribbean woman is seen on her day off engaging in productive activity for her child's and her own benefit (provision ground rendered garden) but Hopkins's racial alliances, the ethnicity of the subject at the center of her eighteenth-century political economy, cannot allow this black woman and child equal citizenship: the name for the young of the ape-worker people-species is "pickaninny," always distinguishable from the term "child" reserved here primarily for the white, therefore human and therefore developed, people of the master('s) race. This characterization of the child-animal and the woman-animal as part of the landscape returns when Montfort later sees his beautiful, cherubic heir astride a horse in North Carolina and remembers this emblem of the Bermudan landscape: "As Montfort watched him, the picture of his last Sunday in Bermuda arose before him: the little Negro child astride his mother's back, spurring her along like a rider his horse" (48). In the beatification of male children, the woman straddling the hyphenated space of Afro-Caribbean motherhood becomes a horse in the planter hero's nostalgic imagination.

Hopkins's clear objective, however, in the opening four chapters of *Contending Forces* is the brutal and primitive construction of race in the barbaric southern antebellum United States: the masses of "crackers" (chapter 2), and the fall of the beautiful and noble Grace Montfort from the pedestal of true womanhood because of the baseness of white men, federal indifference, and U.S. hysteria over purity of blood (chapters 3 and 4). If Charles Montfort is gendered through property as capital, Grace's gendered capital lies in her beauty and her whiteness, preserving the Montfort patrimony for another generation of white men:

> Grace Montfort was a dream of beauty even among beautiful women. Tall and slender; her form was willowy, although perfectly molded. Her complexion was creamy in its whiteness, of the tint of the camellia; her hair a rich golden brown, fell in rippling masses far below the waist line; brown eyes, large and soft as those seen in a fawn; heavy black eyebrows marked by a high white forehead, and features as clearly cut as a cameo, completed a most lovely type of Southern beauty. (40)

That Grace Montfort is described in terms of white southern, rather than white Caribbean, womanhood is indicative of her lack of a country and hence the extent to which she is at the mercy of society and the nationhood of men, including poor white men. Woman here is a symbol, ubiquitous, and as such Grace is immediately marked for expulsion from southern society by the men who constitute the poor white masses: her skin is suspiciously "creamy," indicating an impurity of the blood contaminating the ruling classes and thus the race/power nexus of the national horizon. So it is Charles who hears the subsequent rumors of his wife's mulatta background and of the impending attack by the white mob on the plantation, and it is he who often thinks nostalgically of returning to Bermuda as his home.

Grace adapts: her public persona is eminently successful among the southern elite, and it is only after the destruction of her reputation through the work of the character of Anson Pollock that nostalgia for the climate and fragrances of Bermuda overwhelms her in her boudoir. She is, however, fated to live the life of the "tragic mulatta," the staple of white abolitionist fiction in the United States at its inception.[12] Grace's charm, her whiteness, and her quick acceptance into the upper echelons of white southern society all work to depict a life of grace and social success among the Great Houses of the South. The Caribbean slaves, for the sake of whose ownership the Montforts emigrated, are now transplanted to the borders of the plantation, "picturesquely visible at a convenient distance" as we move among the Montforts in the Great House (43). For Grace's sake, the house has been beautifully outfitted with the trappings of culture that are the business of wealthy white women to acquire and appreciate: a harp, "a volume of Goethe in the original," "the score of some then-popular opera," a grand piano (44). Despite all this, the lust of a white man, the powerful and brutal Anson Pollock, brings about her enslavement and the enslavement of her children.

To have a wealthy white man lust after and assault Grace opens onto the questions of sexual violence against women that are obscured in the depiction of Bermuda's mulatto society. As Hopkins's commentators have noted, the figure of Anson Pollock is a direct rebuttal, via historical truth, to the white southern charge that black men, driven by uncontrollable lust, raped white women and so brought lynching on themselves.[13] The plot is also a mark of Hopkins's sophisticated manipulation of dominant stereotypes, however, that she has Anson Pollock plot Grace's downfall as revenge against his rejection by her as a mulatta.

In other words, just as black men and women were attacked by gangs and mobs of white men for taking upon themselves the social and capital formations reserved for whites in the United States, so Grace Montfort, the white mulatta, is seized by Anson Pollock, the white man behaving as black men were reputed to do. When the assault comes (heavily foreshadowed), it is attributed to a greater force, a final justice gendered as woman in anticipation of the powers accruing to the seeress Madam Frances that we will explore later. But whereas in the attack Charles is shot and his patrimony taken by the nascent Ku Klux Klan dubbed "the committee on public safety" (53), the plantation and its chattel are seized by Anson Pollock, and Grace is subjected to torture and humiliation in Charles's place in the ritual restoration of the old southern administrative policy, of order and purity in the ethno-ideological terrain of power.

We have shifted here from the role of white women in the Caribbean political economy to the political economy of the mulatta, one in which the woman carries the burden of contamination and the threat of new administrative horizons. The political economy of the United States therefore finds woman/mulatta/nation at its center and traces its effects. In fact, throughout the chapters on the Montforts, excepting the first from which she is absent, Grace is constituted as the linchpin of Charles Montfort's success in the new territory, a crucial aspect of survival that Charles's Bermudan friends had warned would be difficult to maintain in such a savage territory as the southern United States. Thus the Bermudan's implication is particularly Caribbean: that rich white Caribbean women, as rich white Caribbean women will later attest, belonged in the urbanity of the islands rather than the wildernesses of the United States or even the cold cultivation of England and Europe.[14] The place for women is in the city, rather than the wilderness, the zone where men discover themselves. For Hopkins, the 1790s are reproduced in 1899 as mulatto nations are denied their social and economic inheritance, and the fate of the nation is here inextricable from the fate of its women.

Montfort's investments are doing well when the "committee on public safety" attacks, but it is a lack of social acceptance—specifically the combination of slavery, bad white blood among the ruling classes of the slave South, and envy and political pride among the white laboring classes—in confrontation with the social enlightenment among the rich white immigrants, the wealth in money of Charles and in beauty of Grace, that brings the Montforts' destruction. A fact that remains unexplained in the book is that the Montfort children's white skin, historically, would have provided necessary cover in the United States for their subsequent escapes from slavery; that is, for Charles Jr.'s adoption by a wealthy Englishman and for Jesse's escape to Boston, an event inevitably helped by the fact of his color because dark skin throughout the New World could turn a freeborn into a slave.[15] It is a mark of the profound transformation, if not elision, of national identities managing racial tensions and the violence of slavery built into Caribbean class and personal identity that Jesse, raised as a white Caribbean planter's son, chooses to align himself with the black community in the United States, and in so doing becomes the ancestor of the black family at the center of the narrative, a center preoccupied with family as much as strategies for political and economic empowerment.

From the 1790s to the 1890s, the intersections of race and gender shift with the accumulation of history. If the hope of the New World African nation in the period of agro-industrial slave labor was the force of nature holding the reins of justice, a utopian administration, then in the face of the new arena, the ape-worker transformation of agrarian society has been displaced by the worker-citizen transformation of industrialization. The mechanics of this transformation count among their effects new investments in the relationship of nation to country: the nation exists in a separate relation to the state, where to have a country assumes the new administrative relation promised in the hyphen of the nation-state, grounded in the collective territory. The use of antislavery rhetoric in the Civil War and the passage of the Fourteenth Amendment held out promises backed up by federal armies, with the equation of proslavery forces with internal enemies built into the Constitution legitimizing the occupation of the South in the name of black inclusion.

But the transformation of the people-citizens to accommodate the new administrative policy requires the recognition and conciliation of divergences in the national body. At the end of the nineteenth century, the black social body was still divided along the lines of an industrial North and an agrarian South. If strategies of the black intelligentsia historically required analyses of both North and South, it is because the administrative policies of the federal government still split the territories between these two poles. Hopkins's women come from both of these administrative traditions, and it is a mark of the meaning of "progress" that their physical and psychological migration is from North to South for Dora, but from South to North for Sappho, from agrarianism to industrialism and beyond. Sappho becomes the hope for the future, the preferred paradigm of the new woman, and she displays it in her technical training as a clerical worker (knowledge labor[16] over physical labor) and in her up-to-date requests for heat to be included in her rent. The concept of the mulatta subject thus includes not only the union of white and black genotypes in the biological sphere but also the union of an agrarian past and an industrial future. Grace, the mulatta subject at the center of the eighteenth-century political economy, is thus superseded in the face of the twentieth century by Dora and Sappho.

Further, if within a woman-centered political economy marriages are

the equivalent of mergers, then Dora's marriage to Arthur Lewis, propo-
nent of the transformation of agro-worker into industrial worker, finds
its counterpart in the union of Sappho and Will, the exemplary advocates
of the new knowledge workers, the new managerial class that can carry
the black nations into the twentieth century by marrying the feminized
historical memory of the South (McCann's "woman as vessel of the past"
[793]) to the new masculinized knowledge worker within the industrial
administration of the North (embodied in male leadership in the public
sphere).

Just so, Sappho's deterritorialization as a victim of rape and a single
mother mirrors Will's as a worker in an industrial society. Dora, the
woman trained in the old agrarian trade for women, managing a household, marries Dr. Arthur Lewis, the man who is tied to the land, coming
out of the old agrarian structures. The resolution of the interethnic
tensions between the people laboring under these two administrative
structures is, then, a task Hopkins's novel undertakes as a mark of the
conflictive horizons of the past that must be transformed in order to
enter the new era.[17] The production of the new woman must not only
take into account the split between agrarian cultures (associated with
people-species, the primitive, the sensual, the sexual) and industrial
ones (worker, developed, asexual, neutered yet masculinized), but confront the dichotomy between paradigms of womanhood and political
administration.[18]

The boardinghouse run by Dora and her mother, Ma Smith, becomes
as much a metaphor for the development of the new black nation as an
answer to the search for territory. "You ought to thank God every day,"
Sappho tells Dora, "for such a refuge as you have in your home" (128).
Out of this territory, this "refuge," Hopkins founds her new nation. In
the move from the rooms and the community of the boardinghouse
through the sewing circle in Ma Smith's back parlor out to the church on X
Street and beyond, the first half of the novel structures an expanding
series of territories protected by marshaling capital and the laws of private
property in the North.[19] At the novel's center, where history again makes
its mark, is the community meeting called to strategize a national-political
response to southern rape and lynching, and held in the church building
that it is the business of the women of the sewing circle to acquire.

Thus Hopkins's political economy is concerned to resolve the problem
of territory and house the gestation of new strategies as much as the New

Black Men who are propelled into Boston's corridors of power, from there to the world, for the uplift of the race. In these schemes, the common agendas of the New Women are characterized by heterosexual marriage and middle-class virtues that teach women on the one hand to follow their men for the sake of the race, and on the other to complement and serve their men's private professional development for public collective amelioration. Like Delany, Hopkins heralds the birth of a new black bourgeoisie—rich, traveled, educated. But unlike Delany, and convinced of the superior might of the white nationalist armies and the state's ability to foreclose on white public opinion, Hopkins opts against turning the nation into an army. In place of war she marries African-American progress to the double agenda of labor and lobbying the ruling elite to transform the intersections of blood, race, nation, citizenship, and gender within the borders of ethnicity in U.S. territory. Management, administration, the missing definitional term that for which labor labors and that which will realize the changes for which lobbies lobby, is the province of mulatto culture: birthing a new black capitalism to cross the new frontier and uplift a nation.

Hopkins plays out the dynamics of womanhood oscillating between these interactive poles in the relationship between Dora and Sappho. Dora, the daughter of Ma Smith and heir to the patrimony of the boardinghouse, is already being trained in its proper and profitable management under the guidance of her mother. In this industrialized, matrifocal family, Will, the son, is expected to leave for college, marry, and set up house on his own, and so Dora is expected to govern the boardinghouse, at least until she marries. Should Dora be widowed like her mother, she can capitalize on her skills and her virtuous—and therefore profitable—reputation. The tenuous economic position of women in the public future of the nation in the United States thus marks the future of this refuge, the site of the production of new, productive black social subjects.

In the chapter immediately following the Montforts' demise, Dora sings the praises of the new boarder, Grace, and gives her pride of place in the house by putting her in the front room, a superior location that is earned by her beauty and grace. At the turn of the nineteenth century as much as in the 1790s, then, beauty is still the repository of capital for women: "She's too beautiful for that dreary back room. I know that it is not business to let a good-paying room go under our usual price, but she's a 'steady'; she has the best references. Father Andrew gives her the best of characters, and so I'll chance getting my money back out of the next cross-grained old bachelor who comes along. See how mercenary I am getting to be since I undertook to direct the fortunes of a lodging-house" (81). In this construction of the border (between outsider and insider, profits and community, men and women, then and now) the boarder's appropriate place in the geography of the household is negotiated among women for women. In keeping with our governing metaphor, we can extrapolate nation from house and see the rules of the house as a metaphor for government, with Dora and Ma Smith at its head. What is hinted here emerges full force later: Dora's investment in the welfare state, guided by laws governing woman's value: reputation, feelings, virtue, work, a room of one's own, empathy with unmarried, therefore working, women, the approval of the Church, and the distance from unmarried men who it is assumed will have money.

At the same time, the narrative of Sappho's past, on which her reputation ought to be based, is slowly revealed as crisis-ridden. Again, it is her beauty and womanly virtues, quickly ascribed to her southern birth, that provide the counterpoint against which her past is to be judged. What is clear, however, is that she has no home; that her deterritorialization as a working woman is inextricable from her apparent disinterest in her marital status and from her black blood combined with her southern heritage and her buried past.

The mulatta worker carries with her the stain of the chaos of antebellum history into the industrialized Boston of 1899 and so is blocked from participation in the areas of the workforce—marriage, light industry—afforded white women. In Hopkins's Bermuda the mulatta/women-species were natural resources for the growth of capital, the workforce, and the nation; in the horizon of the 1890s as well, their involvement in the workforce is integral to the progress of the African-American nation proper, although citizenship for women is only dimly glimpsed on the new horizon. U.S. North-South tensions replay themselves here in the polyculturalism of the ethno-nation, as the culture grapples with the reformations of gender and politics inherited from previous horizons. The new mulatta culture thus leases a zone for itself within the borders of the refuge from which the new social subjects can emerge. If home is nation, the boardinghouse is a foster home, suggesting again that women have no country.

The metaphors for the sexualized woman, especially the mulatta, are telling: to have a past is to have a reputation. This is precisely what Sappho lacks, a silence on history consistently remarked and whose erosion constitutes the major thread that develops as the "plot" over the course of the novel's denouement. Until that past is revealed, Sappho's status and trustworthiness will always be in question. Behind this silence in history lies an agony that reduces her to tears and undermines her belief in her own worthiness, threatening to disrupt the marriage to a New Man that will consummate her life and close the novel.

As the second half of *Contending Forces* makes clear, Sappho becomes a metaphor for black womanhood/nationhood in the South: she has no home, she has been raped by a wealthy white man and then abducted in the attempt to decriminalize the rapist's crime and seal her fate as she is abandoned in a brothel "in the lowest portion of the city of New Orleans" (260). Sappho's virtue, like black women's virtue in the South, in under constant assault for pleasure/profit from rich white men. Sappho comes to function as a metonym for all women with black blood (including Grace) living in the South under white men who sever all family ties and invade at will the refuge of black homes and black women's bodies/ virtue, and thus invade the black nation.

This violent conceptualization of blood, race, and gender transforms even the finest southern women, as "the beautiful pet of [the colored planter's] household" is made into "a poor, ruined, half-crazed creature" (260) by her abduction in the city and her incarceration in the brothel as "a prisoner in a house of the vilest character" (260). As the antithesis of virtuous womanhood and the site of the enactment of subhuman passions, the brothel is cast as the forbidden zone to which only men and whore workers of the woman-species have access, in which black womanhood, taken from its home, is locked up and sold for violation.

In the crisis-ridden history of the nation the violent rape of black women marks the threshold of sexuality under the rule of white southern men. At puberty, then, inaugurating the gendered emergence of black womanhood, and thus the central question of the nation's reproduction, is a historical violation, as the practices of individual violence accumulate to national proportions. This historical violence wreaked on the black woman's body constitutes Sappho's secret past—nation building as rape[20]—the public/private history that must be expunged from the New Woman.

In keeping with the beatification of male children as a proper function of the woman's sphere, what compels Sappho to face her origins/identity is the fact of a son born of that violence whose existence is construed as proof of her shame and devaluing and thus birthed in that other refuge for women, the nunnery. To return to her past before she can face marriage she must return first to her son, to "mother-love" (34), to the violence that marked the death of Sappho's identity as Mabelle Beaubean and her rebirth as Sappho Clark; she must reconstruct her life on the virtues of true womanhood as motherhood before she can reconstruct her disrupted future of marriage to a New Man, wifedom.

For her part, Dora, daughter of the North, is trained in the financial independence and Yankee womanly virtues that govern the novel: work for women, Christian forgiveness, tenderness, the importance of marriage and heterosexual values (women's submission to men who represent marital-financial prospects), and from there to social organizing and to racial uplift. In her discussions with Sappho, the young Dora voices the laws of women's gender in northern upbringing, even as Sappho's accumulation of historical memory of the southern experience of violence against the black woman/nation challenges the paradigms of the political economy of gender for the new national horizon. For Dora, after marriage to the novel's version of Booker T. Washington there is the return to the South; for Sappho there is first the reconstruction of her womanhood, then marriage to the novel's version of Du Bois, and then travel to England to collect an inheritance. But in the quiet of Sappho's room, the zone in which the character of the New Woman is most generatively conflicted, Dora is confronted with the interrogations of an intelligent, battered woman on the laws of gendering and on the constraints imposed on the mind and body of woman in the name of marriage and heterosexual virtues as keys to national progress.

As noted earlier, the front square room is accorded pride of place in the house, where the woman/nation confronts the meanings of its unwritten history. The front square room becomes the site of the organization of the emotive sphere, a site of gestation for the rebirth of the New Woman, where women transgress the limits of the old conceptualization of mulatto nationhood to recognize the poly-ethnicity of the black nation in planning its programmatic integration into the state and the acquisition of citizenship. This act of separation, an act that will allow the New Women to question the configurations of the old, is signed by a breach in the relationship of women to the phallocratic nation (as in Delany) reproduced in parental relations of obedience and transparency. Thus the good daughter breaks from her role and lies to her mother in order to access and preserve the secret borders of the room as the emotive sphere.

If the house is a black woman's refuge, this private space for a friendship between women becomes a pregnant fortress for the emotive founding of the new social subjects: "By eleven o'clock they had locked the door of Sappho's room to keep out all intruders, had mended the fire until the little stove gave out a delicious warmth, and had drawn the window curtains close to keep out stray currents of air. Sappho's couch was drawn close beside the stove, while Dora's small person was most cosily bestowed in her favorite rocking chair" (117). In this perfect picture of domesticity men are not only absent but locked out; they are discussed, their use is managed, but they are not missed. If the house stands as a metaphor for the nation, in the scene above we have approached a frontier, the horizon of a secret zone for freeing women from the normalization of the laws policing women's bodies and habits, predicated on the desires of men:

> "You'll be fat as a seal, and then John P. won't want you at any price. Take warning and depart from the error of your ways before it is too late."
> Dora laughed guiltily and said as she drew a box from her apron pocket: "Well, here are John's chocolate bonbons that he brought last night. . . ."
> Sappho shook her head in mock despair. (120)

Just as the contradictions of women's roles in both cooking and receiving food they cannot eat without losing control of their value has led in many cases to bulimia and anorexia, so the gendered quotidian realities of marriage, the threshold of the reward for value in women, quickly comes under fire: "What troubles me is having a man bothering around. Now I tell John P. that I'm busy, or something like that, and I'm rid of him; but after you marry a man, he's on your hands for good and all. I'm wondering if my love could stand the test" (121). The unraveling of the founding concept of marriage, a woman's natural incompleteness, posits a reconceptualization of the terms of womanhood, a reconceptualization, Sappho explains, that reverses the order of things: "The men get tired of us first. A woman loves one man, and is true to him through all eternity." Dora's response is telling of what Hopkins will characterize as the danger of girl friendships and the social construction of gender: "That's what makes me feel so *unsexed*" (122).

Reconsidering the old laws governing domesticity and marriage begins to unravel them, and, with their unraveling, sexed/gendered identity is unraveled as well.[21] The role of women in the uplift of the race becomes reconstituted in the secret zone, negotiating the poles of true womanhood (dependence/independence) founded in and funded by alliances to men, a negotiation of the regulations of gender dividing the women as they oscillate between these poles:

> "I'm willing to confess the subject is a little deep for me," replied Dora. "I'm not the least bit of a politician, and I generally accept whatever men tell me as right; but I know that there is something very wrong in our lives, and nothing seems to remedy the evils under which the colored man labors."
>
> "But you can see, can't you, that if our men are deprived of the franchise, we become aliens in the very land of our birth . . . an alien people, without a country and without a home." (125)

Although the regional differences between Dora and Sappho are consistently observed, an important precept is remarked in this debate on gender in a political economy centered on middle-class black women. For both Sappho and Dora, behind the struggle for the production of the new nation it is understood that women have no country: the disenfranchisement of their men is the disenfranchisement of the race, even if for Sappho it is the right of women to bother with issues beyond "the mysterious link which would join love, marriage and the necessary man in a harmonious whole" (123) and embrace political economy and the advancement of the race.

The nature of the resolution of tensions within gendering and women's roles in formulating the racial agenda goes a long way toward explaining the disappearance from the rest of the novel of a woman space without men, thereby resolving the danger of "girl friendships" and the anxiety that "a close intimacy between two of the same sex was more than likely to end disastrously for one or the other" (97–98). When men begin to invade the sanctity of the front square room, when the configuration is no longer Sappho-Dora but Sappho-Will, or its antithesis Sappho-Langley (Langley as the brutal descendant of Anson Pollock), the room ceases to function as a refuge, Sappho's flight to her geographic/biographic past leaves a breach in the house/nation that must be healed before the plot can be tied up. The split between Dora and Sappho is marked all the more powerfully in the split between Ophelia and Sarah Ann, the two freedwomen who occupy and work in the basement, as the upwardly mobile Ophelia marries a young man of the Church, supplanting the financial and emotional union of two women.

Jean Franco argues that the power of the "oppositional potentialities of these territories [home, brothel, nunnery]—whose importance as the *only* sanctuaries became obvious at the moment of their disappearance" is often forgotten ("Killing" 420). For Dora and Sappho the dismantling of the barriers to the front square room is tied to the moment in which they find men, entering the privileged circuit of marriage in which women leave one house ruled by a man for another. In the early spiritual autobiography of freeborn Jarena Lee (1836), upon the death of a husband to whom she is dutifully bound but whom she does not necessarily love, she leaves the children with kin and abandons the domestic sphere to testify on the margins of the Church. In another case, freeborn Nancy Prince traveled to Russia with her husband and then to Jamaica as a widow concerned with the international uplift of the race. But by the time of the autobiography of Harriet Jacobs (1861), the home is already the refuge Hopkins claims for it, and from grandmother to great-granddaughter the generations of women nurtured in Jacobs's *Incidents* plot the constitution of a home. Rooms that lock invaders out also lock women in, and in the horizon of free women the house can function as a jail, just as in the horizon of slave women the concept of a home functions as a refuge. It is a mark of the tenets of political black womanhood that neither the nunnery, as the zone of spiritual marriage to God removed from the secular world, nor the brothel, as the zone of financial marriage to the flesh, are centrally embraced as national options, although they mark the parameters of the zones of conflict in the birth of New Women. In the occasional mention of a woman persistently allowing her virtue to stray for profit, there is always the narrator's despair.[22] The psychohistory of the national/family drama between the flesh and the spirit of the law or, better, between emotive desire and the political becomes a central question of the novel: if these are not embraced, then what can be embraced? Dr. Lewis and Dora return South and Will and Sappho are left on the open sea, following the path of capital in the Atlantic slave trade on its final leg.

At the height of black women's power in Hopkins's political economy there is a breach between the mystical and the material.[23] Madam Frances, mystic, crone, southerner, aunt to Sappho, is the woman who confronts and bests John Pollock Langley, descendant of Anson Pollock and Grace's maid who is leader of the Colored American League and the most powerful black politician in the book. Counterpoised to Madam Frances we find Mrs. Willis: widowed, secular, shrewd, politic, a product of an accumulated "racial development" ongoing since before the Civil War among free blacks, both those born free and those who freed themselves (*Contending Forces* 145). If Dora and Sappho represent the New Women for a coming era, then these New Women signify the achievements of a generation of women now in power at the unraveling of Reconstruction, public/political maternal figures of the race. Mrs. Willis's authority stems from the successes of her husband as much as from her intelligence and her veneer of culture, the constraints of her gender adjectivized as "the brilliant widow of a bright Negro politician" (143). Although Hopkins writes her as barely educated, the narrator finds her impressive in her ability to spin her rudimentary education into eloquence and the impression of advanced schooling in order to gain authority. Her sphere of power is the sewing circle, the center for women's political organization in the book. It is through the sewing circles and women's clubs that the community of women organizes the fair to pay off the mortage on the church on X Street.

If the narrative is propelled, then, by the expansion of territory (room → house → Church → World) on the one hand, and on the other by Sappho's return to her past, it is the work of the sewing circle that provides the catalyst for the romantic plot as much as the political one. It is at the fair that we meet Madam Frances and Alphonse, Sappho's son. For Hopkins, however, such a formidable figure as Mrs. Willis cannot be trusted with private dilemmas, a concern central to Madam Frances's sphere of power. When Sappho feels moved to confide in Mrs. Willis, a response to her presence and authority, she feels repelled, as if Mrs. Willis's interest veils a political maneuver with a personal veneer.

The relation of women to power is critical for Hopkins's project. If a new administration for the *oikos* is posed as the base of sociopolitical change, it is the *polis,* the sphere of men and national administration

(Will, Langley, et al.), within which the New Woman must negotiate the position of clientele: employment in light industry and information processing, the transformation of the private house into the public house whose reputation is managed like a woman's. In the end, Hopkins's women must reject public administrative power in favor of liberal education for women, or training as managers of a (petit) bourgeois household (Dora, Mrs. Smith, Grace) or contract work (Ophelia and Sarah Ann, Sappho).

Power, then, is phallocratic, and to the extent that northern women have the upper hand by their knowledge of industrial society, the northern woman is always in danger of becoming "unsexed" in negotiating the terms of the marriage contract (Dora, Mrs. Willis). The ideal body of the worker in industrial societies, then as now, is constituted as centrally male: childbearing and childrearing become disruptive to career advancement, and it is interesting that neither Mrs. Willis nor Madam Frances is seen mothering her own children, but rather the nation instead.[24] The realm of the feminine, accruing to the mulatta, is itself associated with the agrarian societies personified by Sappho and Grace. The extent to which these women are victimized by the men of the Pollock/Langley clan is a mark of their inability to see their place in a male plot to extrapolate power/pleasure from the chaos surrounding womanhood in slave societies.

If the line of power from *pater progenitor* (Pollock) to descendant (Langley), and hence South to North and antebellum to post-Reconstruction, suggests the mobilization of patriarchal forces untouched by new administrative policies, the battle between the emotive and the political comes back to suture and retrieve the (r)evolutionary subject(s) into hegemonic patterns of social relationships. The intimacy of women's most clandestine spaces (Sappho's room, Ophelia and Sarah Ann's basement floor) does not carry, then, into the larger space of the women's organizations, and this is borne out in the battles among women for prizes at the fair.

Hopkins's most powerful arguments for the status of black womanhood as a national fulcrum and the reasoning that will vindicate the African-American/mulatto nation of its history as the focus of a new national policy—"I would not worry about the fate of the mulatto, for the fate of the mulatto will be the fate of the entire race" she tells the sewing circle (151)—we find in the mouth of Mrs. Willis, despite Hopkins's reservations toward her. In a conceptual leap, Hopkins shifts the idea of mulatto/a from metonym to metaphor for the race:

> It is an incontrovertible truth that there is no such thing as an unmixed black on the American continent. Just bear in mind that we cannot tell by a person's complexion whether he be dark or light in blood, for by the working of the natural laws the white father and the black mother produce the mulatto offspring; the black father and white mother also, while the *black father* and *quadroon* mother produce the black child, which to the eye alone is a child of unmixed black blood. (151)

But if there are possibilities here of a group interest becoming the interests of the masses, displacing the concept of a common front in favor of mulatto leaders (the New Men) then the centrality of patience in woman's upward mobility, and therefore personal/political/racial happiness for women, determines the horizon and closes Mrs. Willis's talk: "Remember one maxim written of your race by a good man: 'Happiness and social position are not to be gained by pushing' " (152).

Although Hopkins's national agenda leans toward Will/Du Bois, her agenda for women is always a liberal one based on the virtues of modern petit bourgeois womanhood: patience, cheerfulness, reputation, hard work, the accumulation of capital, marriage. It is these characteristics, mingling the emotive with the political, that allow Mrs. Willis to ascend to her heights, and it is the political edge to her calculations, her personal ambition as much as her veneer of generosity, that both propels her to power and opens the "abyss" between her and Sappho. Although Hopkins admits that Mrs. Willis gives good motherly advice, the unfurling of history, here the agent of nature/woman (recall the Montforts' demise), backs Sappho's instincts to engender the plot structuring the second half of the novel. Hopkins's centering of women in the political economy thus carries with it contradictory effects: women cannot be women (emotive, companionable) and also be political because the Subject of national politics is still male: politics in a woman requires deception because it concerns itself with the negotiation of power and conflict rather than generosity and cheerfulness. The political woman is, then, unevenly assimilated into the twin peaks of politics and femininity, either unsexed (Dora's fear) or living a lie that will inevitably be discovered (Sappho's fear). In the end, Hopkins decides that selfish worldly ambitions (work, repression, self-containment) and even gendered duplicity may ultimately help uplift the race.

If Madam Frances's power is greater than Mrs. Willis's it is because it is metaphysical and otherworldly, confronting politics with nature and the knowledge technologies of a vanquished nation.[25] As if to find a sphere for women outside of the "manly" pursuit of political enfranchisement, Hopkins contrasts the political maneuvering of Mrs. Willis with the power of mysticism, the ability to read the text of a final justice coming out of African/agrarian/slave culture, as we see again in the person of the church's watchman, Dr. Peters. Hopkins further pits Madam Frances against John Langley, the paradigm of the outmoded industrial men characteristic of the second half of the nineteenth century; that is, the black politician prepared to exchange the political future of African-Americans for his own professional gain. If power is what is exchanged—black power to the parties of the white elite, state power to John Pollock Langley—the currency from the perspective of the black nation is treason. It is only in this context, in which John Langley surmises Sappho's/the nation's secret past, and thus the methods of read-ministering the extrapolation of pleasure/profit from the female of the animal-species through the rule and practices of an old paradigm, that we see Madam Frances at work and confront the extent and limits of her power.

Hopkins's Langley plays a crucial role in the novel as the old guard in the political recuperation of black organizations, as, for example, when against the national interest he cuts political deals with the Hon. Senator Herbert Clapp to prevent the colored population from rallying independent political force against the Union in exchange for his appointment to the office of city solicitor. It is in this discussion that Hopkins confronts the frontier of organized black power and the nature of white ruling interests in controlling and maintaining black alliances as much as the maneuvers of power politics among the cadres of the ruling elite. As Langley, cigar in hand, informs Colonel-*cum*-Senator Clapp of the black political agenda—"our men given something beside boot-blacking in the employment of the state . . . our girls given a chance as clerks" (236)—the colonel reveals the white power structure's fear of a race war as chaos: "All right! be pig-headed; don't listen to reason; plunge the country into a race war in spite of all we've done for you, especially for your leaders; and when your race is exterminated, put the blame where it belongs" (147).

At the macropolitical level, it is clear that Hopkins puts her worst suspicions in the colonel's mouth: the seduction of black leadership, their treason against the nation on behalf of the enemy-state, her frustration with the broken promises of the Democratic and Republican parties, her sense of the (im)possibilities of black revolution, her belief that national black violence would lead to the extermination of African-Americans as a people. At the same time, it is also clear from the senator's speech that the black political elite has particularly benefited from negotiations and power politics on the back of just such threats of black national violence. When Langley agrees to keep the meeting in the newly owned church on X Street from becoming explosive by derailing certain speakers and silencing others, the betrayal of the people, as well as the failures of black advancement toward citizenship, is laid at the feet of the old leadership, still male by definition. In the town meeting, and at a banquet at a private club for the white ruling elite to which acceptable African-American leadership may be invited, Will bests Langley as the New Man for a new century, leaving the betrayals of the old guard behind.

When Madam Frances confronts Langley with his dismal future, then, she becomes the only figure in the book capable of undermining his political machinations, wielding knowledge as a power greater than his. As such, although Madam Frances's power is mystical rather than political, she is able to wield the power of women/nature/nation over the emotive sphere and bring even Langley to the point of "desperation" and powerlessness (285). Like the forces of nature that brought vengeance against Montfort for defying the British government and refusing to free his slaves, Madam Frances reads a greater power, a command over future history and the repository of judgment handed down from the annals of justice as the locus of a promised utopia. As such, Madam Frances holds the power of an old African aristocracy as a state of nature, rather than Mrs. Willis's state imposed on nature that requires administration, politics, retreat, and the masculinity of power.

The emphasis on standards of youth and European beauty as indicating women's capital has already been noted. Holding the power of revelation and justice as perfect knowledge, Madam Frances is outside these economic circuits governing the value of women: she is a "crone" (285), a "seeress" (284), a "wrinkled, black face, and gaudily turbaned head" (284) who brings the history of the power of conjure, which is also wielded by the conjure man in industrial societies, ex-slave Dr. Peters, to its most powerful fruition.[26] As an old woman, Madam Frances is situated outside the circuits of women's value, unruly. There is a bond here between capital as pleasure and women as labor, in which the political economy of women is bound up in the relationship between Sappho as a southern belle, Sappho as a black woman, and Sappho as giving over the power of political strategies to Langley by surrendering the territory and the nation in her option for the feminine as passive, the body victimized by politics. That Madam Frances, like Dr. Peters, comes from the South, and that she is the fruition of another notion of mulatto culture for southern womanhood, is suggested by her double maternal relation to Sappho (mother's sister turned mother), the New Woman, although her body has produced no children. But despite her ability to best John Langley, despite her ability to see the future and read the characters of men and women, Hopkins's narrative confronts the fact that Madam Frances's own material political power is effectively null, just as Mrs. Willis's emotive power is undercut by personal ambition and the deception it engenders.[27] If Madam Frances surfaces first at the fair, secretly as coded through messages brought by a child who will come to represent the inheritors/inheritance of the black future, it is Mrs. Willis, the one whose emotive femininity has been ousted by political strategy, whose sphere is the territorial boundaries of the fair within which Madam Frances can emerge into the communal sphere.

Still, Mrs. Willis unsexes as she moves through spheres as a political woman, a worker for the race. I argued earlier that the transition from ape to worker required a conceptual transition from flesh to machine. Here again, in the transformation of a woman into a politician, the flesh of the feminine is irresolvably conflicted with the power brokering of politics, the establishment of territory, the raising of capital, and the motivation of the people toward that end, because politics requires traits accorded to the masculine. Mrs. Willis confounds the male politician in that political power accrues in the body of woman, just as she confounds the figure of the woman with the signs of political mastery that her body accrues.[28]

Although Hopkins cannot help but decry the failure of conjure to render the Civil War redundant, her repulsion from Mrs. Willis requires a figure who accrues the marks of a feminine power coming out of slave/African culture; that is, Madam Frances. It is important to recognize also that this feminine is secret, hidden, internal, and must be offered but cannot be manipulated, and is in direct contrast to Mrs. Willis, who wears her femininity like a transparent cloak, the politician inside her betraying itself. These figures thus mark the points of tension in straddling the middle passage from African to American, from the flesh of chaos to the machinery of the productive worker, from the victim-woman to the woman-worker. In the end, like the witches of Macbeth invoked in one of Hopkins's epigraphs, the conjure woman may hold the secret of the future, but her power is stalemated in the arena of political and economic freedom (citizenship) for the race, if not for women, a stalemate stemming from her status as a nonproductive worker, as chaos.

## The New Men

For this part, Will, the new man, has his manhood defined in old terms: capital accumulation and politics. Jesse Montfort, father to the Smiths and grandfather to Will, is "unmanned by recurring misfortunes . . . and never again seemed to have the ambition to try to retrieve his [financial] losses" (384). Charles Montfort was similarly defined by a recitation of his private property. Masculinity is thus constituted within the conventional rubrics of gendering—the man of means to supplement the woman of beauty. The question of capital accumulation links the two families—Montfort and Withington—as much as the question of blood, and it is also a mark of proper and appropriate gendering that Ma Smith inherits "so excellent an address and manner . . . [and] a superior intelligence" (373), linking her character to her home (the *domus*). To obtain the inheritance of Jesse Montfort through litigation against the U.S. government for reparations for the assault on Charles Montfort, modern men bring the case before the Supreme Court with the arrival of Mr. Withington, son of Charles Jr., in tandem with the "money [that] flowed from his lavish hand, and all the legal machinery that was essential to prompt action" (379). Without yet having money himself, in the clubhouse of the white political elite Will relies on political administrative policy to reengender the black nation: " 'Agitation will do much,' said Will calmly, unruffled by the [white southerner's] display of anger. 'It gave us freedom; it will give us manhood' " (300).

In putting these words into Will's mouth Hopkins opts for the constitution of nationhood as manhood that Hazel Carby denounces, almost a hundred years later, in *Race Men*.[29] Yet the separatist rhetoric of Du Bois, the Douglass of the "Speech on the Fourth of July," and the antebellum Delany are forgone in the face of the National Guard. Consistently, then, power in men is a function of the constitution of masculine identity as black men access the terms of the masculine ideal of self-reliance and achievement that Martin Berger finds particular to hegemonic fin de siècle U.S. masculinity. Carby takes black men and black political (re)presentation to task for the persistent exclusion of women and the feminine from the national agenda. Hopkins's men, although they engage with the politics of Du Bois and Booker T. Washington, engage "race women" with what Rodríguez calls *tendresse*, a tenderness that comes to suture the relationship between genders and generations. Thus Will, the New Man, is a good and loving son to his mother, and it is through him and his determination that the past is incorporated into the future in his marriage to Sappho and adoption of Alphonse as his own.

The patriarchal rage that leaves Delany's geopolitical paradigm so conflicted finds in Hopkins its resolution in Will as Janus-faced paterfamilias: tender at home, but in the masculine spheres of power a strong intellectual, principled and committed to the race. Sappho's grateful love seals the bond of the hearth that Will once lit in her cold room. In the revolutionary subject leading the new national strategy, this mixture of intellectual capital, the threat of a free political mind coming into his own at the head of the black vanguard, and the submission of women to dominant metaphors (wife/mother/virgin), will structure manly political identity down into the twentieth century, to splinter African-American politics in the face of the millennium.

### The Wreckage of History and the Politics of an Open End

Women's investments in hopes for a better future/utopia for black women are located in the promise of Will and Sappho as the New Man and the New Woman of the race in (re)building a nation. If Sappho's story is over, Will's is yet to begin, suggesting that women plot their lives in romantic narratives (Sappho, Dora, Grace), men in history (Will, Charles, Dr. Lewis).[30] The radical Will, like Du Bois, completes a degree at Harvard and Heidelberg, returns to the United States, and leaves again for Europe. Sappho leaves with him as his wife: the southern man marries the northern woman and the northern man marries the southern woman in the healing mergers of a new nation. As Sean McCann points out, "the traffic in women is the traffic in heritage" (793). But beyond this, in the transformation of the agrarian ape-worker to the worker-citizen, the Christian morphology of "America" must interpellate the revolutionary subject. The economic movement from flesh to machine is thus countered by the political spirituality of the black Church, and so the transformation of the flesh raped in its transition to sex/pleasure worker-machine supplements the politics of the New Man with the spiritual promise of the new nuclear family.

In closing, then, I want to trace two issues: the reconstruction of gender and the interpersonal relations of the new black couple, and the construction of the black political structure that births and supports the New Man for a new era. Between the lines of this new leadership we will see the inheritance of Delany: capital and the search for a territory for black empowerment return to unravel the sense of security and empowerment established at the crest of the book.

Like Delany, the rebirth of Hopkins's central character is linked to Christian mythology. In a move that marks Hopkins's fin de siècle liberal agenda rather than Delany's antebellum radical one in relation to the U.S. elite, as much as in the issue of gendering, Hopkins's Sappho is metonymic of her Christian counterpart in Will's dream: "He dreamed that he stood in a grand cathedral, and listened to strains of delicious melody chanted by an invisible choir. *Christie elision, Kyrie eleison,* floated to his ears, and the glad strains of the *Gloria.* Presently upon the altar before him appeared a vision of the Virgin and Child, but the face of the mother was Sappho's, the child by her side was the little Alphonse" (386–87). At the center of Hopkins's nationalist Afro-Christian morphology of women we find the family, rather than the individual leader, and we find spiritual progress governing the secular. This marital/martial split is indicative of Hopkins's engendering of the organization of the black community for mass empowerment. Sappho's flight South from the refuge of the boardinghouse, as well as her mentor's proposal of marriage to her, occurs at Easter, foreshadowing the rebirth of black womanhood. When it comes, it is attached to the dream life of the New Man's imagination. Where Delany's Henrico Blacus is hailed as the Savior himself, Hopkins's New Woman is displaced from both direct assimilation into the Godhead and the threat of marital violence. In its stead, we find the marital, Sappho as mother, as supplement and the beatification of Alphonse as the hope of the future utopia.

To cast Sappho as the Virgin is to baptize her, to absolve her of the sins of being raped and imprisoned at her origins, and beyond this to cleanse her of the stain of physicality at the source of her degradation. If the hope of heaven is justice, and if black womanhood, mired in a sexuality marking the flesh, is to achieve the virtues of true womanhood, then Sappho's rebirth inaugurates a new paradigm for black womanhood. Concurrently, this new womanhood is inextricably linked to motherhood and the rape of the black nation as a "primeval" body (332), to healing the violence at the birth of the new mulatto nation. If women have no country, the litigation that follows in the wake of physical violence marking negotiations between the nation and the state here finds its place in fiction, its judgment handed down in a dream that draws on the promise of Afro-Christian Armageddon, condemning white violence and absolving the black body. The New Woman oscillating between the virginal body and the whore locked in the bordello repeats the structure of the neither/nor: a whore is not a virgin, a virgin is not a mother, a not-virgin not a mother is a whore.[31] In the process of assumption to the place of the revolutionary woman, Sappho must be unsexed or, better, unfleshed.

Black women who are raped are seen in the eyes of the laws of the state and the nation, then as now, as the repositories of the crime, hovering between chattel and personhood, the gendering of violence judging woman as the territory of sin and men's weakness, intricately suspect of rights, volition, and reason. In 1899 as in 1790 as now, the law assumes (black) women bring this violence on themselves, an unclassified species or a category of mutants stuck in the passage from one form to another. If it is a central struggle for Hopkins to absolve the black woman at the center of the black nation (and thus the black body) of the violence of slavery and the archaeology of the human sciences, then this redemption is seen at a double remove.

Women carry the marks of violence against the black nation in the very mechanics of the (re)production of race in New World territories, and absolution must precede the founding of the new nation; yet women can only be absolved by the men who are the products of that violence, and the alternative spaces in which women form their own communities (Sappho's room, the Convent of the Holy Family, Ophelia and Sarah Ann's basement room/workshop, Ma Smith's boardinghouse) are always privileged initially then discarded as superseded administrative modes in the name of progress. Consistently the progress of black national identity seems to proceed on the incorporation of women as passive, heterosexual, and married.

If the rebirth of the New Woman is predicated on acceptance of the mulatto nation and the violence on her body toward the paradigms of true womanhood, marked by historical memory as much as marriage to race men, the rebirth of the New Man is marked by forgiveness, fidelity, and marriage in his private life, and publicly by political and economic ambition in accepting responsibility for the freedom and empowerment, read as the (re-en)gendering, of the African-American nation.

The fictive/historical revelations of Luke Sawyer at the meeting at the church on X Street, then, provided a model. Preceded by Dora's Arthur Lewis, a paradigm of the old man (agrarian, disenfranchised, self-effacing), Luke Sawyer's story tells first of upwardly mobile black merchants lynched for competing successfully against local white men, and then of a wealthy agrarian woman brought low by rape for carrying black blood. On this public witness of the truth behind lynching and rape, under the auspices of the territory secured by the industry of women, Will forges the theory of the new black nation:

> My friends, it is going to take time to straighten out this problem; it will only be done by the formation of public opinion. Brute force will not accomplish anything. We must *agitate*. As the anti-slavery apostles went everywhere, preaching the word fifty years before emancipation, *so must we do to-day.* Appeal for the justice of our cause to every civilized nation under the heavens. Lift ourselves upward and forward in this great march of life until "Ethiopia shall indeed stretch for her hand, and princes shall come out of Egypt."
> (272)

If women's work expands the borders of black territory from the boardinghouse to the church/meetinghouse, what remains unresolved is the question of the next step, the move from meetinghouse to world. For Dr. Lewis, and therefore Dora, the answer is the return south to educate the black nation as industrial workers, as human resources for capital. For Will, the education required for New Black Men can only be handed down outside the territorial United States; that is, in Hopkins's other wild space of this novel (the first was Bermuda), a utopic England. In her last novel, *Of One Blood,* that hope will be transferred to the mother-land/site of contestation of the races (woman will equal territory) on the other continent, Africa, in the wild space of Egypt, birthing ground of the transition for an old world order: Ethiopia → Egypt → Greece → Rome → Europe → global domination. At the turn of the nineteenth century, when the extended family leaves for England at the novel's conclusion, it is Will, and therefore Sappho, the hope for a new nation, who remain deterritorialized.

The church on X Street, as property acquired by the women/community, is left in the pastor's care. The boardinghouse, as property inherited by women, is rented to Ophelia, the slave turned worker/washerwoman turned landlady, moving up from the basement floor to the back parlor. As if in a final gesture toward the primacy of capital accumulation across genders, Ophelia, who took money as well as clothes left by the mistress fleeing the Yankee troops, marries and leases the boardinghouse. Sarah Ann, who would rather retreat to the Great House kitchen than sit with the white family in the front of the white church at the white wedding, and who took only money and no clothes (to make the woman), disappears altogether. For Ophelia, however, the transition from labor to management must also be accompanied by marriage, here to the young pastor. Ophelia, with her dialect and with her insistence that she is thirty-five and therefore born in the year of Emancipation, is a metonym for the transformation of the ape-worker to the industrial worker, freed black women who came North and made good. Her marriage to the young pastor thus signals the marriage of black working-class womanhood, newly born with freedom, to the values of the Church.

For Sappho and Will, in the last lines of the book, there is only the nuclear family and an open end:

> Sappho was happy in contemplating the life of promise which was before her. Will was the noblest of men. Alphonse was to him as his own child. United by love, chastened by sorrow and self-sacrifice, he and she planned to work together to bring hearts crushed by despair.
>
> They stood upon the deck that night long after the others had retired to their staterooms, watching the receding shores with hearts filled with emotion too deep for words. (401–2)

Transition, the nuclear family, the open sea, the commitment to healing a people, and the accumulation of historical memory and education together with the final leg of the triangular trade route lie at the foundation of the plans for the new national strategies. But confronted with the indifference of the Democratic and Republican parties, the threat of genocide from the government in the face of black liberationist violence against the state, and the fear of the enfranchisement of black men uniting the citizenry of the United States, the planners of the new nation turn their backs on a future beyond the horizon, inextricably linked to the possibilities of the Old World, a people exiled by the shambles of Reconstruction, without territory, watching the wreckage of history recede in silence.

# 3

## From Larva to Chrysalis:
## Multicultural Consciousness and Anticolonial
## Revolution in Ralph de Boissière's *Crown Jewel*

■

Young people, not having lived in that time, will be apt to think of the book as a
true historical record of events. Well, it won't do them any harm.—Ralph de
Boissière

In the late 1920s, a group of educated young Trinidadian men began to
hold literary meetings, which later resulted in the publication of a local
magazine called *Trinidad* (1929–30), a title that reflects its nationalist
impulse. Returning from a two-year stay in New York, white Trinidadian
Albert Gomes joined the flourishing discussion group that gathered together some of the leading local liberals and socialists of the time, including Alfred Mendes and C. L. R. James who had jointly edited the by then
defunct *Trinidad*. Ralph de Boissière, budding socialist militant and son
of the French Creole elite, was among the members of the group. On its
face, both *Trinidad* and its more famous reincarnation under Gomes, *The
Beacon* (1931–34), were to be forums in which West Indians, concerned
with the future of the nation, could express their views and exchange
ideas. The political slant that *The Beacon* took on almost immediately,
then, arose not from a desire to destabilize the colonial regime, but rather
to allow discussion of the colony's status and future by a local community spanning the political spectrum.

Within the colonial context, however, any rhetoric that positions itself as concerned with local needs and issues must speak from the place
of nationalism, because the welfare of the local population (the new
"people-nation" and its new social subject, the impoverished "barefoot

man") takes precedence over the territory as a British colony increasing the wealth of the mother country. The *Beacon* group, as they have come to be called, thus saw the birth of a democratic, black-oriented nationalist intelligentsia.[1] Because literacy is strategically a province of the elite under colonial rule, the birth of an educated, politicized (black) nationalist group advocating social changes to include the subject population became a force with which the colonial administration had to contend. In their dialogue on the logics of government and the living conditions of the local population, then, the implicit political-intellectual project founding the *Beacon* group became nation building, just as the "barefoot man" became a metonym for the black central subject of the newly developing paradigms of the government's functions and responsibility to the local majority.

Black middle-class agitation in Trinidad for reform to ward off social upheaval had been developing sporadically for almost a century. Even before the abolition of slavery in the British territories, the wealthy and educated colored planter J. B. Philippe had written "An Address to the Right Hon. Earl Balthurst by a Free Mulatto" (1823) calling for political liberalization of colonial policy toward the colored bourgeoisie and advising the secretary of state for the colonies to suppress the document from public scrutiny lest the revelations and arguments it contained result in mass unrest.[2] But like his political successor and liberal late-century counterpart J. J. Thomas—author of the explicitly anticolonial *Froudacity* (1889) and *The Theory and Practice of Creole Grammar* (1869)—these calls for political liberalization remained couched, on the one hand, across territorial borders toward a Pan–West Indian sociopolitical consciousness, and, on the other, within the terms of the existing class structure. Both Philippe and Thomas argued for a paradigm shift recognizing the inherent humanity of the black population, a shift that would lead to the relative empowerment of the black bourgeoisie and perhaps petit bourgeoisie, but certainly not the working classes and the unemployed.[3]

In 1937 the Trinidadian working class exploded in waves of rioting that spread from island to island up the island chain of the West Indies, shaking the colonies to their foundations and marking the start of the decline of British colonial rule in the Caribbean basin.[4] As an educated nationalist cadre, members of the *Beacon* group could thus find common political sentiments with the rioting poor. With an exposure to the role of race in world politics brought on by the deployment of West Indian troops in World War I as well as migration within the Caribbean and from the United States, both middle-class and grassroots militancy began to take on a new urgency at the beginning of the twentieth century: on their return from World War I, for example, black soldiers in the Trinidadian contingent of the British West India Regiment refused to participate in the imperial victory parade. Discovering they were not to be given live ammunition, the soldiers mutinied—they had intended to shoot the governor.

Unlike many other Caribbean territories, the wealth that Mother England extracted from Trinidad was growing healthily in 1919 when the newly developing industrial working class, spurred by the independence of the returning soldiers, began to take action. The emergence of cocoa production on a global scale (Trinidad accounted for 10 percent of world production in 1906), together with the development of the oil and asphalt industry in Trinidad by London-based corporations, had expanded the territory's economy at the turn of the century. The veneer of "progress" and "development," however, came hand in hand with an increasing awareness on the part of the workers of their exploitation under the reigning political economic order. Most historians of labor unrest and of the development of unions and labor legislation have credited the extreme repression of the colonial regime, in tandem with new patterns of migration to the city and the industrial outposts, with creating a proletariat proper that could then develop a class consciousness capable of bringing pressure to bear on management—in this case, the governor on the one hand and the chamber of commerce on the other.

In *Smiles and Blood*, Trinidadian economic historian Susan Craig points out that in fact the proletarianization of the laboring population went hand in hand with a growing black nationalist sentiment (e.g., Marcus Garvey's United Negro Improvement Association had opened a thriving chapter[5]) as much as it did the creation of an exploited industrial (rather than agro-industrial) class. In narrating this new black/national consciousness, in Craig as in Ralph de Boissière's *Crown Jewel*, marxist historiography thus meets the crucible of black anticolonial thought, fused in a territory marked for unequal exchange in the global marketplace since 1492.[6]

Much of the laboring population in Port of Spain, the capital of Trinidad, and its environs lived in areas known as barrack yards, which were built up over decades from the 1860s into the twentieth century. The hardships encountered in the yards were very real:

The city was compact and well laid out in blocks fronted by tolerably well built houses and shops. But behind the perimeter of each block were barracks, often simply long wooden structures set against the walls dividing lots, and chopped up into rooms each of which might contain a family grouping belonging to the labouring classes. . . .

    Accommodation is such that there can be little privacy, and the yard in the centre becomes a common living place. Water and latrines are common facilities, and there is competition for their use. Deep antagonisms develop which burst out at times, but are largely restrained. Few actions escape its scrutiny. An order of domination is built up in a series of encounters between rivals. . . . Antagonisms are relaxed from time to time by fêtes. . . . At other times the antagonisms are projected into hostility to the outside world, particularly into sharp conflicts with rival yards. (Pearse 191–92)

Although the barrack yards themselves were hidden from the view of polite society, there were in fact complex, and often clandestine, interrelationships between the world of the elite and the world of the laboring poor that exacerbated class conflicts:

> It must be borne in mind that barrack-yard society was not isolated in one quarter of the town, but back to back with the houses of the middle and upper classes. Its members were not only constantly confronted with the display of cultural standards of the higher social ranks, and thus aware of their distance from them, but paradoxically closely associated with them, especially through the women who were servants and often the predominant influence in the lives of the children. On the other hand, middle-class men would seek liaisons with the women. (Pearse 192)

Living conditions in the barrack yards were of great concern to the members of the *Beacon* group and expressions of outrage about the poverty there appeared regularly in its pages. Alfred Mendes's second novel centers around life in a barrack yard; another such locale figures prominently in de Boissière's novel; and James Cummings, himself from a barrack yard, published several pieces on the subject in the *Beacon*.

    Politically, report after report for government as well as industry tabulated and analyzed the devastating socioeconomic effects of management's exploitation of its workers and of the extremity of the extraction of surplus value from the subject population. Colonial Office records evidence that in Trinidad by 1920 real wages had dropped by 120 percent, while the cost of living had increased by 145 percent. Further, the combination of a 50 percent increase in worker unemployment coming with the 1930s world depression, the shortage of skilled labor that meant more people competing for low-paying jobs in the absence of labor legislation, and the hostile climate of worker-management relations in the absence of any structural allowance for airing worker grievances meant a downward spiral for wages and living conditions (Samaroo 31).[7] Nevertheless, as British journalist Arthur Caulder-Marshall noted during the 1937 riots:

> If Trinidad is a true example of Crown Colony government, the theory is a myth, covering a history of savage exploitation. Trinidad has never been a poor island. Since the English seizure of it, wealth has constantly been drained from the island, a toll taken from the various peoples imported there to be exploited. . . . It is a rich island, with 90% of the population impoverished. . . . The benevolent tyranny which is supposed to be superior to the interests of exploiting capital, has in fact legislated throughout in the interests of that class. It has been the political side of capitalism, with a different personnel but to a common aim. . . . The benevolent tyranny, close to the demands of big business but distant from the workers, has blundered on, deaf to the cries of distress because it has not tried to listen. (*Glory Dead* 284–85)[8]

Marshall's comment in fact conflates the two competing strands of administrative power in the colony. Trinidad's position as the single most important source of oil in the British Empire, especially for fueling its new defense technology, made the colony's administration critical as both a governmental and an economic problem, and the response to the riots was in fact revealingly bifurcated. On the one hand, government officials saw the riots as a reasonable response to the people's living and working conditions, whereas the representatives of the investors and industrial management saw it as a problem of law and order—that is, as a military problem. De Boissière's *Crown Jewel* is in fact at pains to mark this bifurcation, as evidenced in the battle in the novel between government interests (the governor, the city council) and business interests (Dollard, Major Bottomly).[9]

Although the militant 1930s union activist Uriah Butler, spokesman for the black masses of his time, has gone down in national/labor history as a radical emerging from the rioting masses, the traces of the maintenance of class structure and privilege—the opening up of the capitalist system for the upward mobility of the black and brown middle classes— remains a crucial parameter that Butler's demands do not dismantle. In de Boissière's *Crown Jewel,* however, by developing the leftist political inheritance of Uriah Butler and Jim Barette, a leader of the Negro Welfare Association, grassroots protonationalism will break from its liberal tradition to incorporate the redistribution of wealth as a corrective to history, tied to the concept of Independence. Here nationalism = socialism, although the struggle between a nationalism that places the oppressed black man at its center (yielding the welfare state that will ameliorate the conditions of the majority) will always be embattled by the nationalism of the brown petit bourgeoisie that wants to localize ultimate control of the economy and society (yielding the liberal state that will protect the private accumulation of capital). For the *Beacon* members, the pressure exerted by the Crown Colony administration brought liberals and socialists together; once the winds of nationalism began to be underscored by riots, however, the fault line beneath the *Beacon* coalition began to shift, and so socialists like de Boissière and James split from liberal reformists like Gomes and Mendes who were later elected to pre-Independence political office.[10]

Ralph de Boissière's *Crown Jewel* (re)writes the history of the 1937 riots as the birth of a Trinidadian nation in the same way that the struggle waged on the streets of Port of Spain and in the industrial outposts came to constitute the beginning of the end to colonial rule. If the riots in Trinidadian history mark the beginning of a mass black nationalist putsch in the West Indies, and the *Beacon* group marks the birth of an educated black nationalist West Indian cadre, then *Crown Jewel,* as Trinidad's "most important political novel . . . [and] the fundamental work of fiction in [Trinidadian] society" (Sealy 3), marks the zenith of the first phase of West Indian black nationalism as a literary fact. De Boissière's characters incorporate, within the horizon of a revolution that sees nationalism as a corrective project logically socialist, the key figures who have come to stand as historical signposts of a nation formation catalyzing a regional transition. Thus *Beacon* member Albert Gomes, subsequently elected to the city council and then the legislative council, dethroned only by the spectacular rise to power of Eric Williams in 1956, appears in *Crown Jewel* under the name Joe Elias, along with his trou-blemaking magazine (the *Beacon* itself). The famous historical figure of Cipriani, a white Trinidadian who began the process of legislative liberal-ization, appears as Mayor Boisson; Corporal Charlie King—a policeman infamous for his brutality in the service of empire—appears in the figure of the policeman Duke. Le Maitre, the hero of the novel, incorporates both the historical role and the personal qualities of union leaders Uriah Butler and Jim Barette (Sander 130–31).

In the process of writing labor riots as the birth of a nation, Caribbean historians and social scientists make it clear that what is recovered is the reconceptualization of the world. As in de Boissière, for the enraged black masses the birth of the nation will be coterminous with conscien-tization, a transformation of personal consciousness as a political force that, given the colonial context, will take on a socialist and international-ist veneer in the rhetoric and the demands of the new nation. At the macrological level of nations and states, what is at stake is a political redefinition of the people in terms of law and subalternity; that is, a debate as to whether or not the people deserve a voice in the administra-tion of the colony as a business enterprise.

Written and rewritten between 1939 and 1950 at a time when Trinidad was still a colony, de Boissière's seditious novel found no publisher until 1952. In fact, the publishers of the milder *Beacon* and *Trinidad* were pressured by local interest groups supportive of the status quo to stop the solicitation and publication of such disruptive and radical material. The seditiousness of de Boissière's act of writing the novel is underscored by the fact that the nation whose coming into being he describes did not gain the sanction of a state until 1962. In his correspondence with Rein-hard Sander, de Boissière is explicit that he wrote the novel as an inter-vention into West Indian historiography: "The events happened, but not necessarily in just that way or at just that time. Young people, not having lived in that time, will be apt to think of the book as a true historical record of events. Well, it won't do them any harm" (130). Between a "true social history of the period" and "not a historical record of events" lies, then, the project of nation formation through the creation of national history, where sensibility comes to fill in the gaps and rewrite the na-tional narrative of transition, of its own birth. The slippage between de Boissière's novel and official history is thus intended to be politicized, a characteristic typical of Caribbean literature from the 1930s and beyond into the present day.

Given this connection between historiography and literature, it is therefore no surprise that in the 1950s and early 1960s—years leading up to Independence in most of the West Indies—a second generation of West Indian writers emerged. By finding the public that *Beacon* writers sought, at the moment when the British government and the cultural and publishing elite began to find value in the literature of West Indian exiles in London, this second generation of nationalist West Indian writers was published as a revitalization of the literature of the empire, as the poetry of Caliban. In chapter 4 of this volume Guyana's Wilson Harris is the representative of this second generation of educated West Indians grappling with nation formation and the prospects of statehood, but it is revealing that for both de Boissière's and Harris's generations colonial rule and underdevelopment made painfully clear the international division of labor and the effects of globalized racism and Eurocentrism on the policies of local government and the lives of individuals. Nevertheless, as we will see in chapters 4 and 6 on national transitions in Guyana and Jamaica respectively, it is not until the 1970s that the impasse between West Indian self-determination ("Independence") and the global economy will force the rethinking of the parameters of national planning incorporating the promises of black nationalism as socialism into the constitution of the subject/citizen at the center of the West Indian state.

In what follows, I examine three macrological issues that *Crown Jewel* addresses by beginning from the micrological. First, I untangle, at the level of macropolitical relations, the function and vectors of power as capital management under colonialism and the seeds of the paradigms of national transition that the novel identifies. To this end, I read very closely three carefully crafted textual moments: a speech by Joe Elias, a debate in the capital's city council, and the interviews with people in the boardroom of the industrial elite. All three passages display the terms and dynamics of the struggles over power and political epistemology. The first slice of evidence, Joe Elias's speech, comes very early in the novel so as to explicate the links between social relations and power relations at the level of everyday life. The second textual moment, the debate in the city council, allows a consideration of how these issues play out in the council chambers in confronting a rebellious subject population through the agendas raised by a debate over a minimum wage. The third scenario, the interviews held in the boardroom by the Minimum Wage Committee, allows us to analyze the relationships between the local representa-

tives of white international magnates, the colored up-and-coming "national"/political bourgeoisie, and the racial and ethnic spectrum of "the
people," a relationship revealed in the dynamics played out in the space
of the waiting room and in the boardroom of the power elites.

In the second section of this chapter, I explore de Boissière's representation of the politics of the home front, analyzing the position of love and
domestic relationships across the racial/political economic spectrum in
order to uncover de Boissière's understanding of the place of the *domus*
in the process of nation formation and power politics. In closing this
section, I look at the narratives of nation formation along the lines of
protonational organization within the parameters of industrial/class
structures and the men who form and revolutionize unions (unions as
political cells). From there I move to an analysis of the groundswell of the
people's rebellion as nationalism becomes a mass movement expressed
in riots (crowd = mob = nation). Finally, I return to the *domus* of the
emerging colored national elite to discern the seeds of the future of
underdeveloped countries (domestic policies and the politics of gender
→ national politics).

Through de Boissière's *Crown Jewel,* then, we can trace the birth of the
nation as a latent feeling of unrest among the people, note how this new
protonational feeling registers at the level of middle government, then
reflect on how the protonation is handled by the economic/administra-
tive elite working to suture the space opened up by the remote possibility
of mass black representation in the colonial world order. The strategy I
adopt of moving from the micropolitical to the macropolitical proves
further revealing in analyzing the position of the house and of women
and love in the marshaling of culture as politics in the midst of an
international struggle. In the end, the dialectical move from the micrological to the macrological allows us, with the benefit of historical hindsight, to see how de Boissière's analysis of Trinidadian society between
the world wars points to the future of government and the politics of the
"national" bourgeoisie waiting in the wings for Independence. In the
final analysis, the warnings of de Boissière's creolized marxism that I
uncover come to fruition in the second half of the century, a fruition of
the problems of the split between nation formation and state consolidation that earlier we saw latent in Delany's paradigms in the middle of the
nineteenth century. We will see this split analyzed again in reading Ileana Rodríguez's *Understanding War in Central America.* By reading de

Boissière's 1930s novel of the birth of a nation and a century, we can trace the threads of democratizing unrest from the micrological level of the people through questions of government, to the macrological level of a "national" bourgeoisie managing government policy where the buck stops. This "national" bourgeoisie will prove to be an anxious student of the patterns of capital accumulation and population management, a grim historical precedent for emerging paradigms of the new world order and the corporate state as the very same century came to a close.

### Constituting the Island Nation: The Erosion of Empire

*Social relations = power relations*
From the opening lines of *Crown Jewel*'s first chapter, the mechanics of colonial power in personal identity that constitute West Indian social organization are under scrutiny, an analysis that will incorporate the interpersonal relationships determining economics and public policy. In the book's opening chapter, titled "The Background," history is reconfigured from the Amerindian's encounter with Columbus through to 1935, so as better to contextualize "the foreign oil companies sprawled all over the south of Trinidad" and the one "English company [that] alone controlled the island's sugar" (x). Where the once all-powerful island planter elite now bow "to the wishes of Oil and Sugar," "the people" look on as "bit by bit the land slipped out of [their] hands" (x). Thus some "four hundred years" of history converge in a dockyard, where the subjects of the new national history gather to express their alienation. Colonialism, they complain, seeps through to the marrow of men's bones and demoralizes them, turning colored men into subordinates and white men into masters:

> Joe was saying: "A coloured boy of fifteen gets a job for between three and eight dollars a week. By the time he's twenty he's makin' ten to twelve a week. He sees a girl, and now he wants to get married. He waits patiently for four or five years, saving all he can. Every now and then he goes to the boss and asks for a raise. He becomes a sneak, carries news so as to curry favour with those over him. He gets to sixty dollars a month, he gets married. The boss puts him in charge of some little department now. This poor down-trodden clerk becomes a terror to other clerks. His wife gets a child, two children.

His salary goes up, seventy-five a month, he has reached tip-top. If an Englishman had the job he would get three hundred. Boy, he shudders when he looks down where he came from. He's now fifty with ten children. He starts to feel frighten' for another reason: old age, no pension. He sweet to the boss like girl to teacher." Joe put his finger in his mouth and looked coy, and everyone laughed as he intended. "This time, now, the wife sayin' novenas to this saint and to that, she feels; 'Oh, my, how God loves me!'" Joe clasped his hands as if praying. "At sixty they tell him he's too old. They fire him. Five years later his children put him under the earth. Done!" Joe dusted one thick palm against the other. "What they buried—a man? They buried a stomach!" (5)

In colonial society, male workers' access to social security is raced, classed, nationalized, and gendered; but what rankles primarily is that the position of the majority in relation to the unequal hierarchy built on these terms determines job, station, pay, workload, or even the possibility of employment. Joe Elias, publisher of a troublemaking protonationalist magazine and contender for election to the city council, displays his mastery of the terms undergirding colonial society; and in his rapt manipulation of the crowd of working men suddenly hearing their life/history, he displays his mastery of the patterns governing the modernizing colonial economy. Not accidentally, Joe's transformation of local men's personal life into political life—the writing into history of the man-nation—is the function of a national literature, and so in its inauguration *Crown Jewel* breaks onto its national stage, writing the unwritten experience of its target audience even as it rewrites the world. The irony signified by Joe's humor, denaturalizing the ruling social order as diseased precisely because it emasculates local men, cries out for a new leadership where local men can be men like Englishmen. And just sensing this call is enough to make the workers feel they are party to a nationalist conspiracy against the colonial regime in the person of their boss, one Mr. Dollard.

The two points at which humor is invoked in this (auto)biography of the man-nation are telling, because both find their humor in the invocation of women as types embodying the absurdities to which colonial subjects are driven: the woman who prays to a fallacious God (so defined under marxism and modernity) and the little girl who curries favor with her teacher through coy looks. Women clearly are on the margins of the new nation-state that Joe postulates through a negative dialectic, just as they sit on the margins of the colonial regime, resorting to prayer or to coy sexuality (a parody of the virgin/saint and the whore) in the absence of a voice that can be heard. De Boissière will work hard to distance himself from such masculinist conceptions of social change and social identity, and the hero's arduous journey toward the incorporation of women into the struggle and the new state will be taken at the highest level of the new revolutionary organization—in the inner life of its black leader, Le Maitre. Here in Dollard's dockyard, however, there are no women, and so the discourse against the diseased social order and for a new nation takes as a binding premise the problem of colonial exploitation hand in hand with the position of women in order to gain men's allegiance. The powerlessness of the man-nation finds its metaphor in its women's absurdity.

"Man" in Joe's parable is an economic concept struggling to express himself. In speaking as a political subject, Joe struggles to shift the terms of the scientific conception of black/creole inferiority toward a liberal socialist humanism—inclusion of the colored majority in the universal category of "man" proper. Such a move could transform local men from a subaltern subspecies (black/worker) into "people" as a political concept, contenders with the "people" of the master race (white boss)—that is, as citizens.

Humanity is codified as an economic category because under colonial policy humanity (defined after the division between man/beast, people/subspecies) and economics are tied together as pillars of the social order. Ontologically, then, within a modern colonial industrial paradigm, masculinity (the province of men) is tied to whiteness underscored by access to surplus value, and so the black man here is emasculated (= deprived of capital) not by lynching, deployed contemporaneously by the United States, but by enforcing the transformation of human value into monetary value. Because human worth is an economic question with a political answer, the colonial social order dictates that where an Englishman would be given $300, a local must be paid $75 and the local must know it.

The colonial regime traps men by integrating the hierarchy of Gobineau's "Inequality of the Races" into colonial political and economic policy, rearticulated in 1888 for the British West Indies by James Anthony Froude after the specter of political franchise (citizenship) for the colonies has emerged in the metropolis as social norms, thereby transforming the black man in the colony from outside to inside (skin = biology) and back (biology = destiny). The fragmentation and alienation of the new man-nation struggling to give birth to itself is thus metaphorized by the reduction of the man-nation to its body part signifying biological need, a stomach.[11] What is at stake, then, is the repoliticization of the epistemic chain man = white = citizen-wholeness versus black = subject = stomach = alienation, the fragmentation of the worker as a political subject expressing itself through the discourse of reduction to body/parts.

History, then, resides in people. If the spectrum of colonial subjects gathered in the beginning communicate among themselves with ease and assurance, this freedom in social gatherings is countermanded by the restrictions in the office and the dockyard where the white man rules, in person or in absentia. The workers discussing the state of their society see themselves as transgressing, and this conspiratorial sense is indicative of the politics of productivity: (black) workers and (white) management must internalize the system of epistemes that secures the colonial socioeconomic order through the interweaving of science and political theory (Gobineau + Smith = Froude = colonial policy). In moving toward the internalization of social justice as an equal chance for black men in the socioeconomic order, the workers begin to shift not only the governing terms for thinking about local society, but the relations between a new national "us" brought into being by privileging a majority (democracy => citizenship), opposed to the "them" of the British and their political representation, colonialism. The workers' discomfort over this new social terminology thus points to what will become increasingly clear, that the new politicization of everyday life stands in contradiction to the naturalization of colonial social relations equated with civilization and a proper and productive society. The men, in discussing and defining their humiliation by the reigning social order, thus plant the seeds of social awareness that will, given the strategic intractability of the colonial powers, logically culminate in riots, most graphically concretized in the burning of Duke, the brutal policeman circulating within their domestic social spaces.

The tension on the one hand between the openness of social spaces in which the construction and deconstruction of manhood and identity can be discussed and, on the other, the constrictions of power in the workplace, is underlined by Mr. Dollard's management strategy. The ease with which Dollard puts his arm on the shoulder of the disgruntled light-skinned employee, or smiles with the black workers as he passes, is a product of this tension as much as it is a strategy for managing minority rule. The colonial powers always realize they are a tiny white minority confined on a small island with vast numbers of black and colored subordinates, and it is up to the principles of morality and law and order—the police, the judiciary, the Church, the newspaper, the school system, and the psychology of normality and propriety—to naturalize colonialism, as much as it is the murky visibility of the ruling powers. If the members of the legislative council must engage in running for office and elections, then "the 17 or so men who spoke for oil, asphalt, sugar, cocoa and commerce form[ing] the core of 'responsible opinion' in Trinidad" (Craig 24) who make up the all-powerful executive council hand-picked by the governor pride themselves on this studied invisibility.[12] The pretension of warmth in the relationships between Dollard and his employees is, then, part of the strategy of this invisibility because Dollard is secretly on the executive council governing Trinidad with an iron fist while smiling with his employees as a well-intentioned but sensible businessman.

## The case of the city council

As a site of contention, the city council comes to house the hopes for social change where such reductions of politics and business to nepotism can be abolished: the rebel leaders will join the liberal nationalists in battling for a national restructuring that irradiates from here. Fighting for control of the island's administration will come to be recognized as ineluctably a struggle for Independence, just as the sentiment binding the creole middle classes to the workers will become nationalism, and the territory to be administered for and by locals will be an island nation.

It is a mark of de Boissière's politics, however, that Joe Elias, the only rebel character to be elected to the city council, betrays his constituency and becomes an apologist for the colonial order. The nepotism that prevents government for the people will in fact be reproduced until Independence and after. Thus the city council as a petit bourgeois sphere of social change always comes up lacking, although the place it holds in the political imagination grants it a functional importance that only a national socialist revolution can fulfill, for it is in the meetings of the middle-class members of the city council that the striking workers want to see the gestation of a new nation. Hobsbawm's recognition that states create nations, written into being by an elite consolidating its own power, holds here.

The workings of the city council are sprinkled almost casually throughout the narrative, but with each appearance it becomes clearer that the tensions mounting within the national middle classes against the backdrop of labor unrest in the streets will find no release in town hall. The urgency of political debate on the streets contrasts directly with the ennui of the de jure middle-class council members who have had their own struggle for enfranchisement, and who recognize from lessons learned there that no change will be allowed to take place here. Nevertheless, the very presence of such a debate among the elected and appointed officials points to a split in the social order between the middle classes anxious for a liberalization of colonial policy regarding race in its administrative cadres and those who recognize that the flow of events—as much as the logic of modern political representation—will take the islands toward Independence and citizenship for the masses. Still, the factionalism of precisely this fetal nationalist gold mine serves to derail its realization, and so the engine of modernization seen as social justice is thrown back out onto the street into the hands of workers threatening to riot.

The discussion in city council to set a new minimum wage becomes metonymic of its failure as a vehicle for national political organization. Historically, Chuks Okpaluba reminds us, the Minimum Wage Ordinance, required in the British colonies by the 1919 Treaty of Versailles, was not enacted in Trinidad until 1935, and the report published in October 1936 was summarily ignored (18–19). In *Crown Jewel*, while the newly elected Joe Elias, prospective socialist champion of the people-nation, explains why the mandated Minimum Wage Committee had met only once in four months, the other members of the city council stop listening:

> Two Councillors had suddenly got up and gone into the gallery for a private conference. The stout Portuguese . . . summoned the uniformed orderly, who respectfully took a coin from him and went out. . . . Another Councillor was busy working out a crossword puzzle in a newspaper. . . . Another, a very ugly black man, was intently picking his nose while looking at the tree-tops in the Square outside. The orderly returned with a large glass full of iced grapefruit juice and set it before the stout Portuguese. (320–21)

The national dilemma of wages and mass deprivation in the capital to be solved by the city council loses ground ostensbily to the battle of personalities. In fact, it is not in the interests of the middle class represented in the council to further the interests of the masses, since in the ensuing upheavals, given the social rhetoric gaining international voice through the nationalist intellegentsia and workers' organizations, the structural privileges of the colonial regime to which the middle class are looking to gain entrance may well be lost.

The management of the island's capital (in both senses) is here caught up in the contradictions between a drive toward representation based on democratic rhetoric meant to include the colored middle classes and the ends of that democratic rhetoric in mass political representation. The new democratic rhetoric means the passing away of the logic of Crown Colony rule, but the striking workers' leaders calling for socialism means that a battle must be waged for representation of the new masses emerging as a political force, and in order for the middle-class cadres represented by Mayor Boisson to win a share in power they must synthesize their relationship to the masses' revolutionary call. Here the masses are still subalterns and the struggle for national administration utilizes the threat of the workers to galvanize the pact between the elite and their petit bourgeois managers, even as these managers jostle for a new structure that will direct the democratic impulse toward an appropriative national administration gaining them access to power.

These elaborate conflicts are here expressed as problems of interpersonal relations, and alliances are formed covertly on the basis of strategies for government and overtly on strategies for verbal supremacy and the management of committees that can control national transition. Thus Joe is attacked by the members of the Workers' Party led by Mayor Boisson as "trying to make political capital for himself" by raising the problem of the minimum wage ahead of them (319). The council representatives of Boisson's middle-class Workers' Party, already seen as a threat to Crown Colony rule, go on to attack the concept of raising the minimum wage as a proposal from an enemy camp, employing the arguments of upper management and international capital to bring the political spectrum full circle, as reformists become conservatives: "How could one expect to pay more wages except by raising rates, and who would bear the burden of increased rates but the poor?" (320). After the riots subside at the novel's conclusion, Boisson will call for a New Deal, the strategy developed in the United States to allow workers access to the benefits of capital accumulation while strangling and decapitating the socialist organizational cells that gave U.S. workers a voice and a political organizational structure. The city as colony, for all parties concerned, is run like a business because here the "nation" is in the process of being defined and so the power battle to set local policy between the men of the city council and their workers is waged on the same terms as the battle between workers and the leaders of industry.

Behind the struggle over a minimum wage is, then, the definition of black colonial subjects as a necessary evil, a surplus population, or as citizens. Because citizenship—defined as having a social pact obligating the government—is confined to the propertied, to consider the masses as having the right to a certain standard of living is to reconceptualize the tenets of citizenship and the fact of the poor/black subject (as both a political and a psychological concept), and thus erode the foundation of colonial representation and society.

The black subject public, as opposed to the citizenry (white, therefore elite), is technically to be represented by those in the room, the creole managers drawn from the middle classes, and it is Mayor Boisson's job to keep the outsiders silent—the subjugation of the general public—while the council argues city policy on their fate. The debate over the minimum wage breaks down into minutiae, and here the futility of the motion becomes apparent in the battle between the thirsty Portuguese man on one side and the black man who picks his nose on the other:

"We would like to pay more, but it would be unbusinesslike to allow ourselves to be stampeded into—."

The black man who had been picking his nose said: "Have you read the report [of the Minimum Wage Committee]?"

"Yes I have read the report."

"You read the lists of clothing?"

"Well, I saw several lists—."

The Mayor was striking the table with his gavel, but the black man, ignoring him, continued, raising his voice: "Do you agree that two pairs of panties are sufficient for a woman for one year?"

There were laughs from around the table. From the public benches came a loud "No!" The Mayor, ceasing to smile, struck the table sharply: "If there are any more comments from the public I will order the chamber cleared!" (322)

In the mind of the Portuguese councilor the idea of the workers having a social pact with the government represents a political shift that translates into a depletion of city resources, and so the workers take on less-than-human status. The black councilor's choice of women's panties is not innocent in its turn to the most intimate commodities needed by the lowest in the strata of the working class and neither is its inclusion in the lists appended to the report to justify the recommended wage, which, not accidentally, is markedly less than the wage already being paid.

The black councilor's push for an adequate report is a push for political representation of the subaltern population, and it raises the specter of a national discourse that will shift the administrative terms to black = creoles = white, and the evaluation of the state of the new nation through the condition of its women. Throughout the narrative of the Minimum Wage Committee, the dialogue on women's panties will carry the weight of the definition of the workers as animals—therefore exempt from the right to human dignity applicable to the middle class and the elite—or as people, thus deserving legislation granting equal access to commodities and thus politically represented. From here, it is only a short step between conceptualizing the people as deserving political protection from the interests of the industries to the concept of the people-nation, a shift whose logic leads inexorably to the decline of colonial rule, according to the liberal logic of representation and government. Hence the heat of the debate.

In the minds of the Workers' Party led by the petit bourgeois, the workers represent a necessary drain on city resources that must be limited, and so the idea that a woman really needs only two pairs of panties a year not only seems reasonable on its face but makes the city seem generous, and with it the ruling Workers' Party who can now show their above-minimum wages to be an example of their concern for the welfare of the "barefoot man" as the black subject of the nation under formation. Their New Deal offers access but stops short of guarantees.

Because he recognizes that race continues to be the limit of political representation, it is the disaffected black councilor (who picks his nose and stares out the window) who points to the cover-up and calls the committee's report a sham. For the conservative henchmen of the elite, as much as the nonblack middle-class representatives clinging to the concept of the island as an industrial/colonial outpost, the city is a monumental business opportunity struggling with its workers. Thus the black masses clamoring outside on the streets for a living wage come to be a "stampeding horde" best handled by law and order: the consolidation of the mayor's authority over the public in the city council chamber and of the structure of government by the police on the street. After Duke's burning, he will be eulogized in Parliament (402).

It is, then, only the emergence of the inner struggle in the council, which has been quietly defining the terms of the debate, that the issue of extending the franchise comes up and the responses of the council members confirm in the macropolitical (definitions of government) what was clear in their debate on the micro (the criteria for establishing a minimum wage). The Indo-Trinidadian councilor working on the crossword puzzle, elected on the promise that he would increase the voting populace, reminds the council "with a look of disgust" that an extension of the franchise is beyond the council's authority (323). Joe reminds him that during his election speeches this same councilor had told his electorate "the franchise served to keep the working masses out and deprive them of a voice" following on the logic set in motion by the decline of white colonial rule and the broadening of the franchise to include local owners of a legislated amount of capital.

When the Indo-Trinidadian councilor responds with a personal attack, labeling Joe "the hooligan element" trying to take the country (324), it is in recognition of the national transition implicit in Joe's motion as much as in his implicit understanding of the logic in the democratic transition that got him elected. It is also symptomatic of the problems in forming an Indo- and Afro-Trinidad political alliance that continues down into the present day. But because power is threatening to slip into the hands of the masses, and because the Indo-Trinidadian councilor is for the interests of the newly empowered middle class, the councilor cannot see his interests advanced through the weapon of enfranchising the masses. The "disaffected public" of his campaign rhetoric becomes a "chaotic horde" storming the gates of political representation. When Joe later moves that the scavengers' wages be increased thirty cents a day, declaring "the people's needs must come before all else," it will be the Indo-Trinidadian who will call him "a traitor" "fighting against the interests of the very people who have put you on the Council" (400). Thus the middle classes jostle for a power base within the new political economy, the one seeing power in a pact with the black subaltern majority rising up ineluctably, the other in a pact with the white minority elite working to maintain hegemony in a changing world. Within the colonial political economy surrounding and defining the council's actions the black masses are the source of economic surplus value on the one hand and of power (political surplus value) in a democratizing rhetoric on the other. In either logic, their constitution as a striking mob in the majority makes their productivity and subordination (as inextricably economic and political concepts) an important problem to an administration, local or colonial, in crisis. And so Joe the elected radical, the black and creole reformists, and the white conservatives will all ground their arguments in announcing their ultimate concern for the living conditions of the people. In this new bottom line cutting across the political spectrum, the people have already won the first battle.

*Power/empire*
The elite/business men become the final arbiters of colonial policy, and this is evidenced in the details of the functioning of government, as when the city council's Minimum Wage Committee gathers in the boardroom of Dollard & Co. Committee meetings are held in the offices of all the major sectors of industry—sugar, hardware and dry goods, oil—and from the stance of this handful of white men it is clear that policy dictates that any sudden move to liberalize wages will trigger the downfall of the economy and the collapse of certain sectors. If "oil" is forced to pay too high a wage, "oil" warns, then "sugar" may well fold. The parameters of race, nation, power, and government in establishing a minimum wage for the colored subject-population are thus already set, and the white and near-white government interviewers will obediently emphasize the word as *"mini*mum" (318). Each of the colored colonial subject-workers interviewed will confound the committee, who, living as citizens in the colonial outpost so far from a standard of minimums themselves, find the workers' testimony impossible to hear, and thus to calculate.

The colored workers interviewed run the spectrum of the impoverished: the old Indo-Trinidadian who speaks only Hindi, the young Indo-Trinidadians who speak both Hindi and English, a black man, and a black woman. The black man assumes his authority in the new nationalist atmosphere that has brought this committee into being. He takes control, making it clear from his treatment of the others that he is beyond them, unintimidated by these white men who will determine their wages and their minimum standard of living.

The alienation between white men and colored subjects on a personal level plays itself out as management/worker politics. In deference to the reputation of the empire, local representative-citizens of metropolitan investors and managers keep their blood pure by controlling their marriages and their women—"we try to get away from Africa as much as possible" one of their kind will say (427).

As metonyms of the executive council, Dollard and Bottomly constitute the visible edge of the power group behind the empire after the fall of the plantocracy. The governor, for his part, makes a fatal mistake in believing the implications of colored local (proto)national pressures that representation of the subject-population is a concern appropriate to government and that the "fair play" alleged to British citizens under Parliament can be extended to black subjects. These white and near-white men, managers of international capital, recognize that the actual function of government in the colonies regarding the black and East Indian races is the creation and regulation of workers who will labor for less than a subsistence wage, that the transformation of local resources into capital is for transportation back to the investors' bank accounts in the metropolis, and that the logic that rules the local social order must function rigorously to facilitate these arrangements. Thus "instead of recommending the 'cat' [the whip], [the Governor is] sympathizing with a bunch of unemployables led by Le Maitre," Dollard will rage (416). The eruption of the subject-population is thus a military problem or an industrial one, one for—not between—citizens and government.

Nevertheless, the Pandora's box opened by the liberalization of metropolitan governments gives the colored population ideas. The state and its social organization must thus create and reiterate a nation proper, exemplified and embodied in white skin and its concretization reenacted by corporal punishment as a tenet of (white) nationalism. Subjects are either obedient, and so employable, or they are dross, unusable, industrial waste with the potential for becoming a problem. And because here the suffering body will never be white, the white and near-white stratum beyond the reach of public physical discipline retain the aura of untouchability, and thus an untouchable power and authority to define the social order in the minds of the colored subject-population.

Each of the workers waiting to be interviewed displays the internalization of colonial authority structuring the social order through culture. There is the black woman who douses herself in makeup and perfume and who dresses not only in satin but pink satin—signs of her femininity used to undercut the double masculinization of black women and women who work through her display of women's capital, her access proving her womanly respectability and so her trustworthiness and the fact that she deserves respect. The Indo-Trinidadians who work in agriculture recognize that the Afro-Trinidadians disparage them because they work on the plantations abandoned by the blacks as a barrier to reenslavement, and so they speak among themselves in Hindi. When the old Indian "hawk[s] the phlegm up loudly in his throat" and, no doubt in a gesture to British colonial propriety, walks to a potted plant to spit, the barriers to a cross-cultural Trinidadian alliance become clear as Mrs. Burnett, the black woman waiting to be interviewed by the committee, recognizing the proper marks of British culture and British relations to body fluids, as much as her feminine social function as the bearer of true culture, reacts quietly but "squeamishly" in the face of such un-British vulgarity (311). When she speaks to the black man beside her, she speaks in "a timid undertone" and he, recognizing his masculine role, responds "in a careless, loud voice of an employee who seems to say: 'You may be awed by the boss if you like . . . [but] I who have seen through him can get the better of him any time' " (311).

Confronting the white bodies in power, the subordinates bend to meet them more than halfway, but in the end it will be Mrs. Burnett who breaks from the system and terminates the interview in disgust. The men on the new Minimum Wage Committee recognize and depend on this capitulation, and build on it with the display of their close social ties, the better to control the upstart population represented by the waiting workers. They recognize, to the point that they never have to articulate it, that the committee can only meet in management's offices, that the committee must be comprised of the owners of businesses as well as government representatives who remain constants—the director of agriculture and his near-white therefore upwardly mobile secretary—and when they allow the workers to hear their laughter and their disputes over the intricacies and fairness of the golf courses at their disposal, they are making it clear that their primary alliance is to each other. This alliance extends from the social through the economic to government, deep into the domestic sphere where they meet for dinner, cocktails, and social conversation, and where their children go on to marry each other. The door to the boardroom is shut for their socializing, and the waiting witnesses are meant to overhear the nature of their pact but not, underscoring the role of invisibility in power politics, to see it. When Dollard opens the boardroom's door it is a signal to the members of the committee that their social relationship must give way to its governmental capacity because there is a tense social situation, and so power must wear an official face in confronting subordinates. The committee secretary, in training, is designated to call the workers for interrogation, and in order to mark his importance as much as his fitness for colonial government he musters as cold a voice as he can manage when calling their names.

Nothing of what the workers interviewed tell these men is understood. The mechanics of a barter economy and of depending on picking fruit and working subsistence plots for survival confound the committee. Boisson recognizes the hallmarks of this economy and can read them for the committee to remind them of his own importance and fitness, since the workers' dollar figures do not tally "because some days they don't eat food, they can't afford it" (315). For their part, the workers cannot always understand the committee's questions because their frames of reference are so disparate. The assessors repeatedly refer to them in the third person so that the workers can never be sure, except when directly looked at, that they are being spoken to and are thus required to speak. Nevertheless, empowered by the new atmosphere, and in dim recognition that the committee is only coming to them because island-wide strikes have forced it, they feel free to tell the truth, even as they grapple with degrees of subordination that will help their case while maintaining their dignity. Mrs. Burnett will finally make to leave in disgust when the director of agriculture raises the question of how frequently poor women wear through panties, and Dollard asks her, to further the government's business, to comment on whether or not poor black women really need to wear panties every day.

### Women and History: Keys to the Domestic Sphere

#### Love: a revolutionary catalyst
If the men who run the colony remain invisible, for the most part, when pulling at the strings of power, then women, love, and the domestic sphere are the keys to exploring the psychology and character of the elite, to those spaces where "Big Business, Officialdom and Cocktails" meet (130). In a curious convergence, it is through the question of women that the black working-class hero, Le Maitre, first stumbles as the embodi-

ment of the new man to lead a new nation. And in order to achieve an understanding of the national condition that reaches both into the household and out onto the street, Le Maitre must reconceptualize himself through his relationship to his manhood as a governing concept, thus gaining the love of the new woman, and fulfilling the promise of his name. History will intervene in love relationships, and it will be the function of women to pull men out of history and history-making into the present to confront the internal micropolitics of national everyday life. Cassie and Popito, Elena and Joe, André and Betty, André and Gwenneth, Cassie and Le Maitre, André and Elena: love and coupling will reveal the inner workings of the movement's cadres, and will predict the political trajectory of the new national men and women.

*White family history = territorial administrative history*
Through André Coudray and his family we enter the private circles of power. If the first seventeen chapters of *Crown Jewel* engage us with the social spaces of the workers and the disenfranchised, to enter the Coudray family home we must cross a border into St. Clair, the neighborhood of the elite. Here we will encounter Judge Osborne, who will later sentence Le Maitre to prison; the man who will refuse to defend Le Maitre, Mr. Coudray, Esq. (André's father), reputed to be the island's liberal best; and their guests: the commissioner of police, the debutantes newly arrived from finishing school in England, and the white British custodians of the major industries. At dinner, or over after-dinner drinks, the men who run the island will set the premises for public policy, determine the candidates for the new generation of the power elite, and consider their daughters' marriages the future for the family, as much as their sons, in administering the future of the colony.

The lines of descendance are carefully drawn: Mr. Coudray, André's grandfather, a planter displaced by Toussaint's revolution in Haiti, flees, like his contemporary, J. B. Philippe, to the deserted outpost that was Trinidad at the turn of the eighteenth century. The colony's new British owners welcomed the expertise in crop management, estate farming, and exports, as much as in running a colony, that becomes a leadership in what was still considered a wilderness. At the top of the mideighteenth-century colonial regime, as planters schooled in French culture, as much as the expertise that made Haiti the most profitable of Caribbean islands before Toussaint's revolution, the Coudrays come to exemplify the wealth and sumptuousness of life among the Caribbean plantocracy that we glimpsed earlier in Hopkins's Grace and Charles Montfort:

> Mr. de Coudray [André's father] had pleasant memories of many a boyhood day in the old ancestral home with its retinue of black servants who had once been slaves. When his sisters were to be married, their wedding gowns were ordered from Paris. Besides racehorses, half-a-dozen riding animals stamped their hoofs in the stables. There were entertainments, balls. There was a particular set of delicate Chinaware that was no longer used but preserved in a glass case—some visiting prince, duke or earl had eaten from it long ago. (130–31)

The past holds a premium here, like the mother country, and so princes/dukes/earls are still for the opportunists migrated to the New World colonies a mark of having arrived, the aristocracy passing out of power lending their blessings to the nouveau riche of the plantocracy by dining in their homes. The family preserves the crockery as proof that they have been sanctioned by authentic society. While the Parisian gowns bespeak purchasing power for the best in the world of fashion, they echo again the centrality of women as bearers of capital, as mannequins on whom the family's wealth and stature are hung. Marriage is a socio-economic and therefore political pact, and so when the reigning order shifts from the plantocracy to the professionals, from land and an old family name to money, with the shift from agrarianism to industrialism marked by the abolition of slavery the change is marked by the decisions made in the family home and are reflected in the conceivable couplings. In this way, strategies of colonial government incorporate women as repositories of value later to be objects for exchange, like an investment bond.[13]

It follows, then, that it is men who must lead because women are viable economic entities only under the guidance of men, be it in the capacity of fathers, husbands, sons, or managers: "Papa had died young, and Mama, putting her trust in a manager, was soon robbed. Her affairs became so involved that she was forced to sell the estate and the ancestral home to salvage something for the children. With no estates to leave them, she sent the boys abroad to study professions" (131).

The Coudray family biography thus follows the shift in the ruling classes from agro-industry to oil extraction, from plantations to business and industry. Because the family forms the remnants of the colony's old ruling elite, the family's history is the colony's history, and the transition from aristocratic colonialism to modern industrial colonialism is not without its disasters, near misses, and dead ends for the founding families. Grandmother Coudray's economic indebtedness forces a reconsideration of the patterns of international investment as a family matter. There is still a place for the extraction of local minerals through agriculture, but with the shrinking of the overseas markets, only a few producers can survive and so many of the descendants of the original planter class must find employment elsewhere within the new bourgeois industrial paradigm that finds greater profits in oil. The elite shift from agrarianism to industrialism is marked by disasters that Caribbean literature registers in the white family house: Rhys's *Wide Sargasso Sea*, opening with abolition, recounts a planter's suicide to mark the sudden transformation of his private property into British subjects, capital into a hostile majority.

And where there are no men to manage the households of the agrarian elite, and the task of the paterfamilias is farmed out to the men from lower social circles, disaster ensues. Thus it is a mark of Mrs. Coudray's skills as a manager in the domestic sphere—and the toughness of the colonial clans—that she recognizes the new paradigms for the proper preparation of her children. In order for them to retain a modicum of their sociopolitical rank, the pattern of family professions must shift, and thus she sends her children abroad to study the new laws and modern business management in order to join the pool of new men, competing with the new moneyed metropolitan families, as trained and true members of the old aristocracy.

*Love among the elite: from family to globality*
Representatives of the new ruling cadres, Englishman Justice Osborne, the colonial secretary, and his son, the commissioner of police and the sub-inspector, now carry with their family's future the future of the colony. Gwenneth Osborne's association with the disaffected André Coudray thus represents a familial crisis because of what it might mean for the future of the colony: the mixing of white and mulatto blood and culture; the ascension of new creole (proto)nationalist cadres to the spheres of the elite; and the dilution of the blood/nation of the colonial

elite with the blood/nation of the subject races as equivalent to the political dilution of colonial policy through the mongrelization of Trinidad's administrative cadres. Love and marriages, and thus women, carry with them the weight of social pacts bearing global ramifications with the specter of the collapse of the empire.

The dynamics of controlling the national transition being forced onto government and management by the impoverished in the streets are worked out in the living rooms and on the verandas of the elite. So the terms and twists of Gwenneth Osborne's interrogation at dinner by Judge Osborne regarding André's character and family carries with it the burden of the colony's future, and so André's culture and connections— whether, as the final nail in the coffin the judge builds for their relationship, he is "popular in the district"—are to be inspected (177). If André comes up lacking in the Osborne household for his "modern" ideas (176), the Coudray's are delighted at this sudden turn in the family's fortunes through André's future in his romantic affiliation with the Osborne family, as if "a not too bright son had unexpectedly passed a difficult test and been launched on a promising future" (178).

All the players—including Le Maitre—realize that the test of André's politics, and hence his future in the colony, are in his domestic arrangements. As a mark of his radicalization and fitness for transformation, his relationship with, first, the colored Elena Henriques, daughter of an impoverished Venezuelan seamstress, and then Betty, colored daughter to a Fyzabad oil worker, will be carefully watched by all involved. To marry Elena or Betty—indeed to do anything except perhaps impregnate and abandon them—is to ally himself with the rabble on the street pressing for nation formation and transition and thus to exclude himself from the administrative posts granted in the spheres of the elite.[14] In his trek from St. Clair to the barrack yards, onlookers throughout the social spectrum mark the shift in the colony's future, the possibilities of men from the elite casting their vote for the new mulatto country.

Gwenneth, true daughter of what members of the local ruling class refer to as their "set," recognizes these emerging possibilities on different levels at different stages in her relationship with André in particular, and with all her prospective suitors in general. Recently returned from England, she is initially attracted to André because he embodies for her the romantic sensibility of the lone, brooding outcast juxtaposed with the officious patriots of local government. As Judge Osborne questions her over dinner, however, she begins to recognize that casual affairs with the wrong set in the colony can inflict lasting damage not only to a girl's future but also to the political future of the island. Faced, then, with André's intensity—he wants to take her away, marry her, have her join him in exile from their "set" and walk boldly into the colony's future— she finds it more amusing, and more in her and the family's/island's interest, to explore flirtation with the sons of the administrative cadres, the corps d'elite of up-and-coming English businessmen, the upper echelons of the police, or the son of the colonial secretary. Nevertheless, she finds it difficult to sever relations with André because she enjoys the power she has over him, and because the suspicion that he is a mulatto excites her sexually. This sexual excitement works in an inverse relation to his prospects as a future husband because the hint of black blood makes him at once a sexualized figure and an exile, excused from government and leadership and thus inappropriate for a woman whose prospects are only as promising as the husband to whom she will attach herself. To marry André is to embrace a mulatto country and the decline of empire, and so Gwenneth finds herself at a (proto)national crossroads with global implications.

The process of Gwenneth's education at England's finest schools imbues her with the sense of white self-importance appropriate to the daughters of the island's ruling families, and she displays this in her bearing and in her relationship to the black masses who surround her: "Gwenneth was one of those people whose walk clearly expresses a trait of her character. When she came rapidly towards him on her high heels with her firm short step, holding herself very erect, André felt uncomfortably that she would have her way in spite of anything anyone might say or do" (171).

The daughters of the elite must carry with them the ability to rule, not only as a complement to their husband's role in colonial society, to whose future they must devote their political savvy, but domestically in the management of households. In the description of her father, what is latent in Gwenneth's manner finds a patrimony in Judge Osborne's training as a member of ruling classes experienced with "Negroes and Indians," and so is particularly appropriate to administering the colony of Trinidad:

> Because he was an Englishman it was natural that there should be thousands of poor blacks who would treat him with servile respect, whom he could employ for low wages and dismiss at will. As an

Englishman who had come from an ancient land-owning family and been educated at the best schools in the country he was by nature and breeding superior not only to colonials, black and white, but other human beings in general. He had spent twenty years in India. It was his firm belief that "all this trouble with Gandhi" would not have arisen if England had not "educated the Indians beyond their intelligence." [Negroes and Indians] were intelligent, but far too immature to make proper use of the knowledge England gave them. . . . In addition, there was a set of regulations, The Law, which enabled [Judge] Osborne to define the lot of the impoverished, the natives, and made it unnecessary for him to consider them further. (173)

What Gwenneth realizes early at a preconscious level in her relationship with André will emerge full force during the riots, where she will feel it the duty of "all her set, especially of herself as a close friend of [Sub-Inspector] David Primrose to walk down Frederick Street as if Negroes did not exist" (403). Love relations among the men and women of the elite are political relations, and so a woman's shoring up the ego of a man with whom she flirts is the same as a national political necessity, for country and for the empire.

*Women and national politics in the petit bourgeois creole home front*
Joe Elias, as a revolutionary/political man who enters the spheres of colonial government, such as the city council he joins, becomes the test case for the argument of working within the system of the colonial regime. In this he is in contrast to Le Maitre and his cadres, who call in the end for revolution as the only means for ameliorating the conditions of the people. While it is true that the implementation of the reforms Joe calls for in the city council threatens the structures of the government by forcing a key epistemological shift—from "subject" to "citizen"—his transformation into a representative of the middle-class nationalists seals the revolutionary antiliberal premise that the system always corrupts. Joe's historical counterpart, Albert Gomes, is in fact only unseated by the Independence platform of Eric Williams, and so the revolution premised on Joe's failure to transform finds itself married to a history in which not socialist revolution but liberal capitalist reform under the leadership of an educated marxist-nationalist and the establishing of a Trinidadian nation-state become the horizon of the people.[15]

Joe's transformation from spokesman for the masses to representative of the national administrators comes, literally and figuratively, as his patrimony. When his father, Old Elias, dies and Joe inherits his estate, he begins to see from the inside the wickedness of calls for higher wages and labor reforms, in concrete terms of his opportunity cost. "You would have to do a pretty good job of convincing me that the increase is justified," he tells the striking scavengers looking to the city council and so gathered outside the town hall, "if you are going to be unreasonable and stupid [in your demands] I will wash my hands of the whole thing" (398, 399).

Just as Old Elias's miserliness is depicted in terms reminiscent of the (modern/marxist) ancient racist stereotype of Jews as misers, so we see Joe's transformation from liberalism into miserliness in similar terms. This transformation comes with his inheritance at the death of his father, a trace of the shifting bourgeois power-base from land to capital and from the colonial oligarchy to the new nationalist mulatto petit bourgeoisie. If the Coudrays had to hire managers who failed them and to limit themselves to managers of investments and careers in the law, the managers and sole owners of property would be the elite, a point of entry for the local colored population—particularly, for historical reasons, the local Syrian elite. Joe's patrimony as an economic concept thus plays itself out as a social concept when he insists his mother "have a car and chauffeur" and monthly vacations at the beach (329). Under the care of a doctor who comes highly recommended, as much as the money that greases the machinery, his mother loses weight, her legs improve, and her voice grows stronger, "as if . . . a stifling, malignant growth had been cut off from her spirit" (330). Joe's women's bodies, their condition and the quality of their pampering, become the repositories of his capital.

Suggesting that politics in the petit bourgeois mulatto domestic sphere bear an inverse relation to the politics of black/proletarian nation formation, Mrs. Elias's condition improves with her son's ascension to the role of paterfamilias, and Joe's sharing of the profits from his inheritance is limited to the family, his mother, brothers, and sisters. Circumscribed by the home and family relations, his socialist impulse stops at networks of blood kinship in the finest traditions of the liberal aristocracy, and the workers in the public sphere, where the battle for the country is waged, find themselves betrayed here first. If initially Joe is forced, to quiet his contradictions, into loaning his workers money (one for a child's operation, another to keep the bailiff from repossessing furniture) he quickly becomes aware that the principles and logic of good business mandate that he minimize expenses and maximize profits, and it is classical music on one hand, and the home and its responsibilities on the other, that come to sooth his transition from "liberal socialist reform-ist" to "conservative national petit bourgeois."

The tight relation between money and power as an economic concept and capital as a social concept means that the newly eligible Joe becomes a prospective husband of choice. Just as André finds himself increasingly excluded from the parties and dinners of the local English set, so Joe finds himself seduced into the homes of the local Syrian elite in an imitation of the local white commercial elite: "Rich Syrians, and some business people who were more white than black and thought: 'Better a Syrian for a son-in-law than a nigger,' invited Joe to parties and intro-duced him to their daughters" as the closer to white the better (331). The interests of money and business whitewash colored people—whiteness as a political position, exile from the black/mulatto nation—and Joe finds himself a welcome stopgap against mongrelization among those who have no hope of marrying their daughters to men with an address in St. Clair.

Integration into the social sphere of the moneyed worms its way in-ward to Joe's reconceptualization of himself—adding "a touch of aloof-ness to the air of importance and self-satisfaction that he exuded" (331)—and inevitably to his betrayal of his public platform metonymized in his attitude to consumption. He spends over a hundred dollars on a gram-ophone and records, at first concealing it "from his ill-paid clerks" and then consuming it openly, brazenly, and conspicuously (331). It is only a short step in the rebirth of Joe Elias as his father when he begins to agree to stall the scavengers' wage increase in the city council, as the transfor-mations wrought in the domestic sphere work their way back into the public political arena. Leaving the council chamber, Joe will give his last word to the rabble: "When they put some of you behind bars" he tells them, "you will soon change your tune" (401).

Mrs. Elias's role also suggests the links between the Elias household and the Coudray/Osborne household in the omnipresence and manage-ment of servants. If Mrs. Osborne acknowledges at least cursorily that ser-vants are people who hear and feel, Mrs. Elias and her son afford no such sensitivity. Mrs. Elias hears her son's irritation, and it is a function of her job description that she identifies the problem, takes it out of her son's hands, and manages to make Beulah, their black servant, come running.

Whatever else must be done, the men must be waited upon and done so immediately. Mrs. Elias thus takes her place among the women of the creole elite who must manage households, concern themselves with proper (that is, capital-accumulating) marriages for their daughters, while establishing their sons in respectable and profitable occupations in government or business, and we see this in her battles with her husband over the money Joe must put up to be eligible for election to the city council. Mrs. Elias's threat to stop managing the household represents a defection of middle management. As a child of the household, Joe relies on his mother for services and to negotiate with his father, the head of the house; once Old Elias is gone, Joe's liberalism plays itself out in the household through the body of his mother (her weight, the condition of her legs, her vacations), and the relation between the domestic sphere and the political sphere, encompassing the deprivation of the workers, is turned inside out when he withdraws from advocating policies that threaten to redistribute his wealth beyond the circle of his immediate family.

*Women and national politics in the barrack yard: the mulatta home front*
In Joe's early days as the populist publisher of an anticolonial magazine, and then as member of Le Maitre's Negro Welfare Association, he flirts with Elena Henriques, the daughter of a Venezuelan seamstress. Elena lives in a barrack yard with Cassie (maid to Judge Osborne) and, among others who populate the most dilapidated neighborhoods of the capital city, Rose, a prostitute who will stand for demoralization and the victory of capitalism over poor women's dignity. It is noteworthy that everyone who lives in this yard is a woman, as if they disproportionately populate the underclass. Mrs. Henriques and Elena, as a couple, come to exemplify the patterns of survival and the cycle of poverty that govern the lives of the poorest, and in their attempts at flight and shifts in perspective on the order of things they encapsulate the hopes of the people in the absence of a revolutionary horizon. Cassie, as we will see later, becomes metonymic of women's capacity for revolutionary transformation, but it is telling of de Boissière's remarkably progressive politics that women can be conceived as agents involved in social change without a man, and that woman's conscientization comes from contemplating her own position in the social order rather than through a Delanyesque paradigm of marriage to a revolutionary man.

Elena and Mrs. Henriques, like the other women in the barrack yard, find themselves in repeated confrontation with the economic order, and the representatives of capital and its reigning formations are always men. The interplay of government and business that we saw in industry (capitalists = the law) replays itself, but where the workers in industry are men, here in the city the underclass is recognizably women. The men who come to collect rent or seize furniture in exchange are representatives not only of the property owners but also the law, because they are bailiffs. The law requires the bailiff to be accompanied by underlings, and so the men who come with them come to take furniture as payment for rent. Cassie's house is completely emptied; Mrs. Henriques, having hidden unsuccessfully, has her furniture taken piece by piece.

Mrs. Henriques is the embodiment of the generous but impoverished soul, the romantic concept of the poor woman who will give away everything she has. For de Boissière, the women who come to borrow from her are thieves and liars, and so it is recognized that the underclasses consist of a spectrum of characters on whose mobilization the revolution depends, a move that marks again the creolization of marxist epistemology and the seeds of what will later become the project of underdevelopment theory in the hands of André Gunder Frank. In her growing conscientization, Elena recognizes her mother's gullibility, an innocence born from confinement in a cycle of ignorance and poverty: Mrs. Henriques will lend the rent money then overspend on a feast to compensate for her depression at the lack of rent money; she will allow herself to be bullied and cheated by the wives of the elite.

For her part, Elena succumbs at first to the temptations of girlhood: boys, virtue, the movies, dates; but, beginning with her liaison with Joe, she initiates the process of transformation that will take her toward a mulatta revolutionary paradigm. Her love of literature (English) and history (West Indian) will make her the right match for the newly conscienticized mulatto André, but the process of their union across class lines will be painful and circuitous. If the men, as I will argue later, come to consciousness through the workplace, women achieve a revolutionary outlook through recognizing a parallel victimization operating in both the workplace and affairs of the heart. As if to mark his place in society above the deprivations of hunger and barrack yard life, André's conscientization will also take place through love, although, unlike the women, he is able to wander freely through the spheres of men: the Negro Welfare Association meeting, the countryside, St. Clair, the militant underclass. If Mrs. Henriques marks one set of parameters for Elena's possible biography (reproducing her mother's life) then André marks the other (union with a new man), and their marriage across class and racial lines is a sign of things colonial falling apart. Just as surely, her capitulation to her mother's self-defeating illusions would mean her entrapment in the cycle of poverty. But once she tries to get a job and escape she is forced to recognize the rule of politics everywhere at work to determine and constrict her life, as that of any poor colored woman.

Before André and Elena can marry, each must go on a journey of personal discovery that will take them toward a totalizing vision of the society in which they live and their roles within it, because each must recognize the psychological split that marks maturation in children: André must break from his family, Elena must break from mothering her mother. And since both are caught up in a society in (proto)national transition, the alienation from preexisting kinship relations is coterminous with an alienation from the preexisting social order. In this transitional society, the new domestic relations in which (mulatto?) white men from St. Clair marry brown women from the barrack yards carry with them the paradigms of the new mulatto national consciousness, as much as they help give birth to them in their union.

*Women and national politics in the barrack yard: the black home front*
The paradigm for the quintessence of revolutionary coupling, however, is Cassie and Le Maitre; and if André and Elena must go through a difficult and painful process of personal rebirth before they can break with the social order and unite, then Cassie's rebirth is arguably the most painful of all. By the time we meet Le Maitre he has already been married and had a child, and both wife and child are dead from starvation and typhoid. The new man here must have the experience of raising and supporting a wife and children in order to incorporate into himself the difficulties of the paradigmatic worker struggling to support a family, but, as Le Maitre himself articulates it, to have a wife and family while leading a new nation to take the streets is to embroil a man in the impossible. The split between the home as the domestic front and the street as the site of battle is absolute in the initial marxist paradigms. Through Cassie, however, Le Maitre will come to capitulate this split between the domestic sphere and public spaces, and in crossing this frontier he will take the ultimate step in dedication to the struggle, casting aside his machismo for the sake of all workers and the revolution.

Cassie, when we first meet her, is a meek maid in the Osborne household. She watches from the margins as Mrs. Osborne cheats Mrs. Henriques, her neighbor, out of her due for Gwenneth's dresses. One of Cassie's tasks is to serve dinner, and so we are privy to the dinner conversation in the households of the white elite. By the middle of the book, as the Negro Welfare Association grows in numbers and impact, Cassie moves from a maid on the margins of the narrative of St. Clair to a barrack yard woman pulling her private life together as a political act. She is slowly drawn into the political meetings, and by the novel's end she is making speeches as fiery as Le Maitre's and leading the marching strikers through the city.

The turning point for Cassie comes when she makes the shift from the old paradigm of depending on a man to the revolutionary one of fighting to change the system, a shift enacted through her relationship to Popito Luna, Mrs. Henriques's brother and Elena's uncle. Cassie loses her furniture because the policeman, as a traitor to the (proto)nation as one who had once supported her, beats her and takes up with someone else.[16] Popito, in offering Cassie what little he has, and in loving her, takes her into another paradigm in which rather than being dependent on a violent and abusive man in order to keep the bailiff out, the union of men and women is a partnership in which both parties love, support, and protect each other.

Through this relationship with Popito, a member of Le Maitre's inner circle, Cassie is drawn into the meetings of the Negro Welfare Association, where lip service at least is paid to incorporating domestic servants into the workers represented by the party. It is a mark of de Boissière's horizon that he can conceive of this, following the historical example of labor leader Elma François, but he cannot, like the institutionalization that comes with the Trinidadian nation-state's decriminalization of these early labor leaders, actually incorporate women and servants into the new dominant paradigms. When Cassie achieves her realization as a new political woman, mirroring Le Maitre at the crest of his inspirational marches, she marches "at the head of the workers . . . with long strides, like a man" (393). In counterpoint, Le Maitre, as the police close in for his arrest, will dress himself as a woman, following Cassie's advice, to gain time for the struggle.

Cassie's break from passivity and the rebirth that will allow her transformation into the woman for Le Maitre—the paradigm of the new woman—comes in a double blow to her political self-conceptualization, marked by police violence. If the rhetoric of genteel colonial society says women proper are exempt from physical battles and so from the maintenance of colonial power by brute force, Cassie discovers that poor colored women have no such luxury. Duke, the policeman who swaggers among them, arrests her on no charge in order to intimidate her into informing on her lover. When Cassie refuses to give in, he beats her so badly that she miscarries. At the moment she recognizes she is not a subject of law protected by the ideology of gender, she recognizes that in her blackness she is an object of colonial rule, a subjugation that can only be relieved by casting her lot with the men pressing for a national transformation.

The second moment comes when, on the way home from a Shango meeting, Cassie and Popito encounter Duke, whose vendetta and machismo force him to attack on sight. Cassie runs. When Popito's rotting corpse is found days later, the officials do not know his name; he joins the countless numbers dead at the hands of the protectors of the elite, dead in the struggle and consigned to an unmarked grave. Cassie will no longer tolerate Duke's abuse and, in the midst of a march turned riot because of police brutality, she douses Duke with gasoline and sets him on fire. Here police brutality stands in for the brutality of the henchmen of the colonial elite.

For Le Maitre the shift is more sudden because he is already, as his name suggests, the leader of the new revolutionary movement. When he contemplates his feeling for Cassie—love, perhaps—it saps him of his revolutionary fervor, just as orgasms are said to make men weak. Before he can couple with Cassie, he must first understand the place for women and their relation in the flesh to the locus and agenda for social change in the home and in the street. Le Maitre's dead wife and child prepare him to lead men, but with the recognition that the majority of the underclass is women, a place must be found for them in the revolution. Although there are whispers of love between Cassie and Le Maitre, it is not until they set out on a hunger march to Port of Spain with the oil workers from Fyzabad that something coalesces within him. Cassie insists she come along, even though Le Maitre feels that the march is no place for women.

In her insistence on being included in the revolutionary national body, Cassie breaks through the first barrier in Le Maitre's mind toward a reconceptualization of women's place in society and social change. Cassie knows she has worked as hard as men and has been paid less, that she has been beaten by the police for information, lost a wanted child to the struggle, and that this march of workers, with all it represents, may work for her benefit if her faith in an equal place in the new horizon is warranted. Her invasion of the new social space of the workers' long march becomes a catalyst for Le Maitre's confrontation with what the narrative ethos concedes are his counterrevolutionary responses to spiritual attractions (love feelings), and it is up to Cassie to organize for Le Maitre the complex interstices of love as a public-political concept and love as a private-domestic affair. Thus if Le Maitre leads the workers and the nation toward a reconceptualization of themselves and the world—where they "cast off . . . their age-old submission" (389)—Cassie must lead Le Maitre in strategies of the heart. Once he realizes her leadership and his reactionary impulse, that the negotiations of the domestic cannot be excluded from the strategies for confrontation in the street, the objective conditions for their union as equal partners in the struggle to make a new country can emerge.

### Revolution and the New Men

#### A man to lead a nation

With the entangling of personal lives in the barrack yard—when Elena and Mrs. Henriques have their first piece of furniture seized as rent and when Cassie's furniture is repossessed and Popito and Mrs. Henriques come to her rescue—a hero emerges in the street. The specter of organized subaltern subjects breaks onto the stage like history, and at its head is a black man:

> Le Maitre was a tall, heavily built brown Negro with greenish eyes and pouting, insolent lips. He attracted all eyes with his big voice, masterful bearing and determined, firm steps.
> "We Demand Work For Our People, Bread For Our Children," said the placard he carried.
> "Now and then, stepping to one side and walking backwards, he would look down the column and shout in a ringing bass that he obviously enjoyed using:
> "Come, comrades, crowd up!" Or: "No straggling, comrades. In step! Left, right, left!" (52–53)

In his bearing and biology, Le Maitre carries all the marks of a masculinity in its prime: his deep voice, his firm step, the authority over others that transforms a straggling crowd into a political force, his plea-sure in watching his power unfold. Le Maitre's cleansing leadership seeps through his skin and infects the crowd of subalterns. Written in his leadership, however, the black man-hero brings a multicultural con-sciousness, marking his body as it determines his politics. His green eyes and brown skin register the mixing of blood and of culture; in his jubi-lant militarism and vocabulary are the lessons, if not the imaginary, of the international proletariat. The cultures of the nation find themselves catalyzed at a crossroads here, and in the process a leader is born who is anchored in the mixed blood of the people, transforming the marchers into an army with an iron will as their only weapon: "The crowd, like Popito, felt in Le Maitre the unabashed resolution of a man incapable of more than one point of view and willing to overturn society to impose it. More, the placards [carried by the marchers] said that that point of view was their own" (53). In Le Maitre all of history's contradictions are re-solved, his individual resolution fortifying collective anger in the press for anticolonial revolution. Carrying with him the weight of a new under-standing, he becomes a catalyst for the resolve and thus the transforma-tion of the people's political unconscious.

As much as his sociohistorical position demands from him the quali-ties traditionally the province defining men, it is his ability to assess, to take and give, that sets him apart. Love for the people makes revolution here an emotional as much as a political-historical act, and it is this that opens the door to love with Cassie that acts as a point of entry for his rethinking of the place of love in the home and so women in the new social order. In the macropolitics of overdetermined identity, his ability to feel is connected to his ability to see, and in the relative quiet of making institutional and organizational affiliations, the very same sociopolitical perceptiveness that makes him dare to defend gay rights—speaking against the violence of his community looking for a scapegoat—allows him to recognize that Joe's affiliation is suspect and that he is using the workers' revolutionary organization as a stepping-stone to a liberal politi-cal career.

*Revolutionary industrial organization = nation formation*
The trajectory from black-centered to multicultural political organization is marked in the transformation of the organization from the Negro Welfare Association to the Workers' Welfare Association. The first name gains the organization momentum on two fronts: first because it distin-

guishes them from Boisson's Workers' Party, and so provides a political alternative. With accession to political power, Boisson and his cadres are revealed as careerists, displaying the same disregard for the lower strata providing their rhetorical base as Joe will later reveal. Second, in articulating itself as "Negro," it puts the disenfranchised black masses at the center of its social subject, and thus uses the sociocultural norm of black = poverty to define its political purview. When the Negro Welfare Association begins to swallow up the burgeoning workers' cells organized according to sectors in the economic makeup, it is the pressures brought on by the momentum of uniting the largest possible sector of the social order that forces the vectors of class to supersede the vectors of phenotype, and so the birth of black nationalism is the promise of the birth of a multicultural socialism.

### Crowd/mob/nation

The climactic series of explosions is metaphorized as a natural event, following on the principle threading its way throughout the novel that nature, at a remove from the national/industrial drama, holds the keys to survival. The first march to confront the governor is, onlookers remark, like the Dry River flooding, a local metaphor for a national groundswell: "In like fashion now, this swelling river of workless people flowed down the street. At every step more were sucked in—grinning youth on bicycles, women with loose alpargats[17] which slapped their heels as they ran, half-naked children. Their noise, the curiosity and excitement on their faces, their shouts of encouragement stimulated the marchers" (52). The birth of a workers' organization pressing for governmental representation is a culmination of history, and the birth of a workers' organization as the birth of history is recorded here as a natural event, a feminine metaphor embodied as a masculine force.

History, like a flooding river, transforms everything in its wake, and suddenly a subaltern people become an unstoppable force. The development and expansion of the organization across zones—city to outpost and back, barrack yard to St. Clair and back—comes hand in hand with its transformation from a black workers' vehicle to a national multicultural one. Without arms, the blood shed on the streets marks another transition, the birth of the nation as a living concept, another national transition written in blood.

The bodies pile up. But in a marked break from the rhetoric of crowds and mobs—uniform, irrational—de Boissière's people become (again the syntax of a river) a crowd, then strikers, then a mob, then a crowd again. And throughout the shift in signifiers marking shifts in degrees of politicization and determination—the erosion of empire—the people are always rational, always determined, and they always plot toward control of the major industries and the streets of the city.

## The future of underdeveloped countries

The crack Le Maitre opens by uniting workers and subalterns is sealed by the middle class that comes in to take control as a new national elite, of the people-nation but sharing the interests of the foreign industrial leaders. Boisson as much as Joe, and like their historical counterparts Cipriani and Gomes, will find it in their interests to form and maintain an alliance with the threat of mass action. Historically, although elections gave Butler's party the lion's share of power in the legislative council, it was the British-trained Gomes, ousted by the British-trained Eric Williams, who worked to derail Butler's political agendas. In closing, I argue three points: first, Joe and his father encapsulate metonymically the relationship between the old creole bourgeoisie and the new; second, that embedded in de Boissière's rendering of Joe's domestic politics is the principle that poor women are the emblem of the oppressed and forgotten people-nation; and, third, that Joe's political trajectory represents the political trajectory of government—the transformation of pro-tonationalism into a strategy for consolidating governmental power in the hands of a new elite—Hobsbawm's nationalism.

It is in his relationship to his father that Joe's revolutionary impulses play themselves out; that is, the problem of the nation played out in the relations between men. The description of Old Elias as a miser—a marxist metaphor for the enemy bourgeoisie—counting his piles of money while moaning and groaning is meant to win sympathy for Joe and provide a contrast through which his revolutionary principles can come into perspective. It is his father and all that supports him and all that he stands for—the ruling order—whom Joe hates, whom he tries to strangle for hoarding the wealth and spending it on illicit pleasures, just as the workers taking the street will attack their white employers' assets. When Joe's father gives him the check and property that will make him eligible for election to the city council, Old Elias, like a leader of industry capitulating, recognizes that he must "buy off [his] own son" or face a mutiny, since Mrs. Elias, as the household's manager, has chosen to shift her allegiances and make a social pact with her son and against the old guard's interests.

Mrs. Elias's new alliance, as much as Joe's anger, stems from their discovery that Old Elias keeps other women, even buying them houses, while wailing in the family home that he has no money and that Joe's demands will be the ruin of them all. Old Elias, like the managers of imperial resources, expatriates his profits and can only be made to spend money at home through threats of violence. In a repoliticization of Oedipus, he is threatened by an alliance of the son beneath him in the social order, compounded with betrayal of the one who lies next to him most nights and who manages his central domestic affairs, his wife.

Later, however, when Joe contemplates his father's corpse he begins to excuse him, and nostalgia turns to the reifications of capital formation in identity formation: " 'How can any of us help being who we are? Do we make our own destiny?' He lay limp on the bed, feeling himself completely in the hands of an unknown power which moulded man to its own mysterious, incomprehensible desire" (327). In the end, it is the project of *Crown Jewel,* and the embodiment of the revolution it records, to refute Joe Elias's ennui, just as wealth will be to blame in the corruption of men, as underscored by Old Elias's final capitulation to his son's platform immediately before his death.

Conversely, just as Old Elias turned on Joe for advocating policies sure to ruin the territory (i.e., his financial interests), Joe turns on the striking scavengers. Liberal conservatism comes as his ideological patrimony, adapted for modern times and the shifting place of the local petit bourgeoisie in new administrative principles born of the split between colonial rulers and subjects, with subjects taking the streets as an outgrowth of reconceptualizing themselves as citizens. Joe's initial sense of political exile is tied to his father's rule; thus with his accession to power at his father's death, what was formulated as an external politics comes to determine domestic politics, and what governed his politics inside the home comes to determine his rupture from the oppressed in the streets. André, passing Joe on his way in the opposite direction, recognizes that there is a contradiction in Joe's protests of difference from business as usual and Joe's defense of himself as a "realist"; André recognizes that "so are the scavengers" and that Joe's rhetoric reveals, even as it hides, the class interests that forestall a purely political solution in favor of the masses (332): the question remains as to the means.

In the family home, however, the seeds of Joe's betrayal of the workers who elect him to power—his petit bourgeois interests—are configured early; and if Le Maitre's questions as to Joe's motives are quieted and Le Maitre agrees to make a political alliance with Joe for the sake of the Workers' Welfare Association, in Joe's relationships to the black woman on the margins of his father's house we also see the seeds of his emergent class identity and political sensibility. We can thus extrapolate again house to nation in a novel by a man about men. If Joe's political future is to be uncertain in the beginning, his treatment of Beulah, employed by the Elias family, makes his politics quite clear: his individualism, his seduction into a comfort uninterested in the labor spent to produce it, his ability to lose himself in what money can buy while forgetting—a forgetting on which his pleasure is premised—the worker who provides and who looks on. A simple detail, if we extrapolate politics from the position of women (the personal as political) belies Joe's narrative's attempt—emblematic of bourgeois Caribbean nationalism—to suture the split in the political man as a heroic representative of the poor:

> He took up the evening newspaper, retired to his room, and shouted for Beulah, the Negro servant girl, to bring him iced lemonade. Mrs. Elias, hearing her favorite son's voice raised in irritation, also joined in the shouting for "Beulah! Beulah!" From somewhere in the yard came an answering cry of: "Yes, Mrs. Eli-oos!" on a high, drawn-out note and the slap of slippers from running feet. . . . Joe had visions of a Socialist Party capturing a majority of seats and installing him as Mayor. . . . Beulah knocked and came in with his lemonade. She had a pleasant, good-natured expression.
> "Here, Mr. Joe," she said.
> "Put it there, just put it there," he said vaguely, not looking at her.
> She smiled and went out. From long experience she knew she was not the cause of his apparent ill-humour. She felt the kindly spirit within him, his sensitive regard for the sufferings of her class, and she was fond of him, as all the servants were.
> Joe let the paper fall from his hand and slowly sipped the lemonade. (12–13)

From his relation to the two women we can see the seeds of his betrayal, as well as the parameters of his sociopolitical identity: Beulah and the servants exist as a political concept in his head, intimately connected to his rise to power, but his treatment of the men and women who make up this class is more or less the same as those whose interests he purports to destabilize. Not only does he see going to the refrigerator himself beyond the limits of consideration, but so does his mother, and Beulah's tardiness in waiting on him elicits not sympathy for the work she must do, but irritation. The slap of slippers on the pavement as the crowd turns into marchers then mob echoes in the family home: the lacunae between the oppressed as a political concept and as an intimate human reality become a problem Joe is not even able to recognize, and we can note that de Boissière excuses him by putting loving words and feelings in the mind of the servant woman as a metonym for her class. His rudeness, acknowledged as rudeness, is excusable on the basis of a "kindly spirit" nowhere in evidence.

The riots of women, workers, and children, then, are also a statement from the subjects to the new local management; and it is up to the new territorial administration to ensure that the workers have another means of speaking. In the legislative council's debate on the meaning of the riots and the trajectory of the Crown Colony's future, it is also understood by the mulatto petit bourgeois contingent invested in liberal reform that once the machinery is in place—manned, of course, by men of the local middle class—there will be no more room for a sympathetic response at any level to such disruptions of the production of surplus value, and the left-wing "extremists and the more unstable elements of the population" can be isolated, and so more easily ferreted out by the police (415).

Hand in hand with this fully modern, liberal reconceptualization of the body politic comes the countermetaphorization of revolt and submission through the discourse of mental health and of normality, once the rioters are divided into the majority expressing a legitimate grievance and the handful of individuals, later synonymized as "the ringleaders," who can then be diagnosed as the disease and surgically treated with imprisonment (415).

Even so marginal a reconceptualization of the colonial social order brings the governor's dismissal from his post, pointing again to the powers and politics defining the colony's population in the British Empire. Once the governor is finished, Boisson, referring to the governor as "Sir Richard," praises him for his perceptiveness and calls for a "New Deal" for Trinidad, the importation of U.S. domestic political strategy on the other side of the Monroe Doctrine. This strategy is designed to undermine the unions, in order to ensure that the "unstable element"—the "hooligan element, he preferred to call it"—was not deliberately given a helping hand (415). In making the substitution of "hooligan" for "unstable" Boisson has already made the transition from the liberal metaphors of the governor anticipating the machinery for grievances to the possibilities within the reformist creole political economy that labels those who refuse the process as "criminals," a random but dangerous element that can now be conceptualized without recourse to the language of humanism and problems caused by environmental factors.[18] Naturally, Boisson and his party see themselves as precisely the embodiments of the new negotiating machinery and the arbiters of the new national paradigm.

Boisson, of course, like the city council over which he presides, is of little importance in the policies of the colony. The very concession to machinery allowing workers to speak to management, in itself a concession asserting that the subaltern can speak and management must listen, will erode the foundations of the empire, and so Boisson/Cipriani will be succeeded by Elias/Gomes, who will be succeeded in history by La Roche/Williams and Independence.[19] By then, the legislated liberalization of management's conceptualization of the workers will have eroded profits to the point where the colonies will represent a burden, and so in the end Independence will not be won through (inter)national bloodshed but be granted by the metropolis after World War II, when the colonies become a burden and the paths of capital shift with the birth of the Bretton Woods institutions (including the International Monetary Fund), the entrenchment of transnational corporations, and the reconstruction of Europe.

# 4
## The New Man in the Jungle:
## Chaos, Community, and the Margins
## of the Nation-State

∎

The map of the savannahs was a dream. The names Brazil and Guyana were colonial conventions I had known from childhood. I clung to them now as to a curious necessary stone and footing, even in my dream, the ground I knew I must not relinquish. They were an actual stage, a presence, however mythical they seemed to the universal and the spiritual eye. They were as close to me as my ribs, the rivers and the flatland, the mountains and heartland I intimately saw. I could not help cherishing my symbolic map, and my bodily prejudice like a well-known room and house of superstition within which I dwelt. I saw this kingdom of man turned into a colony and battleground of spirit, a priceless tempting jewel I dreamed I possessed.

I pored over the map of the sun my brother had given me.—Wilson Harris

"You can't be sure of anything in the bush, Mr. Fenwick. . . . The truth is you poring over them chart and tide-map . . . too hard."—Wilson Harris

Flying over Guyana's national territory, the eye traverses hundreds of miles of dense jungle. On morning flights, the landscape is remiss, stoic, and secretive to the urban industrial perspective. Soaring at such imperial heights, borne by technologies imported from the industrialized countries, the impenetrable green is broken only by the occasional savanna or by the vast brown reach of the mighty rivers. At night, the blackness is absolute and overwhelming.

Wilson Harris's *Guyana Quartet* (1960–64) documents and redocuments this confrontation between the agrarian and the industrial, man and nature, to question the concepts of the nation and the state, and the lay of the terrain (national, psychological, global)—as much to inaugurate as to impeach. In opening and closing his recapitulation of the history of Guyana's national projects from the interior, Harris reconsiders the European encounter with the New World, refracted now through the prisms of New World multiculturalist, protosocialist nationalisms that de Boissière had hinted at, with the reflection of the self that hounds a spectrum of trained, industrialized workers in the jungle. From the characters of Donne and Carroll, the brutal yet contemplative brothers seeking a labor force fled back into the interior in *Palace of the Peacock,* the first novel of the *The Guyana Quartet,* to Fenwick, the government surveyor at the head of *The Secret Ladder,* the novel that closes the series, men find their structures of self, knowledge, power, the encounter, and societal forces crumbling under the terrible weight of the jungle to reveal their artificiality and to threaten the most rudimentary clarities. In the *Quartet*'s intervening novels, Oudin of *The Far Journey of Oudin* and Abram/Cristo/Peet of *The Whole Armour,* as emblematic of those disenfranchised in the national project, find themselves the pawns of private economic strategies and the objects of law and order, their bodies demarcated zones cast as the territory for the extraction of surplus and the enactment of power, before Abolition (estate = state) and after (coast = nation). Confronting the history of the pursuit and promise of development as the national patrimony, Harris's *Guyana Quartet* seeks to decipher the history of social relations, of national and nationalist identities, of labor relations, and of the constitution of men and national administration from the locus of the micrological spheres of the jungle zone into which the universe has collapsed.

Guyana's rainforests were propelled into the media worldwide in the 1970s when the bodies of Reverend Jim Jones and his followers were found in the interior. Confronting, like the earliest pioneers, crises in the collective psyche, these strangers plunged into the wilderness, as pilgrims from the center of regional imperialism, and staged their own massacre. The jungle returns to itself, its own ancient cycles of life and fertile rot, to those who live there, eking out a subsistence on the primeval landscape. These broad stretches of undeveloped territory have persistently proven stronger than the men from metropolitan countries who scouted there: the earliest, Sir Walter Raleigh (1595) and Abraham van Pere (1627), were British and Dutch men captured by the secrets of the interior and the prospect of marshaling capital-intensive technology for long-term profits at the time when the South American territory was administered as a "patroon," the property of the Dutch West India Company. The jungles of this patroon were territory ripe for development in the hands of a new man anxious to integrate the wilderness into the global economy under his proprietorship and to find the capital secreted in this particular wilderness: El Dorado, King Sugar, Harris's palace of the peacock, the minerals of the future, all the lost objects of modern men's desire. In the intervening 150 years, the British blocked development of the interior to prevent economic and therefore political competition with the coast and the colonial regime.

At the close of *The Secret Ladder*, the novel I want to investigate here, Harris explores the quagmires of development as nation formation and state building through a collapse of governmental projects to map the interior. Harris himself began an apprenticeship as a land surveyor in 1939, and in 1942 he was hired as part of a team of national surveyors sent to trace the paths of the hundreds of creeks that extend like spider legs throughout the rainforest, in order to better plan its future. It is perhaps not surprising that this procession of metropolitan pilgrims— Raleigh, van Pere, Jones, Harris—all on a journey foreseen and foretold in *Palace of the Peacock*, found in the interior a paradise to prize and pursue for the sake of what it could surrender: gold, minerals, God, secret knowledges, power. In *The Secret Ladder* the deterioration of the socialist nation-state comes at the hands of a de facto revolution by the masses and the subproletariat. In the confrontation between maroons seen as savage agrarian men of the interior and the working-class government workers from the coast, the lowest echelon of the state conspires to murder the leader/government/nation-state in effigy as a surplus population retaking control of their territory. Entrenched in ancient traditions, they meet around fires in their bivouac to discuss the highest points of law and war and strategy, reading the treachery of the state, with which they once had a pact, into the body of a captured woman. Revealingly, the novel's sole female character, Catalena Perez, becomes a metonym for both the processes of the nation-state's development predicated on the maroons' disenfranchisement and the site for an inaugurating act of war.

In this ambient edge of the world of the rainforest, deep purple and royal blue macaws take refuge, and, in the misty twilight, dimly discernible monkeys chatter in the dark upper regions of the overgrowth, resting and then swinging again on branches a thousand years old. Sun butterflies, "wings breathing like fans" (418), deer, ocelots, pumas, hummingbirds, armadillos, sloths, accouri, and hundreds of living species whose patterns and potential are not yet catalogued by Western scientists populate the vast, dense wilderness. Plunged into such remote and wondrous fecundity, Western men and nations have found themselves undone. In *The Secret Ladder*, Fenwick, a representative of the new nationalist cadres in the Guyanese civil service takes up the subject position of the new man in the jungle, voiding the leases and invading the zones held by legendary but subaltern national renegades—descendants of slaves escaped into the bush, Amerindian tribes fleeing the European invasion of Central America—the better to map the terrain of the future and investigate the social body with an eye to the transformation of government.

Throughout Harris's shifting, anthropomorphic figurations of Guyana's interior, settlements of these nomadic, subaltern peoples take refuge deep within a shared strange yet familiar territory, the people like the territory "wild and impenetrable" in the minds of the administrative cadres of agro-industrial processes. They are alien to the prime concern of the colony in transition—the pursuit of the new nation-state's development and primitive accumulation (Searwar 192). None of the developed peoples live here, by definition. The men emerging from the bush some four times a year to trade and acquire manufactured goods have become iconic in the nationalist psyche: "pork knockers" (men who mine diamonds and gold on a small scale) or "balata bleeders," bleeding the sap from the rubber trees.

Gestating a wealth in mineral resources coterminously with the outcome of small, ancient administrative strategies, the rich earth of the jungle houses a scattered 10 percent of the nation's population (1 percent Amerindian) and is refuge to rebels and peoples rumored to be not yet extinct in the British Empire. These black and Amerindian communities have rejected the reconceptualizations of power, government, and the social body in the wake of late-seventeenth-century agro-industrial development, eschewing national integration in favor of a stateless society. A statute of 1902 ordered the creation of reservations for the Amerindian population as part of the portfolio of the commissioner of lands and mines, superseded by a 1951 policy change favoring acculturation, Westernization, the extension of government into the reservations, and the levying of taxes.

Throughout this history, the administration of native peoples, grouped at the turn of the century with territory and natural resources, and at mid-century with colonial subjects, has been accomplished through missionaries. As a strategy of political education, the colonial regime's creation of reservations proved largely successful in transforming the maroon tribes into barbarian worker-subjects, exemplified in 1953 by their unanimous vote for the coalition party of the soon-to-be-displaced colonial elite and the newly arrived entrepreneurs. In Harris's novels, the predicament of renegade communities of nomad/subaltern peoples becomes symptomatic of the national malaise; and out of these new insights, Harris argues, hope might be founded, confronting the conceptualizations of people and government coming out of the metropolis with the "new" in the horizon of Independence.[1] Thus from the margins of the nation-state, from the pregnant refuse of the process of development and expansion, comes the fountainhead of a new national horizon.

The effects of these encounters interrogate the foundations of the new nationalist administrative identity endemic to the Guyanese new men who will lead the transformation of the state and so the nation, and from there the self, in accordance with marxist paradigms charted by Fanon.[2] This centralization of men in the jungle crosses the limit-text of the terms of the nation-state, simultaneously questioning the constitution of madness and order in relation to the inevitability of the state, the new Guyana's men-nation confronting the threat to reason/progress/history that Michel Foucault sought to sketch for France. Here the tentacles of power/knowledge and the institutionalization of the protonational state are plotted through the jungle and its realities, and through deployment of the bodies of workers, criminals and criminalization, and women— people and situations rendered problems of administration. Harris punctuates his national remappings with crises brought on by the rebellion of these subaltern social subjects. It is these subjects whose lives anchor *The Far Journey of Oudin* and *The Whole Armour,* and who are the base on which men plot the trajectory of power and capital in the novels at the beginning (*Palace of the Peacock*) and in the end (*The Secret Ladder*) of his *Quartet.* They are also the base on which Harris plots his political economic-*cum*-philosophic interrogations of Guyana's social structure and political future.

The people at the center of the jungle communities shimmer on the margins as black or Amerindian workers in European texts documenting

Europe's (re)turn to the bush. The most canonized in the British tradition, Joseph Conrad's *Heart of Darkness,* comes immediately to mind for foreign readers grappling with the chaos Harris writes so masterfully. Given, however, Harris's erudition in European as well as Indian, Amerindian, and African traditions, and the inclusion of quotes from English and other European authors for his epigraphs in the *Quartet,* this insistence on Europe as the original reference point is consistently, and pointedly, turned on its head. Both by the *Quartet's* insistent self-referentiality, and by its confounding of Western ontologies, Harris sideswipes, inverts, and implodes the insistence on Europe as point of origin and return. In his writing, Alfred Lopez argues, Harris "ruptur[es] the ontological frontier of the postcolonial [to] disrupt . . . the discourses of empire" (201, 198).[3]

In fact, here history is always an open and pregnant crucible, and Mother India (*The Far Journey of Oudin*) can take the place of Mother England as easily as the local elite take the place of the conquistadors who preceded them by centuries (*Palace of the Peacock*). Harris's agenda in the *Quartet* is a survey of the diverse groups constituting—and tearing apart—the new nation, written with an eye to rethinking the self, the world, and problems of knowledge and nationhood from the perspective of Guyana's conflicted constituencies and densely jungled terrain. Its complexity stems from the fact that it addresses questions of the "Caribbeanization" of ontology, a project directed at—and meant to question— the motives and certainties of the national groups waiting to assume power. Sandra Drake has argued that "Harris' work is concerned with the forging of individual and community in post-colonial Third World countries" ("Revolutionary Hope" 169) to write from a Caribbean perspective what Hena Maes-Jelink calls a re-creation of "the catastrophic experiences of West Indian history both as facts and as psychological states to be 'digested' by the individual consciousness" ("Wilson Harris" 141). For Maes-Jelink and her followers, Harris firmly "ignore[s] the temptations of 'resistance literature'" (141), but given, as she writes, that his novels "present an inner confrontation between a conquerer and/or oppressor and his victim(s) as well as the traumas that resulted from the violation of a people or an individual soul" (141) in what way is Harris's work somehow beyond West Indian national dilemmas?

In the bulk of Harris commentary and homage, it is the metaphysical implications of his work, undone from the matrix of its omnipresent

West Indian/South American territorialization and political implications, that fires critics' imaginations. In fact, I would argue, Harris's "shamanic dialectics" begin in the battles of ethnic conflict as a response to the invasion and brutality that has dominated Guyanese history and to the fierce interethnic rivalry that dominates Guyanese politics and society today.[4] Moreover, Harris's predictions in *The Guyana Quartet* as a whole, and *The Secret Ladder* in particular, of Guyana's chaos and collapse—political, economic, sociocultural, and psychological—proved prophetic.

Even further, I would also argue that Harris's extensive use of blends of Amerindian, European, Indian, and African ancient knowledges and paradigms, of fable and myth, to rethink the nature of man and mankind and of history and human relationships, as well as the questions of the political economics of the jungle staged in his work against the backdrop of Guyana, grows out of his explorations of the complex intersections of the terms of Guyanese ethnonational identities and the political need in plural postcolonial societies for what has been called "deconstructing difference." In a sophisticated and heartfelt rethinking of Guyana's political and sociocultural impasses—in the 1960s as today—Harris's advocacy of "a fiction that seeks to consume its own biases" (even as it reaches into the heart of "a composite picture of Guyanese life" [Maes-Jelink, "Wilson Harris" 141]) represents his early insights into the political and human suffering that an inability to cope with a colonial past postcoloniality brings in its wake.

From this perspective, Harris's overarching concern is to uncover new technologies of knowledge and development to question the terms of national projects, Guyana's in particular, and from what is learned here, to move beyond to a new world. "Guyana sometimes appears as a marginal society" said Harris in a 1987 acceptance speech in Guyana for the Guyana Prize in Fiction, but "it is here—in such apparently marginal societies around the globe—that supreme importance attaches to creative conscience, to the freedom of the person, to the conduct of politics, the conduct of democracy" (19). As an antidote to "a perverse addiction to authoritarianism in Third World regimes"—including the brutal and totalitarian political elite of 1980s Guyana—Harris advocates for the Guyanese a turn to Guyana's "roots in many cultures . . . [for this] could be its greatest resource" (20).[5]

Ralph Premdas's UNESCO discussion paper on ethnic conflict and development in Guyana makes the point with characteristic acuity: "Never really a national society but possessing at various times incipient elements of shared culture," he wrote after the election of Guyana's first national government "the Guyana state became even more clearly bifurcated as a consequence of protracted polarized ethnic politics" (24). This "ethnic nuclear bomb" (22), still ticking in the early 1960s when *The Secret Ladder* was written, threatens to bifurcate the national project.

Specifically, the novel's mounting tensions between the rural East Indian and urban black creole groups point to the impending fallout in the world, and it is from this interested partisanship over "ethnic shares" in the distribution of the national resources that the stage is set for Harris's and Fenwick's meditation on the nature of Guyanese nationhood from the resource-rich interior (9). In 1953, in Guyana's first election for a representative government under colonialism, a coalition socialist party under Cheddi Jagan and Forbes Burnham—incorporating African, Chinese, East Indian, European, and mixed-race representatives—won control of Guyana's transition to a postcolonial nation-state. After just 133 days in power Guyana's Constitution was suspended, and the British evicted the new governmental majority because, they said, of the radical socialist politics of the Indo-Guyanese Cheddi Jagan. In later years the British came to see as more acceptable the radical socialist policies of the Afro-Guyanese Forbes Burnham (who later, after he abolished elections, became the brutal president-for-life until his death). The original coalition then split into predominantly Afro-Guyanese and Indo-Guyanese factions, out of which emerged a new level of ethnocentrist politics leading up to a new vote. The novel I want to analyze here is set after the first attempt at decolonization and on the eve of this critical second election, following the suspension of the constitution by the British.[6]

The *Quartet*, then, is an opus of Guyanese territorialization. As such, to the horror of mothers like Magda (*The Whole Armour*)—a whore-worker in the interior who sends her son for an Oxford education as a way out—or new men like Fenwick the government surveyor (*The Secret Ladder*), the antiagrarian, modern certainties held out as reference points in both the imperial and anti-imperial imagination cannot take hold and always get men killed (*Palace of the Peacock, The Far Journey of Oudin, The Whole Armour, The Secret Ladder*). In Harris's *Quartet*, the jungle and its ancient maroon and Amerindian inhabitants have the last word and speak to national truths as Harris brings the people and the territory marginalized in nation-state formation into dialogue on the meaning of the nation and its interests. Fenwick's dilemmas are the dilemmas of the coming postcolonial state: who, then, comes to constitute the nation and how does the nation operate in the world? After the idealism of early West Indian nationalist strategizing emerging out of the 1930s, exemplified in this volume by de Boissière, is there in fact a coherent national pact, and is there or can there then be a coherent multiethnic national project in alliance with the new men of the postcolonial state? Searching for answers takes Harris deep into the unfinished inner workings of the nationalist psyches and of national frontiers, and into questions of order and impending chaos, a trek reiterated in social scientific analyses of Guyana's fate at the turn of the twenty-first century.

Interestingly, in Harris's return to this encounter, women as metaphors find themselves in an explosive process of transformation, like a zygote, a fertilized ovum, whereas women as physical beings find their bodies the locus of super-overdetermined violence. In closing the reconceptualization of the (originary) chaos at the end of the old state formations, the position of women in the social structures of the national frontiers changes only for the worse. Although Harris openly displays his sympathy for women's conditions, his philosophical heritage mires him in sexist abstractions that I will read against the grain. In this light Catalena Perez shifts from brutalized clientelic adjunct, property guaranteeing the production of sex/pleasure in payment for her husband's gambling debts, to pawn in the savage game of the new Guyana as enemy/woman-nation, her body the terrain on which the nightmare rebirth of men and men's communities, and thus the nation, will be remapped. Catalena becomes the counterpart of Hopkins's Sappho, mirroring the position of the former from the bottom of a minination at the bottom of the colonial heap, rewriting the narrative of woman's exile from the periphery.

Starting with an exploration of state-sanctioned knowledges and state resources in the jungle, from the perspective of the jungle's pervasive countereffects on modern consciousnesses, I move to an analysis of the campsite as a micrological metonym of the minination. It is here that the native intelligentsia, represented by Fenwick, confronts the subalterns who will constitute the new people-nation, represented by the workers. From there, I rethink the terms that the new men attach to chaos (woman, savage, children, jungle) that set up false equivalencies, and in closing I examine the coupling of Bryant and Catalena that prom-ises a new beginning. From the transmutations of the Amerindian Mari-ella in *Palace of the Peacock* ranging to Catalena, the white woman whose coupling might birth a new nation, "woman" like "jungle" becomes the seat of transcendent knowledges. Both of these terms are posed as ques-tions finally unanswered and unanswerable, along with the nature of the revolutionary "savage" remnants of maroon communities in *The Secret Ladder*.

In Harris's novels, history converges deep in "the interior" and then erupts in the reflection of would-be heroes/historians back into their own minds. These reflections refract through the prisms of chaos, through the clash of modern with jungle/maroon realities. This clash is itself subtended by the national project of turning the jungle terrain into a national resource. Reconceptualizing women and maroons as children in the minds of the workers and the new man marks the macrological disenfranchisement of women, maroons, and children, their exile from the social pact in their categorization as resources as a financial and political concept outstripping their status as citizens of the new nation-state. The novel that closes the *Quartet* on the eve of Guyana's Indepen-dence and government of "Co-operative Socialism" then, sees repetitions of the violence of encounters among social groups and with the jungle terrain that constitute Guyanese historiography as cycles of life and rot in the crisis it catalyzes in the minds of a surplus maroon population, the nationalist workers and the cadres of a new administration. Catalena's position in this weave will remain an open question, predicated entirely on her conceptualization in Bryant's mind, Bryant as the new new man Harris advocates, an Adam recruiting his Eve.

## Body/Jungle

In *The Secret Ladder* the new country will be built not only on the terrain of the jungle but on the terrain of bodies as well; hence the new terrain (conceptual/territorial) and new social subjects must be surveyed. Thus in the opening lines of the novel the technology of development is em-ployed in plotting the future of the nation: Fenwick, nationalist govern-ment land surveyor, is reading the gauge installed on the Canje River, noting that it is well below its expected level. The expected limit is prob-lematic, however, because it was determined by an unreliable record and the superimposition of old numbers signifying past water levels onto the stubborn realities of the gauge: "It was the month of September, noon on the Canje River. The gauge against the stelling exposed the greater part of its slender height. The solid black line of the river divided the painted scale, needing seven feet more to rise to brim the deck of the stelling; the river-gauge shot three feet still above this. Fenwick, the government surveyor, was looking up and it seemed an interminable way for the water to mount over his head" (357). Fenwick is expecting a deluge and speculates it could come in seven days, a conceptualization resonant with the concept of cleansing, of divine retribution, and the "oldest fable" (417), casting Fenwick in one sense as Noah, and in another as observer in the re-creation of the world. Indeed, the flood never comes as water but something else: the jungle itself that weeps, perhaps (447), or its effect on men from the coast, or its maroon inhabitants rising up to inundate the government's representative and its developmental strategies. The blackness of the water, its hard opaqueness as a solid black line, already signals an enigma: water is traditionally conceptualized as fluid, predictable, and transparent; this water, like the terrain through which it cuts, reveals nothing, and the educated man from the coast is left to speculate on its possibilities. The landscape yields nothing, and in yielding nothing it yields uneasiness in the government surveyor.

In moments like these when Fenwick is isolated in his confrontation, the jungle functions as a riddle but on the margins of perception; for example, when Fenwick averts his gaze and it is no longer the government meeting the territory but the social being meeting the landscape, the terrain begins to reflect his own psyche. Staring into the black water whose depth and transformations he is to plot, Fenwick sees a black mirror; and in its dead-stillness Fenwick's eye is thrown back onto itself, and his sense of his concrete existence begins to evaporate under the heat of the sun, the white sky burning down on the black water: "He wanted to curse the glaring cunning of the receding heavens, the oppression of the everlasting bowl of sun in the dense white sky. Instead he closed his eyes and his figure drooped a little in his narrow corial [canoe] and shell of a boat. He opened his eyes and looked around him once again. The river was dead-still save where his own paddle had broken the mirror and surface. All at once he leaned down and splashed the liquid on his face to clear away all doubt of a concrete existence" (357).

This unstinting glare of the elements in the "inchoate" Amazonian jungle resolves itself beyond the structures and methodologies of production and national planning, "a latitude of spendthrift furies and intensities" (358). The sun, in scorching its whiteness through to the skeleton of the surveyor, finds the hinges in the key terms in Fenwick's technologies of knowledge: the ability to read, to see, and thence to measure and predict, and thence to map, to implement. The day turns these terms back on him, yielding nothing, like a mirror in his eyes, and the sun is like a burning X ray that illuminates the skeleton of everything, penetrating to the "whitest bone" (359). Daylight, then, resolves everything back into itself, into its own perceptible essence, its whiteness revealing whiteness and creating whiteness. Conspiring with the sun, the jungle promises to reveal itself only in the end to hide itself; it promises to tell and expose everything but exposes nothing.

Caught in this double bind, the stranger Fenwick feels defeated and cannot see. He is forced to project his own meaning onto the jungle terrain, and the jungle betrays him by refusing to make sense and becoming desert devoid of meaning. Thus his readings are a mirage, erasing the certainties it is his job to collect, write down, and bring back to the coast to the government, for reasons he has never addressed. Time loses meaning here, as the elements force their way back to the founding terms of the conceptual contracts of the Enlightenment that say the world is knowable, measurable, predictable; terms that lie at the foundations of science and technology, democracy, development, and history as a narrative of recorded events and of verifiable and dependable facts. Thus Fenwick finds himself on the verge of dissolution, losing his sense of the solidity of his concrete existence at the root of his project, his identity, and his occupation, as well as his contract with the government, and thus with narratives of nation-state history. His psychic economy reveals itself; he finds himself robbed as the jungle resolves itself back into itself and into desert and nothing, thereby canceling out the difference that will make the terrain mappable.

In the bush the jungle becomes jungle rather than desert, away from the boiling sunlight, but here it is the jungle itself that is read as blind, "blind as a shuttered place" (359), an insubstantial counterpart, perhaps, to the shuttered Great Houses of the abandoned plantations that dot the landscape of so much Caribbean literature. In the battles for New World territory, here the jungle won. Some 460 years later, the government on the coast dispatches its own explorers to the interior, but now there is the

prospect of a new native nationalism to anchor the assumption of ownership, the impression that this space belongs to the viewer because it is
viewed, and in being viewed it is known and mastered, measured, secured. If British and European explorers insured these conceptualizations of self/nation through a contract with a British or other European
state for advanced technologies and military backup—weapons, violent
men, decimation, reservations, then knowledge, science—then Fenwick
and his workers, these new men come into the jungle, have the police.
And so, when the men embodying ancient agrarian strategies already
occupying the zone threaten the government workers' claims and contracts—social, personal, economic—these British/Guyanese explorers
opt to call in the state's security forces, to employ the state's technologies
for the management of power through the criminalization of men ob-
structing the territorial claims of the coast.

As that perceptual equation of security between the eyes and ears of
the state and the land Fenwick surveys is broken by human bodies from
the interior—that is, by the descendants of Africans who cast their lot,
given coastal slavery, for subsistence in the jungle, subsequently leasing
an agricultural zone from the new governmental structures—it is the
eruption of history into a plane where there is supposed to be no history.
The ethnicity of the people from both the state and the renegade camps
within the multicultural nation will condition the nature of their relationship to this history. But in the end, as here in the beginning, the fact of
these historical bodies marking difference, breaking the equations set up
with nature by the initial terms of the government's concerns within the
jungle, becomes a catalyst for remapping the terrain to be surveyed,
thereby changing the course of national strategies. The chaotic nexus of
ancient past and violent present in configuring the future will shift from
the jungle to the body of the only woman present, Catalena Perez. Marriage and heterosexual coupling, as technologies of social and biological
administration, will survive as the only viable alternative after the jungle
prevails again over civilization, although the coastal paradigms embedded in the psyches of the new Adam and Eve in the jungle make the return to "progress" and "development" as crisis management inevitable.

In the process of articulating the predicament of the minination, then,
the symbols of technology can mark the division between the bodies of
the two camps, the one from a maroon administrative structure on
whose disenfranchisement progress and development are postulated,

and the other from the workers from the coast, the camp whose makeup reflects all the diversity of the modern population poised to become citizens of the new state—Portuguese, black, Chinese, East Indian, English, Amerindian—the descendants of peoples leaving their homelands in the wake of the global politico-economic reorganization of territories and populations from 1492 to the 1960s. Here the black Guyanese community straddles two poles, simultaneously inside and outside the country: some occupy the jungle while others cast their lot with the coastal administrative strategies, reflecting the split in the social body of the black nation inducted into the administrative gambles of the imperial powers and their local administrators. Bryant, the black worker, recognizes his counterpart and ancestor in Poseidon, "the black king of history" (369) and leader of the local maroon community, and the difference in their positions in the two social structures is very much a reflection of the outcomes of black New World administrative history. There is, then, a sense in which a man from the modern black nation meets his agrarian self, and the novel is careful to trace the nuances of the new social pacts that are the outcome of this reunion.

The technology that stands between the two camps operates on several levels simultaneously, but in keeping with our recognition of the chaos that the terrain wreaks on the conceptual structures inherited from the Enlightenment we can also hold in reserve the recognition that everything will resolve itself into everything, as well as into nothing, just as nothing will resolve itself into everything. This confusing paradigm is perhaps the most succinct encapsulation of the terrain on which the new nation will be built, and we must see it through to the end when Bryant, the man who will finally recognize the destructiveness of dividing the subaltern population between coastal and interior peoples as an assault on new national history, joins Catalena in fleeing the ruins of the minination. But first let us look again at an (artificially) concrete example, Fenwick's gauge.

In the paragraph quoted above, Fenwick is simply doing his job—a civil servant reading the gauge. We noted that he is dissatisfied with what he sees and that he projects something else, something larger, an inundation. The norm for the water level is set by his desire to confirm what he knows are unreliable records, and beyond that (his desire) the gauge rises up toward the burning whiteness. On this gauge, Fenwick as government worker stakes everything: it is a mark of certainty, of progress, of technology and is the spinal column on which the future of the nation—the plans of the state, development out of underdevelopment, and thus history—is built. This gauge becomes immediately marked as the secret ladder of numbers that never achieve measurement and never achieve the accumulation that defines a series as much as wealth, the progression robbed of its positivist guarantee and so its ability to mean and be employed, its efficacy and usefulness. The referents straddle both the material ("actual feet and decimals") and the conceptual by taking the terms of the development of science and technology, emptying them of their referent/guarantee, and pointing the skeleton toward "the glaring cunning of the receding heavens, the oppression of the everlasting bowl of sun in the dense white sky" (357).

The creolization of the state marks this transformation. The gauge itself is a tool developed in the tradition of the West, its measurements and its readings are a mark of the inheritance of Western administrative procedures. That it is made of wood suggests that it is locally produced rather than imported, because the best gauges should be metal. The wood swells as it is left in the water, reacting as a natural substance rather than having been hardened as metal would have been. It is an instrument, then, that marks in its materiality local resources and the fact of the global markets and the hierarchies in the international division of labor.

On another level, the technology that it represents is not simply the technology of the tool itself but the whole administrative structure that it supports and that supports it—surveying trips into the interior, written logs, the contracting of workers, the administration of those workers qua workers and thus industrial paradigms of human relations, and the role of government. The information gathered and read into this gauge will allow for further planning by the state, the readministration of this territory, and the knowledge of the uses to which this water can be put in the transformation of nature into capital once its patterns are known and logged and predictable. It is the predictability of the territory that allows the government to plan and therefore to develop. In turn, it is development that will lead to the emergence here of a new Guyanese history, the incorporation, after 460 years, of the jungles into the country and therefore resources for the state and its elite, and perhaps the nation. If the jungle is as the jungle always has been, then the jungle has no history.

Poseidon—the "oldest inhabitant of the Canje," or its equivalent, the maroon community farming this stretch of the banks of the river—recognizes all that this means. He recognizes, better than Fenwick, if Fenwick is to be believed, the uses to which this information will be put and what the gauge betrays: the government plans to flood the land by building a reservoir to assist the East Indian rice farmers of the coast, and thus the social and legal pacts between the government and the maroons in the interior will be broken and their homes, land, and labor will be lost, and all the food for their community with it. Poseidon's perception is simple, and Harris will make him absolutely accurate in reading the intentions of the government in the sudden appearance of this new technology.

Fenwick's rebuttal, made to Bryant, is complex and evasive, built as it is on reading the power of the state in terms of its place on the other horizon, the horizon of international markets, brain drains, rates of exchange, the flows of capital in the post–World War II Caribbean basin, the prerogatives of the state. The government does not have the money to build a reservoir, Fenwick protests, years and years will pass before any plans can be implemented, the government lacks the technical and managerial resources, the government's maps are too faulty, and so on. But while Fenwick dismisses his accuracy, Poseidon's reading of the gauge makes it clear that he understands better than Fenwick the changes in the strategies of the coast and the nature of the new social pacts being worked out by the government. Poseidon realizes that the combination of the color of his skin, his culture, and his economy, converging with the region in which he lives, means that he is not of the country whose needs are to be met, that both he and the lease he holds with the government are to be voided to secure new alliances in the name of progress and country. The nation of the new democratic Guyana with which the state will bespeak a pact does not include him and his kind. Thus Poseidon and his men destroy the gauges, an act of guerrilla warfare to resecure vital terrain.

The landscape is known by this conflict in conceptual/administrative structures: jungle is always equal to jungle or desert or nothing or everything, but no one who lives in the jungle is equal to the social body of the nation (= coast = city = always already legitimate government). From the beginning, in order to survive, Fenwick must understand the strategies of Poseidon, himself a gauge (370), rather than the other way around. There is, in the encampment, a work site on the banks of the river where the jungle has been cut back. In the bushes, through a dense trail, sits Fenwick's camp. The hierarchy and isolation of management from workers is thus physically drawn up on the landscape: while the place of the worker is the artificial space, the leader's camp is made in such a way that it blocks Fenwick's view of the path from the sphere of the worker. Poseidon's house is invisible from the river, through a dense thicket of bush that Fenwick's eye sees as "cunning" (411). This is the terrain of transition built out of the remnants of the old administrative paradigms, and in its details we can plot the terms of the relationships between the elements on the new horizon.

The clearing as the place of the worker is the site of the production of surplus value in both capitalist and socialist administrative strategies. This artificial space cleared in the jungle, then, is the work site of the new nation, its administrative center once removed. There are only heterosexual men here—women, like maroons and gay men, have no country—and there is work in the day and rough gambling at night. In the first two sections of the book, "The Day Readers" and "The Night Readers," the conceptualizations of this clearing change to reflect the shift in administrative strategies and the gaze of power. But in the process of waging modern technological warfare, the work site of the government's representative expands under Fenwick's leadership to include Poseidon's house through the body of Catalena Perez, the Portuguese worker's wife and the one woman who comes from the coast, for her own reasons, into this zone reserved for men. The body of Catalena Perez provides the link between the old and the new administrative paradigms, a body ripe for treason and useful because the strategy of the state is betrayal, plotted through the difference accruing to the body of a woman as she becomes a tool in Fenwick's strategies of surveillance.

Lost in the wilderness, trapped in the house of mirrors created by Fenwick's own (mis)perceptions, the mystery and resilience of the jungle come to be equated with his uncertainty in the face of women. Woman is early on synonymous with child, childishness, inscrutability. In the colonial social arrangements of *The Palace of the Peacock*, the character of Mariella was the Amerindian worker, an inscrutable carrier of knowledge and a tool to be used for sex or for her knowledge of the terrain. In the *Quartet*'s opening lines, this same Mariella assassinates the landowner/conquistador, and thus woman/savage/jungle breaks into the fray as a warrior, as a metonym of the subaltern nation, the violated terrain, and as a battered woman. In the *Quartet*'s last novel, where the government men repeat the strategies of men gone into the jungle to claim what they see, for both Fenwick and his work crew woman is all that undoes men's plans and their technologies of knowledge, and yet is an object whose use they cannot help but desire. Their treatment of women will represent a gauge of their ability to govern themselves when Fenwick as leader moves to intervene in the workers' camp life; the mark, then, of a series of social, political, and personal limits. Nevertheless, women, like jungle, are conceived as like children (meaning always already unequal, emotional, omnipresent), and hence are critical resources that it is up to the men-leaders to control, the better to properly deploy.

That the entrance to the camp is on Fenwick's blind side and thus reflects his relationship to the workers is also clear, as Kenneth Ramchand has already argued in his *Introduction to the Study of West Indian Literature*. I want to push the implications of this metaphor in a different direction later, but I can say here that in this context it reflects the crisis in government—the split between leadership and nation. The tent, like the strategies and technologies with which Fenwick has armed himself, is misplaced and thus dangerous. Fenwick's position is tenuous, and it is never the jungle (= the Canje = Poseidon) that adapts to the needs of the government man, but rather the spectrum of government workers to the treacherous terrain.

The locus of power in the maroon enemy camp is marked by the harmonious utilization of the jungle's resources as they stand, by incorporating that cunning secretive profuseness as a natural ally against foreigners and invaders. Stumbling upon Poseidon's home, Fenwick is astonished by the claim incarnate in the enemy leader's headquarters:

> It had an air both foreign and native, ideal and yet primitive, at one and the same time; and yet it seemed so precariously and absolutely right, belonging so truly in this natural and unnatural context of landscape, that the thought of an imposition, of pretentiousness or absurdity in the life of the crumbling building, seemed equally ridiculous and impossible. In fact—if it had been the gift of some imposing divinity—it bore a certain generous conception, economic and still humane. There were no marks of exclusiveness—rather a spirit of all-inclusive privacy, the most welcome artifice of humanity. What was at stake here was not the inevitable ruin of an old house, but a perception of depth more lasting than time, the moral privilege and right of place. (411)

Fenwick finds his lost object of desire, the expert, progressive nationalist paradigm for government and nationhood that he has been seeking, rooted democratically and profoundly in the land and discovered in the architecture of a community working to overthrow state control of the territory. The criminal architect of this utopia has declared the social pacts made between the new state and pressure groups on the coast null and void, beyond the capacity of the new government to deliver. Nevertheless Fenwick has an epiphany. For embodied in the structures of the old maroon men is the utopia postulated by the discourse of the new nationalism—yet this same structure stands as a threat to the power of the new state (as to the old) and it is Fenwick's job to destroy it in the name of nationalism as history and development.

## The Micronation

The *Guyana Quartet* opens with Mariella's dream shooting of Donne, the archetype of the brutal explorer/adventurer driving into the jungle. It closes with Fenwick contemplating the possibility of his own murder in effigy by Poseidon's men and the impending massacre of the ancient maroon community by the state police from the coast. The *Quartet*, written on the eve of Guyana's Independence, thus becomes a vast project of reconceptualizing the coming transformation of the state and its tenets through the terrain of the jungle. The jungle becomes the metaphor for that which has always been unyielding to the interests of the colonial state and which the new state must confront; it is that which, in the mind of nationalist government surveyor Wilson Harris, must be taken into account and is at odds with the new conceptual foundations of the state. Just as *The Far Journey of Oudin* and *The Whole Armour* raise the questions of subalternity—of criminals, runaways, and peasant farmers under colonialism plotting the biographies of peoples in the interior, and so simultaneously on the margins of the national consciousness—the crescendo of *The Secret Ladder* looks to characterize the confrontation of the new government men with the peoples left out of the nation, on their own ground, in order to close the *Quartet*. The novel then circles back to confrontations between the workers, the maroons whose lives and labor were disposable in the eye of the colonial state, and those characters shown in the beginning poring over a map of the landscape.

It is a mark of Harris's sensibility that he is not Fenwick, although he imbues the character with a sensibility that allows him to be a witness and thus the conduit for a new national process lost, for the most part, on the men from the coast. If so far we have looked at Fenwick as a pawn in the battles of nation-state formation, there is also the question of Fenwick as a social subject confronting himself, as Fenwick the man Ramchand has described as "the middle-class West Indian with the refined upbringing" who "must accept and come to terms with a debased African heritage, . . . equally aware of the necessity to avoid setting up this heritage as a fetish" (*Introduction* 171, 172). Fenwick, Harris himself has also said, "is a character wholly related to a quest for authority and responsibility" (cited in Munro and Sander 53). The *Quartet* opens, then, with the confrontation of the maps and paradigms of the old colonialist men with concepts of power and the jungle, and culminates in the confrontation of the new national man from the coast with "something from a deliberately forgotten primeval world" that the book has been concerned to humanize, whose history and/of consciousness Harris sought to sketch and incorporate into a new national/global consciousness (Ramchand, *Introduction* 172).

The reconceptualization of the nation toward the elevation of British colonial subjects to Guyanese citizens for the purposes of the new state stands accused of repeating the exploitative practices and imperial paradigms that have marked the colonial period about to come to an end, and it is in the minds of the intelligence gatherers from the coast confronting the inhabitants of the jungle, as much as the strategic implementation of bodies, land, and technology, that the transformation from the old to the new must occur. Ramchand concentrates on the internal transformations and notes the way in which everything is metabolized in Fenwick's mind and through his dilemma—jungle, people, the nation, history, and truth. I want to look again at this dynamic, but with what will amount to a certain skepticism regarding the post-Independence nationalist strategies and the conceptual enlightenment of the surveyor, and raise again the question of paradigms of development and underdevelopment and the place of diverse subaltern groups in the new country.

Rather than accept the disenfranchisement and deterritorialization of the peoples on the margins of the state and the need for a local industrial revolution, there may well be the seeds of a "third path" beyond populism, a path between the Cuban and Puerto Rican models that Guyana's Burnham administration will in 1970 install on paper as Co-operative Socialism,[7] and that Jamaica's Michael Manley will attempt to take up in earnest, as we will explore in chapter 6. Both the Burnham and the

Manley experiments will prove to be failures, although the nature of the social pact and the disintegration of the Guyanese infrastructure under Burnham is already indicated in Fenwick's response to Poseidon's accusations and in his conferences with Jordan, his second in command. In watching the ways in which Harris questions the mind-set of the new administrators, we can bear in mind that the revelation of the totalitarianism at the root of the new conceptual paradigms of the state's relationship to the nation became increasingly explicit in political practice as the twentieth century drew to a close.

The group of men in the jungle becomes a metonym for the new state cadres, with all the social and administrative structures in place. Fenwick is clearly postulating a new government, and Jordan, sequestered with him in the clearing, is clearly the bureaucratic administrator, as the reins of power and advisor to the prince. As foreman, Weng, the Amerindian mestizo, marks the limit of administrative penetration. The workers, including Weng, take their place somewhere else, and it is a sign of the problems of transition that the workers are an unknown to Fenwick and that he must rely on Jordan for information on who they are and what they want.

Further, when Poseidon speaks to Fenwick, Fenwick cannot hear him, although his lips are clearly moving: "Poseidon addressed Fenwick at last. His mouth moved and made frames which did not correspond to the words he actually uttered. It was like the tragic lips of an actor, moving but soundless as a picture, galvanized into comical association with a foreign dubbing and tongue which uttered a mechanical version and translation out of accord with the visible features of original expression" (371). The mind of the government man reels as he hears the subaltern speak.

Fenwick's strategies of authority become doubly complicated by this gap between which of them knows who he is, as opposed to who he seems to be. We can consider the gap as being between nation and state, nation, state and country, interior and coast, and thus inside and outside, fact and rumor, maroonage and civilization, worker and management, the old nation and the new, subaltern and citizen-to-be, nationalism and colonialism. Indeed, as Fenwick's reading of Poseidon's house makes clear, the new national consciousness says it is predicated on its ties to the land, to the question of birthright and the implementation of local paradigms and materials, to a oneness between soil, history, nation, and state that will equal the new country. The problems of concepts and conceptualization, however, come back to ruin the surveyor's plan, and at the close of the book there is a new invasion when the state police come to restore modern law as order in the government's control of the territory and to stave off the chaos of subaltern strategies embedded in the history of a creolized socialist subject at the center of the government's nationalist rhetoric.

In a series of three conversations on policy, Fenwick progressively alienates his strategist. Jordan recognizes that Fenwick's refusal of authoritarian models of leadership will unravel the social order, and he works to shore up the barriers between leader and led that determine all dialogue between Fenwick and the camp community. First is the battle to alienate Catalena when she complains of Perez's abuse; second is on the nature of Catalena—"she's the picture of a whore, skipper" (421)—and the importance of the dividing line between civil and domestic society (thus the place of women in relation to government); and third is in Fenwick's lending Chiung (one of his crew) his coat, with Chiung's request signaling the decay of order as Jordan sees it: "Before now they look on all familiarity you show as a condescending joke—it didn't matter what you do, they knew you had a hard counsellor beneath—but *now* you really showing you care too much. And they know this is the beginning of the end" (429). Jordan knows the workers, and he can hear Poseidon speak from the perspective of state interests—he knows what the rebels can and cannot see (382). When he recants on his pact with Fenwick after Weng seizes control of the battle against the men from the interior, it is effectively a coup, with the defection of Jordan as domestic policy strategist and the rise of Weng as head of a military takeover for nation and for country.

Fenwick never knows the extent to which Jordan's advice is predicated on preserving Jordan's interests or the extent to which Jordan has placed himself at the service of the new government as well as the nature of his alliance. It is clear that Jordan has his own interests in mind as much as he does the interests of law and order learned under the old administration that says workers and maroons must be treated harshly, as noncitizens, or the social system will collapse. At the same time, it is clear (and Jordan admits it) that the grievances of the workers with Jordan are metonymic of the disgruntled mass base founding the new national consciousness, and so the shift in the relations between Fenwick, Jordan, and the disgruntled workers is the shift from the colonial paradigms to the nationalist, with all its scars and learned brutality. The maroon villages, the administrative strategies of the peoples of the interior, are always on the outside of the new possibilities, and from government through to workers the story of the two camps is the story of a battle to the death, although Fenwick the government man tries to deny it.

The campaign between Fenwick and Poseidon crosses a threshold with the arrival of Catalena Perez: on her body the men can project the tensions brewing between them and enact their social pacts with each other and with the rebels, the materialization of all that pulls them together and sets them apart. Soon the entire project of government, and beyond that the distinction between madness and knowledge, is under fire. The gauges marking the government's claim to territory have been burned, and so have bridges and workstations. The government man finds his feet, gaining command of his men in the sudden realization that this is war.

In this war Fenwick's first task is clarity, the identification of facts and the proper methods of communication, then utilization of operating social norms, the historic sanctity of the marriage pact and the ubiquitous preciousness of a woman's body, the better to invade the enemy's camp:

> "Now, Perez, wake up! I'm being frank with you. I can't afford to build a watchman's camp at Kaboyary. We haven't the money for that. What I can do is to install a temporary gauge at Poseidon's landing. It's two miles below Kaboyary and the best we can do. Instead of sending someone every day to Kaboyary to pick up a set of readings, *you* will move in with your wife under Poseidon's roof. The advantage is enormous. At night you'll be sleeping practically on the spot. Once somebody is there, no one will dare to touch a thing . . . and you, Stoll . . . " he turned a little to face the other man . . . . "will take over Perez's morning to noon shift. I will take over your meters and floats . . . Understand?" (400)

The man who questioned his sanity, who stared into the jungle and saw only his own face, has evaporated, and Fenwick's new reading is predicated on his new manhood and, in turn, on his leadership in war. The men give him power, and it is up to Fenwick to manage it. The workers press for a masculine state: the police as a paramilitary force, the recognition of men's property rights over women (domestic society) as outside the public domain (civil society), the legitimate leader as a man who makes firm decisions and never wavers. Fenwick, in softening toward the men and Catalena, wants to espouse a liberal regime, but this feminization of the state will lead to his being thrown from power and to the workers taking the suppression of Poseidon's uprising into their own hands.

The feminization of the state here takes the form of questioning, of empathy and self-reflection, and of rethinking history in remapping the political future of the nation that in the end is a question of power, knowledge, authority, and pregnancy:

> To *misconceive* the African, I believe, if I may use such an expression as *misconceive,* at this stage, is to misunderstand and exploit him mercilessly and oneself as well. For *there,* in this creature Poseidon, the black man with the European name, drawn out of the depths of time, is the emotional dynamic of liberation that happened a century and a quarter ago—to put a rough date on it. Something went tragically wrong then. Something was misunderstood and frustrated, God alone knows why and how. Like an affair between a man and a woman gone wrong. (385)

The birth of the nation in the horizon of Emancipation is seen as shrouded in mystery, although its disastrous legacy is written on the national body. This nation is a woman, and the state like a man, but it is understood that states give birth to nations and not vice versa. The power to gestate is in the hands of the government, and the new socialist pacts threaten to miscarry. The fate of the citizen-worker in the new industrial horizon is always greater or lesser exploitation as the mule of the nation-state, and so when Fenwick looks to excuse the African Poseidon from the process of exploitation, it will only be an inevitable step to exclude him from the social pacts of modernity altogether.

This postulation of the fate of the African is made from the seat of power, in which the mulatto government man believes "the East Indian workers and rice farmers will win a majority of seats in the next General Election against a large number of [coastal] African" workers in the birth of a newly independent nation-state (385). As such, Fenwick's musing in this letter from the jungle to his mother—in his moment as rebel son of the Guyanese equivalent of a failed Mama Coudray—is also advice on the new ethnic subject at the center of the nation, and so it is advice from the old horizon looking into the new. In projecting back into the past and forward into the future, Fenwick excuses himself from the arena of politics, and his advice from this threshold bears all the marks of this double articulation of the scene of writing. His letter to his mother/country is also a letter to a new nation. His political advice on government is cast as "fundamental and psychological" with the appearance of openness and intimacy intertexted with annihilation and the obliteration of excessive national metaphors, of false starts and reconsidered moves. What is at stake is government, which is seen now as equal to psychology, to national history, authority, freedom, progress, and the foundations of the past girding the (masculinist) future of the new nation-state: "What will you say when I tell you I have come across the Grand Old Man of our history, my father's history in particular? . . . But after all, let us not forget he is the privileged son or grandson of a slave. Don't be offended. I wish I could truly grasp the importance of this meeting. If I do not—if my generation do not—leviathan will swallow all" (384).

The flood and creation predicted in the beginning of the novel is now transformed into a nightmare, a monster from the deep. The notion of leviathan also directs us to Thomas Hobbes's new power structures and relationships of man and materiality—power makes right—and his modern strategies of government managing tensions between authority and self-interest. Hobbes's *Leviathan* is advice to ruling men on how to pull a nation, a mother country, out of the chaos of civil war. This recognition of a confrontation—this attempt to decipher the meaning of Poseidon's words, in gestation—is seen as the crux of the new country that is all in the minds of new men, although it is precisely this body metaphor that must be suppressed: "It's a question of going in unashamed to come out of the womb again," Fenwick writes, and then obliterates (384).

Turning, Fenwick casts the prime government man as Jordan, the man, the military, and the river, "a fine head for a prime minister and a governor rolled into one. . . . He knows how to tax everyone and draw blood from stone with dignified irrefutable supporting entries in the mess book. It all looks very neat and tidy on the surface" (386). Fenwick's right-hand man is perceived in terms of the plantation accountants who cheat their workers and cover their tracks, with the exploitation of the masses that passes for good business sense as much as good government, with the clientelism and corruption that will consume Guyana's infrastructure at the end of the century. Without Jordan, Fenwick is lost, destroyed by "senseless worry," as if eaten up and digested by the jungle. Turning for the last time, the jungle is the limit of government, and its "strange murderous" character is only naturally reflected in Poseidon and his men, the "holy rebels," as surely as the jungle inundates "authority" posited as the guarantee of "freedom" (386). After the letter's confession, Fenwick is overwhelmed by his need for "the most thoroughgoing reformation of character" (386).

The reformation called for by what he has written to his mother/country is rewritten on the territory itself, solving the riddle of the jungle in identifying the faults in the state's maps and charts, poring over the misconceptions of the terrain and the mirages created by misreading aerial photographs. In this shift from concepts of gestating nations to concepts of territory, Fenwick discerns his project in the jungle: "The mysterious foundation of intelligence, the unity of head and heart had become for him, Fenwick knew, an inescapable obsession, and perhaps a foolish myth and a dubious vocation of science" (387–88). This unity of head and heart finds itself metaphorized into masculinity and femininity, and so again the questions of the body are equal to the questions of terrain, as much as questions of Fenwick's British/Guyanese head that will determine the strategies of government.

Fenwick moves to consider the terrain as an economic text: the soil's yield, the development of industry, and so social pacts; and finally that Poseidon's reading of why he was sent is right. In the end he admits to himself that he agrees with the government that the country's needs are best served by the disenfranchisement of the men farming the jungle and the diversion of their water supply for the benefit of the modern men on the coast, and that war is justified in the subordination of these lost, barbarian peoples to economic expansion: "Taking all circumstances into account, Fenwick saw that the extinction of the remaining grants and leases along the Canje, and the logical construction of a flood reservoir to meet the increasing demand, along the coast, for irrigation water in the dry season, was perhaps the best thing that could happen to the country" (388). By meeting Poseidon the government meets itself, and the colonial past collapses again into the Co-operative Socialist future.

*Woman ≠ Savage ≠ Children*

The process of Fenwick's coming to make distinctions between women and maroons and children is slow. Earlier, I suggested that in this primordial world everything would resolve itself into everything as well as into nothing, just as nothing would resolve itself into everything. The constitution of outsiders and the preservation of the state that forms the inaugurating pact of the state with itself and the nation thus finds itself turned inside out, its skeleton illuminated. The first three books of the *Quartet* characterize the nation and old strategies of government that constitute Guyana's history. This focusing in on the question of government and administration and the workers they create, as well as who must be left out (categorized as criminals, mad men, women, apes, savages, children), comes back to question the rhetoric of nationalism that posits the "barefoot man," the "oppressed worker," and the "people" as the subject of the national socialist transformation from colony to nation-state. Harris ties the *Quartet* together here in the concluding novel. Thus in *The Secret Ladder* the Demerara/Abary savannas on which the state stakes its claim to territorial sovereignty are Oudin's (363), and Fenwick's boat is *Palace of the Peacock* (367), reinvoking the city of gold/God found by colonial powers in the beginning of the *Quartet*.

The concepts of political economy provide us with three social groups— workers, rebels, and women—who are clearly demarcated by their relationship to capital and so government. It is Wilson Harris's task on the eve of Independence to remind the nationalist cadres that these categories extend to the limits of the concepts of administration (terrain, nation, government). And so in reading the loci of these people as social subjects constituting the masses in concluding the *Quartet*, we will decipher the collapse of the administrative categories for the minination in the narrative's metaphors for the jungle as a body; and bodies, especially women's, as a jungle.

This reading suggests that the collapse of narrative and government in the end is only the revelation of an inability predicted in the structures of the knowledge itself confronting the terrain. Fenwick never knows for certain what has happened or what constitutes the facts, and it is he most of all who is prey to confusion and seeks the security of history and liberal education. In section 1, "The Day Readers," he concerns himself with the management of his team and the differentiation of fact from rumor, for rumor is "savage" (386) and "a lying jade" (403). This focus on management strategies and gathering intelligence, conducted through metaphors of outlaws (whores, savages, barbarians), wants to guarantee the supremacy of the state project through the constitution of new men in the jungle as the micronation, as nationalist colluders leading the workers and embodying the cultural pluralism projected at the center of the new national rhetoric. Nevertheless, neither the workers nor their brutality emerge along the vectors of power embodied by the narrative eye until they impact on Fenwick's consciousness, and so the workers' integration as individuals into the narrative is slow and spasmodic, an exploration and a series of discoveries where the spectacle of their miscegenation is always remarked. In section 2, "The Night Readers," Chiung, Weng, Stoll (the mulatto worker), and Fenwick confront the attack on government by the maroon renegades, which is revealed as retaliation for the workers' exploitation of the maroon traders. Under Weng's leadership the workers will wreak a personal revenge under the umbrella of upholding government and the rule of law. The concepts of worker, rebel, and social pacts, as much as the informal economy that feeds Fenwick and his men in the jungle, suddenly come to light, and Fenwick discovers he has unleashed the contents of a Pandora's box, opening a fissure beyond his control and the reach of his perception. Thus he cannot remember the faces of the two men from the maroon community who stand silently by, watching the scene of Fenwick discovering (his own) murder in effigy, although he does not yet know it. The maroon community, once understood as the social subject "subsistence farmers in the interior," becomes, in the administrator's eye, "a rebel nation."

In the closing section, "The Reading," which describes what the narrative eye / I saw, the inundation of the governing structures of authority and the re-creation of the nation are marked by a workers' revolt (predicted by Marx but undertaken here against the lumpen and for the interests of the national bourgeoisie) where the workers' take government into their own hands against Poseidon and the rebels. It is marked, too, by the flight of Bryant and Catalena, and so the sacred status of the monogamous heterosexual couple—the centrality of proper English morals— although their interracial coupling will be suspect in the eyes of the man who has seen, and been thrown from, power. The symbolic chaos of the novel comes to a head here at its conclusion: the river begins to swell and the gray sky to drip, the Twins of Greek mythology are revealed as maroon emissaries from the subsistence community sent with government leases and titles to prove their legal pact, and the "immortal foul sisters" are named for the conceptual architecture of the future, "hope and progress" to Jordan's mind. In Fenwick's toppling from the center of power, the narrative eye/I takes to a bird's-eye view, and so begins to see into the heart of the rebel nation, and into women, workers, maroons, nations, and history at the dawn of the novel's seventh day.

Jordan's break from Fenwick, signaling the alienation of the mechanisms of the state from concepts of civil service and pacts with government leadership, already threatens Fenwick's liberal regime, the "philanthropic society" Jordan warned did not exist: "One would never be worried to ask who entertained whom, if one always left people's private morality or immorality alone so that it never materially affected the order of government. . . . Jordan did not think a social expedition should ever be so cornered that it had to discover who kept company with whom. This was always the beginning of the end of oneself and everything" (447). The structures of surveillance collapse under the weight of state regulation of the social subject beyond the exchange of labor for wages and Jordan's allegiance to the state, and he predicts the graft and corruption that will threaten to destroy the infrastructure, the totalitarian regime whose paranoia will drive it to spying on its citizenry, abolishing private much less public opposition as well as elections while claiming to represent the people (cooperative republic = totalitarian state). The position of the hidden focal point, the leadership of the masses (now the nation) is suddenly open.

And although Fenwick plans to interrogate each of the workers in turn on the events of the night and its reading, he discovers the rebel workers' leader is not Stoll, the light-skinned mulatto aspiring to be a government land surveyor, as he suspected, but rather Weng the hunter, the Amerindian mestizo who gathers intelligence on the rebels' plans from the balata bleeders. Weng recognizes that the attack on Chiung was meant as an attack on Fenwick in order to relay rebel military strategy to Fenwick. It is he who knows how to manipulate the workers, and he takes command in heading their transformation into a military cadre of civilian reserves spearheading a charge to be completed by the jungle police. Weng hungers to embody the power of the law ("I taking a page out of your book, Mr. Fenwick" [393]), and Jordan early aligns himself with him: " 'Weng will tell you himself, sir,' he declared. 'But the fact is the river people—all the black people from topside and bottomside the river— flocking around Poseidon. They ready to make trouble.' Jordan laughed contemptuously: 'As if they can really make trouble! One good look at them and they scared stiff. A pack of crude children.' He added softly under his breath: 'Savages, too!'" (380–81). When Weng says later, "Don't trust that black old man, skipper. Jordan would tell you so himself. And Jordan can see a thing or two steady and better than most body can," their pact is sealed, and its parameters clearly drawn.

Fenwick never reads beyond the levels of masses and the polite authority of social contracts, and so the workers are always children and the rebels are always jungle or ghosts of a vanquished nation, just as he sees in Jordan the hard face that in governing maintains power—a face that is always Medusa's, a fearful beast-woman turning men to stone. This rebel/madman/beast/woman immateriality reflects the jungle as much as the jungle reflects the immateriality of the social pacts among the masses, and as much as Fenwick's inability to read the workers and to even hear the men from the interior reflects the epistemological limits of the coast, and so too the workers' inability to read Fenwick. In this there is a slippage of unreadable signs: government = worker = leader = madness = boredom = children = insoluble mystery = jungle = coast, or = desert. Children, in fact, are nowhere present in this national configuration, and instead become the metaphor for unsuitable behavior, a floating political signifier that can attach to workers, women, or maroons when their position is to be dismissed in the decision-making process.

For the limits that serve to organize this chaos, the narrative eye becomes omniscient (leaving the limitations of Fenwick behind) and turns again to the gathering rebels. It turns to Poseidon first, and then to their tribal administration, to the constitution of a leaderless society in which hope for any possibility is invested. These are seen as men with "honest uses for everything they own" (441), but also men with a desperate need for cash, to enter the modern system of commodity exchange. They are maroons, but they are also men anxious to retain their social pact with the coastal government; they send emissaries to the government men, yet blend into the bush in the eyes of armed intruders accusing them of treason.

The black settlers of the jungle become prey to leviathan and, from this perspective, ghosts. The march of modernity as capitalism enforced by the West is backed by the most advanced technology of war and determines the future of the territory. As the remains of a vanquished paradigm their extermination is inevitable, and so they are already ghosts in the eyes of the omniscient narrator. In his "habit of aerial contemplation"

Fenwick soars over the landscape and recognizes the ineluctability of the modern state, and so, concomitantly, the insubstantiality of subaltern pacts, preventing him from seeing now that he believes he can hear, and the cycle of confrontation and death seems to roll just as ineluctably to its conclusion.

The social contract that the workers offer to Fenwick is predicated on conceptual categories that demarcate men and that determine the status of the leader, as well as on the dissemination of power into the concept of the self. Men, the victorious model of the new national consciousness, are hard (391) fighters (425) who refuse to submit to sickness (428). They are those for whom losing at manipulation is equivalent to "being ridden" like a homosexual (423), and they are those who have the stomach and the balls to play serious poker all night, where a woman's vagina is now collateral (402). The structures of the state and its technologies (weapons, knowledge, social and political violence, capital, surplus) have already been internalized by the worker-citizens of the new nation. It is a mark, however, of the traces of that transformation that the men/workers can understand Poseidon and the workings of the mad/rebel mind, whereas Fenwick cannot. The space of the center of power, the focal point of the panopticon, is (in)visible to the modern populace but its occupation is assumed, and a real man must fill it. Fenwick's fall from power, his expulsion from that seat and the ascension of Weng the military strategist, is equivalent to public recognition of Fenwick's feminization, a feminization Jordan sees in Fenwick's insecurity, sympathy for women, and counterproductive emotion. Fenwick in turn sees Jordan as feminized in his "grumbl[ing] improvidently like a woman" (448).

The circles of power are redrawn on the terrain as Jordan advises Fenwick against the feminization that will be his undoing. Power here is linked to access, to the process of coming before the law that says Fenwick must make himself unavailable, must treat workers like women and children who grumble and must be ignored and given their orders, and who must be protected from themselves and their own bad government. If the ascension of Weng is read as the revolution of the workers to secure the zone for the state, his love of gunplay and ability to articulate the modulations of power in the clearing—the sector of workers and the expenditure of government labor power on nature—provide a narrative of men and power that can move the masses against the enemies of the coming nation-state.

The reconstitution of the new national subject through the ancient terms of manliness demanded by these new men of the masses leaves no space for women, and it creates instead a nation of men alone at war. Women are trouble (422), an alien species (414), an "insoluble mystery" (413) repeatedly synonymous with savages and children (411, 412, 413, 414, 416, etc.), or with animals (392, 407), or with the land (410). Dead/old women are selfless, invisible healers (449), a flower (413), the repositories for the principle of the feminine as love, and love in the face of all reason is an "ancient madness" (451). Jordan, as the woman-monster Medusa whose gaze turned men to stone, government strategist on domestic policy and manager of the government's resources ("This is no philanthropic society," he informs Fenwick [380]) substitutes for the feminine in functioning as the keeper of the domestic sphere for Fenwick individually, and for the men as a mass. The one woman here, Catalena Perez (= Helen = Andromeda = the Trojan horse), is the property of one man, her husband, whose violent transference of the strategies of men in power for managing the territory and alien communities within the national borders onto the body of woman, becomes the limits of proper government. As a mark of the catachresis between Fenwick/liberal socialism and the men-workers, the figure of Perez—characterized under Fenwick's leadership through an old term for woman-chaos, that which is not of the nation-state, the anticoncept antiman, thus anticommunity/state interest, that is, a "cunt" (442)—in his violent excesses and abuse of women will emerge under Weng as metonymic of the men-nation the workers propose.

We first encounter Catalena emerging from the house of the maroon leader. Fenwick can only see her as a cowering child, a savage/mad woman unaccustomed to coming before the law. Titillated by the welts left on her body by her husband, Fenwick recognizes in her Guyana's poor, white shopkeeping class—selling rum and groceries to workers— and its women with no way out (413). When Catalena speaks and tells her story of abuse, a jungle comes out of her mouth (415).

Woman's exile is thus mapped on Catalena's body and in her autobiography, the lingering remains of the "establishment of trust . . . she had once distantly hoped for but never found" (416). Exiled from her family through marriage to Perez and beaten by her husband/owner, she has no allies and no means of escape. Her social pacts and her position in negotiations of power and representation tell her that men are beasts but she is their property, that the rule of law binding men dictated by men is beyond her reach. Her exile from rights to political representation as a limit securing the social pact is reiterated when she reveals to this stranger Fenwick details of her abuse: immediately she confirms the enmity of Jordan, who sees her claim to human rights and political representation as a rebellion and Fenwick's inevitable sympathy for her as another thread in the unraveling of order, progress, and administration. Alone, Catalena recognizes that her life is always at stake and that in giving this stranger information she is gambling for a new position. When she suddenly clings to Fenwick, he sees her as a mad woman/ child summoning his desire, until he realizes it is in response to her abusive husband's approach.

This micrological blindness is not to say that macrologically women are no longer a national battlefield. From the moment of her arrival, well before we have met her, Catalena became a syntagma for elaborating social pacts. Knowing only of the marriage contract and her arrival at the campsite, Fenwick decides that the best way to spy on Poseidon is to use the premise of woman's fragility as a tactic for stationing one of his men in Poseidon's camp, sending Bryant to ask Poseidon if he will allow her the comfort of his home. Perez, we learn from Jordan in this first strategic moment, beats his wife, and the prospect of confining him with her away from the men may make him kill her, but this is not yet Fenwick's concern.

After Catalena's appeal to Fenwick, Perez beats her more than ever, and she is forced to go begging to Fenwick as an emissary from her husband, under threat of execution if she does not get him reinstated on the project team (453). This threat, along with the worst of the beatings, is the price she pays for appealing to leadership for representation. Her plea to Fenwick is a stab in the dark and, later, delirious and hallucinating, she sees his position as the joker in a poker game; the leadership's response to her abuse as the wildcard in a real man's game among men (workers, Fenwick/Poseidon, Perez/Fenwick, maroons/workers) with her body at stake.

The question of the potential of Catalena's body thus finds its second solution in her coming to Fenwick in the jungle and her ability to arouse him because, like the maroons, she has no cash, no allies, and cannot survive on the coast. The fact of difference in women's bodies, given the psycho-sexual paradigms of the state, marks her body's cavities as capital, as parts of a sex-pleasure machine, and the question is always open whether she is—or will be or was (made)—a whore-worker, because she is of the woman-species. Fidelity is not at issue here, but rather property rights, exchange value, and the limits of the social body and representation. Perez, as part of a husband's private prerogatives that Jordan defends, offers her vagina for sex as collateral in the workers' nightly poker games, just as he sends her to plead with Fenwick for money, a dirt poor woman-exile of uncertain racial ancestry whose body is captured by Fenwick and Poseidon, as surely as the leaderless rebel community declares war and revenge in their battles for the future and control of the terrain.

### Nothing to Lose but Our Chains: Bryant and Catalena

If within the province of upward mobility the preservation of property rights over women operates with the centralization of a woman's value in the hands of the man to whom she is bound by law, so within the depths of the worker's camp, in the process of reading and speaking a locus for the brewing menace, the narrative eye seizes on the control and distribution of Catalena's sex/pleasure value as the locus of a break in the social contract. Fenwick wants to extend his ability to dictate policies to men's relations with women and thus to the exploitation and management of women's value. This is the moment of his feminization, the seed of his undoing, and the jungle is a womb. If Perez disappears from the narrative once he is dismissed by Fenwick, the centrality of Catalena as a new horizon in the national perspective holds her in its grip and she becomes the ruse on which the surveyor's men will achieve the assassination of Poseidon as much as a key to a new future and a new nation, a renegade Eve in the interior.

The rebels know Perez as "that monster, her husband" (456), and Catalena's return to the camp in the company of Bryant, earlier the self-chosen son, is the catalyst for the disaster that will end and then re-create the world, as it will cast them, weeping, out of Eden (452). Bryant, as a black worker, recognizes Poseidon as the limits of his/national history. From the very beginning he understands all that Poseidon says and the nature of his freedom, his administrative choices, as well as his exploitation at the hands of the workers. Bryant, from the start, is the one who sees the men farming the interior as deserving of a social pact and, beyond that, he recognizes in Poseidon his own ancestry. Poseidon in turn sees Bryant as a man he can trust, and Bryant returns this trust with a love that even Fenwick can see. Captured after killing Poseidon, confronting the rebel leader's body dead by his hand, Bryant confesses it openly for the first time. If Poseidon brings Fenwick's gamble with modernism to a crisis—"Time and history have made us all equally ignorant about who really exploits whom" he babbles fearfully to Bryant (375), and "it is still slavery, don't you understand?" (395)—then Bryant recognizes both Fenwick's liberal emotions and Poseidon's desire for fair play, just as the narrative eye recognizes Bryant as Adam and Poseidon's "apotheosis" in modernity (457).

In Bryant's misreading of Fenwick and his commitment to the creole nation-state, he fails to anticipate the destruction of his ancestral community as the ground for the development of the new country. He fails in his stewardship of the social pact between modern and agrarian black men that Poseidon had hoped for in failing to see that when the government man looks at Poseidon he sees dense bush, jungle, a "black wooden snake of skin" (371), a madman possessed by "a runaway African slave who had succeeded in evading capture and had turned into a wild cannibal man in the swamps, devouring melting cocerite flesh" (369). Bryant's oscillation between Fenwick/modernity and family/his ancient roots leads to the destruction of those roots by his own hand. The rebels are in crisis, meeting in an opening in the bush guarded by the stench of dung that burns the lungs of foreigners, a fetid threshold that Weng's platoon, followed by the government's police, is coming to storm. Bryant suppresses his inclination to join the circle of black man-warriors debating strategy in order to cement his relationship with Catalena, and so his betrayal of his heritage locates itself on Catalena's body. Poseidon recognizes he has been used by the ubiquity of Catalena Perez's body—"half-priestess, half-prostitute" (454)—and so strikes out against her as she trespasses into the rebel center. When Poseidon rises to lash out at Catalena as the terrain of his undoing, Bryant, in striking out to defend her, is already "one of the surveyor's men" (456).

Like Hopkins's white mulatta, Catalena is a sacrificial victim in battles between men: Bryant kills Poseidon, the workers declare war, and Catalena believes she is to be gang raped as retribution against the coastals and in redeclaration of the maroon's determination to fight. Poseidon concurs with the men from the coast in projecting betrayal onto her body as an easy target, a body without history of its own, and the depths of her subalternity are clear in this moment: she is beneath maroons obliterated in the name of progress and the social pacts of the new country. According to the lens of modernity (hers as much as the narrative I/eye's) that grafts the workers' poker games onto the maroon tribunal, Catalena's rape and murder would constitute a safe vehicle for their declaration of war against a state that does not represent her (460–61).[8]

Catalena's betrayal of Poseidon is a result of her attempt to free herself, to bring about her own emancipation. Here in the jungle, a penniless, homeless woman finding herself trapped without choices in conceptualizations of proper government that exclude her as a disease, she discovers that the three c's governing women's value, encapsulated by Nicaraguan ruling-class novelist Gioconda Belli as much as by Pauline Hopkins and Frances Harper, still apply: *cara/cuerpo/capital* (face, body, money). Bereft of this last, Catalena capitalizes on her ability to generate sexual and therefore emotional passion in men, through her sex, her breasts, her inscrutability to the male gaze, and her ancient secret of possession, metaphors for (a) precious body part(s) that so far guaranteed expulsion from the citizenry, and from the perception of her need to know:

> Bryant found himself unable to withstand her. His greed for ancient remembrance and love possessed many dormant signals, now coming to primitive life, beauty as well as lust. Catalena was a model of his compulsive derangement, a living projection and vessel, nevertheless, to offset the last impending signal of all, which was to be a god's [Poseidon's; his grandfather's] death. . . . Bryant suddenly fell on her . . . and possessed her with the utmost resolution and rigor. . . . He had been dreaming of her for a longer time than he cared to admit. From the moment he plotted to find room in the river for her. Long before she herself actually knew. (453–55)

The liberating social pact is worked out here in the exchange of sex for haven. For her part, Catalena, a desperate and impoverished Sappho, Guyana's new woman after the (re)creation, seeks only marriage, and so a modern social pact, the power "to work upon and expand in another's governing brain" (454), and that this means freedom: "She would do anything, beg anyone, lie with any man to ensure for herself a flying start" (454).

# 5

## The Masculinization of Mothering:
## The Oakland Black Panthers
## and the Black Body Politic

■

There is an old African saying, "I am we." If you met an African in ancient times and asked him who he was, he would reply, "I am we." This is revolutionary suicide: I, we, all of us are the one and the multitude.—Huey P. Newton

A slave who dies of natural causes will not balance two dead flies on the scales of eternity.—Eldridge Cleaver

The only way that the world is ever going to be free is when the youth of this country *moves* with every principle of human respect and with every soft spot we have in our hearts for human life.—Bobby Seale

Those of us who want to love our country are not anxious to ask whether our police are capable of murder. So we do not ask. We dare not concede the possibility.—Commission of Inquiry into the Black Panthers and the Police

In the anecdotes of oral histories, as much as in the popular insurgent imagination, the founders of the Oakland Black Panther Party (BPP) hold an almost sacred place as embodiments of strength and political insight, epitomes of the New Black Men.[1] In the hands of the BPP, Malcolm X's slogan "By any means necessary" became a call to arms, and thus much of the Oakland Panther lore describes the spectacle of black men policing the police and lined up in military formations. Huey Newton's and Bobby Seale's practice in the early days of their activism of following the police in the Oakland streets at night and reading to those being arrested their rights as a citizens—a practice that helped to win them the enmity of the on- and off-duty Oakland police force—is now considered a basic right of all Americans and the duty of the police.

After some thirteen years of struggle, sympathetic historian Michael Newton estimates, three hundred people died in the crises created by the formation of the BPP (223, 216). In political history, the 1969 murder of the Chicago Panthers's main cadre by a SWAT team in the apartment of Fred Hampton becomes a metonym of the extent to which, on the one hand, the state was determined to exterminate the BPP by any means necessary and, on the other, the threat contained in the Panthers's ability to reconceptualize privatized spaces like ghettos and prisons proved political dynamite, and so shifted the place of inner city blacks in U.S. politics to this day. Here at the beginning of a new century, it is worth noting that several of the points in the Panther program were later implemented at some level by the state.[2]

Black Power's reconceptualizations of the victimization of black Americans take up old terms in order to foster a revolution and throw into crisis the conceptualizations of "blackness" as a political concept. The new black man is recast as antithetical to the interests of the state. Eldridge Cleaver's paradigmatic "Allegory of the Black Eunuchs" asserts that old black men ("Negroes") are categorically condemned because "black rebels his age do not walk the streets in America: they were either dead, in prison, or in exile in another country" (155). The castrated black prisoner thus becomes the paradigm of clarity, and the functions of love and anger in black strategy and mobilization begin to shift. Prison rather than Church, the secular over the religious, exile rather than belonging, revolution over survival, come to determine the politics of empowerment for a new generation of black leadership. Prison is a school; the state is the enemy.

Histories and analyses in the social sciences focusing on the Black Power movement have documented violence operating predominantly in two spheres: the body in the street and the body in the home.[3] As we might predict from the history of black nationalism in the United States, these two terrains are gendered and conflictive: the house becomes the province of women and thus feminized, the street the province of men and thus masculinized. The strategists of the Civil Rights movement across the political spectrum all take up the question of the street as the site of struggle, with the home as a private space invaded by the at best ineffective paradigms of the dominant culture. In Martin Luther King

Jr.'s "love vs. bombs" section of his "Walk for Freedom," for example, the home as the place of wives and children is held entirely sacred. From the politics of King to the politics of Malcolm X, neither devises a political strategy that can cross the border and enter the family house.

The terrain of the national platform is explicitly the masculine domain of the street, the site of male refuge from social and economic exclusion and from confrontations with the armed forces of the state. For the proponents of Martin Luther King Jr.'s Non-Violent movement, this meant marching peacefully through hostile neighborhoods in the North and the South to expose and record through the mass media the violence against the black community that had been hidden or explained away for so long. In direct opposition to the resulting image of the black social body, the new generation of black leadership elaborated their platform with a new dominant metaphor for empowering the struggle: the seizing of "balls" as a metaphor for seizing power that makes men and, thus, a nation (207).

Twentieth-century literature of U.S. black leadership has long positioned black men as trapped in the turgid spaces between the street and the prison. Both E. Franklin Frazier (1948) and W. E. B. Du Bois (1969) diagnosed this problem as stemming from a pathology of the home, positing male hegemony of the domestic sphere as a solution for the tensions played out on the street. The unnatural position of black women thus enters the debate by implication, and as in Delany their transformation into housewives becomes implicitly a national imperative. The main focus of these arguments is that from the turn of the century through the 1960s (at least) black men were considered unclean and dangerous. To cleanse the national space white America normalizes a massive integration of state forces to police the ghettos, incorporating new laws and local, state, and national police forces, as well as the FBI, as not only justified but necessary.

Nevertheless, the questions of the black house and of black women return incessantly as a stumbling block for both the Black Panther Party and the state. Daniel Patrick Moynihan's infamous 1965 *The Negro Family: The Case for National Action* locates the origins of black impoverishment and disenfranchisement in the place of women and the pathological/matrifocal inheritance they carry from slavery into the bosom of the home, and views this as determining the black condition.[4] Pauline Hopkins's appeal for the nation to come to terms with its history, and so with the position of the nation's women, had yet to be heard. Women still represent, on one hand, the suspect term of the black body politic in the national rhetoric, a locus of black pathology; yet, on the other hand, healing the home front for the rearticulation of social spaces and the empowerment of men also becomes a touchstone of black prescriptions and government public policy. For the good of the black nation women must be disempowered, but they must enter into the disempowering pact on their own volition.

This confusion on the question of women and the feminine reemerges in the ideology of Black Power. Black Power sought to transform the operative political paradigm of the black social body from a "woman" into a "revolutionary man," a transformation necessitating arms, which is synonymous with justice, revolt, pride, balls, true blackness, power, the new black body, the new black nation, men, and, theoretically, women. In the process, punks or faggots—and even more certainly, on the rare occasion the subspecies is mentioned, lesbians—must be weeded out as a disease infesting the nation. Sexuality, like gender, is thus a central political concept.[5]

In Moynihan, as much as in the rhetoric of Black Power, at stake in the concept of a coup at home are masculinized women—hence the terror of lesbians and the problem of integrating women into the revolution. This problem with women accompanies the radicalizing of the street as the site of black male refuge, where men find their balls and love each other's company—hence the problem with gay men. In terms of the production of the New Black Man and the "We" of national community that is a groundswell of a people under siege in the ghetto, negotiating these tensions carries the weight of correcting history and of reconstituting the entire black body politic as properly male.

For both black nationalists and liberal Moynihans, pathology resides in the substitution of power in women for power in men. Such conceptualizations of the black sociopolitical condition tie together the disparate strands of the metaphors for women and the feminine traversing the BPP literature (the multiple meanings of "mothers," "punks," "queens," "sisters," "bulldaggers," "pussy") along the lines of disruption and treachery. This proliferation of terms and concepts associated with the private sphere and private parts comes to carry the burden of a national upheaval. The macropolitical sexualization of black people by white culture already sets the terms for society, which then play out in the laws and in the courtrooms of the United States. In elaborating the ideology behind these terms, the discussions begun and documented by the BPP build on the double-edged pillars of psychology and the judiciary, operating to determine the definitions of nation, gender, and national politics and the agenda of the revolutionary and enemy state.

Historically, the fascist antipathy toward blacks and black rights was unleashed again by the BPP's insistence on black inclusion in the rights guaranteed by the Constitution and its amendments. Police officers on- and off-duty engaged in direct shootouts and resorted to a host of methods for harassing and disrupting the BPP's most humane self-help programs like the Free-Lunch Program. If J. Edgar Hoover had used the FBI to attack Martin Luther King Jr.'s passive resistance movement, the organized, confrontational refusal of the BPP to capitulate to white supremacy led Hoover to vent the full might of the FBI toward the strategic objective of the Panthers' destruction by any means necessary (Churchill and Wall 71– 73).[6] Members of the Black Panther Party, like members of all black civil rights groups, were framed and imprisoned by the state, and the BPP's ideological formulations were clearly affected by the pressures of being under siege by one of the most powerful governments in the world.[7]

In attempting to represent the community, the BPP was obliged to formulate policy on women, lesbians, and gay men; my analyses in this chapter focus on the position of these three groups in Panther ideology. Elaine Brown's *A Taste of Power* documents the brutal effects of this ideology in practice. I am primarily concerned here, however, with the politics internal to Newton, Seale, and Cleaver formulating the new black nation and its effects on the BPP's possibilities. Gender theorists of men and masculinities across the disciplines argue that "non-hegemonic masculinities must always be simultaneously theorized along two axes, the male-female axis of non-hegemonic men's power over women within the marginalised grouping, and the male-male axis of non-hegemonic men's relative lack of power vis-à-vis hegemonic men" (Brod 89).

One way of approaching an issue central to my reading, then, is to investigate how much the ideology of the Black Power movement in general and the Oakland Black Panther Party in particular fall prey to subsuming questions of "the relational nature of gender as site and result of interactive negotiations" (Brod 89) between genders into structures of domination that replicate white violence toward black men and women "in order," as Kobena Mercer and Isaac Julien put it, "to recuperate some degree of power over the condition of powerlessness and dependency" (136). Again, New World black nationalist ideology takes up the dilemmas of gendering and reengendering that Spillers articulates as endemic to the mid-twentieth-century macropolitical debate over black families, and thus the gendered structures of black homes as foundational to the new horizon. Where Delany had focused on an implicit reengendering within the *oikos* and explicit reengendering in the *polis,* and Hopkins had turned inward in the face of lynchings and the emergence of Jim Crow to think again how to move back into the public sphere, the new black men dismantling the mid-century status quo return to old codings to rewrite their meaning.

The power of the black male body as a site of confrontation (as criminal, as threat), along with the question of black sexuality as a site of both fear and envy in the dominant culture, lead the New Black Men to confront such white "regimes of truth" in a raced repoliticization of psychology and sociology.[8] Key terms like anger, power, desire, and love take on new political meanings. From this new paradigm of power and knowledge, then, the new nation is to be built, and from there the new national dynamics of the home and the family in the service of birthing the national community (community organization = nation building) is to be extrapolated, performed, and codified.

Reading the ideology and internal politics of Black Power under the signs of women and gay men is not a new strategy. The late Joe Beam, the late Isaac Julien, Michelle Wallace, Ron Simmons, bell hooks, Elaine Brown, the late Essex Hemphill, and Cheryl Clarke, among other scholars, have already taken to task the leadership of the black radical movement for its treatment of women and gay men.[9] I reiterate the question here to broaden it, to ask what comes to constitute the "feminine" in the ideology of the BPP's revolutionizing foundational concepts. This inquiry is made to better isolate the threads of psychology, economics, and the judiciary working to reconceptualize the politics and history of the black male body—according to three key political autobiographical records—to engender it as a metonym for the national community. Pulling at this question to analyze the Oakland BPP's internal ideology, I argue, will account for some of its concrete political failures as a vanguard representative of the people.

*Women as Bodies / Women's Bodies: Love, the House, and the Bedroom*

I want to begin by looking at the question of houses as feminized spaces, as well as the process of coming to birth, in order to explore some of the ways in which the social and biological spheres that women occupy are seen in the writings of the BPP's three leaders. Bobby Seale and Huey Newton grapple explicitly with the question of the family, and although both were raised with a mother and father in the home, the nuclear family must early be rejected in the process of political individuation. So, although Huey Newton has the most stable family background of the three, and although his dedication in *Revolutionary Suicide* credits his mother and father for giving him "strength and making me unafraid of death and therefore unafraid of life" (i), the book opens with a poem of the same name founding the new man on the opposite premise: "By having no family, / I inherited the family of humanity" (v).

A question we can come back to in grappling with this paradox is the place of the family house in the process of birthing the revolutionary hero. Bobby Seale's *Seize the Time* opens with his family house and his neighborhood in telling "Who I Am": "When Malcolm X was killed in 1965, I ran down the street. I went to my mother's house, and I got six loose red bricks from the garden. I got to the corner, and broke the motherfuckers in half. I wanted to have the most shots that I could have, this very same day Malcolm was killed. Every time I saw a paddy roll by in a car, I picked up one of the half-bricks and threw it at the motherfuckers. I threw about half the bricks, and then I cried like a baby" (3). We can extrapolate from this moment of crystallization a paradigm of the terms on which the New Man gives birth to himself, and we can think through the national political resonances of his points of reference. Here love = anger = war, as it is his love of Malcolm, itself predicated on Malcolm's love of the community, that gives birth to the anger that makes him attack the state. The imperviousness of the police, dispatched through the black neighborhood in the wake of the assassination reputedly engineered by the Nation of Islam with the FBI as an accomplice, already predicts the military superiority of the state's forces, as well as their strategy for debilitating Black Power by targeting its leadership and forcing armed confrontations.[10] The question of an armory will become a crucial one, making or breaking the BPP and the revolutionary agenda. Already there is the shortage of weaponry, as much as their poverty in the broken bricks the extent to which the militarized men who will form the cadres of the BPP must scramble for weapons out of what is available on the streets. Anger, here linked to the political pain that brings tears, expresses the love that authorizes Malcolm's stature as *pater progenitor,* and seals tight the new fighting body.

Although the house initially functions as a psychological anchor, its function as a safe haven is only dimly on the margins of the new warrior's worldview. It stands as a reminder of an absent mother, one who gardens, and it is only by reading back to the source that we can begin to see a place for women or love in the family house. Although Seale's mother is looked upon intermittently as a barometer of the community's response to the BPP in *Seize the Time*, Seale's earliest memory is of his father beating him unjustly and making him wash his father's shirt (women's work), and this is the beginning of the injustices that lead to his conscientization. In search of his mother here, at this birthing/breaking point, we can see that she has built a garden—perhaps as an escape from the violence in the house and the larger U.S. society—and because she gardens Seale can find ammunition, although at this critical moment the trajectory is away from solidarity with his mother and the family house as haven. This elaborate conflation of anger and love, pain and birth, the transformation of the borders of the gardens and what they represent—haven, women's work—into missiles, goes a long way toward explaining the internal politics of the new black nationalism after the assassination of Martin Luther King Jr. and, more particularly, Malcolm X.

The process of birthing the New Black Man is thus caught up in a dialectic between the protectors of the white supremacist state and men trapped in occupied spaces. Eldridge Cleaver describes his own process in a notorious passage from *Soul on Ice:* "The term *outlaw* appealed to me and at the time my parole date was drawing near, I considered myself to be mentally free—I was an "outlaw." I had stepped outside the white man's law, which I repudiated with scorn and self-satisfaction. I became a law unto myself—my own legislature, my own supreme court, my own executive. . . . I became a rapist. To refine my technique and *modus operandi,* I started out by practicing on black girls in the ghetto" (14). In the struggle to give birth to himself, the New Man of the ghetto returns to the body of woman as a substitute territory, and black women in particular as territory for war games. Like the tyrannical enemy-state, Cleaver's new black state, in and for itself, is predicated on the brutalization of predetermined segments of the population. Gender takes the place in Cleaver's new regime that race held in the old.

Although Cleaver will later reject rape as a political strategy, the place of women's bodies as territory in the (inter)national struggle is never obsolete. In his love letters to Beverley Axelrod, published at the center of

*Soul on Ice,* "love" for Cleaver entails a loss of the self to recover the self, or in less romantic terms, power: "The reason two people are reluctant to really strip themselves naked in front of each other is because in doing so they make themselves vulnerable and give enormous power over themselves to the other one" (148). These private letters written under a public eye (first prison officials, then the readership of a bestseller) struggle with the questions, for Axelrod, of his honesty and hidden motives. And in this reconceptualization of himself for his own purposes, he encapsulates, Huey will come to realize, the relation between the BPP and the black community they sought to represent.

Cleaver's "love" leads him to declare his feelings "one for the books, for the poets to draw new inspiration from" (149), but the prospect of loving also erodes his sense of himself as a revolutionary, undermining the ultimate project of giving birth to "Eldridge X" (150). After Beverley Axelrod's "transfusion" of compliments (142), he is "humiliated" by what he wants to write (143), as the language loses what both see as his "hatred," a driving force amply exemplified in the essays published on either side of this "Prelude to Love." For Cleaver, this "love" as tenderness is a private affair made public by the fact of the urgent need for a black rebirth, but tenderness is never a public-political affair, an affair for the street. If for Newton, Seale, and Malcolm X, an "infinite love" as tenderness is the founding precept of the revolutionary subject (Newton iv), for Cleaver, love as tenderness is locked up in a drama between two people: a man (imprisoned) who hates and a woman (lawyer) who frees him. In the transition from private to public the meaning of "love" shifts from tenderness to rage, yet women are always central. Still, through the judicial (public) as much as the psychological (private), the conceptualization of women ties the private love letters to the final, public one where Cleaver speaks to "all black women" on behalf of "all black men."

In Cleaver's influential essays, especially "To All Black Women, from All Black Men," the terms of the new relationship between men and women come to set the terms of the BPP with the nation. Women come to stand for history through their wombs in (re)producing the race and their function in the lives of the men, and for Cleaver, revolutionary black men in turn must rise to their proper place—hegemony—in order to be worthy of that womb/history. Women as metaphors for the nation deserve the first and last apology, given in the suppliant public love letter that closes *Soul on Ice.* There, woman is "Queen—Mother—Daughter of

Africa" whose womb has given birth to civilization as much as black liberationist heroes since the onslaught of slavery. Yet woman as black metaphor of black victimization finds release only in the black man's regaining of his "balls" "from the teeth of a roaring lion" (207). With black men's rise to power the violence of history is set right, and so the end of the glory of the power of black women is equivalent to the success of the revolution (207).

Cleaver's infamous characterization of desire for white women as a pervasive disease that burns in every black man's chest is, then, less a return to community than an expulsion of contamination. Here the white woman becomes a metonym for the enemy, a symbol of his property and his pride: "Rape was an insurrectionary act" in light of "the historical fact of how the white man had used the black woman" (14). And as a political guerrilla strategist Cleaver recognizes that women form a weak link in the vectors of power because "from the site of the act of rape, consternation spreads outwardly in concentric circles" (14).

The revolutionary shift from individualist revenge to a communal black nationalist agenda thus requires that the white (woman) be expelled from the heart of the black social body and that the local black version be exalted in its place in public rhetoric, if not necessarily in private life. In either case women's bodies are crucial, but only as the terrain on which men discover themselves and their own internal workings in a world typified by battles among men or, in Cleaver's case, where men find their souls as private beings and their sexuality as public men.

In Seale's testimonial on the BPP, women as bodies in the flesh become objects promising sensual pleasure deployed for cadre control and recruitment, as when Bunchy Carter has the women in the party "turn a cold shoulder to all these fools who came around late," or when the men on the corner "whose curiosity was aroused . . . rapping with some of the other sisters, and got the same answers"; that is, no membership, no play—and so join, to his delight (396). For their part the women internalize these dynamics, for the party and the revolution, and Bobby Seale recites incidents of black women struggling to tie their sexual availability to the BPP program (is he a real Panther, does he know the ten-point program, and if not ought she to have sex with him) and it is left to Seale, he explains, to arbitrate the sexual drama in the office as in the bedroom, to guide the New Women toward an understanding of their sexual role as their political role based on principles developed by Huey Newton (393–403).

The principle that monogamous heterosexual relationships = bourgeois capitalism comes early in the life of the party's founder, although it gains a patrimony after Newton moves in with Richard Thorne. To test the reliability of women's commitment to "mutual honesty and the elimination of jealousy"—revolution in the black family house—Newton and Thorne within "a given period . . . would sleep with more than one woman to see if they could deal with this without regressing to their old values . . . considered outdated and bourgeois, as well as mentally unhealthy" (Newton 93). If in looking back Newton recognizes an exploitative relationship, exploitation for him resides not in the interchangeability of and experimentation with women; these women may or may not be able to make the grade and must always be replaced anyway. Rather, exploitation resides in "practical reasons"—which here mean the acquisition of money—if what Seale calls "good loving and good screwing" are assured, because life without the latter "can be bad for a man's mind" (Seale 197). The liberation of women from the cage of the "imprisoning, enslaving, and suffocating experience" of "the bourgeois family" (Newton 91) into Newton and Thorne's social laboratory, where the political frontiers of the uses and habits of the domestic sphere (and for Newton of women as sex partners) are programmatically explored, becomes on reflection "a kind of 'God experience,' when I was 'free'" (93). Newton's freedom in the home is complemented by freedom on the streets, where he was supported by prostitutes and his work as an outlaw "pulling small-time armed robberies with some of my 'crime partners,'" men on the street who will make up the pool from which the cadres of the Black Panther Party will be drawn (93).

In the process of giving birth to themselves as political men, both Cleaver and Newton move from the capitalization of black women's bodies on the street (as rape victims or prostitutes) to white women's bodies (as rape victims or prostitutes) and, at least rhetorically, back again (as deployable sexual partners in revolution). This is always done with their eye on the displacement of white men's propriety through conceptualizing women as black men's property, the object as well as the subject of appropriate black anger, and the recapture of black balls in the reunion.

If this is indicative of the conceptualization of the revolution then it stands to reason that all the revolutionary models in this universe will be men: Huey Newton, Bobby Seale, Eldridge Cleaver, Fred Hampton,

Bunchy Carter, Malcolm X. The mechanics of the exclusion of women from the revolutionary pantheon—as from equal citizenship in the new nation and the revolution—are already clearly laid out in Malcolm X's testimonial: " 'You can never fully trust any woman,' he said. 'I've got the only one I've ever met whom I would trust seventy-five percent. I've told her that' " (389). The underlying premise here is that women stand for treason in the black national front as transnational frontier, and the metaphor reveals itself fully through Malcolm X's metonym for treason drawn from the history of the "mother" country: "Do you know why Benedict Arnold turned traitor—a woman!" (389). Nevertheless, women as metaphors and bodies are inextricably intertwined in the discourse and ideology of the new nation, although always on the margins in the essays and testimonials of the revolutionary heroes.

At stake in the question of women is the model for love internal to the black community, a concept that will underwrite the authenticity of the revolutionary hero as true representative of the people. A tie that binds must be read at the source of the revolution, and so a place must be found for women in the new model (because men must relate to other men only as minds and ideologies), and therefore the ideological implications of the concept of the feminine and all that accrues to it must play a critical role in reformulating the nation.

It is no surprise, then, that in those instances where Cleaver and Newton explicitly address the concept of loving it is not the love that the leaders hold for the people (in the tradition of the New and Old Left and *Guevarismo*) but rather of men for women, extrapolated again from the micropolitical into the macropolitical and reexemplified in Seale's relation of "babies that come out of the pussies of women" to "the dudes that put their dicks in the pussies of women" constituting "the correct social order" (254). Or as Cleaver puts it, the revolutionary relation of "all black men" to "all black women."

The private situation of black men in the home and the bedroom, which here means with women, is thus central to the BPP agenda and to the ties that bind the vanguard to the nation, although the men do not recognize it in their battles with the state. Women as metaphors constitute history, the (re)source of the nation, victims of the struggle, the territory lost to the enemy that must be won back, the element on whose alliance the struggle will triumph or fall. But although black women are integral to thinking the state of the nation, the terms on which the New

Man identifies himself and the struggle—as, we shall see, eunuchs, anger, warfare, and balls—predetermine the marginalization or exclusion at best, and victimization at worst, of black women in the movement for black liberation, unless they become New Men.[11] There is thus a profound contradiction at the heart of conceptualizing the "We" of the new revolutionary community, and women become as crucial and as overdetermined as they are interchangeable. Nevertheless the program for the home front takes up the question of women and the bedroom, and it is from what is discovered there that their program for the nation takes its metaphors governing the relationship of black men to the state and to U.S. history. Through these governing metaphors, these three men at the center of the BPP leadership rehearse their paths in their autobiographic constitutions of the revolutionary hero (the new "I") and the new nation (the "We"). Collectively they strategize to embody a new black subjectivity as a model of health (the new "I/we" which will yield national revolution, which will yield international revolution, which will yield a new, manly, colored world order).

## Male Bodies: The Struggle, the Street, and the Prison

Bobby Seale matures as a political man when he is pushed out of the system of the white supremacist nation-state, when he is expelled from the army for talking back and having too much pride for a black man. A bill collector pursues Seale while he is in the army. Because his commanding officer and the bill collector come from the same racial and social circle under a racist system, the military officers and the military police combine to force Seale's hand in the dispute. His refusal to submit to such an invasion leads directly to his being psychoanalyzed by army experts as disturbed, and thus he is given a dishonorable discharge. Then because of the record on him that the state forces accumulate and disseminate to his employers, he is fired from job after job. The power of the white nationalist nation-state combines its assaults on black men by politicizing and instrumentalizing the concepts of "madness" and "sanity," "freedom" and "criminality," "sickness" and "health."[12] Under the tyrannical state, the rebellious black man becomes a dangerously chaotic subspecies that it is the duty of a network of white nationalist forces to police, as earlier Delany had argued from his own horizon.

At some point all three Panthers are imprisoned. Each is seen by a psychiatrist, although only Cleaver is driven to a clinical nervous break-down. Each is physically brutalized as well, and each finds that his free-dom is always within easy reach of the law. Money + white cadres (capital + army + law) = power, as Delany had noted and the Panthers re-discover. Money is the path to physical freedom in white America, and money is always demanded by the state from politicized black men in bail and fees as quickly as it can be accumulated, an FBI strategy dele-gated to local police. The state's charges rarely stick, but constant harass-ment breaks morale and eats into organization time and resources. Money must be exchanged for the freedom of black men's bodies, be-cause both sides recognize that the freedom of the New Black Man's body is fundamental to black revolutionary political action. At stake is the body as a site of male power. Further, it is the performance and regulation of the black male body toward docility and criminalization that is at the origin of the battle between black men and white state cadres. What is policed or breached at the local level, as the local and state police, Gover-nor Ronald Reagan, and FBI Director J. Edgar Hoover all agreed, deter-mines the strategic positioning of the black male body in the economic, juridical, and sociopolitical order of the United States. The black male body becomes central to a new kind of struggle.[13] It is the (re)formation of the new body and the struggle that I want to explore further.

### The struggle in the street
"The people in Detroit" argues Huey Newton in an interview with "The Movement," "learned that the way to put a hurt on the administration is to make Molotov cocktails and to go into the street in mass numbers" (Meier, Rudwick, and Bracey 511). The "people on the streets" = "the activists" = "the real vanguard of change" (513), and so the movement seeking to represent the people becomes defined as an urban guerrilla movement that takes as inspiration the models of El Che and Fidel, and of the Vietnamese under Ho Chi Minh. The home is the place of women and nonviolent men and so constitutes the rearguard, the place of "older people" who have been "beaten into line" (513). In the minds of the revolutionaries houses offer no protection, and so the United States itself becomes "a burning house" (510), as rent strikes for better housing bring not white sympathy (the key political hope of the rearguard) but the police, the "strongarm men" of the administration (the state) "to throw the furniture out the window" (501).

The ready invasion of the house by these armed and dangerous "protectors" of the "corrupt exploiter" thus sets the terms of the revolt. The cadres of the BPP find themselves caught in an armed struggle between "a nation of 'black slaves' and a white nation-state hostile to democratic black freedoms" (Meier, Rudwick, and Bracey 501). To "deal with the corrupt exploiter you are going to have to deal with his protector, which is the police who take orders from him" (501). This invasion of the home, and thus its negation as a refuge, takes its place in the collapse of narratives of history as progress in black-white relations stretching back to slavery. From this perspective, there is no progress in U.S. black history.

The masculinization of the state, and the feminization of the black home in its violability (exemplified in the rape of black women) and lack of defensible borders, becomes key in the new black political economy: "In order . . . to assert his manhood [the master] would go into the slave quarters and have sexual relations with the black women. . . . Because if he can only satisfy the [black woman] then he would be sure he was a man" (Meier, Rudwick, and Bracey 505). The violability of the borders of the house-nation means the rape of black women = castration for men (= non-men = punks ≠ real men), and makes raped women's treason inevitable, "because women want one who can control" (505); that is, they like it.

### The struggle in the prison: men gestating men
Cleaver outlines his rebirth in terms of self-hatred and revolutionary violence in the form of the rape of women's bodies, as we have seen, but also through his experience in prison. His writing "to save myself" (15), as well as reading Fanon's *The Wretched of the Earth*, Williams's *Negroes with Guns*, the speeches of Malcolm X, and the teachings of the Nation of Islam contribute to his rebirth. The prison community thus provides the forum in which true black men's consciousness is formed because power relations become naked. Cleaver details the factions within the prison, and his allegories of power in *Soul on Ice* all take their reference points from within this sphere.

Peculiarly, in Cleaver's prison men have no bodies except as metaphors. Here the body never stinks, never defecates, never feels sexual desire except as an always already operating internalization of macropolitical forces—racist or revolutionary. And so the process of rebirth is the process of purification in a reconceptualization of race and penises and vaginas (= souls) and propriety, which is legitimate property rights, which is Cleaver's revolution. Hence his vitriolics against homosexuality and the obsession with sex as a metaphor for macropolitics. Cleaver's body may be contained; it is, he confesses, contaminated by unclean interracial desires but at least it never functions except as a vehicle for the revolutionary mind and so revolutionary politics.

For Huey Newton the body functions much differently, and his experience in prison alienates him, as Elaine Brown documents, in forcing him to either die or be reborn in the dissolution of the mind/body split ascribed to the pathology of racist capitalist paradigms, forcing his mind back into itself to take back control, and in so doing save his life. The body for Newton is initially conditioned by the social contract with the enemy-state as a weak point, and its desires are weapons the state uses against revolutionary—that is, real—black men.

The chapter "Freedom" in *Revolutionary Suicide* relates Newton's process of revolutionary rebirth, and after the fact he discovers that his philosophical reference points are Gandhi and the East. Newton is reborn in solitary confinement in the Alameda county jail, in what everyone calls the "soul-breaker": "Four and a half feet wide, by six feet long, by ten feet high. . . . I was always kept in the dark, and nude. There was no bunk, no washbasin, no toilet, nothing but bare floors, bare walls, a solid steel door, and a round hole four inches in diameter and six inches deep in the middle of the floor. The prisoner was supposed to urinate and defecate in this hole" (100).

Against the state's attempt to break him he reconceptualizes his relationship to his body. First his body must be instrumentalized, ingesting just enough nourishment to stay alive while producing a minimum of waste. As punishment for political activism, the prisoner is forced to confront his body as a contaminant of the social space and of psychological organization, and so Newton finds that survival means his body must be mastered like a machine. Here the ultimate terms of the social contract resolve toward the mind confronting control of the body and the isolation of its by-products.

The horrors of this brutal level of disenfranchisement, then, amount to the confrontation of the body with itself as an irretrievably physical phenomenon, and now property of the state; a confrontation the authorities have discovered can be withstood at best for two or three days before the prisoner begins to scream and to beg. Newton recognizes that his own refusal to submit comes not from any "ideology or program" but something else, "stubbornness" perhaps (101), and so the revolutionary leader recognizes that the male body stands before the ultimate point of politicization, in itself "the 'last' end of the world" (100). To drive him to madness or submission the prisoner is deprived of light, of space, of nourishment, of stimuli: "During the day a little light showed in the two-inch crack at the bottom of the steel door. At night, as the sun went down and the lights clicked off one by one, I heard all the cells closing, and all the locks. I held up my hands in front of my face, until I could not see them. For me, that was the testing time, the time when I had to save myself or break" (101).

The second point in the survival strategy is that the mind must be controlled to reproduce its storehouse of images and connections at a pace. This, the relay of the incarcerated mind, marks the inner sanctum of the body. To survive, the resistant body in solitary must be sublimated and controlled, and this space before ideology and political programs, with its isolation of the body from a sense of anything but its own weakness, its own filth, its own needs, must be recognized as the last weapon of the state against political black men who are "arrogant" (103) and refuse to "abide by the rules" (107). It is this weakness that leads to the capitulation that the state wants to see Newton make, opening the doors for the internalization of the power of the state that makes men submit and beg to be allowed the small place allotted. These doors that open within the mind relentlessly confronting the body are explicitly linked through the mouth of the prison captain to the doors of solitary confinement: capitulation is the path to the prison community and from there back out into the street.

To this end, the protectors of penal institutions are authorized to disempower by the amendment to the U.S. Constitution that bans slavery everywhere except in the prison. The much remarked on fact that the prisons are filled to overflowing with black men traces an unbroken line from the antebellum agrarian project of torturing slaves to turn a man into an ape-worker to the modern project of turning a black man into a model prisoner, into one comfortable with the social spaces allotted the black male subcitizen determined to die of natural causes. The agrarian barbarity of the overseers in one administrative paradigm is replaced by the modern barbarity of the police and prison administrators in the other. In both, the clause in the social contract with the state that ought to protect the black body—"all men are created equal"—is voided, and this loophole becomes the administration's greatest tool. For this reason, prison is the space of black revolutionary rebirth, where black men realize their place in the hole in the nation reserved for them, and so their excommunication from the promise of the American Dream. Thus, Newton argues, "the nigger out of prison *knows*," and "has seen the man naked" (Seale 4), although any alliance to revolution remains to be seen.

The state, to protect itself from public scrutiny of the discrepancy between the (then) official rhetoric of prisons as "rehabilitation centers" and its private strategies for the policing of inmates through tyrannical repression (now), pulls the political prisoner every fourteen days and has his body washed and mind checked. Madness is the anticipated response to such punishment. He who continues to think as he did before solitary confinement is seen as beyond the reach of reason (therefore humanity); in the person of the state psychiatrist and in the conflation of pathology, politics, and race, the prison as the madhouse become political limbo. The male body cast into this "hole" most often breaks, as when a man "screamed night and day as loudly as he could" (104). Newton cannot recommend his own path to freedom to young comrades.

## Power in Men

### (Dis)seminating revolution and the birth of the panther

The power of black revolution as a grassroots strategy begins in the reconceptualization of the self—in relation to history, to the social pact between government and the people—that transforms. And as we saw in looking at the place of women, power is a masculinist prerogative. In creating a public persona in relation to black community, and in order to capture the black public's imagination as much as to consolidate its own transformation, the revolutionary New Black Man is secured in a series of metaphors embodying itself as itself, the birth of the new nation.

The panther as a political image has an elaborate genealogy in the Civil Rights movement that preceded the Black Panther Party. The meaning of this image shifts dramatically in black American political history: for the 1966 Mississippi Freedom Democratic Party it functioned as a call to register and vote, in its way as radical a response to the political situation in the South as were the Panther guerrilla tactics in the ghettos of the North (Carmichael and Hamilton 98). The image moves from defining an electoral agenda to a description for Malcolm X as a thinker, for his physical presence as a political black man. If the Mississippi Freedom Democratic Party symbolized an almost utopic strategic integration of men and women into the political empowerment process, by the time it registers the power of Malcolm X, women are already suspect. Problems immediately arise for the Oakland BPP in defining the relationship of the BPP leadership to those they seek to represent:

> When we started passing the platform around the poverty center [in Oakland], they'd ask, "Why do you want to be a vicious animal like a panther?"
> Huey would break in. "The nature of a panther is that he never attacks. But if anyone attacks him or backs him into a corner, the panther comes up to wipe that aggressor or that attacker out, absolutely, resolutely, wholly, thoroughly, and completely." They didn't *want* to understand that. (Seale 65)

And so the problem of the tie between the revolutionary "I" and the "We" of the impoverished black nation, of love as tenderness and its absence, and of a willful silence in the relation of the Panthers to the community ("they didn't *want* to understand that") sits at the very heart of the BPP's concept of power and representation, of the "I = We = nation" structuring the revolutionary vanguard's self-definition.

*Power and balls*
To birth the black militant, as we have seen, for him to transform himself from an Uncle Tom negro into a new black man, black men must reconceptualize themselves, body and mind, in terms antithetical to their determinations by white power and its state. Within the terms of the dominant discourse of race and power/knowledge, the black man must become a New Black Man, and so an outlaw. This is typical of how what the state considers a "criminal," or how "client" is transformatively called "prisoner" or "inmate" (the latter two terms recoded as signifying "one who has seen"), and so perhaps a new man, a "real" man (Newton 120). What is recaptured here is "balls." For Black Power advocates this means recognizing the problems of black-white coalition politics and the systemic betrayal of black empowerment by liberal whites. To take back one's balls is thus meant to be only a metaphor for strength in resistance and for thinking for one's (black) self rather than being suckered into

working for the white nationalist agenda, and therefore against black people.

Nevertheless, given the BPP ideology formulated by Minister of Information Eldridge Cleaver, and taken up by Newton and therefore Seale, as well as the general problem of integrating women and politicizing what comes to constitute the feminine, it is not by accident that Cleaver's new outlaw-state's first target is women and its first tactic is rape. Struggling, since at least Delany's time, with deterritorialization, Black Power's black nationalism seeks control over community resources, and in a community within which people have nothing but each other and the spaces in which they live this means controlling women as resources and custodians of the home. Taking territory comes to mean controlling women's bodies and social spaces. Because white women are symbols and carriers of white men's property and status, white women can be attacked as territory/strongholds are attacked, in a war between the races. Looking to operate outside the law, Cleaver reconstituted himself in terms set by the enemy-state, and just as law and order are still structured in terms of the three branches of government established in the U.S. Constitution, so women and all that accrues to the feminine (homosexual = criminal ≠ citizen) are still exiled to the margins of the liberationist struggle and the "new" nation. As in Delany a hundred years earlier, these three founding bodies of the state—legislature, court, executive—and gendered and sexual hierarchies within the nation inextricably work toward a similar ethno-nationalist agenda for both sides.

This paradox between the enemy-state and the new black nation is written into the BPP platform, where the climactic demand for "land, bread, housing, education, clothing, justice, . . . peace . . . [and] a United Nations-supervised plebiscite [to determine] the will of black people as to their national destiny" (Seale 68) is explained by reciting the Declaration of Independence as an African-American Declaration of Independence from Anglo-America. Here again, the enemy-state's strategy for the pacification and marginalization of black men and the ghetto community determines the reference points for thinking about both the strategy and the internal politics of the revolution. So the state's coalition of armed forces come to be termed simply "the Man," as if summing up that state of mind black revolution calls for, since black and white Men = arms = balls (≠ the feminine = gay men = women ≠ subjects of law in both the white bourgeois and black revolutionary states).

Huey Newton's strategy starting from the founding of the BPP was always to follow the laws to the letter in order to expose the fact that black men in the ghetto were not allowed to take up their rights as citizens, and so the Oakland Panthers always carried law books that detailed both their rights and proper police procedure. The state responded with legislation enacted at the local and federal level to ensure their prosecution. To reconceptualize black manhood by taking up the gun, the very terms on which the state operates overtly and covertly to ensure its power, was thus a direct and public refusal of the disenfranchisement of black men: if the Constitution guaranteed the right to bear arms, then the Panthers, as black men who were citizens of the state, would exercise that right, although from the beginning Newton knew that the state would see this as a confrontation that could only end in death.

Thus, in relation to the state, the political strategy of the BPP under Newton and Cleaver is a series of public confrontations with the forces of the state—the Panthers on the state capitol grounds making Governor Ronald Reagan run for cover (like a black man should), the BPP on the floor of the state capitol armed to the teeth (like the white police in the streets of the ghettos)—although Newton will recognize that while such tactics mesmerize the public and capture the media, the sensation allows all sides to ignore the political issue of the covert war against black men and their disenfranchisement (Newton 149).

I will argue in the end that the paradigm of manhood as power equated with Black Panther revolution as a process, and the Black Panther revolutionary as a member of the black community, prevents the articulation of a communal agenda beyond the politics and advantages of sheer confrontation with the armed forces of the state. What is at stake in their definitions of bodies and the feminine is the fundamental definition of both nation and power, because under Cleaver's direction the BPP leadership's allegory of power is founded in the body, organizing national relations through power relations, and power relations through metaphors of gender and sexual relations.

*War + history => women*

The effective enslavement of the black man by the state must include the attempt, Newton tells "The Movement," "to bind the penis of the slave to show that [the white man's] penis could reach further than the supermasculine menial's penis. He said, 'I, the omnipotent administrator can have access to the black woman'" (Meier, Rudwick, and Bracey 505). Power is equal to the word and its metaphor is the reach of the penis unbound to access women, as we saw in the B P P's deployment of women as political rewards, the enslavement and humiliation of the black nation metaphorized as the reach of white penises into black vaginas.

The terms of battle come full circle when the black man is characterized as responding with a "psychological attraction to the white woman . . . for the simple reason that it was the forbidden fruit. The omnipotent administrator decreed that this kind of contact would be punished by death" (505). Here, again, women are the battleground across which warring factions meet, and so the struggle of racial power relations for the rights of men is equal to the historical struggle between black and white men for property rights over women.

In the process of black men taking power, the overthrow of the white penis is equal to white men's feminization. The feminine = the weak and the disempowered, just as white men feminized black men by constricting black penises/power, and so Cleaver will call the disempowered white man-nation's penis a "clitoris" as an act of counterhumiliation, a verbal enactment of the revolution (184). The parameters of power are then already set, and just as it comes from above to claim the streets and invade the house, power determines the most intimate units of the black nation in controlling the relationship of the body to the mind: "If he can only recapture his mind, recapture his balls, then he will lose all fear and will be free to determine his destiny. This is what is happening at this time with the rebellion of the world's oppressed against his controller" (Meier, Rudwick, and Bracey 506).

The mind and body must form the whole in characterizing the split between a white power state and an oppressed black nation. The unity of mind with body on both fronts—the state and the revolution—is thus defined as manhood, ownership of the proper penis, and power as the ability to define and enact definitions (= balls = courage = arms = freedom). In turn this leads, in nationalist history, to the alliance of women who cling to power/nation—as white or black men—as if, like Hopkins, in recognition of the exile of women as subjects of law in the revolutionary paradigm.

The victor takes all and women are the prize booty, thus war + history => women. For Newton the reconceptualization of the black man—and so black power and a new black political strategy—begins in this domestic dialectic. Women's bodies as national territory and sexual objects in the liberation of black men from white men in the home are to be superseded in the street by a dialectic between revolutionary men's bodies, guns, and upholding the laws of the state against its criminal protectors. "The perfect man" is thus the uniting of the newly freed mind with the (male) armed body which = control of the country = the guerrilla as a political man, defined as he who knows how to properly deploy the body: "The guerilla is a very unique man. . . . The guerilla is not only the warrior, the military fighter; he is also the military commander as well as the political theoretician. . . . The gun is only an extension of the body, the extension of our fanged teeth that we lost through evolution. It's the weapon, it's the claws that we lost, it's the body" (Meier, Rudwick, and Bracey 507). Thus the ability to define = the ability to make things act according to definitions = power = MAN = revolutionary vanguard = body (balls) = mind (arms).

### Sex, power, and men: the primeval mitosis

The defining sociopolitical concepts in Newton's dialogue with "The Movement" are developed from Cleaver's essay "The Primeval Mitosis." Cleaver coins and defines the key terms in a narrative of class and caste struggle in the United States that again begins in the home, which is again equal to the bedroom. White men rule and black men labor; black women work and white women are repositories of surplus (leisure time, capital, culture, grace). Here administrative/mental power exists in inverse relation to labor/physical power, and within what Cleaver sees as the caste society of the United States this means that black men and women are "Supermasculine Menials" and "Subfeminine Amazons," just as white men and women are "Omnipotent Administrators" and "Ultrafeminines" respectively.

Cleaver's analysis of social imagery defining civic relations and public policy thus takes him from sexuality to class and caste, and so the mind is whiteness, which is "weakness, frailty, cowardice and effeminacy," which is the feminine, which is antithetical to the body, where body is "strength, brute power, force, virility, and physical beauty," which is blackness, which is the masculine (180). Each of the social subjects thus conceptualized suffers from a bifurcating confusion over the location of power. On the one hand power is in the heads of white men as administrators and in the bodies of black men as the laboring force but, on the other, a black man taking back administration of his body takes power out of the hands of white men. Thus power, divided between white minds and black bodies, is either split among men or monopolized. Women black or white, attracted or repelled, can only oscillate between these opposite poles defining social relations (= world).

The poles of attraction as loci of power are predicated on these oppositions, where white women seek the real men, therefore black men, created to "touch that magic spot in her mind which triggers the mechanism of her orgasm" (188). For their part black women seek white men because "the urges and needs of the Amazon's psyche move her toward the source of power" (188). At the same time, however, the black woman can never find fulfillment, because she is also attracted to the "Supermasculine Menial" (= body) although she cannot respect his disempowerment (= castration), and so Cleaver leaves black women "lost between two worlds" (188).

Although this construction means that both black women and men are exiled, the equation of power with balls and penises with weapons means the black man alone is the hope of the nation, since of all the elements it is the "Menials" who are "least alienated from the biological chain" that determines the proper sociopolitical order (188). If in the late nineteenth century and early twentieth century white men implemented biological sciences for policy to diagnose the politically disenfranchised as a national disease, as a mid-twentieth-century black nationalist, Cleaver reverses the qualities attached to black and white men's bodies, and nothing is in fact displaced because women as metaphors and bodies still serve as the (impure) ground on which men debate each other's nature, sins, and condition. And in a perfect catch-22, it is precisely their status as objects of national/men's debates that makes women biologically impure, politically suspect.

Power here is desire + the ability to (en)act, the prerogative of men, the facility triggering desire in women. Thus, as a sexual concept lesbians, as women desiring women and generating desire in women, become a political concept, the penultimate of power unnaturally oscillating among women. The sexual, and so in Cleaver's eyes political, exile of men—the negation of the equation between penises, balls, and power— makes lesbians uninterpolatable by the national(ist) narrative, cold to the man-nation's call. Because sex = politics, lesbians are "frigid," which is the absolute of woman's treason through failing to acknowledge the terms on which the war is constituted; their sexual disinterest in men becomes a political failure to fight for men's power over women as territory. What is implicit in Newton and Seale is explicit here: the terms of the black national front require the centrality of and submission to the heterosexual black male body as a measure of national and personal health.

Cleaver's metahistorical narrative is ultimately the apotheosis of his personal sexual dilemmas, narrated in "On Becoming," where evolves the supreme desirability of the sex of the black male body into a locus of power and strategy for liberation, and its terms are taken up by both Huey Newton and Bobby Seale as gospel. If in writing the process of giving birth to himself Cleaver cited LeRoi Jones's command to rape the men (violating enemy ranks) and kill the women (unstable elements in the enemy population), his love of men and of "the beauty of the brute body" (164) return in the prophetic language of his metahistories, elaborated in "The Allegory of the Black Eunuchs," "Convalescence," and again in "The Primeval Mitosis." There he describes in detail the "strength, brute power, force, virility, and physical beauty" (185) of the black male body in the act of giving sexual satisfaction, which is for him the culmination of black manhood, the pillar of revolution: "It will be no big thing for him to do since he can handle those Amazons down there with him, with his strong body, rippling muscles, his strength and fire, the driving force of his spine, the thrust of his hips and the fiery steel of his rod" (185). As a political narrative, this carries the old teleology Cleaver claimed to have abandoned with apologies as he moved from having conquered black women with his penis/weapon to seeking white women as a metonym for the enemy-state. The ecstatic description of the physical beauty and sexual prowess of the black male body becomes the vehicle for the apotheosis of public-political revolutionary aesthetics.

In Cleaver's allegory, none of the other players can match him, although everyone wants him. And since sex is power and desire is politics, the climax of his sexual desire (political power) takes on the terms of national development as it builds. The complex interactions outlined above are crystal clear as the sexual union of black men and white women becomes a revolutionary apocalypse: "But what wets the Ultrafeminine's juice is that she is allured and tortured by the secret, intuitive knowledge that he, her psychic bridegroom, can blaze through the wall of her ice, plumb her psychic depths, test the oil of her soul, melt the iceberg in her brain, touch her inner sanctum, detonate the bomb of her orgasm, and bring her sweet release" (185–86). Because for Cleaver "race fears are weapons in the struggle between the Omnipotent Administrator and the Supermasculine Menial for control of sexual sovereignty" (190) (that is, control of women's and men's bodies) white women who surrender become terrain on which the development of the black nation is predicated.

Struggling to capture the moment of orgasm when black men rescue white women from the "imprisoning, enslaving, and suffocating experience of the bourgeois family" (Newton 91), Cleaver's narrative fragments and grabs at snatches of national metaphors as if for ground or air. Thus the white woman's vagina becomes territory that is drilled for oil where the black penis is the technology of development; the white woman becomes the terrain of the world, stretching from the "Arctic" to the "Antarctic" (184); the insertion of the black penis into the white vagina becomes the invasion of the "inner sanctum" of the "Omnipotent Administrator's" territory, treason on the part of "the women of the elite" and so victory for the black man; the fiery steel of his rod is allegorized in making her (white territory) recognize she was always his; the munitional superiority of the U.S. state that brought World War II to an abrupt end becomes the mushroom cloud of her orgasms, closing the circle split at the beginning of time, "The Primeval Mitosis." Coming together, the black man and the white woman "achieve the supreme identity in the Apocalyptic Fusion" (177). All narratives converge in the black male body, and thus biological/sexual miscegenation—the counterpart of white men inseminating black women—here is mirrored in the politics of black men reclaiming their minds.

In societies based both on and beyond racial class/caste oppression, it would seem, the mulatto, as a subject signaling sexual/biological/political union, is at the silent center. To claim the concept of mulatto as an end or an origin, however, as in Hopkins, is to acknowledge transculturation as a national historical/biological fact, and so accept the history of white U.S. strategies, paradigms, and language in conditioning black culture as much as the terms of revolt. Because there is "the Primeval Urge to transcend the Primeval Mitosis" (188) white culture is in historical decay—"the attribute of sovereignty was reposited in the male hemisphere"—and so the black penis is the weapon of choice. History, including the history of biological/political cross-fertilization, becomes a paradigm of malignancy, and sex a paradigm for war. "Power comes out of the lips of a pussy," a revolutionary Cleaver tells his rallies, and "Power comes out of the barrel of the dick" (Seale 247). These elaborate metaphors become the precepts for conceptualizing power and revolution because they serve to transform the old new men into revolutionaries. For Bobby Seale, *Soul on Ice* and "The Primeval Mitosis" must be read and reread by BPP members, as it is essential to bringing "history to the threshold," "to the front of a liberation movement . . . right here . . . in the belly of the monster" because it "unbrainwash[es] *everybody in society* . . . black, white, blue, green, yellow, red, polka dot" (262). For Seale, *Soul on Ice* is key to understanding the extent to which these pathological ideologies, disseminated through institutions and backed by the armed forces, have the power to run the world in running black/white/mulatto consciousness, and the social imaginary.

*Love among the Troops: The Problem of Male Bonding*

*The masculine "We"*
Despite the consistency with which the constituency of the vanguard was narrowed, both Seale and Newton spoke out in broad terms to characterize the leadership (the "I") and its relation to the national community (the "We") in order to displace the accusations of isolationism aimed at Black Power groups—as to all nationalist groups—from the Congress of Racial Equality:

> I can always talk about myself as an individual. Huey can talk about himself as an individual. At the same time we always tell black people, "We don't give a fuck whether you're wearing a pimp suit, whether you're wearing an African gown, whether you've got a natural on, whether you're wearing a Black Panther uniform, whether you live in Africa, whether you're over in Vietnam, because wherever you are, the racists and imperialists will brutalize, murder, and oppress you, because they've been doing it for 400 years and they're still practicing it." (Seale 252)

This recognition looks to conceptualize the position of the black community in an international frame. It writes their platform, born in love as anger and the drive to connect the divided world community of color, as complementing an attempt to take back black neighborhoods in order to feed, clothe, educate, and nurture as elaborated in the BPP ten-point program. Their platform's actualization requires love as tenderness, in Newton's insightful terms, the revolutionary recognition that "I, we, all of us are the one and the multitude" (332).

Newton had said that there could be no compromise, and so there are only two alternatives for the future. Both are termed "suicide," the one "revolutionary," the death of the individual and his rebirth as the community (love as tenderness), the other "reactionary" (love as anger) as defined in Eldridge Cleaver, the refusal to nurture, leading to defection from the community, exile. The language here is again of a black state, but Newton sees in Cleaver that "his ideology was based on the rhetoric of violence; his speeches abounded in either/or absolutes, like 'pick up the gun or remain a snivelling coward'" (331). The militarization of the BPP initiated under Newton and Seale and carried to the extreme by Cleaver was meant initially as an act of love as tenderness, to show the people "the colonizers and their agents—the police—are not bullet proof" (329), and in the end the BPP was concerned to implement "military tactics made public for political reasons" (330).

Newton was not speaking of Cleaver alone, however, when he recognizes that what "appealed to him were force, firepower, and the intense moment when combatants stood at the brink of death. *For him this was the revolution*" (330–31).[14] For Newton, this means Cleaver was in political exile long before he was in physical exile, and in a typical move Bobby Seale will try to heal the wound. This political alienation that Newton identifies in Cleaver, putting confrontation with the state over the birth of the revolutionary community and nurturing the nation, Newton recognizes as a "suicidal gesture," and so signals that the quality of the (nurturing) relation between the BPP cadres and the men on the street will make or break the revolution (331).

The ability of the BPP to organize and recruit what they called the lumpen proletariat stands as an unimpeachable testament to their commitment to grassroots black organization and liberation.[15] But because the terrain here is the street, the players are all men. Although the Black Panther Party program calls for liberation on ten fronts, the reconceptualization of the black nation for the transformation of the old men into new men fixes on one: the deployment of the gun, the conception of national cadres as military cadres. And in the new theater of the electronic media and the community, BPP confrontations begin to unravel the place of black men in the Constitution; opening, like the Los Angeles riots of 1992, onto the deconstruction of the national dialogue on race relations. Thus the barbaric South is revealed in the West, as in the North: antebellum dehumanization persisting in postbellum police procedure; the responses of the local police and white mobs in the South reproduced in the enemy-state's police departments, including Hoover's FBI; the exile of black citizens from the rights mandated by the Second, Ninth, and Fourteenth Amendments to the Constitution, concretized in the image of armed state forces at a local and federal level marshaled to harass and massacre black men who dare to organize segments of the black ghetto community within the social spaces reserved for white citizens. There are two logics at work here: the laws of the white nationalist nation-state and the dynamics of BPP epistemes.

The contradictions in the rhetoric of the relations between men and women, women and women, men and men, and BPP and community resolve themselves for Newton in "death born in love." The strategy of revolutionary suicide he gives as "an old African saying" (332) but the resonances of Latin American revolutionary language are not accidental, and neither, to a certain extent, are the resonances between Newton and Che Guevara, both of whom are worshiped by their cadres for their capacity to love and, by means of this love, their ability to birth a revolutionary nation.

Complications immediately arise because the concept of love, the key to King's non-violence movement, is tied up in the concept of the feminine; woman to woman, man to woman, woman to man, love must always be tied to women's bodies, or among family, or to the family house. In practice, love as tenderness among (political) men becomes a suspect thing, and between black men and "the man," intentionally or not, defines punks—that is, betrayal as both a personal and a national political concept. Love elevated to black national strategy is thus political homosexuality, according to the terms on which nonviolence is rejected, contaminating the virility of love among the troops, of cadres of men organizing through love and faith by denying them weapons—bodies, penises, claws.

This feminine contamination asserts itself through the specter of political weakness as homosexuality; and so Martin Luther King Jr., James Baldwin, Baynard Rustin—leaders from the earlier generation—are accused of softness and of a willful femininity (tenderness toward the white nation) as opposed to real liberation through the recognition of black men as castrated (anger toward the white nation), or else of accepting castration as fact rather than engaging in warfare to reassert black manhood and win back black men's balls, and so black freedom. Nevertheless, in *Seize the Time* consistently, and *Revolutionary Suicide* persistently, it is love and tenderness that are called on to structure the New Man's relation to the "We" of the black community, as surely as anger and rejection structure the New Man's relation to the dominant ethno-ideological stance of the enemy-state. In Bobby Seale's testimonial, Huey Newton, and to a lesser extent Eldridge Cleaver, gain their heroic status on the basis of their tender love for the people, and thus their ability to speak to and for "the brothers on the streets" considered criminals and hooligans by the enemy-state. Cleaver even goes so far as to postulate to Seale that Huey Newton is to Malcolm X as Jesus Christ was to John the Baptist (Seale 264).

### The baddest motherfucker ever to set foot in history

Bobby Seale's testimonial from prison of the Black Panther Party is also a story of a love between himself and Huey Newton, as much as the story of a love between Newton and the community. The inaugural chapter of *Seize the Time* tells "Who I Am," a recitation of Seale's alienation from the nationalist narrative of the United States, first through the lever of identification with Native Americans, then through a fascination with rediscovering Africa, and so himself. But chapter 2 is "I meet Huey" and this is where the story of Newton and Seale begins, before the story of the BPP; indeed, the friendship of Seale and Newton becomes the paragon of men bonding in revolution, the new "I/We."

Newton becomes all things to Seale: lawyer, political prisoner, "philosophical theoretician," "practitioner," "head director," "top official spokesman," "Minister of Defense," "leader" (13), "nigger," "descendant of slaves," "the baddest motherfucker ever to set foot in history" (xii). It is only after Cleaver defects from the BPP and tries to take its leadership from him that Newton sees Cleaver as a reactionary, in love with the gun but not with the community. Seale sees the problem with Cleaver in the beginning, but defers to Newton because he "just had a tendency to follow Huey" (133). Seale points out he is not ashamed of this, suggesting some discomfort with public perception of his position, his definitional feminization as a follower perhaps, but it is also like Bobby Hutton to Bunchy Carter, another paradigmatic relationship in the training of new men, a child, a student, an apostle, an admirer: "I just followed him, and listened to him and tried to understand what he was saying. If I disagreed with him, I tried to disagree properly" (133).

For his part, Newton looks for Seale when he gets out of prison. Seale's alienation from the black organizations at hand (particularly the "punks, intellectual, jive, motherfucking cultural nationalists" of the San Francisco Black Panther Party under Roy Ballard,[16] and the "cultural nationalists" and "pig, black racists [who] really work with the structure against their own people . . . out of a psychological need to hate white people just because of the color of their skin" [271] of Ron Karenga's United Slaves organization) becomes the catalyst for a new relationship. They meet to solve some of the ideological problems of the Black Power movement, "chew[ing] over the political situation, our social problems, and the merits or shortcomings of other groups" (Newton 111), which means discovering why no black political strategy has succeeded and what kind of black organization could.

But in narrating the details of this alliance, it is clear that wherever Newton goes Seale will follow, and that Seale, with the martyr Bobby Hutton, becomes a metonym for the "thousands of us," the "We" within whom the revolutionary must lose his individualist self-conception in order to birth a revolutionary nation, and nurture it into freedom. Seale's dedication is for Newton, Newton's is for Bobby Hutton.

*Either way, their desire is always criminal*
Inherent in the concept of new men (I, leaders) loving men ("We," man-nation) is the expulsion of the "punk" as the locus of disease, the sex metaphor in BPP ideology for black men enslaved and turned by the enemy. Behind the political concept of the "punk" sits the sexual concept of homosexuality. According to Minister of Information Cleaver:

> Many Negro homosexuals, acquiescing in [a] racial death-wish, are outraged and frustrated because in their sickness they are unable to have a baby by a white man. The cross they have to bear is that, already bending over and touching their toes for the white man, the fruit of their miscegenation is not the little half-white offspring of their dreams but an increase in the unwinding of their nerves—though they redouble their efforts and intake of white man's sperm. . . . Homosexuality is a sickness, just as are baby-rape or wanting to become the head of General Motors. (102, 110)

The familiar terms replay themselves, and in Cleaver's investigation into the politics of interpersonal relationships, homosexuals are criminals to be expunged from the black body politic. And, as we have seen, because sexual submission to the penis as a body part is the equivalent of surrender in macropolitical power relations, carrying the weight of betrayal, homosexuals, like women seeking control, misappropriate men's balls and thus are treasonous in the midst of a revolution. The black body and desire properly belong to the Panther ideology, even as the Panther revolution claims itself as a haven of black freedom.

The black gay men and lesbians under deep cover within the cadres of the BPP are invisible to the leadership of the revolutionary community. Chief among the reasons they remained in the struggle is inevitably the recognition that the details of the reasoning behind Cleaver's macropolitical analysis are the same as his analysis of the position of all black men. And although Cleaver does not realize it, his distinction between homosexuality and heterosexuality—a difference structuring a revolutionary universe of men meeting men—evaporates: "The white man has deprived him of his masculinity, castrated him in the center of his burning skull" (103).

When Cleaver is not transforming gay black men into women, then, the position of gay black men is the position of all black men, although Cleaver wants to see capitulation as the reason for the pathologization of homosexual desire. When gay men are seen as women, the terms for their dismissal are the same; that is, sexual difference as political betrayal, expressed as their willingness to take white men to bed. Either way, their desire is always criminal, sexuality joining the place of gender in Cleaver's outlaw state and race in the status quo. James Baldwin's criticism of Norman Mailer and Richard Wright, then, becomes attacks on "black masculinity," "a despicable underground guerilla war" (109). The community of the exiled coalesces in the figure of the "punk" in whom the treachery of women reaches critical proportions because it is cased in the body of a man, an embodiment of the nation betraying itself.

The meaning of "punk" as a political concept becomes even clearer when Martin Luther King Jr. is set against the true manhood of Bigger Thomas and comes up lacking—the former's treason and womanly nature exposed in his "self-effacing love for his oppressors" (106). But having exiled from the revolution women (which would include lesbians), gay men, and "Martin Luther King-type[s]"—together making up the statistical majority of the black community—the irony of condemning "North American reality" for having "hate hold sway in love's true province," "a rank perversion" that turns "the two-dollar trick of wedding violence to love and sex to hate," is, like the concept of democracy, lost on Cleaver (108). Because there are no people here, only pawns and concepts, there is, as we have seen repeatedly, no distinction between love as a personal act and collective love as politics. In its place we find men gestating a (man)nation, the masculinization of mothering.

The problem concepts of a black homosexuality (= men ≠ men) permeate the militarization of the black community so conceived. Cleaver's revelatory concept metaphors of black male failure recur in his public love letter to black women in describing himself and "all black men" as "a snivelling craven, a funky punk, a vile, groveling bootlicker, with my will to oppose petrified by a cosmic fear of the Slavemaster" (209). The disease in Cleaver's eye when he looks at Baldwin, and by his own extension black gay men in the nation and so the movement, his sense of self-hatred and loss of black manhood, combined with his helplessness in the face of the black male body in the sex act, thus finds its articulation here in the struggle to express his loss of his balls, in black men's betrayal of the black body politic, the black "eunuch" and his love, his drive to connect. To capture the diseased body of the "punk," like "woman," is to seize the emblem of national defeat, a treasonous impulse within, and the defining interlocutor is always the white male penis and the power of its offshoot, the might of the enemy-state.

*The politics of homosexuality*

In this world of male fixation with the company of men and male bodies to the point of exclusion of women (except as reproductive organs, prizes, and helpmeets), a pathology emerges, a phobia, within which sexual desire emerges as an epistemological crisis when facing the social order, characterized by a cultivated need by some in male culture—gay and straight—to withhold from women equal access to power, with men predicating their value on the subordination of women and the feminine. The constant, defensive emphasis on the performance of masculinity, a performance eroticized, if differently, in both gay and straight male culture, leads in the end to men's alienation from women.[17] This "hommosexuality" (a term I present to mean homosociality combined with a blunt sexism), as a sociopolitical concept incorporating masculinist power, desire, and sexuality, we can postulate as the obverse of something we can call "homosexuality," a term defined by Huey Newton as men seeking "tenderness and vulnerability and love" from men (252).

We can look briefly at two polemical writings from two of the strongest black male voices of the late 1960s, and see how the terms of hommosexuality and homosexuality elaborated by one of the old men and one of the new, James Baldwin and LeRoi Jones, operate in the shifting terrain occupied by the new men and revolutionaries. Baldwin's *Tell Me How Long the Train's Been Gone* (1968) takes up the recognition and rearticulation of relations between three generations of men through the terms of love and anger in men loving men. Here, just as Leo Proudhammer represents the old men in his dreams of troubled integration, Christopher represents the new in his refusal of the American Dream for a new revolutionary movement that demands black men pick up the gun. Their love affair renders explicit Baldwin's perception that for the leaders of the 1950s and 1960s the healing of the man-nation is equivalent to acceptance of love between men, and the love of fathers for sons and sons for fathers, as much as sexual love.

In this novel of healing, however, women are consistently exiled. Black women disappear from the penultimate configuration altogether; Barbara, the white woman standing with them in the triangle of companions anchoring the novel, becomes once more the ground across which both men struggle and with whom sexual relations must be superseded by the struggle for what is ultimately only an alliance between them. Barbara becomes a metonym of the American Dream for the older man, and a proving ground of manhood for the younger.[18] The pact between the two men in the end is a healing. Yet this healing, in which their mutual recognition creates a political bond that stretches into the bedroom and out onto the street, rests on something one step removed from a vanguard given its exclusion of a meaningful social pact with women. The emotional pact between Leo and Christopher as a social pact between the old men and the new, whose political position incorporates homosexuality, thus looks to concretize a phobia that persists at the root of the men-leader's conceptualization of a revolutionary movement for civil rights, a hommosexuality of black male politics at mid-century. In the end Leo finds himself offstage waiting for a cue, and Christopher disappears into the anonymity of the enraged urban black masses of the ghetto.

In making this choice Christopher must opt to make secret his sexual desire. The assault on the body of black gay men has been seen as the ritual projection of a historical violence burning in the black man's chest, a desire always already operating as an internalization of macropolitical forces. Yet all of the players, including Huey Newton, recognize this projection back into the community as black on black crime, and gunplay between men the elaboration of micrological battles on a macrological stage.[19] Imamu Baraka's (LeRoi Jones) infamous playlet "The Toilet" (1964) takes up the problem of love between men as well, but in the terms of the New Men faced with a crisis within the ranks and in the constitution of the black community: the leader of the gang loves the man that he orders abducted by his cadre and finds beaten in the public toilet, a social space reserved for the disposal of the unclean, a public space itself unclean.

In the closing moments of the play the leader, "weeping and cradling the head in his arms" (404), comes back to kneel and embrace the beaten black body of one he loves, but only in private. The scenario, set entirely in the toilet to which he as leader has brought them, characterizes the anger that makes black men assault black men and drag them down into the "impersonal ugliness" of the wet and stinking room (389–90). Within the nationalist context this toilet on stage comes to function as a "liberated area," a black-controlled equivalent of the white prison's soul-breaker, a privatized hole in the new nation where men must confront their bodies, power, love, and mind-body relationships.

Baraka's playlet recognizes that there is no public or secure private place in the new nation of new men for a love that binds the leaders to the most violently oppressed within the black man-nation. At stake here again is the (re)constitution of masculinity and the superceding of fear that makes the new man. In flight from the feminine, political black masculinity at mid-twentieth century becomes predicated in everyday life on the homosocial anxiety of failing to suppress homoerotic desire, the failure to bond with and be equal to the patriarchies of the world.[20] In the psychology of black sociopolitical movements, for both Baldwin (circuitously) and Baraka (explicitly), gayness and women "become the 'other' against which . . . men project their identities, against whom they stack the decks so as to compete in a situation in which they will always win, so that by suppressing them, men can stake a claim for their own manhood" (Kimmel, "Masculinity" 134).[21] The political dilemma of this contradiction encapsulates the tensions between violence and tenderness within political black male communities in its focus on the psycho-social and political cost of (black) male fear, and the problem of love. For as Cleaver points out in his diatribe against Baldwin, black gay men ("punks") suffer the violence at black hands that black heterosexual men ("niggers") suffer at the hands of the police, the Klan, and the white mob.

*Men seeking tenderness and vulnerability and love from men*
Huey Newton analyzes encounters with sex in prison in his testimonial, and what he sees reveals that he cannot see these men as they cannot see him, and that this blindness causes his own reconceptualization of him-self, the world, and the prison in terms recognizable as the feminine. His reading of these encounters begins with the usual emphasis on sexual desire. Here, as in Hopkins, the architecture of this privatized space will carry with it the architecture of the nation. The locus for these sex crimes is not the house in the city but its obverse, the prison in the country. We have already noted that in the mind of the revolutionary who has seen, however, the distinction is precarious, and the prison is only an extreme and naked embodiment of the ghetto as a colony.

In this particular prison, where Newton will encounter men seeking sex with men, there is a difference he seizes on to explain his political exiling of the inmates that raises questions about the extent to which he sees the enemy-state ideology working to divide the nation. As opposed to a norm of "more than 50 percent of the prison population" fewer than 10 percent here are Black or Chicano, and so there are no riots, and it becomes "a model prison" in state propaganda. White men, remember, degenerate into the feminine. If the physical architecture divides this population into four quadrants that never meet, the sexual-therefore-political architecture "very important" to its model status is 80 percent "homosexual"—a term I put in quotation marks because Newton's defi-nition constantly shifts. Here "homosexuals are docile and subservient; they tend to obey prison regulations" (Newton 251). At once we can recognize the terms for the old men, the domesticated ones.

If the problem of the revolutionary vanguard is to convert a population acculturated to subserviency, Newton dismisses the founding tenets of the BPP's lumpen ideology to fall back on nineteenth-century biological determinism.[22] For these men, politicization is hard because they are "men who lived largely for the next sexual encounter" (251). If, as we noted earlier, one of the functions of women's bodies was to use desire for sexual encounters to bring the lumpen on the street into the BPP offices for training, and later to control BPP members through the denial of sexual favors, then these men take on the face of these lumpen so conceived.

But without the sexual promise of women's bodies in the flesh, Newton finds himself put in a woman's place where he is seen as a body primarily for sex—the street strategies of male-male consciousness-raising breaking down—and so Newton is at a loss. Men seeking "love and vulnerability and tenderness" (Newton's ultimate definition of "homosexuals") from men imprisoned with them are seen less as responding to the violence of incarceration—or articulating "tenderness" and "love" within an oppressed community that Newton later recognizes the state has taught the nation to scapegoat—than in terms of the old rhetoric of the state, a "perversion" that puts men seeking men beyond the rights of citizens. In seeing gayness as beyond the reach of the revolutionary, and gay men in the position of drug addicts, Newton's "revolutionary rhetoric" reproduces the logics of the enemy-state, justifying incarceration and disenfranchisement. The leader of the New Men thus falls back on the epistemes of a sexual degeneracy that white supremacist ideologues ascribe to blacks as a race, genetically beyond responsible politicization, and so their embodiment as "perversion" takes them, like Cleaver's black women (188), to the other side, lost between two worlds.

Nevertheless, the terms by which these lost men are known remain the same as for the old nation and the lumpen, "exploited and controlled by the guards and the system" deprived of the "normal yearning for dignity and freedom" (251–52). Although Newton's stated percentage of gay men in the prison seems more to refer to a basic fact of prison life than to a position on the spectrum of sexuality, the primacy of sexual desire over political redemption puts Huey himself in the position of a woman who finds all attempts at political dialogue a pick-up under duress. And so attempts at conscientization for mutual liberation are defeated by men's overriding interest in sexual encounters, in "love and vulnerability and tenderness" that Newton sees here "distorted into functions of power, competition, and control" (252) and not in his own experiments with women's behavior and psychological and emotional limits.

The encounter with what Newton considers gay desire in prison thus takes us back to the problem of revolution in the family house. Definitions of love, freedom, body, mind, school, house, and prison, key terms in elaborating the dynamics of black exploitation by white nationalist policies, come back to haunt the movement. In locating black pathology in the exile of black men opposed to or invested in the use and abuse of black women as political subjects, the narrative of liberation spirals back, with an ever-shrinking circumference, until the only ones left standing are the men-leaders and their mirror image. By meeting FBI strategies—of isolation, of turning the revolutionary community against itself—halfway, the revolutionary defense group devours itself on one hand, and on the other withdraws at each epistemic turn from a fundamental inclusion of the social groups together constituting the black national majority.

*Love among the troops*

In the end, the community programs born of the revolutionaries' love binding the leaders to the community were forgone in favor of point 7 of the BPP platform, the "immediate end to POLICE BRUTALITY and MURDER of Black people," which meant the arming of the BPP and its definition as an urban guerrilla group, although Newton, like other Panther group leaders coming later, will recognize this as derailment. In hindsight, Newton sees that the Panthers succeeded most in making public the police brutality that was a routine part of ghetto life, and still is. Calls for employment, housing, education, the trial of black citizens by their peers, community input in policing neighborhoods, and an end to the exploitative inevitabilities of capitalism fall by the wayside, and by 1973 Newton notes, even as he attacks Cleaver for his defection, that the Panthers "were looked upon as an ad hoc military group, acting outside of the community fabric and too radical to be a part of it" (329).

Even as Newton struggles to understand in political terms what has happened, the gap between the "we" of the Panthers and the "We" of the community widens:

> We saw ourselves as the revolutionary "vanguard" and did not fully understand then that only the people can create revolution. At any rate, for two or three years, our image in the community was intimidating. The people misunderstood us and did not follow our lead in picking up the gun. At the time, there was no clear solution to this dilemma. We were a young revolutionary group seeking answers and ways to alleviate racism. We had chosen to confront an evil head on and within the limits of the law. But perhaps our military strategy was too much of "a great leap forward." (329)

Ultimately the split between the "we" projected by the revolutionary vanguard and the community they sought to represent, precisely the problem of democracy that Newton and Seale had identified in earlier, competing black political vehicles, is vast enough to swallow up the BPP as it then stood. The intimidation of the ghetto community by armed men (the white police) was thus ultimately reproduced as the means to the end of liberation.

# 6

## A Politics of Change:
## Sistren, Subalternity, and the Social Pact
## in the War for Democratic Socialism

■

Ah wanted di leadership to base pon some better foundation dat tek account a women and children. Ah wanted we as a people to work togedder by some principle and not just like a outlaw business. Ah wanted leaders dat would look pon di way how dem do tings and not just what dem preach or di tings dem give we.—Sistren

Up to 1976, the .365 Magnum was the deadliest weapon in common use in the political battle. . . . The 1980 campaign was to be dominated by the M16 rifle. —Prime Minister Michael Manley

In the 1970s, some twenty years into the history of development theory, the emphasis on strategies for raising per capita income and gross national product (GNP) had led to an emphasis on the macroeconomic sphere.[1] "Development" was seen as coterminous with "industrialization," and "backwardness" and "underdevelopment" with an agriculturally based economy.[2] Social welfare, in many instances the ends of conceptualizing "development," was expected to arise naturally as a byproduct of industrialization.[3] Up to the collapse of the Soviet Union, perhaps because of this concern with the national welfare, "progressive" or "people-oriented" development theory had, taking marxism as its base, sought to develop a theory of economic growth that would bring workers from the countryside and workers in the cities into the social and political process, and thus used strategies of national mobilization in the internal implementation of developmental targets. It is here, in the specifics of implementation, that the gender neutrality of the language broke down in taking account of women and children.[4]

Such questions about the integration of women into developmental paradigms provide a critical context for Prime Minister Michael Manley's program of Democratic Socialism in 1970s Jamaica, as well as for Sistren and *Lionheart Gal: Life Stories of Jamaican Women*, the focus of this chapter. For lurking behind the terms of "agriculture" and "industrialization" is a gendered division of labor. In cases where data has been gathered, it is women in the underdeveloped countries who do most of the work associated with agriculture. And in the industrial sectors, apart from the superexploitative export processing zones, men are given pride of place over women seeking employment. The problem is that women's work remains invisible in much of the data gathered until very recently.[5] Further, as Hilary Beckles points out in confirmation of Wilson Harris's suspicions of the notions of proper governance at the moment of Independence:

> The construction of the nation-state as the final victory for anti-colonial forces carried within its very conception and design several layers of enforced agreement that quickly emerged as the new and revised oppressive hegemony. Emphasis upon national unity as the ultimate social condition meant that political contests over inequitable ownership and control of productive resources, women's objection to masculinist domination of public institutions, resistance to racism against peoples of African descent in everyday life, and the critique of socio-cultural privileges attained by representatives of white supremacy ideologies, were oftentimes presented as hostile to the national interest. Newly politically empowered men, described as "founding fathers" of nation-states, who in fact were essentially leaders of political parties and corporate institutions, defined and declared what was the national interest and how it should be protected. They alone finally determined who were the supporters and enemies of the nation, and which discourses were nation-building and which were subversive. . . . Tokenism [toward women's issues] and paternalism . . . ran rampant within the formative years of post-colonialism. ("Historicising Slavery" 48)

At the intersection of poverty and women, the largest single social sector in underdeveloped countries, a cycle of disenfranchisement feeding underdevelopment emerges: the women reject government politics as undemocratic, the politicians neglect—if not reject—poor women's knowledges and their role as national resources and as people, with the women's rejection feeding the latter as surely as the latter feeds the former. Patriarchal dominance by men in the household often seals the severance of the social pact within the home itself. Certainly, the critical microeconomic work of the reproduction of labor has been rendered irrelevant or taken for granted, and thus invisible at the macroeconomic heights.

At the macrological level of national statistics, the unpaid work of women in the agricultural sphere, particularly at the subsistence level, has gone largely unrecorded. Janet Momsen tells us that in the eastern Caribbean, where there is a high rate of male migration to the cities, women control 35 percent of small farm production outright (*Women and Development* 50). In the highly patriarchal East Indian community of Trinidad, however, that percentage plummets to 0. Indeed, although men undertake 100 percent of the work of soil preparation and 84 percent of pest control, women are left to undertake the majority of the work of weeding, fertilizing, harvesting, taking care of livestock, and so on. Lurking behind this "and so on" is work that includes prenatal care, child rearing, overseeing children's growth and education, feeding the family, and serving the sexual and ego needs of the husband. Gender's role in the division of work, as a form of social control, thus directly affects production. Women as a whole remain super-disenfranchised in these processes, in terms of accounts of labor expended and the range of tasks for which they are held personally responsible in relation to decision-making power and visibility in national surveys of farmers, land use and resource implementation, and programs for ameliorating the living conditions of "the people."

The preponderance of women workers in the export processing zones, with their emphasis on service industries opening the way for women, merely compounds the problems with the veneer of "progress." Women workers make up the majority of those employed in this futile attempt at regional development, but only because they form a large labor pool inexperienced in manufacturing whose socialization has revolved around deference to men, and it is not by accident that it is men who in turn make up the managerial cadres.[6] Locally, in turn, when training and modernization programs are offered as part of agrarian reform projects, men have received the lion's share of places and materials because they are seen as the decision makers, and because women are seen as less trustworthy.

The position of women in the conceptualization of national development has been changing, however, as a result of pressures from within and outside the evolving Caribbean state (Barriteau 186). It was Ester Boserup's *Women's Role in Economic Development* that proved to be the turning point in rethinking "development" from the perspective of the equal inclusion of women as women. As Lynn Bolles argues, after Boserup documented a division of labor by sex through empirical evidence, feminist development economists have contended with the idea that "modernization and development policies have more often than not resulted in a deterioration of women's status which was akin to their exclusion from 'productive' economic activities" ("Theories of Women" 23). Roughly twenty years later, after most of the West Indies gained political independence, Peggy Antrobus's 1970 "Women in Development Programmes" traces a similar problematic with the old New International Economic Order, where women's integration was addressed as an addendum, exemplifying the West Indian states' resistance to recognizing that there is a division of labor at the level of sex as well as nations (37).

Introducing gender as a central vector of analysis, as we saw earlier in Pauline Hopkins, turns agendas and assumptions inside out because it introduces not only women as a component but the centrality of the domestic sphere as well. These conceptual problems bear down on government and World Bank policy with a vengeance.[7] Within the 1975 development strategies jointly designed by the Inter-American Commission of Women, the Women and Development Unit at the University of the West Indies, the Women's Desk of the Caribbean Community and Common Market, and the Adviser on Women's Affairs at the Economic Commission for Latin America and the Caribbean, for example, three principles were established worth quoting in full:

> a. *existentialist*, focusing on the creation of new human relationships,
> b. *egalitarian*, focusing on a list of concrete claims and demands intended to "integrate women into the mainstream development activities,"
> c. *anti-capitalist*, which sees the inequality of women as the conse-

quence of economic and social structures embedded in the capitalist system and which would subordinate the liberation of women to the overthrow of this. (Antrobus, "Women in Development" 40)

In other words, the joint commission sought a new social pact for women with the nation-state, one that Democratic Socialism would attempt to incorporate into a new political economic agenda for development.

With attempts at implementation, however, it became clear that the distinctions posed in the catchwords of the Mexico City World Conference of nation-states—"Equality" (First World advocated), "Development" (Third World advocated), and "Peace" (Second World/Eastern bloc advocated)—break down when brought to bear on the case of women in development programs. Peggy Antrobus tells us that women working on specific development projects recognized "the intricate connections between the three goals": "For instance, the link between the existence of gender hierarchies in the home (*Equality*) and women's access to resources which would determine the quality of their contribution to *Development;* or the link between male-female sex stereotyping (*Equality*) and violence at personal and social levels (*Peace*) or the link between the level of expenditures on militarization (*Peace*) and the availability of funds for social and economic programmes (*Development*)" ("Women in Development" 44). Jamaica under Michael Manley was a notable exception in the struggle to integrate women into the political restructuring of Caribbean countries and reconceptualizing national development.[8] It was in this new political climate that the social and political condition of poor women became a national concern. Democratic Socialism, as Manley's program has come to be called, lived a short and violent life (1972–1980). In its aftermath, Manley was chief among those seeking to explain its logics and the reasons for its failure.

As a group of life stories coming out of Democratic Socialism, however, *Lionheart Gal: Life Stories of Jamaican Women,* a collection of fourteen testimonials produced by a Jamaican women's advocacy group known as the Sistren Collective, holds the seeds for an alternate history and evaluation of the events of the 1970s. At stake is a battle over history, and the nature of the social pact with the nation. Manley's developmental schemes for Jamaica, starting from a reconceptualization of "progress" as the democratization of the state, tried to assimilate this new understanding of the position of women in development to integrate women into a new national agenda. The new political climate signaled by Democratic Socialism is thus the result of a renewal of the promise of a democratic social pact between the government and the people.

In the rest of this chapter, I put the testimonials of Sistren as women's narratives in dialogue with narratives of Manley's Democratic Socialism. Here the political narratives of Democratic Socialism's chief architect and political economic histories of the Jamaican government's experiment have come to constitute state histories as narratives of failure. *Lionheart Gal* offers a reading from the perspective of the nation's poor, in whose name Democratic Socialism was launched.

I have arranged my readings in this chapter into five interwoven sections. I begin with a very brief reading of Michael Manley's analysis of Democratic Socialism. In the process, I touch briefly on the statistical records of Democratic Socialism (1972–1980) to raise the issues of women's role in state narratives, of subalternity, of what I call "higgler" economics, and of the question of violence in the social order as it relates to women. In the second section, I go on to analyze the political emergence of Sistren out of Democratic Socialism's policies as a women's theater collective of, for, and by the people, and *Lionheart Gal* as women's testimonial and as women's political history. The first part of this section grapples with the place of language and ethnicity in West Indian national literature—the place, then, of the culture and historiography of the Caribbean subaltern masses. The second part grapples with the political implications of rethinking history through these testimonials, through what I call "Patwah politics." Central to the project of Sistren and of *Lionheart Gal* is thinking through the position and politics of subaltern women, and so in the third section of this chapter I read the construction of "woman" through a collective autobiography as the concept appears across the testimonials in *Lionheart Gal*. In this process I articulate some of what is unearthed about women in culture and underdevelopment, as well as about gender, power, struggle, and identity in the process of reconstructing womanhood, as a way into poor Jamaican women's experience of the national community in the 1970s. Another history of Jamaica emerges from centering the life stories of subaltern Jamaican women, and I suggest some of the implications of this through the lens of the autobiographies of empowerment presented in *Lionheart Gal*.

In the two final sections of this chapter, I single out two testimonials that specifically engage with putting women and the concept of woman at the center of the debate over Democratic Socialism's history, inviting a reading of the failure of the social pact that Manley and the People's National Party sought to establish. In closing, then, I offer two close readings of testimonials from *Lionheart Gal,* "Veteran by Veteran" and "Foxy and the Macca Palace War." Through "Veteran by Veteran" I trace first a story/history of women under Democratic Socialism to argue that the real effects of Manley's project were cyclical. Vet's testimonial in "Veteran by Veteran" also records the history of a ghetto/national community. In closing, through the testimonial in "Foxy and the Macca Palace War," I argue that if we follow Foxy's lead, in the story of the rise of one man from the ghetto community to national politics we can trace the cracks that have led to the current breakdown of the social pact between state and nation in Jamaica. This also points to the ways in which the failure to think through the masculinization of politics and subaltern culture at the micrological level leads to the total chaos that enveloped the national community and led inexorably to the self-destruction of Democratic Socialism and, arguably, of the Jamaican government's social pact.

### *Democratic Socialism as a Narrative of Macrological Failure*

Narratives of Michael Manley's Democratic Socialism (1972–1980) are by and large narratives of failure. Manley himself wrote perhaps eleven books about the political experiment, analyzing and reanalyzing the programs attempted and the crises confronted. Certainly, by the time an exhausted and angry electorate voted Manley's sole opponent into office the country had plummeted to its lowest point: the economy was devastated, the national debt had skyrocketed, the dollar had plunged, the managerial classes had migrated to the United States, the ghettos had reached the state of civil war in which they still remain today, and the shelves in the supermarkets were almost completely empty. What, then, had happened to the dream of a new Jamaica?

In a scathing review from the Left, Fitzroy Ambursley reports the following statistics: "Real income fell by 25 per cent, while the cost of living rose 320 per cent . . . [and] net foreign reserves stood at minus J$900m—a fall of 1,014 per cent [since 1972]. Real investment fell by 65 per cent. Unemployment went as high as 31 per cent in October 1979, although [by 1980] it had been reduced to 27 per cent" (85).[9] Jamaica's share of the world bauxite market, aided by the world recession, had plummeted from 27 percent in 1970 to 17 percent in 1975, while Guinea's export share rose from 2 percent in 1970 to 23 percent in 1975 (Ambursley 83). The growth rate of the gross domestic product (GDP) in Jamaica's mining industry fell from 14.0 percent in 1973 to 8.5 percent in 1974, and then to −20.2 percent in 1975 (Stephens and Stephens 390). International capital (in terms of international market shares and the accompanying crucial foreign exchange) thus flowed out of Jamaica and into Guinea—from one embattled Third World community into another.[10]

The reasons for this devastation were hotly debated, but it was clear to all involved that without a change of government both the United States and their allies among the local Jamaican elite would continue the relentless assault within the United States, both in international forums (particularly the International Monetary Fund [IMF] and the World Bank) and within the country itself, in order to destabilize and alienate Jamaica from the world community and sources of capital. In the 1980s, President Ronald Reagan and Jamaica's newly elected Prime Minister Edward Seaga both depicted the Manley regime as "almost communist" and "a tool of Cuban expansionism" (Stephens and Stephens 2).[11] This is tellingly far from the truth, but what is clear from all accounts is that Manley's experiment with a "Third Path" between capitalism (United States) and socialism (Eastern bloc) shook the premises of development theory in the Caribbean and provided an alternative to the U.S.-backed Puerto Rican and Soviet-backed Cuban models of development that had previously set the terms for the Caribbean/Latin American–U.S. debate.[12]

In his 1982 postelectoral defeat observations, Manley reflected that when he and the People's National Party (PNP) were swept to power in 1972, they declared four basic goals:

> Firstly, we wanted to create an economy that would be more independent of foreign control and more responsive to the needs of the majority of the people at home. Secondly, we wanted to work for an egalitarian society both in terms of opportunity and also in the deeper sense of a society in which people felt that they were of equal worth and value. Thirdly, we wanted to develop a truly democratic society in which democracy was more than the attempt to manipulate voters every five years. Finally, we wanted to help, indeed accelerate the process by which Jamaicans were retracing the steps of their history. (*Jamaica* 39)

The process Manley described in 1982 is primarily a process of decolonization, of moving to change the "public" represented by state government from the (local and international) financial elite to the bulk of the population, as the proper role of national government. Nevertheless, the literature that grapples with the events and their causes and explanations documents the extent of the furor raised by the United States externally and by the Jamaica Labour Party (JLP) internally in their opposition to the PNP's strategies and rhetoric. Although it is true that the PNP lost the 1980 election, the electoral figures bear witness to the historic involvement of the masses in the political process: out of one million registered to vote, a record 86.9 percent voted. In defeat, Manley's legacy was the realization at some level of his early campaign slogan: "Power to the people."[13]

*Higgler economics*

Narratives of Democratic Socialism by both local and foreign political economic analysts all revolve around a set series of terms: the GNP; major exports; the business elite; the question of sabotage by the business elite in tandem with elements of the JLP and the CIA;[14] the government's international banking strategy (to borrow or not to borrow); capital flight; and the role of the largest daily newspaper, *The Daily Gleaner*. "Soft" concepts that appear repeatedly, however, particularly among those from the sympathetic Left, include "mobilization," "the resilience of the people," and "love." These "soft" terms, elaborated as the real keys to the success of the struggle to realize the promise of independence and decolonization, usually have only the vaguest referent, but in tandem with (neo)liberal and marxist epistemologies it is the national as "we" or "our" that is specified. I would argue that statistically the referent is women in general and poor women particularly, not only because they constitute the largest segment of the nation broken down into social groups by class and by gender but because of their central role in the social and economic order.[15]

With increasing shortages of food and consumer goods and services during Manley's first term, it fell to women to find ways to keep the domestic unit together, the indispensable basis on which macrological state projects depend. Lynn Bolles has documented some of the strategies that poor and occasionally middle-class nationalist women developed to "make do" in a besieged, ever-shrinking economy: "With a modicum of cash they buy fractional amounts of goods at one time, exchange and network in a total effort to provide food, shelter, clothing, school fees, etc. for those dependent on her. In the countryside, we might include growing food on a garden plot as an essential part of subsistence. Or selling beads and bracelets, coconut oil and hair-braiding—goods and services produced domestically in tourist areas as the ultimate visual portrayal of the inequality derived from capitalist accumulation" ("My Mother" 32).[16] Bolles and other feminists studying development theory point out that in many attempts at using standard economic indicators to explain and incorporate data on women into national statistics, analysts have confronted the "futility and inapplicability" of neoclassical models of economics and social patterns (32). Indeed, especially given its dependence on neoclassical economics, I would argue the same holds true for marxist epistemologies.[17] Much of the flow of goods that keeps the bottom from completely falling out in Caribbean and Latin American societies comes not from the sources predicted by either neoclassical or marxist economics but from a group of women who thrive throughout the region, known in Jamaica as "higglers."

These women who sell goods on the sidewalks and roadsides have become integral to providing a wide range of commodities more cheaply and more accessibly than the more formal outlets. Armed with U.S. currency often purchased on the "black" market, they would (and still do) fly to Miami, New York, Panama, or neighboring islands, shop, and return with boxes of goods in short supply to sell. Through this economic activity, they provide a critical buffer when the government and the official sector are at a loss. In their production and marketing strategies, developing since the market days and provision grounds (Hopkins's "garden") before the abolition of slavery, they have consistently provided a buffer zone for the vast majority of Jamaicans, a stratum of Jamaican economic independence that has survived all the major administrative transitions of the region's history. They also represent economically successful women from the lowest classes, and their role in the lives of the women of Sistren is documented throughout *Lionheart Gal*.[18]

Women are, then, at the center of the concept of "the resilience of the people." The place of women in Manley's paradigms is not so clear, however. In 1974's *The Politics of Change*, an initial attempt by Manley to elaborate some of his ideology for the public in book form, the nation is metaphorized as a family, and mobilization and strategies in the program for national development are elaborated through this means. Nevertheless, it was women who most felt the harshest effects of the failures in the PNP's initiatives.

The Bureau of Women's Affairs, established by the PNP in 1974, was set up "to seek methods of improving the status and promoting the development of women in society; to identify and publicize the status and conditions of Jamaican women; [and] to assist in promoting policies and programmes to integrate women into all areas of national development with particular emphasis on the integration of rural women into the rural economy" (Antrobus, "Women in Development 37b). The first government in the Caribbean to establish national machinery directed at the problems of women and their integration into society and development programs, the Bureau of Women's Affairs nevertheless was staffed with only a part-time director and a secretary. In 1976, after the PNP's reelection, the staff had increased to only nine, including, Antrobus reports, an education/communications officer and three rural coordinators (39).

During its eight-year course, however, in accordance with its commitment to creating a genuine democracy, the Manley government instituted a number of significant changes in a direct attempt to ameliorate the conditions of women's (particularly single mothers') lives, including food subsidies, a minimum wage, tuition-free education from primary through to the university level, compulsory recognition of trade unions, the legislation of equal pay, a family court, maternity leave with pay, and community health clinics (Manley, *Poverty of Nations* 83, 84; Girvan, "Notes" 117). Women were also highly involved in protests against the cruelty of the imperialist demands imposed on the PNP government by the IMF and in support of the breakthroughs in legislation and social programs benefiting women (Rhedock 66–67). Simultaneously, however, the unemployment rate for women rose from 34.6 percent in 1972 to 38.7 percent in 1979 and then to 43.5 percent in 1981. For men, the figures are tellingly lower (1972: 13.6 percent; 1979: 19.9 percent; 1981: 14.2 percent), although government census figures consistently show women outnumbering men in the labor force by thousands. The murder rate dropped from 40.7 per 100,000 in 1980 to 22.0 per 100,000 in 1981 and felonious wounding from 29.8 to 26.4, but reported rapes decreased only 1.1 points, from 35.1 to 34 per 100,000 (Stephens and Stephens 387), suggesting the role of sexual violence against women as a baseline indicator, a revealing index of social unrest.

The consistently high levels of sexual violence against women reported even after the electoral defeat of Democratic Socialism underlines the importance of poor women's bodies as a metonym of the nation in ideological struggles and as a touchstone of power in Jamaica's popular masculinist imagination. The incorporation of domestic workers into the formal economic and statistical system, a project conceptualized as early as the 1930s, remains largely unsuccessful, although domestic work is the largest single sector of women's employment (Wiltshire-Brodber 149). Yet, in a move typical of the paradoxes of his narratives of Democratic Socialism, Manley's *Struggle in the Periphery*, written "just ten months after the debacle" (208), notes that the "soft" issues of pride and ennoblement are among the handful of successes, summed up in the feeling that "household helpers enter a house by the front door now" (215).

### Sistren and the Politics of Subaltern Autobiography

One of the Manley regime's responses to the destabilization campaign of the United States and the deepening global economic crisis of the 1970s was the Impact Programme designed to give short-term work to displaced workers. Honor Ford-Smith and Elean Thomas both report that in 1986, 60 percent of the unemployed were women (national unemployment stood at 25 percent) and over one third of Jamaican households were headed and supported by women whose real income percentage dropped 109.1 percent between October 1976 and November 1980 (E. Thomas 67; Sistren xvi–ii; C. Thomas 235; Kaufman 248). At the petition of the Bureau of Women's Affairs women were assigned the lion's share of the Impact Programme jobs, in keeping with the new government statistics showing a clear predominance of women-supported households among the poor. Of approximately fourteen thousand workers hired, ten thousand were women (Sistren xxii). Among the women hired to clear ditches, cut grass from sidewalks, and similar tasks, were fourteen women who would form the theatrical cooperative Sistren.

### "We want to do plays"

When the Sistren participants first met, with organizer Honor Ford-Smith, in a "broken-down schoolhouse in Swallowfield" (Ford-Smith 88) to organize their participation in a 1977 Worker's Week concert, they said "we want to do plays about how we suffer as women. We want to do plays about how men treat us bad" (Sistren xxii). In this work, they engage with the democratizing of national culture, for they engage in cultural production in the language and narrative strategies of the people. An early production, *Bellywoman Bangarang,* addresses the issues of unwanted pregnancy for an audience of poor women and men, grappling with the ways in which the lack of basic information among women in rural subaltern communities perpetuates the victimization of women by men as sexual predators, and women's subsequent entrapment in the cycle of poverty.

In Sistren's testimonials a clear pattern emerges as basic facts of everyday life between the pressures of (a surprisingly calculated) male sexual pleasure and women's economic function as precapitalist resources in a system that forces them to bear the burden of working and raising children—predominantly girls, but all replenishing a cheap surplus labor pool. The lack of information about sex and women's bodies can become critical and ruin, if not end, women's lives. Thus *Bellywoman Bangarang* (roughly translatable as "pregnant woman's picaresque") was improvised through Jamaican folk proverbs, riddles and games, and songs and storytelling techniques developed by the women out of their daily experiences and through their own culture. In this way, they were able to raise crucial yet taboo topics like menstruation and teenage pregnancy, while articulating their message within subaltern cultural norms and ontologies.

All but two of the women of Sistren represented in *Lionheart Gal* come from the bottom of the social ladder. Reading their testimonies, we encounter the human lives behind the statistics used to calculate the state of the national economy and the status of poor women, of peripheral women, of women in development. Recent postmodern critical theory in the humanities has taught us to be suspicious of the value of the term "real life" in social and political debates as a caveat against epistemological violence. In the logic of the social sciences, individual testimonies are too often marginalized as anecdotal.

However, even if we allow the concept "real life" to be a "discursive construct," discursive constructs inevitably house their destructuring other; and in this case that other describes its limit in the body. Moreover, within the foundational principles of national and international development planning, the sheer accumulation of detail and incidences of everyday life for Jamaica's poor challenge the inappropriateness of current developmental blindnesses on the difference made by gender.[19] In *Lionheart Gal,* as in so many Caribbean and Latin American testimonials, the body predominates as a limit—that is, it hurts: for food, for sleep, to be held; for rest, for medicine; from beatings, from torture, from rape. The ever-receding problematics of discursive constructs thus meet a limit in the attacks on the body that mark these texts. Narratives of the body, and of daily life prior to its disciplinization for governmental and economic purposes, granted a concern for human welfare, then counter other kinds of narratives (e.g., statistical narratives) as a lesson, as a contribution to history, as a commentary on the strategies of development and "progress."

It is a goal of Sistren as a collective to teach poor women strategies for combating problems of violence in their homes and communities, given the ideology of convergences Antrobus outlines above. These intricately connective strategies for women's personal empowerment work to facilitate women's integration as women into the political process. This becomes the final trajectory for their work, as a new model of "progress" and "development" and as, interestingly, the proper march of history.

Since 1977, when the group was first formed, Sistren has come to represent a prominent and successful small-scale Caribbean alternative to traditional models and voices of development methodology. Primarily a political theatrical group, the Sistren Collective produces textiles, comic books, and videotapes that inform women on topics ranging from women's history in local and regional labor movements to the dynamics of sexual violence in the home. Their journal, *Sistren,* covers issues from women in development projects and proposals to working poor women's responses to government working papers, as well as offering workshops on women's health, sex education, handling teenage pregnancy, and so on. They have organized marches and protests in the streets of the capital against the working conditions of women in the export processing zones, and they have taken to conferences, training sessions, and performances in the Caribbean region as well as Europe and North America their struggle to break the silence surrounding women's exploitation and government complicity.[20] The stories and events included in their collective autobiography, *Lionheart Gal,* provide us with the opportunity to look for the historical events behind the figures calculated at the national level and offer an alternative reading as to the failure of Michael Manley's strategy of a Third Path to development.

## Subaltern historiography

History is a constant interlocutor in Sistren's theatrical performances and their autobiographies, entering as a form of collective women's remembering of women and extending the concept of the family—as Ileana Rodríguez notes for Central American women's testimonials—from the biological to the national as history.[21] Toward the end of Manley's second term, the CIA mobilized to destabilize his administration. To that end CIA operatives swelling the ranks of the U.S. embassy in Kingston made an alliance with the disaffected local capitalist contingency of twenty-one families and the JLP (headed by Edward Seaga), and proceeded to incite, fund, and arm civil violence and unrest.[22] Together, they imported large shipments of guns and distributed them to their cadres in the ghettos. Strategies of FBI infiltration for the destabilization of U.S. black empowerment groups thus find their counterparts in CIA destabilization campaigns abroad. The result in the Jamaican case was the transformation of gangs into political terrorist groups with a sophistication of weaponry unheard of in Jamaican history. Manley describes how the explosion of gang warfare and civil war converged on a tenement yard with a fury and tactical sophistication that shook the nation:

> A member of one gang was killed and reprisals began. In due course, the leader of the other gang was shot dead on a main highway early one evening. Before we [the government] knew it, members of his gang had surrounded a huge tenement yard in which over 500 people were crammed into some 200 small rooms including areas to wash, cook and do all other domestic activities. Fires were set at several points on the outer perimeter of the old buildings and shacks that comprised the yard. The whole place went up in flames. Eleven people died. The victims included five small children, and two babies, who were trapped in the flames and died as their parents listened helplessly to their pitiful screams. (*Jamaica* 138–39)

Apart from the aphasia signaled at critical moments by the passive voice, what Manley leaves out is that those who tried to leave the burning yard were massacred with machine guns, and that the nation by and large saw the event as a political act. When the Kingston Alms House, a poor house for old, infirm, and retarded women, burned down about a week later, the word on the street was that it was political revenge for the Orange Street fire.

For *QPH*, a play performed by Sistren in remembrance of the women who died in the Kingston Alms House fire, members of Sistren improvised a structure from a ritual practiced in rural west Jamaica for celebrating the dead by drumming and dancing and telling family histories through movement and music with drinking, singing, and feasting (Ford-Smith 90). *QPH*, as developed out of Etu-based patterns of rural subaltern culture, stands as a celebration/remembrance for three women, two of whom died in the fire: "Queenie, a preacher who is removed from her church; Perlie, who is banished from her family and driven to prostitution after becoming pregnant by the gardener; Hopie, a servant who, after thirty years of service spent on one family, is left destitute when her employers move" (90). Throughout their many theatrical productions, Sistren records women's lives on the streets and in the tenement yards to reveal and analyze problems that beset women at the bottom of the social ladder in the periphery. They find themselves actualizing many of the problems of underdevelopment in their lives and their bodies, including the isolation that besets underdeveloped countries and the difficulties in supporting self and offspring that can so easily swallow up what looked to be personal and political progress.

The primary audience for Sistren's theatrical productions is comprised of poor women like themselves, and their topics pertain directly to those issues that most affect poor Jamaican women. In this light, Sistren has developed as a tough political empowerment strategy for both those who formed the troop and those who had not been or could not be afforded such an opportunity. In the shift from drama to printed autobiography, however, the group leaves the popular sphere of drama in which the choice to retain Patwah as the oral vehicle is mandatory for communication as much as their political agenda, and enters the sphere of autobiography, of the (petit) bourgeoisie. In crossing the frontiers internal to the nation—class, language, ethnicity, history—they register multiple displacements of what has become the nationalist norm.

Since at least the 1930s, when, as we have seen, West Indian literature began gaining a democratic (black) nationalist momentum, through the Caribbean Boom period of the 1950s and 1960s, the region's literature has grappled with the problem of the gap between the language of the rulers and the language of the ruled majority. Although many of the region's novels include local speech as the language of the majority at some level, it is always in direct speech, and the place of authority—of reported speech, commentary, and plot development—is in English.[23] In writing their book in the language of the majority, the women of Sistren underscore the contradiction in a nationalist literature that claims as its subject and concern the plight of the "barefoot man" and/through poor women. In writing their lives, they challenge the images and mythologies out of which subaltern Caribbean women were presented as the core of the nation in the nationalist novels of the 1930s, or as peripheral figures in the novels of the 1950s and 1960s where the representatives of the "barefoot man" fashioned a political identity of the new nations. The "barefoot woman" here enters the stage of national literature to be counted, to shed new light on subaltern women's realities in the national and developmental process, and to speak for herself.

*Patwah politics*
Most of the voices of *Lionheart Gal* speak in Patwah not only to mark the class/culture division but to speak the language of the subaltern class from which most members of Sistren emerged, and to whom they insist their productions be primarily accessible. Protagonists of these testimonials speak as one among many. This is in part to avoid the isolationism of bourgeois individualism and maintain the volume's collective spirit, and in part to protect the women involved, some of whom had been physically attacked and others called lesbians—that transnational name for women who refuse a central primacy of the male ego and masculinist psychological domination as the parameters of woman's identity (Sistren xxv–vi). At one stage, the life/stories of their collective autobiography were all to be recorded oral narratives initiated by a questionnaire.[24] However, for the two "middle-strata" women in the group the interviews format did not work well because they were "accustomed to standard English and conventions of academic expression" (Ford-Smith xxviii). Thus two of the testimonies are in standard English, eleven are in Patwah, and two, "Criss Miss" and "Ava's Diary," use both. The form and textual heterogeneity of "Ava's Diary" is explained by editor Honor Ford-Smith in material terms that open onto the multiple jeopardies in Ava's life: " 'Ava's Diary,' for example, began from a detailed statement she had written about her experience of domestic violence to give to the police. We decided to keep the diary she had created herself and to extend it back through the other interviews" (xxviii). By positioning this voice at the end of the volume, Sistren and Ford-Smith open onto

several different sets of issues, but I will point to only one—the way in which the "diary" operates to construct a language/subject on the borderlands of class strata and points to a collective subject where differences interact without one erasing the other. To make my argument, I will provide further contextualization here.

Patwah is the language spoken by lower-class Jamaicans. The official language of the government and the bourgeoisie—managers and narrators of the macrological sphere—is English. This means, among other things, that poor children are faced with another language altogether in the educational system, whereas for bourgeois and upwardly mobile middle-class children it is a question of reading and writing in the language they and their families speak. Patwah, then, as the bearer of the poor and therefore majority realities, is a mark of culture/class identity rigorously expelled from official discourse and the strata of the elite, with calculated exceptions—for example, political speeches at election time.[25] It is the language of an economic strata that maintains, in the face of extreme poverty, indigenous cultural forms, concepts, assumptions, and strategies for survival in an oppressed and oppressive society. It is a language initiated in the emergency economy of slave culture, where alliances had to be made and a language/culture constructed that could maintain a sufficiently broad base of intertribal African understandings to keep one another alive and be able to go on.

In the 150-odd years since slaves and maroons like Jamaican national hero Ni ("Nanny"), "Rebel/Queen/Mother" and Maroon "General," won Emancipation, many Patwah-speaking Jamaicans have continued to live under crushing poverty on the margins of a (hostile) plantation and urban economy, despite a long history of participation in anticolonial uprisings, agitation for home rule, and the elections of a range of labor-oriented administrations. Needless to say, women have predictably suffered the worst of this poverty.[26] To be unable to speak standard English is to be found lacking in a society dominated internally by a postcolonial patriarchy of the middle and ruling classes, and externally by the imperialist policies of countries like the United States and England. Access to the English language and institutional education is a passport to the track of upward mobility in the private and public spheres. The situation is much more complicated than my sketch here allows but it is perhaps sufficient to register some of what is at stake in the heterogenous flow of language(s) in the borderlands between oral/written Patwah and written English as appears in "Ava's Diary."

The difference in the relation of oral to written culture leaves its mark on the life stories of the Sistren community. In the penultimate moment of "Ava's Diary," before the glossary that translates Patwah at its most illegible to English-speaking readers, there are acknowledged parameters of difference in the relation of oral to written culture that leave their marks on the transcription of the life stories of the Sistren community, the configurations of the "rebel consciousness" of Lionheart Gal. The epistemologies and strategies of oral culture, as part of the heritage of the Patwah-speaking community, are invested in the oral interweaving of life stories. Oral culture, as part of the heritage of the Patwah community, lends itself to the telling of life stories, drawing on the epistemologies and strategies of subaltern Jamaican culture. The effect of institutional education is to foreground the issues of writing's relation to and control of consciousness and speech, the need to construct oneself within the discourse of the written word. In the difference of the displaced middle-strata stories in English, class leaves its mark, openly, on the (re)construction of the social text and in Lionheart Gal, the final product. The language of the other mixed-language piece, "Criss Miss," marks the fluid intersection of the identity/class relations bifurcated and policed in "Ava's Diary."

"Ava's Diary" also foregrounds identity/class relations by the privacy of the diary context and its relations to the survival of generally middle- and upper-class women's culture in many parts of the world, including the Caribbean, a forum often recording hidden scenes of domestic violence against women but interspersed here with the official language, a constant reminder of the divide between Ava and the state.[27] In this "Ava's Diary" again oscillates on the borderlands as it is meant for public consumption—initially by a police force notoriously unconcerned with victims of domestic violence, then by a national and international readership of Lionheart Gal.

As editor, Ford-Smith's structurations are not always this successful—for example, the subtitles that attempt to fill in the hinges of the story " 'Exodus' A Run." Faced with breaks in the text, she inscribes phrases from the upcoming passage to make the silences speak. These subtitles can serve no purpose other than to calm the alienated reader's anxiety over what might lie behind such silences. However, if the politicized collective Jamaican subject signaled by the voice of the diary and the "we" of Lionheart Gal is problematically utopic, it is at least problematized in terms of class, race, world, history, ideology, and culture and always only pointed to in the process of performing specific educational, empowering, and healing activities.

"Rebel consciousness" becomes a space where differences can be acknowledged and sifted to interact productively for quotidian change. The infusion of privatized violence into the (inter)national public sphere constellates with the political urgency of their lives/stories and the (re)cognition of the class interests hidden in the Patwah/English division to create a heterogenous space of sister subjectivities. And as a mark of the persistence of subalternity, although the English passages in "Ava's Diary" bespeak the language and authorized concerns of the state, it is the voice in Patwah that tells of the connective tissues, left out of the official record, in Ava's and the nation's mother tongue, in the voice of the people. On the materialist side of sisterhood, then, lies the alienation of the social pact between the state officials and the subaltern masses recording their life/stories. Whom, then, does the nation-state represent?

As a corrective, the cultural base, rather than obfuscating or denying the elements of unofficial culture, allows the women to speak of their own exploitation, linking their consciousness of their oppression to their mother's and grandmother's lives—and so to history—as well:

> Di family used to lease land from di estate and cultivate it. Our family used to plant food crops and Icilda used to sell at Sav-la-Mar market. She always have Mama like a slave. She wuk her out in di field and use her to carry di excess load pon her head when she going to market. She send her children to school, but Mama continue working in di field. All Icilda children can read and write, but up to now Mama can only sign her name.
>
> One day, Icilda send her to buy carrot in a man field. Di man rape her in a hut in de field. She get pregnant. Dat is how my madda have her first child, my bigger sister. (62)

Rape conflates with labor exploitation to determine the lives and family histories of a woman trapped in a pocket beyond the reach of the law—a violation (re)marked in Pauline Hopkins's work that questions again how much things change, and points to rape as a form of women's torture and male pleasure across national borders and national cultures. The voice seeks to (re)cognize the possibilities for women's lives and reterritorialize the concept of womanhood toward liberation/decolonization. As part of their work in breaking the silence, they recognize that the social sanction to exploit and abuse may be linked to men's genitalia by cultural tradition but that it need not be so, as when the exploitation of child labor by adult women re-creates something of the same scenario, a return to slavery.

If sexual abuse is at least not generally a threat in all-women networks, the threat is supplied by a random man, one who, himself exploited, sells food to workers and is thereby himself at the mercy of the workers' employers and the wage levels they set. Underscoring the complex networks of (dis)empowerment in a rural subaltern community, in the telling of her sister's conception, there is no sense that official or unofficial retribution is a possibility. For her part, Icilda recognizes that education is one of the basic requirements for escaping the poverty trap and so makes sure her children are in school and learning. But at the subsistence and marginally capitalist levels of society, where bodies = labor power, many families cannot afford to give their children the free time needed to attend school. Thus Icilda supplements her income by substituting a girl child's labor for her children's, as if this girl-child not her own, and so owned, were an expendable resource.[28]

A goal of Sistren is, then, to educate by drawing on—validating and empowering through—the vehicle of subaltern culture as national culture. In their performances around the world, the marches they participate in in the streets of Jamaica, their publications, and their videos, they break the silence about the impact of internal and international economic and political struggles (particulary metropolitan and national elite political and economic supremacy) on the poor, especially women and children. If under (neo)colonial regimes, as we saw in de Boissière, the white/local bourgeois family history was the territorial history, here that history as the beginning of national history has been turned on its head.

The lessons to the managers of Independent democratic development multiply: in this pocket the violence extends from the economic language of the public sphere—of the expenditure of labor power and its transformation into capital accumulated—into social relations. Collectively, these testimonials denaturalize daily violence against, and exploitation of, women and children, and suggest ways of turning the anger that comes from the recognition that women have a right to self-interest toward productive ends. Patwah politics is a politics that begins again from the specific experiences of the people, moving from the micrological realities of subaltern Jamaican culture to the macrological issues of democracy, political economics, the social pact, and government through the chasm into which subaltren women are flung in daily life.

### Under the Sign of Woman: Lionheart Gal

As a treatise on the condition of women in Jamaica, *Lionheart Gal* becomes both an implosive and an explosive text. As one of its authors, Foxy, describes it, Sistren itself grew from just such a recognition of the difference woman's politics makes: "Tings develop so-till we start meet more people and talk bout woman and work and woman and politics. We discuss what is politics and how it affect woman. After we done talk ah get to feel dat di little day to day tings dat happen to we as women, is politics too" (253). The larger narrative here implodes because it destroys all the traditional generalizations of women's nature and provides ample evidence that, from one perspective, to be a woman in Jamaica provides no givens. Women exploit women and men in the pieces "Veteran by Veteran," "The Emancipation of a Household Slave," "Country Madda Legacy"—indeed, in every one of these testimonials. This is not the paradigm of bourgeois womanhood on which feminism, as much as patriarchy, is predicated, and on which gender planning and World Bank development programs are predicated. We confront, then, the discrepancy between Caribbean reality and Euro-American ideology to which the Caribbean people are still held accountable. At the intersection of working-class and bourgeois patterns of coupling, identity, and reproduction, and the relay between Caribbean reality and (neo)colonial ideology, the women of Sistren inscribe their life stories.

At the same time, this gathering of life stories is explosive because it tells the stories of abuse, of deprivation, of politics particular to women, and in the telling of details and small events it makes it clear how much the policies of the government, the poverty and underdevelopment of the nation-state, and the problems of internal mobilization converge on women's bodies and women's consciousness. Quotidian dilemmas (re)enacted in the plays performed in the countryside, neighborhoods, and in the spaces of the city's theaters cross a frontier in their written autobiographies.

The importance of the everyday comes to answer questions only guessed at by those setting policy and determining the course of the ship of state. Bit by bit, the details of daily life, of assumptions, of solidarity, of abuse, of deprivation, of who works and who doesn't and for whom and when, create a picture of Jamaican society that starts in the countryside and works its way toward the city and thus the seat of government. In gathering local knowledges toward action and a reconceptualization of politics, the life stories of the women of Sistren turn the conceptualizations of Jamaica and Jamaicans upside down and toward new ideas of the national social, economic, and political experiences of the poorer classes. If the march of the majority of the women from the country to the city mirrors the guerrilla's trek from the mountain to the plaza in Central American socialist narratives, these women's lives contain the seeds to effect just as much of a revolution, although, predictably, they never see state power. In what follows, I want to read across the testimonials to plot a macrobiography from the women's collective testimony to discern some of the issues at stake in determining the trek toward empowerment that is traced in the individual autobiographies as much as in the collective. At stake here is a biography of the oppressed majority.

*"All my life me live in fear"*
These words inaugurating *Lionheart Gal* cut to the heart of the matter. Revealingly, however, the first testimonial is not a story of withdrawal and self-denial but rather of violence. The speaker ends the stories of her childhood, for example, by describing the events that led her to stab her cousin for picking a fight with her in defense of someone else. Each of the women feels, and penultimately finds, herself alone to face the world. If Betty resorts to attempted murder, Bess allows herself to be forcibly estranged from her baby's father as a source of crucial prenatal financial support and transportation to the new family planning clinic by her mother. All three of these women are driven by fear of domination and abuse by subaltern men.

The issues of poverty, ignorance, and children's exploitation, for example, raised in the play *Bellywoman Bangarang*, converge again in the testimonial "Rock Stone a River Bottom No Know Sun Hot":

> To how [mi madda] gwan is like seh she never waan me fi chat to no man at all. She no must expect seh me would a tek a man inna some way? She feel dat by telling me "man a green lizard" she would prevent a situation, but she mek it worse. Madda fi really siddung and talk to dem daughter inna certain ways of life. No just

mek she go out deh jus go drop pon it so. Mama did really waan lickle teachment for she did backward. Inna Mama time if yuh no white, yuh couldn't go a high school and so all dem tings mussy mek her believe di colour of yuh skin haffi do wid yuh ability. Yuh know weh did happen to she? She did feel sey she would a live forever, so [mi son] Craig wouldn't want no faada. She could a never no seh she would a dead. (57)

If one of the problems of underdevelopment is the lack of educational resources for the majority of the people, in "Rock Stone" it impacts on daily life in a way particular to women. Fear comes to characterize Bess's mother's relation to the relatively empowered gender, as if what power men's genitalia allows men across class divisions within a patriarchal society is used as a weapon against women. In the absence of resources such as access to birth control, sex education, a woman's right to choose, and paternity and child-support lawsuits, a mother resorts to a desperate attempt at studied ignorance for her daughter. Her strategy fails, as Bess is seduced in confusion. As the title of the testimonial suggests, women's ignorance about sex, power relations with men, and reproduction creates a situation in which the overprotected child cannot guess what the outcome of her actions nor the drives of her inevitably maturing body may be. One of the crucial lessons of "Rock Stone a River Bottom No Know Sun Hot" is that women's bodies and women's sexual desire cannot be erased by repression.

This is a lesson the new Democratic Socialist state itself was struggling to learn, just as it struggled to come to grips with the difference in women's bodies and women's position in the division of labor and the sociocultural order. Bereft of social support services, working within a system whose trajectory includes formally and informally institutionalized patriarchal deceit and sexual violence, the mother responds with fear and denial. Like the state, mothers must move beyond the concept of the genderless citizen whose body is de facto (if not de jure) male, and so in telling the story her daughter recognizes the need to break her mother's silence, and that it falls upon women to educate women, not only about biology and reproduction but about the intricate realities in the power relations of seduction and the domestic sphere.

But what also stands out in this passage, as in so many others in *Lionheart Gal,* is the primacy of fear. Bess's mother has been taught not only to repress her daughter's sexuality and difference as an act of will, but to devalue blackness, which means in the end devaluing herself, her daughter, and the majority of the community. Her mother sees it not as a personal devaluation, but a public, sociopolitical evaluation: white people succeed and so are smarter, white people are smarter and so they succeed; black people, especially black people with nappy heads, fail. Even 150 years after the abolition of slavery, the legacy of slavery's social policies negate the government rhetoric of democratic (black) nationalism.

A mother's fear is here so strong that when her daughter's pregnancy begins to show, she locks her daughter out of the house, refusing to give her access to food, shelter, or clothing. In doing this she denies the young girl whatever marginal gains keep her from homelessness within an agrarian pocket of society—in short, the girl is exiled from the house into the surrounding bush to fend for herself. And although initially the baby's father together with his mother appear devoted to helping her access prenatal care at the government clinic and to providing support for new mother and child (a would-be disruption of the pattern of father-children relations Rodríguez identifies in the Latina testimonials she reads) Bess's mother drives them away in a hysteria brought on by years of fear and oppression. The ignorance and fear for her daughter that makes her shield her from the world and knowledge of (the difference in) women's bodies turns back into the family home to sever the very mother-daughter bond she had devoted herself to, and her precious hope for the future becomes an outcast and a torment. Her daughter's first struggle to free herself will involve grappling with a fear of sex and of men as a legacy particular to women.

Fear cuts across the social text, then, as it cuts across the psychology of the women involved. It comes often at the hands of the father. In *Lionheart Gal,* fathers in women's childhoods are masters or overseers, as for example, when a child is hung from a tree and whipped. The problem of fathers as masters over children extends from the realm of childhood and children deep into the realm of adults, when mothers attempting to defend their children find themselves susceptible to the same abuse. Power in these narratives, as I argued, sticks close to the body, and so the familial conditioning of children that begins in ideology, again echoing Rodríguez, and moves through biology to psychology represents a studied and socially sanctioned policy to establish men's word as a pillar of law (defined as discipline and punishment), a lesson for the wider social world to teach adult women that as women they can easily be abused like children. Thus the text of woman's lives is riddled with brutal domestic abuse as symptomatic of women's political disenfranchisement as proper and appropriate.

The use of violence as a control does not stop at the hands of men, however, and men are not the only perpetrators. In the testimonial "Rebel Pickney" the child Betty, already abandoned to her grandmother, is ambushed and beaten by her mother on the way to school because the mother feels both her children and her mother have destroyed her life. In truth, it is fear that determines the mother's life as much as the daughter's, because her own body's betrayal has brought children into the world that only unravel her future plans to get out, to get away, to decamp to the city as hope for a new beginning. Repeatedly, pregnancy configures as a woman's disaster, and violence always ensues.

The threat of rumor as the means of communal knowledge, and its direct corollary, reputation, as the means of determining social standing and rights, further extends the confinement of women out into the larger world of the village community. In recasting information in retelling the story, ideology refashions the oral text. In the end, the policing of women serves conservative ends: the silencing and domesticating of women as women's responsibility. The politicization of women's biographies at the heart of the book is thus a direct attempt to counter the normative narratives that attack women who act out or act up to confront the norms of girls' socialization through silencing and contradictory messages about women's bodies that threaten through ostracism.[29] Gender and sexual politics determining women's lives and freedoms thus come out of the mouths of the empowered in the community, as the disempowered struggle to make sense of the abuses of their bodies and their trust predicted by these politics. For this reason, women are always starting out afraid.

### "It no mek no sense you be licky-licky"

*Lionheart Gal* illustrates that the process of woman's maturation becomes the process of overcoming fear as a central dynamic in women's lives. To be a grown woman comes to mean taking one's life into one's own hands and being prepared to suffer loss and alienation because of it. To be "licky-licky" is to be needy, to come begging. As children, for example, two of the women in the book found themselves forced out of the family house—wattle and daub with mud floors—into the bush to live off of roots; to sleep, terrified, in trees; and to watch the world of their families from exile. In the city, to which the women of the country gravitate, there is the possibility of domestic work, of living in a room of one's own, and of creating a better life, but city life is fraught with its own dangers, where women who hire other women work to cheat them of their wages, for example, or send men to extort rent with threats of violence.

In both the city and the country, through a dialogue with the premise of refuge within women's community these testimonials document how women exploit women as part of the efforts to fulfill a woman's responsibilities: managing the house, ensuring their children's education, producing at least subsistence crops. To be a grown woman thus requires great strength in these testimonials because it means taking a stance for oneself, alone and without money, against a hostile world.

Over and against this is a legacy of women's strength. Several of the mothers of the members of Sistren encourage their daughters to find their own resources, to engage with the inevitable attacks out of a tradition of women fighting back. As Foxy, benefiting from family history, recounts it: "Him feel seh him a man and me must abide by him. But my madda was a type of woman weh fight. Me no see why me should a come out a fi-her school and cyaan help meself. So me fight him. As a argument develop, him nah get di chance fi lick me, me first start it. My Granny say no man could beat my madda. My madda always say, 'Yuh no fi mek no man rule yuh or turn yuh inna no football or batterstick. Yuh fi help yuhself'" (258).

### "Member seh man a green lizard"

Relations with men, as we saw in the case of fathers and again in the case of fathers of babies, more often than not come to embody woman's recognition of herself alone in a hostile world. If (petit) bourgeois narratives of womanhood tie women to men who lock them up in the house, repeatedly in these narratives men pull women down by drawing on their labor for sustenance, psychological as well as sexual and biological.

It is clearly part of the group agenda, however, to avoid a homogenizing maligning of men. If there are everywhere stories of male violence, there are less frequent—but all the more accentuated for it—instances of men nurturing loving relationships with women. With tenderness, a father is remembered for nursing a child's wound, for working hard, for being a good father; a grandfather remembered for singing and dancing with his granddaughter and encouraging her to think. These men who support and nurture, however, are also frequently the men who beat, who rape, who abandon. The lesson to be learned is thus that men change their colors like a green lizard, that a woman can never depend on a man, that a woman must stand on her own, and that no man can be trusted. The preacher who beats his wife, the husband who steals his wife's wedding ring to buy rum, the playmate who rapes, and the lover who extorts with threats of violence dot the pages of the testimonials. Because of men's instability, women must have their own house, their own bed, their own job, and this is critical advice.

Nevertheless, the process of patterning a healing social and psychological space also includes struggling with relationships with men. As Rodríguez points out in her analysis of Latina testimonials, a democratic drive toward the social wants to incorporate a concept of society as an extensive political family. In *Lionheart Gal*, this means recognizing the privileges of men implanted in woman's consciousness from childhood. As one woman puts it, in a poem she writes after refusing the assistance of her baby's father,

> Without a man,
> I am a man's woman.
> Without a husband,
> I am a wife.
> Without a father,
> my children must grow. (140)

The trajectory from a primary definition of woman as man's property, through women without a man in the family house, to children without fathers extends to women in life, and into a philosophy of life: "Without life, our lives must go on. / Without hope, we're not hopeless" (140); from being in negation, then, to being as negation of the negation. Despite this affirmation, in the constant repetition of the negations in sphere after sphere of life, there remains a spiral of zeros that nevertheless will amount to something, emerging from a series of paradoxes:

> Without a reality, we shall emerge
> from captivity.
> Without all we can stand tall, firm and strong
> in what we believe in. (140)

Ground zero becomes a premium productive space.

The question of men's relationships to women still comes back to haunt a woman's being through her sexuality in her grappling with the equation of men with power. In the very project of empowering women, of reading into women's lives something on the order of macropolitics, there is always, as a logical extension, the charge of excessive masculinization. Lesbianism enters the debate in *Lionheart Gal* here, as a charge leveled by men against women for focusing their attentions on the condition of women. And out of their mother's mouths homosexuality enters in also as a curse, where men refuse or cannot match violence, an inability attributed to women. One speaker's mother, in throwing her husband into the ditch for cursing at her, finishes her dismissal and the severance of any possibility of respect with a local epithet ("faggot") that can get someone killed in Jamaica if it is believed to be a sexual practice and not a metaphor for total disempowerment, in a man who is a woman. Subaltern Jamaicans make clear their capacity for regurgitating violent disciplinization and punishment on unruly women's bodies, taken to the extreme at the thought of identifying the bodies of gay men and lesbians.[30] Yet a small voice breaks through: as one woman puts it, she might have become a lesbian if only she had known it were possible.

*"All who know what o'clock strike already"*
The endpoint of *Lionheart Gal*'s testimonials is, then, an elaboration of the process of woman's liberation as a living fact—biologically, then critically, psycho-ideologically, then politically through solidarity, as Rodríguez has it, then economically—to the equation of woman's liberation with the accession of woman to a sense of her own power, built out of an understanding of the vectors and meaning of her oppression. History enters the circuit of autobiography toward this end, and it has two faces. National history is the history of men who are worked to death on the big plantations or who revolt and rebel extrapolated into the history of worker's unions and the transition from slavery to "freedom" to Independence. Foxy's testimonial recounts the collapse of men's progress as historical progress. But, consistently, more integral to progress than men's history is a knowledge of women's history stretching back through the family as a legacy of people's empowerment. That story of preceding events and generations is threaded through mothers and grandmothers, and consistently in these testimonials it is women's mobilization (the

recognition that "if yuh tek yuh pickney to hospital and it die in yuh han—dat is politics" or if "yuh man box yuh down, dat is politics" [253]) that provides an alternative to the war and violence that escalates or abates. Remember that if the statistics for murders and felonious woundings fell after the 1980 elections, the rape statistics hardly budged. Knowing one's own best interests and place in the world comes to mean also knowing one's position in relation to one's mother's life. Mothers figure prominently in every one of these autobiographies and almost all end with advice on mothers and mothering. The meaning of being a woman, coming into one's own—knowing "what time it is"—thus hinges on (knowing) the meaning of a mother's life.

We move in the end back to the questions of politicization, of coming into one's own as a political being and a subject of the state. The history of the working class, and of rebellions and strikes, enters here at the point of breaking into the larger political structures. If these testimonials are simultaneously political narratives, economic narratives, and autobiographical narratives, they are also gendered historical narratives. To know and come into one's own—power in women—becomes to teach, to be independent, to nurture children, to politicize them into understanding their place in the larger structure and to take it seriously. It also implies the ability to speak openly about women and sex, to free oneself and teach children to free themselves from victimization, so that each successive generation can achieve more than did their parents, "to come togedder and keep on demand what dem want to see change and work hard to get it change" (87), and, perhaps, to find love and community at home with men (women + men = nation) in security and in affirmation: "Me nah pull up neither for me develop a lot since me first know him and him accept it. Him no try hinder me. To me is like di security draw me closer to him and den it becomes love, yuh understand?" (218).

## If Woman = Nation: The Implosion of the Kingston Ghetto

I want to close with two readings of two testimonials from *Lionheart Gal*, "Veteran by Veteran" followed by "Foxy and the Macca Palace War," as alternate narrativizations of what happened to "the masses" read under the sign of woman during Manley's experiment with Democratic Socialism, a metonym of "the people" for whose welfare Manley and his cadres struggled against overwhelming odds to reform the policies of the state.

Because poor women are the majority of those most oppressed, in their involvement in the political process we can see some alternate meaning for the term "progress" and "development" in populist terms, on a human scale. In *Plotting Women,* Jean Franco offered a reading of what she calls "the loneliness of the gendered subaltern" (178), a notion seconded by Gayatri Spivak.[31]

Certainly, the comparative interest of the Manley regime in alleviating this "loneliness" accounts for some of the relative integration, as well as the hierarchical range within even so narrow a category as those consigned to subalternity. The implicit dialogue between Franco's reading of Jesusa's life in Elena Poniatowska's *Hasta no verte, Jesús mío;* Ileana Rodríguez's of Lea Marenn's *Salvador's Children: A Song for Survival;* Elizabeth Burgos-Debray's of *I, Rigoberta Menchú;* Margaret Randall's of *Todas estamos despiertas: Testimonios de la mujer nicaragüense de hoy;* and my own of Vet's and Foxy's life stories in *Lionheart Gal* raises questions of the conditions maintaining subalternity as a transnational condition, as much as the upheavals in spheres stretching into the most private spaces in the wake of the massive restructuring necessary to alleviate this condition, touching on a range of factors that oppress women from the bottom of developing societies.

At first Vet, the protagonist of "Veteran by Veteran," refuses to involve herself in the political battles around her, convinced that no one in the political structure is interested in working with her to ameliorate her living conditions. As Vet describes the neighborhoods in which she grew up, she textualizes the marks of class, nation, history, and the tenuousness of the social pact with the ghettos in the capital city's topography:

> I grew up in di area of King Avenue, di main road [in downtown Kingston]. On di odder side was Flowers Town. Further over behind Flowers Town was Rock City. I live in Rock City, Greenfield Town, in front of People's Theatre and further up. Me also live near a standpipe beside di area dem call almshouse burying ground—later known as Ghost Town. . . .
>
> Round by The People's Theatre and Love Lane, di living conditions were worst of all. People raise hog and fowl and let dem go an mess up di place and it stink.
>
> Brown's Lane lead round to Flowers Town area. Yuh find a mixed multitude living around dere. Yuh find people who cyaan afford fi

pay rent. I hear dat place used to be woodland. It have wholeheap a dildo macca.[32] People who come from country and no have no money, might meet up over deh wid dem friend and decide fi capture a piece of land. If yuh no strong, yuh cyaan live in dem deh area. Yuh haffi strong fi defend yuh piece a capture land, and yuh house. . . .

Sometime dem use box weh fridge come in or stereo or electric appliance dat come from abroad and mek dem house. . . . Some dig pit toilet. Some don't dig no toilet. Dem use di bush. . . . If yuh live mongst dem yuh haffi live wid di situation or leave. Sometime yuh cyaan leave, cause yuh no have noweh fi go. (157–58)

The place names in this passage are telling: the People's Theatre from the nationalist era; King Avenue, the main road, from colonialism; Ghost Town, from outside governmental structures. Later Vet will live on the border of two zones called "Palestine" and "Lebanon" to reflect the civil war. It is clear, however, that in the ghetto there is already low-intensity warfare, evidenced both in the language and the social condition it is meant to convey—the "capturing" of land; and what it takes to survive— "defending" the seized territory. The state's control of the area is already strained, and the rule of law here is the rule of brute force. This will again characterize what amounts to the next step up the socioeconomic ladder, the tenement yard, itself captured, in this case by a woman, with the help of her sons, who extorts rent from the people in the yard just as the bailiffs did in Trinidad in the 1930s.

Governmental presence here amounts to putting up a standpipe to provide water for the squatter community, a service that both exemplifies and points to the limit of the government's resources and their populist reconceptualization of the state's relation to the people. This represents "commitment" only in that previous administrations would have ignored the squatter communities altogether, except to bulldoze them when those holding the official titles and leases complained. In the detail so subtle as the standpipe, then, lies the difference between a government for the elite exiling the poorest levels of local society, and a government committed at some level to alleviating conditions. The standpipe stands here as a mark and a limit, then, of Democratic Socialism for the squatter communities.

As such, the pipe runs from the government standpipe to an individual house is a sign of privilege, and here the language is both social and military: "If yuh is a Ranks living in di area, yuh can run a pipe from di standpipe to yuh yard.[33] A Ranks is a person who advance in a sense more dan some—or dem might be from a family living dere a long time. Dem know dat dem can attach a piece of pipe and run it to dem house. If government ketch dem, is trouble, but dem know how fi do it—use night and do it" (158). If "Ranks" suggests a superior physical force—remember it requires brute force to remain within the squatter community—it also suggests the strains of a militaristic hierarchy within the subaltern community.

The next two sentences register two crucial points in configuring power: "Later on di government decide to set up pipe inna di different people dem yard. When di bwoy children from dose areas start growing up, dem gang up and go pon di corner" (158). In the battle to both win back the social pact with the community and to alleviate conditions, the government takes what was at first an illegal activity meant to signify social superiority guaranteed by force, and then democratizes it. In engaging with the poorest in the city, the government tries to diffuse the potential for hierarchical relationships, supporting and supported by the emergence of a power group within the squatters' communities. There is again the question of the strength of the government's pact, and in capitulating to the laws of brute force the best the government can do is put the modicum of privilege taken by the emergent leaders back into the hands of the people.

The group of young boys from the community who begin to gather on the corner forbodes the creation of cadres of angry young men, and they will reappear later from someone else's neighborhood, transformed and armed with .365 Magnums, M16s, AK47s, and SLRs, precursors to the men "disguised" as soldiers who will terrorize the women of the community. Within the ghetto neighborhoods, even the police function as another militia group: "Di police know seh no bad man no live on my road, but still while we a talk one a dem turn di gun pon di little youth [I was talkin to] and say 'Move yuh what's-it-nots-it.' Dem rain down gunshot pon him, dat we haffi run go inside quick-quick. When me see dat me say, 'Yes, Lawd. Might be dem all mek up dem mind fi kill out all di youth inna Palestine' " (172). The community is splitting away from the nation, if the "nation" is seen as the social body holding a pact with the state. Similarly, the confusion surrounding events and motives at the micrological level reflected in Manley's books on the period are predicted in their failure to dehierarchize the community. Although the war will not break out until later, its preconditions—cadres of disaffected men on the margins of the community, the rule of force rather than communal social relations, the inability of the government to regulate, the tenuousness of the social pact—are already in place.

These preconditions are in part a product of the patronage both parties had earlier used to cement their ties with the labor unions formed after the 1930s riots, and thus get elected. If Manley courts the men in the ghettos as New Men to cement the social pact, further down the infrastructure the mentality has not changed, a crisis in the process of conscientization addressed by both Harris and de Boissière. That what rules is factionalism rather than nationalism is integral to Vet's socialization by her mother. The politicization of everyday life takes a fairly comic turn early on:

> One PNP woman used to live side a di yard and a JLP used to live a di next side. I used to hear di PNP come out a morning time, when dem a wash and a spread di clothes pon di zinc fi burn.[34] She used to sing:
> Old clothes government
> A weh me do yuh?
> Me no waan no salt fish
> Me no waan no weevil flour.[35]
> Den di JLP one come out and find something else fi sing and dem start throw word and dem sing and cuss all day. (161)

If openness, humor, and work characterize political battles between most of the women within the community, secrecy, violence, and deception will later characterize most of the men's, because the political bosses arm only men, and women are recruited to cook and serve them (shades of *Guevarismo*). Then the women's political affiliation becomes irrelevant when facing the military invasion that characterizes the emergence of political violence among men:

> One night, me see some guy a run up and down all bout. One uproar out a street and when me look me see one guy run come in di yard. Him run inna di bathroom. Me see a next guy run come in di yard. Him run inna di bathroom. Me see a next guy run through di

gate. One woman in di yard name Miss D. She say, "Oonoo cyann tan inna me yard, yuh know. What oonoo want in yah? Oonoo a leggo beast.[36] Oonoo no come in yah!"

And dem a say, "Madda, yuh see one bwoy run come in yah?"

"If yuh see anybody run inna dis yah yard, dem run go someweh else. Beg you come out a me yard!" And dem lef. (162)

The men are here engaged in a struggle to the death, and it is their machismo combined with their disaffection from the social pact, as much as what they stand to gain from the support of their political bosses, that drives them. Notice that the territory on which the war is staged is occupied by women, and that the men are strangers, perceived as invaders. In the end the community of women will lock themselves in their houses.

The stories of escalating political violence are tellingly interspersed with stories of domestic warfare in which Vet struggles with men, with a landlady who does not own the land but extorts "rent" nevertheless, and with raising children. "When yuh done wid me yuh graduate from college" the father of one of her children tells her (163), but he proves trainable; Vet's father, a Cuban, wanted to marry her mother, but she declined, foreseeing trouble, and he, like the father of Vet's baby, soon disappears in the United States. For men living in the war zones there seem to be mostly two options: join the (official or unofficial) military cadres, or emigrate. The exceptions are few and far between, but one man stands out in imploring the youth to stop the violence and increase the peace:

Starman was one a dem man who used to fight gainst di war and di propaganda. Him used to love di youth and try see to it dat no fight never gwan in di area. We used to respect him for him used to stand up and defend di community. . . . One morning . . . me wake up and her seh police shoot Starman inna dance di night before. Me stand up out a me gate and one lickle bwoy deh side a me tell me what happen. Me say to meself, "If dem kill all a activist like Starman who supposed to safe, dat mean from yuh live down yah anyting can happen to anybody." (171–72)

For women, the history of the political struggle from the perspective of life in the war zone is double-edged, encompassing both the domestic and the political spheres. The men who invade neighboring communities will be their sons, their brothers, their lovers, the fathers of their children. Vet's community is attacked in a way that marks the fact that women occupy the territory and men are the invaders: rape is the weapon of choice and it is applied indiscriminately to women and girls alike. When the women respond by bringing in their own men as protection, they implicitly acknowledge that they are living in a battle zone, and that men make up militias. In her growing conscientization it is Vet who recruits and strategizes a defense force from the community to secure their bodies and their homes from invasion by marauders and political gangs. Still, any hope of survival within the war zones requires bringing in men for protection. More and more people are forced to leave the yard until the local JLP political boss holds a meeting and instructs their cadres to call a ceasefire, or else no one will be left to vote: the agenda here is to take the territory, neutralize the population, and commandeer their votes.

Moving to a board shack becomes "like heaven" because it is in a "socialist yard" which promises, in its political homogeneity, that there will be peace. But because the woman who owns the yard is a "Labourite" (JLP), as the 1976 election draws near the yard quickly becomes a front in the political battle—PNP men threatening retribution to protect the territory; JLP men searching for socialists to exterminate, and to rape and exterminate if they are women—and so, in search of peace for herself and her children, after the election Vet is forced to move again, to "tek one a di government house for me couldn't tek the friction" (169).

But in running Vet finds herself on the border between two communities called "Palestine" and "Lebanon." Here having access to food becomes a mark of betrayal: "One drunken woman named Madda Pinnacle from down deh used to say, 'If yuh go a town and buy a pound a steak and put it inna plastic bag and walk wid it come up yah, dem say yuh a CIA'" (171). Having gone next door to buy three eggs from a friend Vet finds herself trapped by volleys of gunfire. When the gunmen arrive in soldiers' uniforms, it is only by grace of her faith in the state that she believes them disguised; for armed and instructed they form militias, terrorist groups raised by the political bosses to take and retake the ghetto territory. And because most of the households here are headed by women and the heavily armed militias are made up of men, within the war zones it is clear that the battle for control of the state is a battle of disaffected men against women who hold territory. This territory is gained through a pact with a modern politics that recognizes that poor women head a majority of impoverished households, a modern politics possible because power is in the hands of Democratic Socialism, which establishes a social pact directly with these women.

On the day of the 1980 election, when Vet goes to the police station for protection, she finds the station is deserted; in the police's place only Labourites wield batons. Arriving at the polling station to work for socialism and democracy by noting voter turnout, monitoring the voting process, and fighting voter fraud—the inclusion proper of the people in the democratic process—she finds the roads and the polling station have been seized by a platoon of Labourite men armed with machine guns. When a Labourite woman tries to take her papers, turning them from a voting list into a hit list, Vet is forced to run for her life.

After the election she refers to as "di Deliverance" (172), terrified for her life and her children now that she is known as a political woman, she borrows money and leaves the house the government had provided. She moves back into the network of extortionist tenement yards, coming full circle but for the lingering fact of her politicization: "Is like di politicians no waan working class people fi live good for when dem have dem political differences is always inna di working class area dem fight it out" (170).

### The Macca Palace War: Power in Subaltern
### Democratic Socialist Men

The engine for political mobilization and development as a human political concept must confront what I have called Patwah politics and the condition of subaltern women as a deconstructive locus. It is the insight and knowledges provided by subaltern women's culture that brings me full circle, to look again, in light of Vet's life story, at narratives of Democratic Socialism and the reasons for its failure. For Manley, de Boissière's conjunction of Patwah politics with socialist insights is precisely the aim of the reformation of government, and it is this that brings the wrath of the hegemony, especially that of the U.S. government. Consider, for example, the following reflections: "Between 1972 and 1974, the People's National Party government sought to institute social changes which would reflect these objectives [i.e., the democratization of the nation represented by the state. . . . In 1974, however, the price of oil rose. The impact of this was deleterious on the Jamaican economy" (Jamaica 83).

This is the narrative of the failure of Democratic Socialism in its pre-eminent form—that is, as an economic narrative. The factor I want to focus on here is the relay between this economic narrative and the other dominant narrative, that of politics. This focus takes two forms, one concerned with internal issues, the other with the external:

> At the same time, the government had begun to talk to the bauxite companies about renegotiating the operations of the mineral companies. These negotiations did not proceed without acrimony and in the end the government had to impose by law in parliament the Bauxite Levy. The negotiations with the bauxite companies commanded wide support across all classes in Jamaica. [Note the implied political economic fallout reflected in the statistics quoted above—that is the unspoken end of the story.] The government had sought to increase Jamaica's share of the benefits of industry. Perhaps, however, it was the PNP's redeclaration of socialism and the beginning of the ideological debate in society which triggered a process in Jamaica. . . . At the public level, more radical pronouncements set in train deep fears.[37] In a real sense, society was unprepared for this ideological debate. ( *Jamaica* 83–84).

The power of the local elite in coalition with the business elite heading the multinationals—their ability, as documented by de Boissière, to manipulate the international economic order and so the economics of local everyday life—is intertwined with an "ideological debate" and "deep fears" presumably among the elite and government officials. This is the narrative of the problems of the first term (1972–76).

The second term (1976–80), the one Manley noted elsewhere was dominated by the M16, is narrated as follows: "For the next four years the country went through a difficult period. The attempt by the government to deal with internal questions of social justice led to the 'revolt' of the bourgeoisie. The attempt to articulate a foreign policy that was based on a concept of non-alignment and involved Jamaica dealing with Cuba became a point of great controversy in relations with the United States" (85).

The coming to voice of the women of Sistren records another perspective on the events of these years. The "difficult period" was not simply a matter of a revolt by the bourgeoisie, although they played a large part in derailing Jamaica's democratization. In fact, a central question raised by the Latin American Subaltern Studies Group—who is the subaltern and what does she or he want?—comes back to haunt the historiography of

Manley's experiment.[38] Contrast, then, the following as a narrative of the failure of Democratic Socialism:

> One night when di area was under curfew, we was outside chatting. Di soldiers come. Dem run we off a di street. We go inside and when di soldiers gone, we come out again. Me and a youth name Babyface did a run some joke, when me see some soldier man come round di corner and smash di lightbulb.
>
> "What's di position?" dem say. When me look good, me recognize a man who come from down Limbo. Me realise seh a di Limbo man dem dress up demself as soldiers and tek time come inna fi-we yard. Dem mussy did walk through di cemetery. Das what dem do when dem waan terrorise di area.
>
> "All a oonoo turn oonoo face to di wall." Me never fraid a death. Me only fraid dem a go rape me. Me would a prefer dem kill me, more dan dem rape me. Dem make Babyface go one side. "Go inna di house," dem tell di rest a we.
>
> Den one a dem stop me. "Mek me see yuh finger." Me quail up, cause me a tell yuh, me fraid. It was only me leave back wid Babyface. Di boy open mi hand gently an tek off di ring. Him go fi tek out me earring. It wouldn't come off. Him pull-pull till him split di ears and draw it out. Dat time pee-pee a run down mi leg. "Go inside," him say. Me go in and run straight under di bed. Den mi hear three shots. Me see di light from di shot dem clear.
>
> Ah hear a voice calling. "Mr. B. Mr. B. Me get a shot!" Ah recognize Babyface voice. Mr. B. a my uncle. Him jump up and tear through di window. Ah come out and follow him. When a look ah see Babyface a draw . . . draw go under di house. We try fi draw him out, but we couldn't do notten. Di whole a him side tear off. Him dead same place . . . in front of me.
>
> Di incident wid Babyface affect me bad. He was only around twelve, thirteen. We find out dat dem kill him because dem tek him fi mi stepfadda. Dem did have on di same colour shirt. (250)

The disconnection between the dominant and the subaltern narratives forms a chasm into which Democratic Socialism collapses. Foxy, the member of Sistren from whose life this narrative is extracted, is herself concerned to enter the debate, to engage and find a voice in thinking about the history of Jamaica between 1972 and 1980. Indeed, in her testimonial the structural relations between Foxy watching Manley make history and the battle between men in the night of the Kingston ghetto converge. Foxy's story is a history from the margins of men from the ghetto taking the new democratic opportunities created by Democratic Socialism for re-creating society: through her history of one man from the ghetto we can subtend a history in which the people are not empty vessels, pawns in a battle between Manley and the native elite and powers behind imperial politics in the West and the international division of labor. The macrological narratives of the kind governments use to display development come immediately under fire vertically instead of horizontally.

The focus of Foxy's history is Spangler, a man from the subaltern classes who becomes a politician and wins the support of the people for his character and his family's history of intervening in police brutality on behalf of people from the neighborhood, as well as to "calm di people" themselves in such crises (243). The community, the working-class Wrongoose Penn, decides they have had enough of corruption and party factionalism: "We say outsiders always come inna our areas and reap di sweets. Now we waan show di rest a di world seh good people come from di ghetto. We waan show seh we can lead weself and do it good. We chose Spangler fi our candidate in di election, because him is one of us" (243).

The historical backdrop to this new beginning, in one sense, is the new possibilities opened up by the government's democratization of party politics. This is subaltern history as a history in which the government/ state politics is the protagonist. On the other side of government, however, is subaltern history as told through Patwah politics:

> A cyaan prove it, but what ah understand is dat Cyclops [the reigning politician] was di first politician in dis country to use guns fi fight him campaign. Him do it because him wanted was to control di people living in di Underworld. Di Underworld was a place where people live inna house mek out a box top and ole car skeleton. Dem never have notten. Him give di Underworld man gun fi go shoot off di man dem wat support Sassafras him rival. Sassafras man kill Cyclops boy wid stone and tek way dem gun. So a him first establish di gun and Sassafras polish it off. (244)

There is a war brewing, then, led by local male politicians attacking the voter base of a rival politician by killing the voters. Sassafras's men, not to be outdone, do them one better by retaliating with stones to seize their enemies' guns. The scenario reiterates in 1970s Jamaica the 1960s scene that opens Bobby Seale's *Seize the Time;* here too, it describes the rebirth of men that is the birth of a movement to shake a nation.

At one level, politics in Foxy's history is waged in terms of making good on the social pact. In concrete terms, the people seek benefits: Cyclops razes the Underworld and builds the "Mount Olympus" housing project, work is given away, the people are encouraged to participate openly, to join the debates, to have faith in the new political program and its possibilities. On another level, however, Foxy documents a story of power in men, and of an internal politics of gender that equals the Black Panther Party.

In the beginning, Spangler is described in terms reminiscent of de Boissière's Le Maitre: "Spangler was a handsome man. From yuh look pon him face, you could see seh him is not a man of wrongs. Him look innocent. Brown skin, tall beard, medium build" (243). In his relationships to the people, too, he is clearly of them:

> Sometime even Spangler himself used to come [to the local campaign office]. Him was friendly. Him go round from house to house eating and drinking wid di people and talking to dem about what and what him wan fi change in di area. Him say him a go build school and house fi di people dem weh live inna ratta castle wid di bunchy-fowl-house a pickney, weh a run up and down pon street. Him say him a go build park fi tek dem off a di street. Him say him going try promote youth employment and bring in laws to help di working people—like minimum wage and rent restriction. (244–45)

Spangler's politics is a people's politics, translating Manley's agenda into the specifics of his constituency. This is, then, the crystallization of the opening up and redirection of the state that Democratic Socialism saw as its radical political agenda, the seed of the new social pact between the poorest in Jamaican society and the government from which a new alternative to the Puerto Rican and Cuban developmental models would spring.

The introduction of Ananse, a man also from Wrongoose Penn with roots in the countryside, brings another element. Ananse, like Harris's Jordan, is a man who knows how to balance the books, a manager of the people, a right-hand man: "Ananse get one a di contract weh a give way. But me no see him do no work none at all. Him tek di big money and get one lickle labourer fi do it and give him lickle bit a money" (245). Ananse is nevertheless also a man of the people, a follower of Spangler's politics.

But in Foxy's astute analysis lies the seeds of trouble, the crisis, we could say, between modern politics that equates profits with progress, and beyond with popular representation: "Him a follow Spangler who a preach bout di rights a di small man, but him a imitate di worst ways a di Big Man" (245–46). These "ways" are endemic to the politics of masculinity that equate access with machismo: "Him get big car and start drive up and down all over town wid woman and a spend big money" (245).

Ananse's assimilation into Spangler's political cadre takes place offstage, but its effects are immediate. The armed power struggle between Cyclops's party (occupying Limbo) and Spangler's party becomes war as soon as Spangler wins the election. The political party in power now has to cope with attacks on its constituency with the kinds of shootouts and burnings Manley historicizes in the passive voice. The transition this effects on the political hierarchy is dramatized in Foxy's only slightly metaphoric description of Ananse as "di general" (247), and as in Harris, the man who runs the day-to-day political struggle for control is also "di gorgon" (247). This is not to say that the politics of Spangler have disappeared, but that enacting Spangler's politics through the prism of machismo identity means the two are inextricable, so that "for instance, if yuh are a lickle sufferer in di area him will give yuh a fifty dollar" (247). Foxy's critical aside that Ananse then expects something in return could also be seen as the party expecting loyalty from its people in times of crisis.

The situation is further complicated by the involvement of the police and the army in the fray. The neat distinction between the police and army as apolitical forces beholden only to the state and the law, on one hand, and the troublemakers beholden to neither, on the other, immediately breaks down. From the very beginning, the police are pulled into the war. At a victory march for Spangler, Cyclops's men start firing into the crowd. Foxy's mother is an eyewitness:

> "Fi-we man never have no gun. Dem only fling bottle," Mama say. "A di plain clothes police dat support Spangler. Dem was inna di procession. A dem did a fire dem gun."
>
> Lickle while after, we hear seh Cyclops candidate fi di area call down soldier and police pon Spangler supporters at di constituency

office. Di soldier dem come down and start beat up di people dem. Di people tek revenge. Dem bun up di car dat belong to Cyclops candidate and dem mash up him office. (246–47)

The arming of the people thus becomes a necessity for survival, and the people themselves demand it: "Dat same evening people a walk up and down di community and a say, 'Me no know weh Spangler a deal wid.' 'A full time him arm him man dem' " (247).

Spangler's reappearance bears the hallmarks of the change, and Le Maitre with guns is not as de Boissière would have hoped: "Ah notice dat when Spangler pass, him car full up a bad man. Him start lose weight and wear plenty jewellery. Him always have on a snake head ring. Di more di war gwan is di more attention di bad man get from Spangler. Is like dem start to live off a di fighting. . . . Di fighting give dem something to turn to Spangler wid. Dem can say, 'Me do so and so last night' " (251–52). The discrepancy between Spangler as the hope of the people and Ananse as trouble has closed, and the two become interchangeable, except for Spangler's greater access to the state and the fact that Ananse is in charge of the trenches.

As we saw in the Black Panther Party, it is only a matter of time before the violence that restructures the definition of the community and its relation to the state turns inward. Predictably, from machismo politics the devouring of the community that the armed men are supposed to represent starts with a man's desire for a woman: "Di boys visit Sufferer. Sufferer disappear. Sufferer woman go fi talk, but she know if she talk dem come fi she. Lickle while later, yuh only hear say Ananse deh wid Sufferer woman" (254).

But women's bodies are not only territory to be won as proof of Ananse's power. Ideological reformulations embrace a new inclusion of women as political partners and Ananse follows the party line, although Foxy's cynicism in recounting the story lays bare the schism between cosmetics and real political enfranchisement. The resonance between her complaints and the complaints of the women of the Black Panther Party are startling: "Di party Spangler belongs to talk bout woman, so [Ananse] bring in more woman fi camouflage. Whole heap a woman used to follow him. When dem waan we fi cook and run up and down fi dem, den claim seh woman a di backbone a di political struggle. But when we waan fi more dan serve dem, dem no tek no interest" (256).

Power in men means war, and the language of women's inclusion without dismantling the constitution of masculine identity from the previous horizon means the patronizing marginalization of women, except as cooks, as helpmeets, as sex partners, or metaphors for these new men's progressive superiority, designed to foster women's allegiance as cooks, as helpmeets, as sex partners, and as voters since here, unlike in the Black Panther Party, control of the state is a real possibility. The limit of political representation is marked by the treatment of the body, as in the case of the enemy-state in relation to African-Americans and to subject peoples under colonialism, and so it comes back to haunt the cadres of Democratic Socialism.

Men's abuse of women is not considered, as Harris's Jordan had said, the business of state politics, and the debate between Fenwick and Jordan is reiterated in a debate between Foxy and her politicized lover, a disciple of Spangler's democratic agenda, when Foxy asks: " 'Wah mek him [Ananse] ask fi di gal? A kill him waan come kill her?' " Her male partner responds: " 'Wah happen to yuh. Everyting yuh fight di man inna. Wha mek yuh no mind yuh own business. Yuh hate di man so-till yuh gone inna all di man private affairs' " (254). The failure of Spangler's cadres to include women is succinctly encapsulated in Foxy's retort that the men supposedly fighting "to bring welfare and educate people bout dem democratic rights" (256) "use di word 'private' fi buy pass and cover up all kind a slackness" (254). Jordan's politics win out when Foxy is no longer able to come to Spangler to gain an audience in her realization that Spangler "have him favourite" and that literally—although we can see clearly the politics of its metaphorical implications for identity in struggle—"him favourite is pure man" (256).

From the perspective of the inclusion of woman (a mark of difference on which the PNP's new ideology was predicated) and the betterment of the people's lives (the other mark of difference on which Democratic Socialism was predicated), there is no difference between the old and the new regimes. Democratic Socialism thus failed to redefine the nation toward national unity and in so doing militarized the social pact between the working class and the state; women are left superexploited and marginalized in the political process while also bearing the brunt of the failures of the system. And this is perhaps why Foxy does not bother to name the political parties but focuses instead on the actions of party cadres who operate in their names, which amounts to the same in the end.

For women in the ghetto, nothing changes, and so Foxy is as liable to be a victim of random police abuse as were the women of de Boissière's Trinidad, where, in the service of who knows what if any political affiliation or state agenda, "dem beat all belly-woman and carry dem go jail" (249). Progressive politics in the ghetto as in the nation must go back to the drawing board and think seriously about the incorporation of women, because the men "only rob and scrape. Dem not fighting fi di society better and fi we children better. Dem only go out deh and shoot off a lot of people and when dem fire di gun done, dem no care if di rest still hungry and ignorant. Dem no care if we is no better off" (256).

# 7
## Geopolitics/Geoculture:
## Denationalization in the New World Order

■

In its [postrevolutionary] descending curve, "difference" comes to occupy the site of conflict between the individual subject and his social milieu.—Ileana Rodríguez

If we go down, we go down together. The Los Angeles upheaval [after the Rodney King verdict] forced us to see not only that we are not connected in ways we would like to be but also, in a more profound sense, that this failure to connect binds us even more tightly together.—Cornel West

At the climax of the African-American and West Indian traditions, represented in this volume by the radical experiments of the Black Panther Party and Sistren under Democratic Socialism, we come to a geopolitical frontier. Plans for revolution, state managed or through heightening contradictions, yielded chaos. Revolutionary rhetoric had promised a new social pact; but in both cases the people-nations that the revolutionaries claimed to represent returned to liberalism, rejecting the transformation of social spaces into the war zones that revolutionary principles bring in their wake. And as we move into the twenty-first century, less than twenty years after perestroika, glasnost, and the breaking down of the Berlin Wall, the only viable political alternative to capitalism is more capitalism.

In *The Borderless World* Kenichi Ohmae makes the following formulation of the new relationships between people, governments, and industry: "If this book has another purpose . . . it is to show how multinational companies are truly the servants of demanding consumers around the world. It is these customers who are driving them to operate, develop, make, and sell in many countries at once and who are in the process helping to create a borderless economy where [national] trade statistics are meaningless" (x). Ohmae's depiction of the new multinational logic is in fact through terms once used to describe the role of the state—that is, in terms of the social pact between people and government. If globalism succeeds in rendering meaningless national trade statistics (and thus the concept of the national economy) then globalism succeeds. Then, the American-born Ohmae continues, "you will agree that it is time to throw the bureaucrats out" (x).

The redefinition and reduction of the role of the nation-state—the subsumption of the nation-state to corporate logic internally, complemented and superceded by the rise of the global megacorporations to a global legislative hegemony institutionalized in the World Trade Organization (wTO)—is then a necessary function of the new political economic realities of what Hardt and Negri call "Empire." "Government" accordingly becomes a "bureaucracy" whose job it is to get out of the way of corporate industry, to concern itself with providing a facilitative infrastructure, with the wTO to police it. And for Ohmae, true to the rhetoric of capitalism, it is the "people" who hold the power.

"Democracy" as a system granting equal rights to human beings thus becomes a purely economic concept—the people's right to consume—in which the consumer and the fiction of "economic man" replace the political concept of the people-citizenry, but the power of the consumer is unshakable. Nevertheless, the age-old partnership between the industrialized liberal state and the bourgeoisie, particularly from the United States, dominates the Bretton Woods institutions. These institutions bear down with a vegeance on the countries—now "economies"—in the periphery, those nation-states and populations scrambling to dismantle the putsch toward their political-economic irrelevance in a political world dominated by capitalist ideologies, including "every man for himself" and "my advance at your expense."

From Senator David Coore, Jamaica's minister of foreign affairs and foreign trade in the 1980s, one-time minister of finance under Manley, on the other side of the international division of labor, comes the following cry:

Partly by deliberate design and partly by default, the multilateral institutions have come to exercise a controlling power over the basic economic and financial strategies and even the detailed micro-management of the economies of the developing world. They are using this power to enforce, often in the most extreme form, a specific ideological model of economic management. This not only conflicts with the basic expectation of people that their sovereign Governments have the responsibility for taking fundamental economic and social decisions, but it is not necessarily relevant to the needs and capacities of all countries to the same extent. (qtd. in Ryan, "The Caribbean State" 6)

Government thus becomes a service industry, the secondary partner in an unwanted "global alliance," or in the language of the horizon preceding globalization, entrapment in a new neocolonialism; and it is these "multilateral organizations" (here the World Bank and the International Monetary Fund [IMF]) whose function it is to manage globality in the developing world, with the WTO having ultimate authority over the possibilities of trade. With the decline of peripheral state sovereignty through mortgage and the accompanying rise of the new ideology of global imperialism, the threat of invading armies in the service of cold war politics in the old neocolonialism is thus replaced by the threat of increasing exclusion from the world market, and megaarmies or megacoalition armies in the service of the circuits of capital today.

From either side of the North/South divide, there are two sets of conceptual categories, each with conflicting demands and conceptualizations of success. But what is nevertheless evident is that for both, the key concepts examined in this volume have once more shifted meaning and weight. Gender, New Men, New Women, nation, citizenship, the international division of labor, and, perhaps most dramatically, the state are no longer operating under the same paradigms as have been developing since the seventeenth century.

Bearing in mind David Coore's concern for the interests of the Jamaican—and indeed postcolonial—voters struggling under the blows of decades of "structural adjustment" programs, Gayatri Spivak's view of the West's ultimatum for neoliberal political-economic alignment in decolonizing countries seems particularly apt: "You can knife the poor nation in the back and offer band-aids for a photo opportunity" (*Critique* 371), because, she writes, the "general ideology of global development is racist paternalism (and alas, increasingly, sororalism); its general economics capital-intensive investment; its broad politics the silencing of resistance and of the subaltern" (373).[1] If, as Immanuel Wallerstein argues, the primary conflict in the world system was once between a supranational system that negotiated the role and rights of nation-states on one hand, and the demands of nationalities promised representation by governments on the other, in the twenty-first century that paradigm becomes obsolete. As the new global corporate men debate new supranational structures that acknowledge—even as they push for—the end of the nation-state's control over national economies, so the "people" once referred to as nationalities come to represent "markets" and "consumers." The language of global corporate logic and the language of the state go head to head. Here there is no longer a division between "barbarians" and the "civilized" except in terms of their respect for—and feasibility as—markets and resources.

In the relation of the U.S. state to the people, "nationalism" remains rhetoric designed to bind the people to an allegiance to the state, rather than vice versa, creating a market for the state agenda. Government, too, marries the market, as in the case, among others, of the Gulf War and the invasion of Panama to arrest its head of state packaged and marketed as a "Desert Storm" and a "Just Cause." For the state, "barbarian" is, then, a national-cultural term also used in packaging and marketing war; for the new global managers it becomes an economic concept encompassing those still culturally unabsorbed or unabsorbable into the global circuits of capital. Thus in the new financial world order, determined by the maneuvers of global corporations in an interlinked economy, "people" is a postnational term and "culture" is tied to a gloss of consumption patterns and market conditions.[2] Subalternity remains endemic.

Samir Amin points out that "a country's position in the global hierarchy is defined by its capacity to compete in the world economy" (3) in an unequal fight for control over a share in five global monopolies: technology, worldwide financial markets, natural resources, media and communication, and weapons of mass destruction. Governments based on principles of nationality and the concept of the sovereignty of nation-states in the name of "the people" become a hindrance, like a woman taking too much power to herself and who cannot be thrown out of the house. Governments must accordingly find "global alliances" as well: consider NAFTA, GATT, NATO, the WTO, the G-8, the Trilateral Treaty with Asia, and states making pacts with states to pave the way for the market and to keep up with the paths of industry.

The work of nongovernmental organizations, in tandem with the extraordinary activism of people and organizations like Randall Robinson, TransAfrica, and Amnesty International, becomes the horizon of international social justice and human rights in the Caribbean.[3] The rest of the world's population, particularly in the Third and Fourth Worlds, become increasingly subaltern by force of the dynamics of globalization, even as "the rhetoric of their protest is constantly appropriated" (Spivak, *Critique* 373).[4] The nagging questions of (re)presentation become exacerbated as global inequality escalates.

As some have argued, academic cultural studies may well be in danger of aiding and abetting this project of escalating and normalizing inequalities.[5] In this new global village, the new social pact is marketed as security for people as consumers, and governments and global corporations compete as providers. Following paths cleared by the work of scholars such as Rex Nettleford, Gayatri Spivak, or Hazel Carby, this book has been an attempt to question the role of cultural studies in globality, thinking across the international division of labor. The international literary production of the African diaspora is, like all others, necessarily caught up in this dynamic, and in interrogating the texts I have chosen, I have worlded the texts through the possibilities within cultural studies and textual analysis to see how these texts interrogate their world and the power relations within it, even as the terms of such communal projects and their paradigms are increasingly overwhelmed and undone by the projects of financial and trade globalization.[6]

Globalization, Hobsbawm reminds us, was projected as inevitable since the days of Adam Smith. That Ohmae discusses the nature of strategic alliances between corporations in terms of a "marriage" is revealing of the patterns of power relations in critical pacts, and the patterns of capital's penetration into the domestic sphere to suit its needs. Equality in (corporate) partnerships, Ohmae argues, is critical for the development of the global order. The worsening position of women in the sweatshops of the periphery would then seem to be the dowry, and their organization, betrayal. Corporate practice bears this out.

Ohmae's "marriage" as the hinge in managing transition takes us back to the models we have seen within the literature of African-America and the Caribbean where coupling carries the weight of the social order.[7] Indeed, from Delany through to Sistren coupling has borne the burden of representing the building block of the future. The ends and implications of such couplings, of course, shift from paradigm to paradigm.

Delany, for instance, subordinates coupling to the problems of war, in a military model taken up again in the Black Panther Party. For Delany, and, more explicitly in the case of the BPP, the place of women as bodies in both cases is on the sidelines, one whose ultimate function is service, a refuge from battle should the man-hero want it. At the level of rhetoric and metaphor it is with women as vehicles for national disgrace that women find themselves included throughout the conceptualization of the nation as army, and then as a sign of weakness, men's (therefore national) victimization at the hands of its constituting enemies.

Gender, then, cuts a (national) border. In this, de Boissière's paradigms become the most progressive, for he includes women's bodies at the scene of battle as warriors and as heroes. Although de Boissière's model is also a military one, because women are included in the nation as army, in his novel's final moments he can dress Le Maitre in women's clothing as an act of camouflage and a guerrilla stratagem. At Cassie's suggestion, cast as an instance of brilliant tactics for a common front strategy, Le Maitre overthrows gender bending as a contamination and its copula, the subordination of woman as disease, to advance the cause of the people. If coupling signified a form of internalized authoritarian repression in Delany and the BPP—breaking the pact of equality in the home for the good of the people-nation—for the couple at the vanguard of de Boissière's new nation marriage already signifies a strategic alliance between genders. The same is true in Harris and Hopkins, where marriage is a new beginning for the community yet to be born, and in Sistren, where the failure of Democratic Socialism is linked to the failure of healthy domestic relations with men and thus a gendered civil war. In all cases described above, the status of the national couple reflects the status of national representation, now the battleground for gay rights, the end of social programs, and right-wing elites on both sides of the international division of labor.[8]

If marriage and coupling come to signify the national pact, the inverse processes of denationalization yield orphanhood and homelessness. The grim scenario that opens Rodríguez's retrospective of revolutionary Caribbean writers is duplicated in "At America's Door," a 1993 editorial in the *Economist:*

They dash across the freeways in San Diego, zig-zagging to avoid the traffic. They labour in long rows in the Michigan fields, keeping their heads down. Shiploads of them, huddled in blankets, arrive on the beach in New York. Open the door of a sweatshop in Los Angeles, a garage in Chicago or a hotel kitchen anywhere, and their faces stare out: tired, wary, slightly defiant. Their language is not English. The laws of the United States are mysterious to them. All they want is to work, earn money and be left alone. (11)

In Rodríguez, however, the paradigm of the nation-state as a vehicle for progress and development has failed. At the end of the promise of a revolutionary reorganization of the social pact in their home country— perhaps we could call it a "repatriation" of the social pact—the orphans following the international path of capital are already refugees, dying, or corpses.

The promise of the new social pact between subalterns and the nation-state, in each of the cases we have examined in this volume, was wrapped up in the question of the models of leadership and the revolutionary subject. In all but the paradigm of Sistren, the struggle to give birth to this new subject was a struggle led by males to seize power in the name of the people, the subaltern classes. Just as men remained unquestionably in control of national leadership, women, with the exception of those in de Boissière's final chapters, found their position in the social imaginary unchanged. Even in the case of Sistren Democratic Socialism was an ideology founded and implemented by men with whom the Sistren Collective engages when they speak of the meaning of progress and the nature of the national agenda. And in every case, the metaphors for the new nation are resolutely heterosexual, floundering in negotiating sexual difference within the national community, although here, again, there are progressive moments in Sistren and de Boissière where an attempt to rethink the politics of desire is made at the level of speculation.

The notion of difference, then, structures the heart of national strategizing on the micrological level. Macrologically, if black nationalism, as Moses and Gilroy argue, is a direct response to oppression by Europe and its New World descendants, then Rodríguez's argument holds here too: on the question of women, and more vociferously, on the question of lesbians and gay men, for the most part the paradigms of national leadership incorporated repressive elements from the sociopolitical order they sought to overthrow. The revolutionary leadership repeats learned structures of authoritarianism and repression.

Because of this, we could follow Rodríguez's study of revolutionary

Central American literature and align the disenfranchised. The subaltern masses in Delany, Harris, and Sistren, gay men and lesbians in
Sistren and the BPP, and women in all but the examples of de Boissière
and Sistren are disciplined and expelled. In one instance after another
when we came to the role of women and the feminine in each of the
strategies we found the subaltern expelled under the attributes under the
sign of "woman" as analyzed by European feminists such as Hélène
Cixous, for example, or in another moment, Luce Irigaray.

We confront a cultural dissolution of the borders between us and
them, between the black New World and white Europe, between Central
America, African-America, and the Caribbean—that is, hybridization,
the notion of mulatto as denationalization, the critical counterpart of
reterritorialization and the erasing of borders. Yet the people's determination to gain democratic rights brings the repressed women (including
lesbians) and gay men to voice from within the proposed new national
configurations. The logic of government in the United States creates
ever more fragmented political identities. In the calls for national unity
through inclusion of those previously exiled as difference, new democratic transitions also mean the dissolution of identities premised on the
hegemony of one gender/sexuality nexus over all others.

We can return, then, to the macrological concepts I have followed in
reading nationalist literatures from African-America and the West Indies
as points of entry in grappling with (geo)cultural and (geo)political difference in the new world order under construction. Against the backdrop of
the contradictions and shifts at stake in our own transition, attentive to
the patterns of the national literatures we have explored, I want to read
Ileana Rodríguez's *Women, Guerrillas, and Love: Understanding War in
Central America* (1996) as an elegy to the revolutionary nation-state and
to the promise for social change that it once embodied. It was in the state
that the disenfranchised—from Delany to Sistren—once held out all
hope for equality and justice.

In counterpoint, I want to read African-American novelist Julian's *Just
Being Guys Together* (1992) as a black gay text grappling with utopias.
Julian approached, before his death from AIDS, the dilemmas of the texts
of the African-American nationalist tradition, and he wrote his novella
with an eye to the impasses we carry into the twenty-first century—the
age of AIDS, globality, and the questions of sexuality and identity that
have dogged both traditions. In this, the text represents a vanguard in

that it recognizes at the level of fiction seeking the future what Rodríguez documents at the level of the writing of revolutionary culture of the past, on the border between being in and being out of the African-American nationalist tradition. Finally, I want to read Rodríguez's and Julian's texts through Cornel West's *Race Matters* (1993). In particular, I will follow a path suggested by Rodríguez's paradigm of gender as a sign of denationalization and Julian's novel as plotting hope among the professional cadres through the lens of West's analyses of race, class, and culture in politics, in writing as articulating a new public policy.

As my strategy of reading I want to triangulate these three texts with my analyses in the preceding chapters—a conversation that points to one of the possibilities of interlinked cultural economies or instances of possible strategic alliances across borders. My argument is that the three texts reflect the status of the key terms we have been following from Delany to Sistren. Reconciliation with difference will come to mark a new frontier, as together we move inexorably into a postrevolutionary, postnational world order, and a global turn to neoliberalism. West and Rodríguez will have the last word.

## The Failure of the State

For each of the authors we have studied in this volume, representation by (if not control of) the state was the end point of their nationalist paradigms, and in the state's constitution was invested the solution to the people-nation's problems. At the end of the century, Caribbean nation-states discover from experience that control of the state itself, as a mechanism of popular representation, fails to deliver. Perhaps for this reason the joyous hope of West Indian governmental control that underlies the grim narrative in de Boissière is replaced in Harris by the sudden recognition of the chaos of the nation. In Harris, once control of the state starts to become a concrete reality, the narrative eye begins to see all the difference that divides the national body from itself. It is this crisis of nation formation and popular representation that Sistren's autobiographies document in response to Democratic Socialism. Sistren's testimonials demonstrate that Manley and the People's National Party administration's attempt at a corrective, given control of the state to put it in the service of the national majority, led to an exacerbation of the social pact's disintegration, to more chaos, more civil war, more exiles, more corpses.

The drive toward the nation-state in the periphery as the guarantee of social equity and improved standards of living thus comes to a stalemate.[9]

The faith of African-American narratives in the U.S. state follows a similar trajectory, and given the Caribbean experience Delany's about-face from a strategy of founding a black nation-state with the advent of the Civil War may underscore the viability of his perceptiveness, a perceptiveness we saw everywhere apparent in his macrological assessment of the position of blacks in antebellum New World political economics. The nineteenth century was indeed the heyday of the imperial nation-state. Waging war to force state representation, for Delany as for de Boissière the first step in nation formation was the (re)constitution of the people into an army. Military strategy returns as the vanguard with the guerrilla insurgent model of the BPP, but because the critical objective of territory in state formation remains unresolved, the military forces of the federal government—intelligence and infiltration by the armed forces from the police to the National Guard to the FBI—send the black national agenda into disarray with a series of pivotal murders, arrests, and internal destabilization projects.

In turning away from such military strategies because they represent suicide, the logic of Hopkins's investment in federal power takes her out of home and country, thereby eliminating the escalation in the black body count that armed confrontation would entail. Yet her heroic couple's territorial exile, mirroring black political exile, underscores the entrenchment of white nationalism in state policies. For liberals as for revolutionaries, in the African-American cases of Hopkins, Delany, and the Black Panther Party hope sits in the lap of representation through the nation-state and through incorporation as a subject—rather than object—of law. What is most explicit in Hopkins lies implicitly at the foundation of both Delany's and the BPP's concepts of statehood: the Declaration of Independence, the promises of the Constitution, the tripartheid division of state power as a system of checks and balances. The United States provides the model, and the political horizon is the (re)formation of the liberal state.

The difference between Delany and the BPP and Hopkins is that for Hopkins the problem of territory is immediately confronted, rather than deferred. Thus her tactics for integration through minority rights are based on espousing the virtue of liberal over revolutionary strategies, because without a clear military objective armed mass confrontation can lead only to national extermination. At the outer edge of the struggle for state representation, then, lies national suicide, and it is on the negation of this possibility that the revolutionary military models of Delany and the BPP, as much as de Boissière, are predicated. Because the military narratives threaten death, revolutionary coupling comes to signify setting the world right and national health. For African-America, the failure of the state to grant civil rights leads to a rebirth of nationalist sentiments trapped in a culture in transition, and for the elite, as for the elite of the Third World, partnership in the global order.

*Paradigms of inversion/invagination*
In the cases of paradigmatic inversion in Hopkins, Sistren, and Harris, coupling comes to signify in the opposite direction, and it is revealing that two key terms are chaos and woman. For Hopkins, the chaos of contemporary social relations—the exacerbation of the contradictions of Reconstruction—can only be resolved by struggling toward the liberal horizon. Nevertheless, in the end, clinging to the principles of a state that has abandoned them, the black nation embodied in the heterosexual couple at the vanguard of the new horizon finds itself exiled. For Harris, the nation finding itself in founding itself devours itself. Here again, within the paradigm of chaos, militarism, and the "us" versus "them" of nationalism as a mass movement, it is in the monogamous heterosexual couple that hope for the future of the nation resides. And in both, marriage replaces the pact between women and the state, signaling the political exile of woman. Sistren, extended the hand of government with the promise of Democratic Socialism, finds the woman/nation abandoned to the guerrilla tactics of petty party-bosses (now the "dons" terrorizing ghetto communities, transshipping cocaine and marijuana, brokering elections, and threatening to supercede the capacity of the security forces of the Jamaican state). Poor women find themselves on the other side of a battle waged, in its best instance, by Jamaican men who would reproduce the strategy of the BPP, except here the possibility of radical men taking control of the state is taken much further. The failure in democratic nation formation leads to the failure of the state and the social pact—that is, the promises of citizenship.[10]

Rodríguez's *Women, Guerrillas, and Love: Understanding War in Central America* traces the rise and fall(ing apart) of the new democratic struggles in 1960s Central America, first in the testimonials of guerrillas in the mountains, then progressively in the transition to state power and the articulation of a new social pact, a journey at once realized and meta-phorized as a trek from the country to the city. In some fourteen of the texts Rodríguez reads, consistently the new revolutionary state has as its primary interlocutor the old paradigms from which it seeks to distin-guish itself in critical ways. And although there is no question that the Sandinistas, for example, are antithetical to the sick brutality of the Somoza regime, in seeking to work out the new social pact and the na-ture of the state the blind spots in the gaze of the new revolutionary government come back to separate the leadership from the polity they seek to represent. Hence we see Rodríguez's terminology of deconstruc-tion and the emphasis on the process of invagination, despite the fact that in the Caribbean deconstruction as a technology of knowledge repre-sents what many Caribbean critics consider "white people's business."

As the difference of the revolutionary leadership from the people grows, the gravity of the bond between the vanguard and the people for whom they struggle in war time (Guevara, Borge, Ramírez, Cabezas) comes progressively to be replaced by irony (Borge, Dalton), and then absurdity (Ramírez, Morales), and then chaos (Naranjo), undercut only by the unmitigated gravity of the condition of the people as subaltern and unrepresented by the state (Arias, Asturias, Argueta, women's testi-monials). The revolutionary state becomes a simulacrum—an elaborate representation of itself to itself as a fact of both internal and external realpolitik. In this sense, the narratives of Central American revolutions, like Manley's Third Path and BPP strategy, are again narratives of failure, due, indisputably, to the unrelenting efforts of the powerful right-wing alliances in the U.S. state (Ronald Reagan, George Bush, Oliver North, Jesse Helms, Bill Casey, etc.), but due, too, to the failure of the new states to see, and thus to know, the people they sought to represent. The battle in the international arena of nation-states that Fenwick resorted to in blinding himself to Poseidon, and that Manley frequently resorted to in historicizing his Third Path, would seem to become endemic to nationalist-*cum*-socialist Caribbean governments.

These gaps in revolutionary social pacts held out in African-America by Delany as much as by the BPP, become, as I have argued, critical flaws—lacunae through which the vanguard ideology loses sight of those it seeks to represent, the people-nation promised citizenship. For the BPP, the narrative of history and so of the condition of the nation resolved itself in a racialized story of gender and sexuality determining national organization, and from there a strategy to build an army and take back the streets of the ghettos. Their strategies proved sufficiently powerful to bring the potential for fascism/authoritarianism at the root of the U.S. nation-state to the forefront, but it was fascism/authoritarianism that BPP leadership exemplified in its relationship to black women, especially black lesbians, and to black gay men.[11] For Sistren under Democratic Socialism, again suggesting the inversion signaled by a focus on women, or all those included under the sign of woman, it is local forces aligned with the U.S. state (and as such an international common front) that arms the lumpen of the community, and so Democratic Socialism travels the same road but in the opposite direction.

In 1960s and 1970s African-America and the Caribbean, the attempt at revolution confronts the might of the U.S. state as much as its own internal blindnesses, and in both cases the people-nation reject the vanguard to return to more liberal paradigms. And if throughout the New World liberalism becomes the people's choice after the revolutionary language of the 1960s and 1970s, it is also because the U.S. state has openly declared its intention to undermine all revolutionary agendas at home and abroad. The role of the U.S. state in the return to liberalism is thus pivotal.

The United States backed up neoliberal politics with armies, and fledgling revolutionary societies were infiltrated and destroyed when not outright invaded. Cuba, the last standing revolutionary Caribbean nation-state, walled in on the verge of starvation and atrophy, becomes a case in point. As the squeeze tightens, food shortages slowly starve the people. The Castro government, angry, macho, and determined to go down like a "real man," refuses to relinquish power or brook internal calls for political change, and people seeking to leave the debris of socialism remain trapped behind an iron curtain of ideology. In refusing to confront the new (geo)politics, Castro's revolutionary government, abandoning all semblance of representation of the people, is dragged kicking across the epistemic frontier: nation = corpses; revolutionary state = fascist state; country = concentration camp. And on the other side, the collapse of the "nightmare" of the socialist alternative, Senator Bob Kerry will argue in opening a 1993 Senate Intelligence Committee hearing on Cuba, comes as a "meltdown," the "evaporation" of the revolutionary social pact; in other words, the incorporation of military terms for the aftermath of an atomic explosion to describe the collapse of revolutionary governments and all that they promised to transform for their people. Here, too, in the war against Caribbean sovereignty—against democracy, equal rights, and the rights of citizens of Caribbean nation-states—capital deprivation substitutes for armed invasion.

At the same time, the revolutionary state's failure to transform social relationships within the nation, as much as in the pact signaled by the hyphen joining the two in the term "nation-state," has severely undermined the confidence of the people in the ability of the state to resolve their dilemmas. In the new century, the magnates and the subaltern classes, as much as the petit bourgeoisie, concur in abandoning the failing paradigm of well-being through the mechanism of the nation-state.

### State/city, country, and home/territory

Looking back, like Walter Benjamin's angel of history, all roads to what was once called "country" at the core of Rodríguez's macronarrative lead to and from the wreckage of the history of the state/city, and in following these paths she finds a failure, blindness, and insight. Julian's novel *Just Being Guys Together*, the end of the twentieth-century African-American text I want to introduce in counterpoint, travels in the opposite direction, in that all roads to what was once called "country" lead to the constitution of home. The *fin de siècle* (de)consolidation of a democratic nation-state in Caribbean literature at the end of the twentieth century finds itself counterparted by the (re)consolidation of a home in African-American literature. Globalization provides the platform for a strategic alliance for coupling.

Of course, these associations of state/city with the Caribbean and home/territory with the dilemmas of African-America can also be reversed. In truth, what fuels political transition in the Caribbean nationalist narratives is also a sense of home, and here the problem of territory is also the first priority. The revolution (in Rodríguez, in Harris, in de Boissière, in Sistren) starts with the abandoned zones, the zones of jungle as both a metonym and a metaphor (territory), and then moves to the state territorialized as the seat of government in the city. The terms nation, city, territory, and state thus become inextricably intertwined in the Caribbean sociopolitical scenario.

And on the other side, what is at stake in Julian's novel is the consolidation of home premised as the consolidation of control over territory, but here jungle and bush are replaced by the house and the possibilities of the cities, from macroeconomies to microeconomies. Hopkins's trajectory is out of the home to the Church to the world; for the Panthers, as for Delany, the house offers no refuge from sudden and random assault by the enemy, and so alienation from house = alienation from history = exile. In Julian's novella, the crisis of political exile from the state is resolved, post-1968, in Hopkins's logic of the fin de siècle, through circumventing the hostility of the state by using the laws of private property to win a place from which to gain social, psychological, and from there political, health. The terms of city/state and home/territory thus follow the patterns Rodríguez observes of opposition = equivalency, patterns we will see again, although the roads to the equation for African-America and the Caribbean are obverse and inverse of each other.

African-American literature by women at the end of the twentieth century often documents the difficulties for black women in building a home (single black men are all in jail or gay) even as black men document their exile on the streets, the self-destruction wrought by the influx of drugs through white supremacist engineering for the radicals, and by the inability of young black men to find role models or to access the system of upward mobility for the liberals. Faced with the failure of the home/territory and the city/state to serve the interests of the nation, the terrain of "country" is thus written as an impasse. Thus it is, perhaps, revealing of the place of gay rights as the twentieth century came to a close that Julian's novella of two black gay men building a home, starting from "a house standing alone at the end of a dead end street," came to suggest a new beginning, a new utopic paradigm that can address the structural dilemmas in the African-American debate with an eye to the new world order.

With the demise of state sovereignty, Caribbean literature also documents "a dead end street," the debate, even, of whether state sovereignty was ever really established, the problem of mass migrations to the already overcrowded cities, the flight of middle management to the First World metropolises, the dangers of drug trafficking and the false hope of hard currency injections through drug traffic, the debt crisis, and the decreasing per capita incomes throughout the region. The hope that fuels the fight for a share in the export processing zones, a much sought-after opportunity for linking up with the global economy, is undercut by the victimization of the (women) workers and the absence of corporate interest in regional development. The result of the collapse of the state is thus mass migration, the legal and illegal emigration of the managerial cadres, and, as the 1998 U.N. *Human Development Report* put it, the displacement of 21.5 million of the world population as refugees, sub-altern, dispossessed. Rodríguez's book looks back to remap national/state histories, urgent with the hope for new strategies to reintroduce the agenda of social justice, although her book finds itself in deadlock.

African-American and Caribbean literature grappling with the role of the state as much as country, generally speaking, is a literature of stale-mate and of a conceptual cul-de-sac.[12] It is a fact well noted by African-American political rights groups of the symmetry between racist argu-ments and homophobic arguments in the U.S. Congress, as much as in the Caribbean, that the silencing or total absence of debate complements quiet gay and lesbian disenfranchisement, when not systemic brutality. Not surprisingly, then, Julian's is a novella of the African-American com-munity that traces success precisely to securing a home/territory. Fur-ther, it accounts for, as it moves toward, health in the (micro) social body, with the aim of providing a new kind of (re)solution. In the tradition of black nationalist literature, Julian's novella is at pains to represent a carefully thought out and worked for utopic refuge given the myriad oppressions with which the black main characters, on a daily basis from all fronts, have to contend as people deserving civil rights. The demise of revolutionary macronarratives leaves the public spaces abandoned or stalemated, and so there is the retreat to private spaces in search of utopia, to the romantic paradigm and clusters of couplings as a vehicle for progress.

True to the black nationalist tradition, the two men at the center of Julian's novel, Ernest and Bernard, live in a zone of conflict where differ-ence means disenfranchisement. The blood shed on the streets in the Non-Violent and Black Power movements in the name of national up-ward mobility has given them more choices as to where they can live. But a generation later, the state still does not provide a meaningful social pact—a lack here even less at the level of sexuality than of race—and so the forces marshaled against them are many and varied.

These forces mirror negativities—that is, failures of the social pact with the state at a series of levels. There is the failure of legislation, captured succinctly in the title of Derrick Bell's 1987 history of African-American U.S. civil rights laws, *And We Are Not Saved*. There is the failure of the constitutional rights to equality, equal protection under the law, and to privacy promised to U.S. citizens in the homophobia that encircles them. And at the broadest level, even though propagated in its advice to other nations, there is the failure of the state to educate the public as to the damage social prejudices wreak on the social order, exemplifed in the epistemic exile that comes out of the mouths of the people around them—that is, the single white character who, not accidentally, is the boss (racism + homophobia), and blacks in the persons of the African-American family-nation (homophobia). Within the white community that encircles them, the house at the end of a dead-end street comes to house a new national couple, and in this sense they represent the nation. Because the nation must incorporate women, the novella also grapples with alternate forms of coupling and sexual politics for women in the new strategy. Still, the retreat to private spaces is pervasive—from house to car to plane to house—as the nation's fragmentation reorders relationships to community. There is no state for them. As I have argued, at the end of the nineteenth century, Hopkins's women moved from house to church to world, finding exile; at the end of the twentieth century Julian's men return home and police the door. Here there is no longer hope for a pact with the state, except home as a refuge against orphanhood and death, and community based as much on inclusive, connective relationships to difference as on race.

## The U.S. state as simulacra of democracy

As a metonym of the failure of the social pact in the abuse of state domination at its worst, or representation of the people-nation become simulacra (Rodríguez's "masculine I" = government = the "masculine I"), in the corridors of power Senator Jesse Helms's political work has tied the African-America and the Caribbean and all these issues together. On the international front, his blocking of the funds promised to the Nicaraguan people through the vehicle of the Chamorro government—in exchange for an end to U.S.-created civil war with the defeat of the Sandinistas in an election forced and overseen by the U.S. state—was matched, if not exceeded, within his home territory by his determination to block not just women's and ethnic minority rights (that is, the majority of the citizenry) but most vociferously of all, gay rights. As gay black men and as U.S. citizens, Julian's characters find themselves at the center of elements of the social order marked for subordination by the politics of the status quo. Helms thus comes to embody the enemy-state represent-ing itself in and for itself, against which the vast majority of the people-nation under the baton of the U.S. state must struggle. And in this moment, come full circle, we find that here, in Rodríguez as in Julian, gay people = women = men = people = resources => democracy becomes the utopian (re)conciliation of difference as sociopolitical equal-ity, a paradigm, curiously enough, whose future depends on its making its way, slowly but surely, into the revitalization projects of private institu-tions under the new global corporate structures.

### Nation as (Atte)n(u)ation

In the new globalism the concept of "nation" becomes progressively obsolete, although nationalism still carries sway. Spivak argues acutely that in the Third World "fundamentalist nationalism arises in the loos-ened hyphen between nation and state as the latter is mortgaged by the forces of financialization" (*Critique* 364)—that is, the tremendous debt burden of Third World countries and the relentless imperative toward privatization and structural adjustment. As the borderless economy for-mulates itself in the developed and developing countries, nationalism comes to signify chaos and self-destruction (Bosnia/Kosovo, Northern Ireland) or reactionary household management (Western Europe, Israel, the United States). As such, the problems of the "nation" become prob-lems of managing infrastructure on one hand, and managing internal difference on the other. The cure prescribed by UNESCO is pluralism.

   In a sense, the central importance of managing internal difference is also the lesson of the two traditions we have been exploring: although each successive paradigm has grappled with the relationship of the na-tion as territorial community in relation to the world, it has also been forced to turn inward toward the incipient divisiveness that creates treason—real treason in the cases of de Boissière, Hopkins, the BPP, and Sistren, or as a hallucination as in Harris and the Panthers. Either way, the fear of betrayal leads the national community to devour itself, pitting each element against the other for domination as it splinters the commu-nity. In all the works I examine, the final interlocutor is civil war. As the Caribbean and African-American communities brace themselves in the age of globalization, the final self-curative cry of national leadership is paradoxically toward an inclusiveness, the breaking down of barriers that divide one element of the community from the other, "us" from "them"—that is, the deconstruction of nationalism as its salvation. Only by resolving the impasse of internal difference can the community survive. In this the liberal politics of Julian converge with the revolutionary problematics of Rodríguez and Cornel West.

On the external front, the front of community relations toward other nationalities, the paradigm shift of globalism has reterritorialized the world. Ohmae explains that capital is no longer the province of transnational "national" bourgeoisies. The world, as Umberto Eco described it in the 1970s, is moving "towards a new middle ages," with communities reduced to deterritorialized bands and with capital transnationalized in the extreme through a handful of key cities.[13] Ohmae's description of the increasing independence of the massive foreign exchange market from government control exemplifies this: foreign exchange linkages determine the statements of governments, not the other way around. Power as an economic concept has left government behind, and so government must redefine its purpose to survive.

Under these conditions, nationalism becomes a destructive force, disrupting local market conditions at worst and fostering protectionist policies at best. The recognition of this destruction is signaled in the shifts in strategy and administrators at the top of the national organizations (states in the Caribbean, the political black bourgeoisie in the United States). West Indian Carnival, for example, was once fiercely protected by Trinidad as its own lucrative nationalist concern. Carnivals staged by other countries (Jamaica, Barbados, Guyana) were thus seen to be undermining the national cultural supremacy in Carnival, and thus the nation. Now, however, the paradigm has shifted, in part with the persistence of the regional tourist industry aligned with governments and a vibrant, established, already Pan-West Indian cultural sector. Carnival is, then, a component in a new strategic alliance. For following on the path of erasing borders in economic strategy, tourism becomes a key industry interlinking the region's national economies. The region and the culture become commodities produced and marketed by strategic alliances for a globally conceived consumer base. "Carnival" becomes a postnational, regional event in the face of the increasingly urgent developmental targets across national frontiers toward the formation of linkages for a borderless world.

On the other side, in the developed countries, with the success of the antiapartheid struggle, elite African-American executives make it their concern to invest for the long term in the new South Africa.[14] In facing the logic of these examples, we face the end of nationalism, for the political borders representing national borders have already been exceeded by a transnational economic order. The chauvinism of U.S. black nationalism toward other countries—inclusion of another element of the diaspora, especially "Africa" and the Caribbean island nations as simulacra for self-gratification—is substituted by strategic financial and cultural alliance; by the strategies, if not necessarily the tactics, of the corporate agendas for the twenty-first century. In the new global paradigm, "balancing payments"—the new term superceding "progress" and "development"—requires the end of the blind "us" versus "them" that structures nationalist identity.

### Difference as (atte)n(u)ation

Reading into the negative spaces of Rodríguez's narrative, the "moment of disillusion" cuts both ways. Hobsbawm emphasizes that states create nations, not the other way around, and following this logic, with the failure of the state, it stands to reason that the disintegration of the social pact leads inevitably to the attenuation of nation as a cohering concept. Looking back through Rodríguez's readings, in hindsight the nagging questions of the difference between revolutionaries and people, people and women, government and people, revolutionaries and the revolutionary state, " 'revolutionary'ism" and romanticism unravels the national social pact at every stage of its constitution.

Granted the relative advantages of living in highly developed zones, the new generation at the center of Julian's novella has also broken with the paradigm of the "nation." In its place we find a community horizon of smaller, attenuated social groups, an interconnection of households whose interconnection both supports and constitutes them as a political family. The subjects signifying health in Julian's utopia are coupled and productive, developing community more along the lines of the Sistren experiment against the "I" of the revolutionary hero of Black Power or the party bosses of Democratic Socialism. Yet the break between the revolutionary and the romantic narrative yields a critical difference in the fragmentation of the community and reorganization of the way domestic units connect. If in Sistren we find women who organize collectively outside the home to change the nation and the pact with domestic space, in Julian men and women organize to create a transformative home and engage with a new, privatized social order.

At the level of the people, there is, then, for African-America and the Caribbean already an end to nationalism. There may be a pleasure in regional or ethnic culture, but the dogged alliance to the nation-state, and thus the concept of nation, is no longer individually viable, except as a commodity, a simulacrum. The elites of both groups have long followed the global path of profits beyond the national interests, except at times in name only. The petit bourgeoisie, typically, has followed suit, as shown by the fetish for Miami, New York, Mercedes Benzes and suvs, the latest designer label in jeans and shoes, and "appropriate neighborhoods" "safe" from the increasingly restless and violent subaltern classes.

The widening gap between elite and subaltern that allows, as much as it fosters, the new strategies of the elite similarly determines the new subaltern strategies, those men and women the *Economist* describes as wanting only "to work, earn money and be left alone." As we cross into the new century, the sufferers, traditionally at the mercy of government and the nation-states, have taken their lives and their futures into their own hands. That is why, according to a U.N. report on migration, the women migrating to the developed zones outnumber the men. Further, it is a sign of the role of gender missed in "nation formation" then, and in "global (i.e., postnational) economics" now, that women are twice as likely to send money "home" than are men, and that they contributed in 1992 some US$60 million to the territorial economies, as opposed to the US$45 million disbursed in foreign aid.[15] The flight of capital and management from the underdeveloped zones is matched by the flight, whenever possible, of people classified as "unskilled labor."

As the underdeveloped nations spiraled into greater and greater impoverishment, self-preservation for the group through class allegiance— cultural/economic but no longer national—has taken its place. Thus "Haitians" will band together to build a boat and risk probable death trying to cross to the United States, and Latin Americans will sneak across the U.S.-Mexico border by land, also risking death. The postnational group may reconstitute itself in the metropolis, but here community is a question of shared culture and experience, and so nationalism as a separatist concept loses much of its popular sway in favor of economic assimilation. In the northern metropolis, the postnational identity expresses the attenuation of personal/national identity in its hyphenations—"Haitian-

Americans," "Mexican-Americans." Those remaining at home in the Caribbean increasingly debate party loyalty, and, in African-America, the disillusion with the electoral system in all but the worst-case scenario has become a truism in the mass media, a forum generally oblivious to the political trends of the African-American community.

Nevertheless, community persists through culture and experience, and so the world Rodríguez explores is, she proves indisputably, inextricably linked across national boundaries, just as the vehicle for Bernard and Ernest coming to know one another is jazz as a sublime expression of African-American culture, a home-grown forum for the black experience gone global.

### Rethinking New Men and New Women

In traveling back to the source of the failure of national representation, both Rodríguez's and Julian's texts grapple again with the problem/concept of New Men and New Women, of the paradigms (social, psychological, political) for exemplifying leadership in the new globalism. If in Rodríguez this is a double-edged narrative of some success but much failure at the macrological level (hence the narrative of chaos/authoritarianism and the persistence of subalternity we also found in moving from Harris to Sistren) in Julian there is the trek toward some failure but much success once the social sphere has shrunk to the home, and the trajectory into the public sphere incorporates the global marketplace.

Rodríguez's "New Man" struggles with the relationship between the "I" of the guerrilla and the "We" of the people. For Guevara, the "New Man" is at once tripartheid and of a piece. Nevertheless Rodríguez finds the New Man is fatally split between his equivalence to "the people" and his difference from them; that is, between the New Man as "one who shares the longing of the people for liberation" (equivalence) and the New Man as "a guiding angel, who has fallen into the zone, helping the poor" (difference) (42). The split between the New Man and the people-nation begins to breach.

As a percentage of the population, women and gay men make up the majority of the people. When the BPP in African-America, like the *guerillero* in Central America, lambastes as a fundamental precept in the formation of the New Man-as-the-vanguard that the New Man (Panther, *guerillero*, zygote of the new nation) not be "a bunch of little women . . . a bunch of faggots" (Rodríguez 45), the political pact with the majority—that is, with democracy—is already broken. Delany's project betrayed the same breach with barbarian culture taking the place of gayness. At birth, then, the new man in Central America as in African-America alienated himself from the people. Sistren, the Panthers, and Harris record the effects of this breach. Revolutionary nation formation fails despite the fact that, as Rodríguez remarks, the new men believe that in seizing power they are exercising *tendresse*, love as discipline, and as such, *"tendresse* is proposed as an instrumental term mending a rift" between the vanguard and the people (33).

On this precept of subject/vanguard formation, Rodríguez points out that to construct

> the New social subject with religious attributes, repressing the emotive components of the psyche, leads to the denial of that which represents the intervention of the subjective element in the revolutionary lexicon's social revolutionary formations. Language plays logical tricks, and makes A = −A: in proposing the conjunction of the individual/collective, they projected those same attributes of the masculine I onto the collective. In making emotive personal-social expressions clandestine they favored the economies of false conscience and made a simulacrum of daily political life. It is this characterization of resistance as repression, and of strength as endurance, that stymied the New in the New Man. (48)

Rodríguez points to the problems of language as knowledge technology in grappling with the failure of the revolution to equal the people for her own reasons. For ours it is the last series that comes to be the crux of the revolutionary dilemma: resistance to repression = more repression; strength = more suffering, more endurance. The New Man thus incorporates into the paradigm of the central social subject the psychic structures of authoritarianism. Harris recognized this in Guyana's transition to Independence, at the level of political logic translated into problems of epistemology. It is this, in one sense, that generates the chaos of the social world—jungle as metaphor for the relations between social classes/forces—when each segment of the national community predicates its own progress on the marginalization and disenfranchisement of the other social groups. Given the lens of socialism that claims to substitute equivalencies for differences, the social pact is impossible to fulfill because the people reproduce the structures of authoritarianism en masse, but against each other. De Boissière's history proves mistaken, impossibly utopian.

This dilemma comes to structure the learning process of social relations and progress for the two men at the center of *Just Being Guys Together*. The psychological trek in the guerrilla literature is from "faggots" and "little women" to men en route from the mountain (exile) to the city (home/territory) in search of country. In Julian's novella and short stories the trek is toward a realization of the difference difference makes, a critical rerouting between men and men, between women and men, between women and women. Houses and couplings consummate the national narratives of Delany, Hopkins, de Boissière, and Harris. Following on the extrapolation from house/coupling to nation we could read the shifting relationships between Ernest and Bernard, Wanda (Ernest's sister) and Stephanie (Ernest's friend) in terms of a macrologics for social relations renegotiating differences and equivalencies in the name of fairness, empowerment, and respect. The fact that (with the overdetermined exception of the boss) all of the characters in Julian's novel are black, and that the novel struggles with the establishment of community within the paradigm of family, are indicative of such a reading.

We have seen marriage as a metaphor throughout the nationalist works examined in this volume, with the exceptions of Sistren and the BPP for whom coupling represented the repressiveness of the preceding paradigms. Marriage as a metonym, however, takes us to the other side of constituting social relations as equivalencies. In regard to coupling, revolutionary culture must inevitably come to grips with the play of (revolutionary) social forces in sexual/interpersonal relations. Rodríguez points this out in reading Roberto Morales's novel *El esplendor de la Pirámide* (The splendor of the pyramid), in Manlio Argueta's novelized testimonial *One Day of Life,* and again in reading three Central American women's testimonials. In Morales, for example, the woman excluded in vanguard formation becomes the crux on which the success of the struggle turns, the novel ending with the question always already answered in the affirmative in Argueta and in the testimonials. At stake here are the concepts of nation and community metonymized as family and couple. In Rodríguez's reading of *One Day of Life,* and again in her reading of the testimonials, however, she finds that in the hands of subaltern New Women, beyond the paradigm of the biological family, lies the political family; that is, the convergence of the "I" with the "We" that the revolu-tionaries fought to enact. Here the BPP and Sistren are reincorporated into the paradigm of marital relations as progressive national/commu-nity relations. As the testimonials of the three groups under scrutiny (Sistren, the BPP, and Central American women) make clear, however, the potential for real-life mergers of the biological with the social to yield the political family is fraught with tensions.

And it is in the alienation of people from people that the forces of repression take root: in Sistren as in the Central American women's testimonials, for example, the alienation of men from women is a famil-ial and political fact. It is telling of the sense of a massacre both ongoing and impending, perhaps, that Huey Newton's revolutionary paradigm eschews marriage and the family as reactionary, in favor of suicide. As Rodríguez points out for the testimonials, and as Julian exemplifies in his novella, in fact the distinction between the nuclear/biological family and the political family is sexual access. Thus that limit to sexual access that Newton and Seale sought to break is reconsolidated in the utopic moments of (re)union, advocated and exemplified in the testimonials (Sistren, the three Central American women's narratives), as much as in Julian. Monogamy comes to underwrite trust in the most intimate of pacts. Conservative ideology succeeds.

### Reconfiguring the national community

In two critical scenarios, Julian describes a key transition from a pact between couples to a political familial pact. In the first, Ernest has invited Bernard and Wanda to an all-black gay and lesbian setting. All three find themselves alienated from each other (difference). Bernard complains vociferously about Wanda's presence as an outsider at an event organized on the premise of the centrality of black gay and lesbian culture. Ernest's response to Bernard is a mixture of silence, refusal, and patient rebuttal. Yet for Ernest, Wanda is his sister and Bernard his lover, and so each is the other's "in-law" (marriage yields equivalence). In response to the tensions that arise when Bernard and Wanda must negotiate each other's difference Ernest leaves them more or less to elaborate their own rela-tionship, while making the importance of their finding value in each other clear to both of them.

Bernard reads all the alienation of white from black America in Wanda's alienation from the people around her, in her bearing as much as her words, in "her off-to-see-the-carnival-sideshow take on the evening ahead" (2–3). The analogy to marriage comes to the rescue in the relationship between black gay men, lesbians, and straight women (groups oppressed by the black community) as an analogy for rethinking the place of gender and sexuality in the nation as a political family, in Bernard's imagining "that putting up with Wanda was like putting up with in-laws. It's only for a few hours, he kept telling himself. And Ernest was worth it" (2–3). For Wanda the same is true, although in-laws represent an unavoidable part of life, when she labels Bernard's suspect remarks as like "in-laws." The centripetal force of the relationship between Ernest and Bernard thus becomes the equivalent of the formation of a healing social pact across warring factions, and so the problem of difference in the figures constituting the nation as family must be worked out.

### Reconfiguring woman

The shift in the relationship between Wanda as a heterosexual woman and Bernard as a homosexual man carries with it the weight of testing the usefulness of the new paradigm of men's relations with men for the community at large. That is, the social test for the new men's relationship and self-conception is in its (their) ability to incorporate its (their) own difference into the struggles of the heterosexual community and vice versa. True to the utopian impulse driving the novel, when several chapters later Wanda appears suddenly at the house looking for Ernest to help dissuade a man who has tracked her threateningly for miles, Bernard, in the second key transitional moment, uses the power of the male body in threatening social situations to scare the would-be rapist away. That is, Bernard inverts the strategy of repressive masculine authoritarianism through the deception in presenting himself to a homophobe as a "real man" and not a "faggot," thereby invoking, in order to rescue Wanda from violation, the threat of violence that conditions men's homosocial relations over women's body parts.

The psychodynamics of this second configuration are revealing. First, Bernard recognizes the social position of Wanda as a woman and as a *compañera,* and this means recognizing the prevalence of rape as a threat men hold against women. For Wanda's part, in seeking out her brother and finding her brother's lover, when she tells him of her situation and solicits his help she is making the equivalence from biological pacts to new social relations at the base of democratic reorganizations of the social sphere. In making such an alliance, Wanda recognizes and appreciates Bernard's strategic use of his male power—a strategy she herself had devised and had come to her brother (a biological pact) to implement, and found his lover willing to engage (a sociopolitical pact). Bernard threatens to attack the unnamed man in defending Wanda as his property. In the battle between Bernard and the unnamed man, the hostilities internal to the black social world determine interpersonal relations, following on the combative logic of the BPP as much as the guerrilla troops Rodríguez analyses: men + men yields resistance = repression; strength = endurance.

To come to this pact, Bernard and Wanda individually and collectively recognize each other as social beings in a hierarchy of race, gender, and sexuality that constantly shifts, and so their new relationship that incorporates each for the other into the family/home is predicated on reading against the grain. And just as Bernard and Wanda worked out a pact through a metaphor of marriage in the first scenario, in the second moment of transition her strategy is to present Ernest/Bernard as her husband. Heterosexual and homosexual men's and women's democratic recognition of difference becomes the key to healing divisive social relations and thus to a new social pact embracing difference in equality.

### The invagination of sexuality

The process of elaborating social justice in equivalencies that acknowledge difference works its way into the question of personal identity, of the interplay between self and other. The two transitional moments exemplify this. In the first, Wanda and Ernest are dining and they are approached by an acquaintance of Wanda's:

> "Wanda!" she exclaimed, leaning down to hug Wanda. "*Alrrrrright,* girlfriend!" she said, giving a knowing wink to Wanda. "It's good to *see* you here. I kept wondering why I never seen you out anywhere. After a while, I figured you must be in a real solid relationship or something." She squeezed Wanda's hand and continued. "Sure is good to see you here. Let's dance!" . . . "I'm not—I'm straight, Lurleen—" Wanda finally said. "Yeah, you, me, and everybody else here come Monday morning!" (2–6)

As a critical step in understanding the positions of Bernard and Ernest as difference, Wanda finds herself, because of her presence at a gay and lesbian social gathering, labeled a lesbian herself. True to the general strategy of the novel, however, the context for such an epistemic violence is turned inside out because her colleague from work, coming out to her as a lesbian herself, greets her with joy as "family"—that is, family as a political concept. In her logical twists to extricate herself from a perceived homosexuality, Wanda finds herself throwing up the prejudices and alienation of homophobia, the desperate emotional and political need to differentiate herself from "them," to remain an outsider, a woman come into alien territory; a woman come, as her brother muses on her epistemological predicament, only "to spy and be fly" (2–6). Wanda finds herself at the inversion of collective sexual mores, included as one of the "us" when her sense of herself is predicated on being one of "them." Or to invert the dynamic, when Wanda (the I/she) wants to equal the collectivity as duplications of herself, and so classify those around her as "them" (them ≠ I-We = nation), Wanda finds herself at an impasse.

In making the connection to the second transitional moment when Wanda seeks protection from Ernest and finds Bernard, Cornel West's explorations in *Race Matters* of the impact of race, gender, sexuality, and history on black politics and culture provides a critique pivotal to contextualizing Wanda's dilemma and subsequent transformation. West scrutinizes, for example, the interdependence of claims to "racial authenticity," "black nationalist sentiments" (as in the BPP), and "the way in which black nationalist sentiments promote and encourage black cultural conservatism, especially black patriarchal (and homophobic) power" (25). "Like all conservatisms rooted in a quest for order," West writes, "the pervasive disorder in white and, especially, black America fans and fuels the channeling of rage toward the most vulnerable and degraded members of the community. For white America, this means primarily scapegoating black people, women, gay men, and lesbians. For black America, this means principally attacking black women and black gay men and lesbians" (27).

Wanda's dilemma in being included as a lesbian is thus a national one, and she seeks to ally herself with black nationalist conservatism in asserting her difference from the people around her. All of this converges, then, on the nexus of politics and sexuality, a distorted inheritance of Black Power rhetoric in the popular imagination, the demand for arms severed from any community agenda: "For most young black men, power is acquired by stylizing their bodies . . . in such a way that their bodies reflect their uniqueness and provoke fear in others . . . and so-licits an attention that makes others pull back with some trepidation. . . . Yet a black machismo style solicits primarily sexual encounters with women and violent encounters with other black men" (88–89).

The other side of the social equation is the fear generated by the threat of encounters with these men. Julian's unnamed man is a metonym for this segment of the black community, just as these men, advocates of post-1968 black nationalism, use their maleness, their heterosexuality, and the threat of violence—conservative patriarchy—to claim primacy; that is, their status as new men, as the vanguard, rulers of the street, members of a family premised on murdering members of the black com-munity. The status of women and gay men as prime targets for assault leads to a pervasive fear for these two groups, creating what Maria Mila-gros López calls a "text of fear" that functions as "a social condition that emerges or disappears as a result of our real or imagined relation to the ex-terior" (97). Throughout Julian's text, anterior to the sociopolitical deci-sions that structure the novel, it is precisely a rejection of and mobilization against fear and insecurity that constitute "a new space of *social consensus* where heterogeneous sectors of the population seem to converge . . . around a sense of experienced fear" (99). The absorption of individuals into capital under globalism and the laws of private property become walls protecting Julian's protagonists against this fear and its perpetrators like the unnamed man—his lack of a name underscoring the fact that he stands as a metonym for a violent sexism and homophobia.[16]

For her part, Wanda's early homophobia, like all homophobia, is based on the distinction that men = heterosexual; homosexual ≠ men. The first and second transitions, then, constitute a copula in reforming the place of gender and sexuality in reforming new political identities. In opening the road both ways Bernard's later deployment of male privilege and the logic of compulsory heterosexuality to remove Wanda from dan-ger disrupts the epistemic chain, and so Bernard is a man as the man who pursues her is a man—hence Bernard's or Ernest's ability to maneu-ver the situation. Here heterosexuality, alienation from women, violence, and repression (social, biological, and political, in the case of rape), tak-ing the place of love in social relations, is the definition of "man" that both Wanda and Bernard must agree is hegemonic to get her out of danger. Yet it is the recognition of the (power) equivalence in both Ber-nard's (gay) male body and the would-be rapist's (heterosexual) male body, simultaneously with Wanda's and Bernard's recognition of Bernard's difference (the reserving of sexual desire + the shared metaphor of family as a founding precept of interpersonal relations) that is at the basis of their alliance, and so the healing social pact.

Persistently in Julian's novella, as if in answer to West, "black cultural democracy" replaces "black cultural conservatism." According to West, "instead of authoritarian sensibilities that subordinate women or degrade gay men and lesbians, black cultural democracy promotes the equality of black women and men and the humanity of black gay men and lesbians" (29). Wanda's transformation thus carries the weight of a cultural revolution, the formation of a new democratic pact across genders and sexualities. The text of fear, rather than serving to cement allegiances to the state and its self-interested narratives of the social body (as in the Anglo-American and conservative African-American communities), becomes a "floating signifier [whose] great potential for collective mobilization" is actualized (López 110).

### The Persistence of the International Division of Labor

Julian's utopia is facilitated by money and the absence of physical violence—that is, a convenient but costly combination of class and nation. The wealth of the United States, we must never forget, was and is accumulated by a history of unequal relationships and ruthless political economic exploitation. If in the African-American tradition the Caribbean functions as a refuge—discursive in Delany and Hopkins, real in the case of several BPP members—in the Caribbean the United States functions as a repository of capital nevertheless de-utopianized in the rumors of racial oppression and the explicitly classist and racist immigration laws that hold sway in U.S. embassies in the New World. In de Boissière, Mrs. Henriques, Elena's mother, plans her escape from the barrack yard to a utopian United States, only to be told that the United States offers no refuge. The Caribbean people's introduction to systemic black exclusion undercuts the narrative of the American Dream as part of the transformation of the people into nation through education and a new awareness of racial politics across national borders. It points, too, to the importance of claiming Caribbean home territory, of claiming country.

In Harris, the United States is referred to only obliquely as the other horizon; indirectly, in terms of the international markets, through the metonym of foreign exchange—that is, a source of hard currency in permanently short supply. The chaos of civil war further ensures this, just as the war is brought on by a struggle over the management of resources and over development as disenfranchisement of the people on the fringe of integration into capitalism. In Sistren, the United States functions as the place to which nomadic men disappear in search of a better life, most often never to be heard from again, and as the source of the CIA arming men in the ghetto. After the demise of the social-ist project, we saw earlier, women will follow the same path as global nomads, but will send hard currency (U.S. dollars and British pounds) home to support families left behind. The failure of the state makes pursuing development, redressing unequal exchange, and negotiating the international division of labor a family affair. Globalism, then, works its way into daily life.

Curiously, this is precisely Ohmae's advice to developing nations. There is no doubt Ohmae delights in the logic of the game of interna-tional capitalism, but, in another example of the odd convergence of evaluations on the Right and Left he is in agreement with the vanguard of Third World development strategists when he emphasizes the critical nature of the paradigm shift, slow to be adopted by Third World govern-ments. This reluctance, as he rightly argues, is an exercise in their desire to hold power at the expense of the people. The hope for development defined as improvements in key indicators (infant mortality, life expec-tancy, expenditure on health, and so on) in the new paradigm lies in the reversal and displacement of the protectionism of Third World strategies in the multinational world order in favor of the creation of a Caribbean regional economy. Such an enterprise presents the opportunity for a model of new democratic relations between countries and across bor-ders, and a new experiment in fairness and respect as mutually beneficial to each of the countries involved. The hope for development thus lies in a paradigm of "us" + "them" as burden sharing—in terms of expertise, infrastructure, and fixed costs in communities as markets. The business of social well-being, of coming together as a community—of politics, in short—comes from the possibilities that integration into the global econ-omy as a global economy allows.

As the project of regional integration outside of NAFTA stutters, the WTO works hard to ensure the development of New World territories as markets for megacorporations by striking down European partnerships with the small farmers in the region and crushing local competitors. The collapse of any viable political alternative to capitalism also means the collapse of any respect for the idea of the right to work, which means, in concrete terms, the resubalternization of the poor in the region. Withdrawal from the global economy is not an option, creating the cul-de-sac of the project of representation and citizenship. This is what it means to say, "capitalism won." "Market calculations and cost-benefit analyses," West writes with prophetic acuity, "hold sway in almost every sphere of U.S. society" (16). Globalization permeates daily life in the ghetto and in the house, as in the transnational corporation. But explicitly in the case of the Caribbean administrative elite, and implicitly if we extrapolate from the Caribbean subalterns' choice of flight and attenuation of nation, the same holds true for the underdeveloped world. As we saw in the *Economist,* from the perspective of the refugee "illegal immigration" is fundamentally a calculated, economic decision based on the status of labor markets and cost-benefit analyses. All parties recognize that old political battles are now resolved on economic grounds, and so the state, gender equality, and postnational communities must all find a niche in the shifting patterns of the international division of labor.

It is revealing that here the state is absent from the strategies of expansion explored in West, Rodríguez, and Julian and is embodied in subaltern migration, and that corporations and cities, as markets for labor as much as goods and services, take its place. For Julian, African-American strategy shifts in recognition of the failure of the nation-state and of it as "not ours," even as the state itself goes into decline as the deconstruction of the prior epistemologies of black power. In West the growth and development of an infrastructure, a political project akin to the economic project of the until recently vilified Booker T. Washington, becomes the hope of the ghettos. For West, alliances are made to institution building, but in Julian, as for the black community permeated by corporate values, personal security becomes once more the horizon and the global marketplace is the terrain. In the ghettos of African-America and the Caribbean the ticket is drugs; in Julian, as for the cadres of new intellectuals (Shelby Steele/Cornell West/Rex Nettleford), politicos (Cornel West/Rex Nettleford), and artists (Toni Morrison/Ice-T/Kamau Braithwaite/Velma Pollard), it is culture.

On the other side of the international division of labor, from the leading Caribbean strategists who must think about Caribbean public policy and its responsibility to help redefine the agenda of the state, this globalization, reconsolidation, and careful diversification for local expansion is the agenda driving a new urgent logic.[17] The disappointment of the Caribbean in the preceding paradigm of "protectionism as an anti-imperialist strategy" that Ohmae outlines comes in the wake of the expectations of the nation-state as newly "ours" and of faith in the nation-state as the vehicle for community development and representation that lies at the heart of each of the Caribbean strategies examined in this volume. Under globalism, the imperialist policies of the cold war era—as irrational and antidemocratic as they were invasive—have given way to a new political geography and new geopolitical strategies with the international division of labor at its heart. And so where once the region could trade off on cold war alliances for its own benefit, now the problem is simply to be noticed by the global players.

It is perhaps in this light that we can read the complex network of global alliances that structure the last two chapters of Rodríguez's book. The work of Indian scholar—and globetrotter—Ranajit Guha on a legal fragment provides the conceptual starting point for reopening the road to empowerment in Rodríguez's reading of Asturias's *Men of Maize*. And in her final chapter on Central American women's testimonials edited by women of the global elite, the work of self-exiled Chinese feminist scholar Xiaomei Chen cross-fertilizes with the work of U.S. scholar John Beverley, U.S. poet of witness Carolyn Forché, Chicano activist/critic Juan Flores, Salvadoran-American critic George Yúdice, international Bengali critic (and expert on French deconstruction) Gayatri Spivak, and the list goes on. In the search for a new knowledge technology through which the oppressed can speak, Caribbean critics draw from around the globe, following on the agendas of breaking the silence and forming community for political and economic relief exemplified in the production of these testimonials, as much as in the work of international institutions critical to what was once a national revolutionary agenda—Witness for Peace, for example, or Americans United with the Congolese People. In the post–cold war global paradigms, it is lobbyists from these groups as much as testimonials produced by international teams that can redirect state policy.[18]

Rodríguez's focus on the status of women's testimonial literature and the role of elite/First World women in it, through the examples of the work of Lea Marenn on *Salvador's Children: A Song for Survival,* Elizabeth

Burgos-Debray on *I, Rigoberta Menchú*, and Margaret Randall on *Todas estamos despiertas: Testimonios de la mujer nicaragüense*, points to the globalization of what were once local agendas whose success depended on blocking northern intervention. Rodríguez discovers that "in situations such as Menchú's—Venezuela/France/Guatemala—and [Lea Marenn]—El Salvador/United States/Central Europe—nuanced by a diversity of political, social, and ideological circumstances ordering national/party mediations in a highly definitive transnational environment, the constitution of the subjectivity of the female subaltern could still be analyzed in terms of the solidarity and commitment of the (woman) writer" (*Women* 170). New paradigms of development and postnational political agendas thus require transnational alliances: the role, in Lea Marenn's instance, of international adoption agencies; the availability of money from financial institutions as well as family members; the role of Witness for Peace in using the power of white skin and a U.S. passport to protect Central American refugees. This is not to say that Rodríguez argues for the death of local community solidarity—horizontal alliances—for it is only in the name of configurations of community that her book finds hope for resolution of the poverty crushing the vast majority of Caribbean peoples. In her, as in Julian, globalization also means that useful strategies for developing knowledge technology can be gleaned from all over the world.

### Gender as a Sign of Denationalization

My closing subtitle above is taken from Rodríguez's opening chapter of *Women, Guerrillas, and Love,* characterizing the meeting of the Sandinistas and the Contras to sign a new national pact, a meeting redefining the nation as "a point of inversion, the space of negation, the realization of the unimaginable" (3). Women's dead bodies come to signify the crisis of the state allegorized in fiction (in the case of Sergio Ramírez's *Castigo Divino*) and in autobiography (Tomás Borge's *The Patient Impatience*). The presence of women's dead bodies as a sign of denationalization raises for Rodríguez the question of the double role of gender in national literature. On one hand, she argues, "woman" comes to signify the loss of sovereignty, transposing the social role assigned to women into the arena of nation-states. And because the nation-state is masculine, this transferal of the man-nation to the position of women signifies gayness as a sign of the loss of sovereignty, defeat, and denationalization, the men-leaders casting their loss of sovereignty as the nation itself "taking it up the ass" (60), or as Amin has it, those states he locates at the "fag-end" of the world system (73).

On the other hand, Rodríguez makes two important points. First, that women form the demographic majority of the people populating the territory of the state (an average of 51 percent of any population). Second, that the position of "woman" (as other, as soft, as untrustworthy, as unfit for inclusion into the military cadres, etc.) is the place assigned to the campesinos in whose name revolutions are fought. Thus with the alienation of the state from the nation and the failure of the social pact, gender, as a sign of denationalization, comes to signify the failure of the state to mobilize, sustain, know, and therefore operate in the name and service of the nation.

Women's bodies as dead, disappeared, or alive have performed the same function throughout the texts I have examined. Interestingly, in moments of nation formation, women are inscribed as alive and present: Maggie and Henrico, Sappho and Will, Cassie and Le Maitre, Catalena and Bryant.[19] In moments of denationalization women's bodies disappear or appear as dead: the women/corpses/history of the BPP, the violated and sold Sappho, the kidnapped Catalena as a sign of national crisis that the workers invade the barbarian camp to rectify. And when women take center stage, as in Sistren, the gender positions are reversed: gender as a sign of denationalization comes to mean an absence of good or innocent men, or their appearance as dead or disappeared bodies.

The reading of the new social relationships in Julian's novella that I have been pursuing here in regard to the ideology of Black Power, in which, as we have seen, the rhetoric of a radicalized new nation deployed the metaphors of women and gay men as treason, is thus also an argument of inversion, of "the realization of the unimaginable." People exiled from the new guerrilla nation—gay men and women—come to the table from a position of strength. Hopkins, also exploring the parameters of race, gender, and sexuality, again provides a revealing precedent.

Hopkins's Sappho and Dora, each drawn inexplicably to the other and locking themselves in the privileged front square room, risk a harmony among themselves that threatens to render men, and so for Hopkins the nation, redundant. If women's longing for women is consistently displaced at the beginning of the novel—one's name/the other's desire—as the circle closes around them Hopkins must break it, and the sanctity of the front square room must be penetrated and surveyed by men. Nevertheless, the discursive threads rearticulate Hopkins's anxiety: although the asexual Will will prove the man to make Sappho whole, to whom she must attach herself in order to give her life fullness and meaning and sew up the plot, his intrusion in turn only prefigures Langley's, the epitome of a brutal desire that is the province of the masculine.

The policing of sexuality, as Foucault contends, progresses on the basis of confessions, on the making public of private desires so as better to allow for their categorization and regulation. Sappho has "a story written on her face" Langley will read, and this reading will recapitulate her violation and reveal his true nature (89). Woman-identified desire never confesses itself among the conflicting factors in *Contending Forces,* except in Sappho's name, and Dora's feeling that Sappho "seemed to fill a long-felt want in her life" (98), and the author's curious remark on the dangers of same-sex intimacy "more than likely to end disastrously for one or the other" (98). The women governing the boardinghouse leave the front square room untouched, but for the narrator it is clear that Sappho can never return: her/their (sexual) awakening—its wicked touch—must be her (political) exile from the (national) family home until she proves her allegiance through heterosexual marriage.

Beyond the trope of the family as nation traditional to African-American nationalist literature, Julian's novella puts the responses and mind-set of the preceding horizons in the mouths and actions of Ernest and Bernard's biological families. This inversion of the central metaphor in national paradigms, an inversion made realizable by the new postnational and globalizing social order, comes to grapple directly through its characters with gender as a sign of national transition, except here, unlike Hopkins, Julian confronts head on the role of (homo)sexuality in the constitution of the nation. Will and Sappho, like Sappho and Dora, remain trapped in a capitulation to the gender norms of late-nineteenth-century Anglo-America mulatticized in relation to African-American politics. As New Men of the dawn of the twenty-first century, Ernest and Bernard recognize, in the tradition of African-American nationalism, identity politics and the reconstitution of gender as part of the territory that needs to be won.

*Homelessness*
Hopkins's trajectory was from the house into the world for empowerment through inclusion in the marketplace. Like mulattos a hundred

years earlier, the black gay and lesbian subspecies is hotly debated as sterile and dangerous, the undoing of the nation for both black and white. Senator Jesse Helms and Minister Louis Farrakhan agree on this. In Julian's utopia for the age of globalization, the black gay and lesbian subspecies fighting in the margins of the capitalist African- and Anglo-American paradigm gain a foothold in secrecy, in marshaling private property and in globalization. And like Hopkins, the ends of the struggle are through participation in the marketplace of goods, services, and ideas.

Inverting Hopkins's politics, Julian's novella abandons public spaces and retreats to the house, but the public spaces and the disenfranchisement of the majority nevertheless persists. For Delany and the BPP, the nation was to take territory, although in the face of realpolitik the utopian military strategy broke down on the problem of territorialization. As Harris predicted in fiction, and Sistren and the BPP recorded for history, the nation granted territory devoured itself. Julian's new community avoids war by marshaling a wall of money and private property in the developed zones—in the limousines, mansions, jets, and international careers at the service of his characters. War—be it class war or race war—is then reified into the field of words and is never a matter of hate crimes, assaults, guns, and public spaces strewn with dead bodies. Dead bodies enter the narrative as already disappeared, a direct result of AIDS but always offstage: even corpses are a private affair.

As a macropolitical democratic paradigm, in turning their backs on the public spaces the exiled retreat into the house. Living and dying without recourse to the street means a retreat to laissez-faire liberalism and a pact with global corporations that ignores the concrete facts of industrial production. At the novel's beginning Earnest and Bernard both work in industry, but our only exposure to this is through interviews over lunch with bosses and in private ruminations. There are no scenes on—or references to—the floor of the factory itself.

As knowledge workers—lawyers, intellectuals, musicians, artists—Julian's characters move to exempt themselves from industrialization to find a foothold in a postindustrialized world of knowledge industries, as new black men for the twenty-first century. In their celebrated sociological analysis, liberal analysts Jerry Hage and Charles S. Powers describe the postindustrial subjects as "complex selves who are comfortable maintaining multiple identities" (81).[20] Ernest signs a contract with a Japanese recording company; Bernard develops his hand-painted furniture business.

The path the novel takes toward utopia is a mark of Ernest and Bernard's access to the transition to postindustrialization, leaving behind—rather than grappling with—the problems of racism, exploitation, disenfranchisement, sexism, and homophobia that led to their retreat. As corporations replace the state, it is only the fact that industry provides health insurance while the state does not that keeps them at the factory. Otherwise Ernest's global career and Bernard's private business in refurbished furniture would provide sufficient income to seal their retreat. The element missing in Julian's paradigm of the house at the end of a dead-end street is, then, not so much antithetical to what West calls "the development of a collective and critical consciousness"—that is ever evident in both the world the characters leave behind and the world they create—as it is an impasse in "a moral commitment to and engagement with causes beyond that of one's self and family" (37). To be fair, Ernest and Bernard, as was Julian himself, are black gay men in a racist, homophobic, and violent society working to invent a life-giving haven for themselves on the palimpsest of their testing positive for H I V. The public plaza shrinks to the private house; the liberated territory contracts to the controllable spaces of the house in the city, protected by the laws of private property.

The attenuation of nation in Julian, then, arises from his character's inclusion in the small black homeowning middle class, after the momentous failure of the grassroots organizations and conceptualizations of community to deal with the violence perpetuated on black women and especially on black gay men and lesbians, a violence documented by Harris and Sistren and applauded by the BPP. The new black professional class writes itself. This points to the internal implications of West's title, where *Race Matters* refers not so much to the persistence of racism (the external front) but the issues and debates internal to the black community. Yet Julian's liberal insights into identity politics reiterate that democratizing gender and sexuality are basic to political success in marshaling community to meet the challenges of the new global paradigms—principles that democratic socialist West is everywhere at pains to underscore.[21] Just as corporations slowly learn to recognize allies and resources in like-minded individuals of all colors, genders, and kinds, and states make pacts with other states to rethink turf and borders in meeting the challenges to inclusion presented by corporate globalism, so the definition of "nation" as "community" must expand and make room for pacts along the lines of collective interest and a common political need for the genuine democracy that West calls for. Julian's insight lies in enacting his utopia as concentric, ever-expanding circles.

By capitulating to the sexism, racism, and homophobia permeating the community at all levels, the majority lock themselves out. But as we noted with Sappho, nunneries and houses may lock intruders out but they also lock the vulnerable in. Julian's utopic dream ignores those excluded from the professional classes in a world in which the middle class is disappearing, and it is this that makes his strategy a retreat into globalism. In Patricia Powell's *A Small Gathering of Bones,* a Jamaican counterpart to Julian's novella, the hero is banished from the family house/nation by his mother/country and dies of AIDS alone.[22]

Abandonment of the state as a vehicle for representing the people means there is little between, on the one hand, those abandoned in shaping the new global paradigm who migrate to compete for low-paying jobs and, on the other, the power of the global corporations and the people privileged to be flagged as the consumer and the market. The latter—people as markets—are the groups with whose welfare all the dominant apparatuses of power concern themselves: in police protection, in legal protection, in political representation, and through the public cultural institutions. Even as the corporations paint themselves in familial tints—felicitously and profitably reshuffling the peoples of the global village—they fire, remove, eject, or ruthlessly exploit and/or ignore industrial workers in deference to the bottom line.

Following on the logic Ohmae outlines, the larger corporations swallow up smaller corporations, mimicking the relationship between big states and little states (imperialism) and macrocultures swallow microcultures (racism and ethnocentrism) under the aegis of modernization. The triad of racism, sexism, and capitalism, Wallerstein argues, organized the social body toward industrial production. Under multicultural globalization, class alliances supercede ethnic differences in the new corporate paradigm of multicultural capitalism. As its price, for the majority of the periphery's population, now conceived as "problem areas," the interpolation of the subaltern as docile worker without rights and anxious to please—shades of de Boissière's Trinidad before the workers' revolts—becomes the other horizon of incorporation into globalism.

Although its successes have been great, the failures of black nationalism are, then, concretely represented by real and political homelessness and by the corpses that pile up in public spaces on land in the cities and countrysides and at the bottom of the world's oceans.[23] Failure is also represented by the history of governments faced with providing representation. Finally, failure at the level of the black subaltern masses is marked by the increasing need to abandon the countryside (the undeveloped areas) on the one hand, and in the stark deprivation and violence that has come to structure daily life in the inner city on the other. Black men become the primary killers of black men ages ten to thirty-five. West notes that whereas for almost four hundred years blacks were least likely to commit suicide they have now become the group at highest risk. When the nation begins to murder itself, we face the ultimate diversion of the national paradigm.

Derrick Bell's *And We Are Not Saved* records the history of governmental attempts to resolve what it calls "the race problem" in the United States. Since the passage of the Civil Rights Act of 1965, however, what has substantially changed is the size of the black petit bourgeoisie and the black underlcass, and the mediating role of money in race relations. The increasingly political role played by pointing to the presence of the black middle class (as distinct from the black bourgeoisie) brings with it its own crisis. For on the one hand it allows liberals and reformers as well as conservatives to point to black access to public institutions as a mark of success, of the government's, the nation's, and institutional concern with black peoples; on the other, the systematic exclusion of blacks from the core groups organizing the nation and national interests has not changed.

The battle to transform this systematic exclusion was waged under the name of a strong "multiculturalism" with the coming to power of those shaped by the international social movements culminating in 1968. But it is precisely the threat of this democratic shift to what Premdas calls the state's dominant cultural core that has rallied the bitterness of both disenfranchised whites and the wealthy conservative elite in the United States. At the highest level of global politics, the parameters of governance and political struggles for community rights, as Lamming argued in the epigraph in the introduction to this book, are still set outside the spheres of government, and the new bottom line is economic, not civil, and set by prevailing global authorities and, in the Caribbean, by global corporations like Chiquita. Hope lies in economic—not civil—citizenship, as far as the managers of globalization are concerned.

The struggle we all face, then, is with the changes coming in the wake of the open institutionalization of tenuous and postmodern social pacts as governance. This struggle stands behind each of the essays in Mosley's edited volume, *Black Genius*. Both Delany and de Boissière were grappling with the incorporation of the masses into the paradigms of modernity (representation in and by the nation-state). Hopkins and Harris attempted to further the debate by raising the questions of inclusion and class dynamics given a small foothold within the modern paradigm; that is, granted middle-class access into the arena of debates over the proper use of land and the distribution of resources, over appropriate educational schemes, and over the position and political role of women within the national agendas.

Hopkins and Harris then register the shift from the macrological problem of exile within modernity—problems of claiming the right to protest—to the problems of crippling internal conflicts. Sistren and the Oakland Black Panther Party grappled with speaking history, public policy, and public and private reality from the bottom or outside, from subalternity. Rethinking community meant confronting a relentless patter of oppression, marginalization, and superexploitation as old as mass African presence in the New World, despite laws and paradigms promising a voice and social reorganization.

Geopolitics and geoculture present a political scenario that is difficult to untangle in the challenge of rearticulating the struggle for human rights and public political representation, against, Spivak argues, the model proffered in the metropole: "Citizen[ship] of a dead-end world" (390). Julian's novel, in abandoning public spaces and concepts of a program for renovation extending beyond the domestic unit, bears the hallmarks of despair at the heart of its hope at the end of a dead-end street. This is nowhere more evident than in the HIV-positive status of Ernest and Bernard, for they are living with a time bomb in their bodies, even as they are dependent on a corporate scientific community to invent or discover a cure. This means dependence on a pact with global pharmaceutical corporations, which in Julian means depending on nothing at all.[24] Ernest and Bernard simply don't bother.

In this sense, West and Rodríguez are struggling for a rebirth of the values of social democracy and the incorporation of the people as people (and not "consumers" or "markets") into the paradigms of civil society and thus the structures of representation that de Boissière and Sistren sought. Neither West nor Rodríguez is laboring under the illusion that the traditional structures of power have ever been primarily or altruistically concerned with the well-being of the majority of the population— the interests of the elitist state always superceded the people's. Nevertheless, coming from a tradition of concern with the disenfranchised, each is grappling with the challenge of the privatization of poverty, violence, and death.

On the other hand, there is the increasingly omnipresent fact of homelessness—that is, people by and large abandoned by the state. In the Caribbean, generally, a lack of facilities and funds leaves many of the insane abandoned on the streets, where they mingle with the children who gather together for safety and companionship and to beg for a living. In the United States, as the middle class hangs on and the working class falls further behind with the impact of the denationalization and massive mergers that become the strategic horizon of corporate agendas, those left out of the process find themselves on the streets without a home to reconstitute as a haven.

The problems of the black poor become the problem of the black middle class (persistent exclusion, difference beyond class barriers) just as the problems of the black middle class (the struggle for inclusion, equivalence on the other side of class barriers) become the problem of the black poor. If there is no alternative to capitalism but more capitalism, negotiating race matters in class structures and class structures in race matters becomes the new political horizon. West prefaces his book with this dilemma. Socialism in West's *Race Matters* is almost always a moral question of providing comfortable access for all to that which capitalism once reserved for the middle classes—in the United States the white middle classes specifically.

Nevertheless, like Julian, negotiating and evaluating the slogan "the market won—long live the market" is West's and Rodríguez's dilemma. If West's purview in *Race Matters* is strikingly national (reconsolidation of the community after attenuation), the deconstruction of national borders in Rodríguez harks back to my point that the ideological effects of the international division of labor are unavoidable in the developing territories. The unfolding new world order means increasing disenfranchisement for most and escalating privilege for some according to corporate logic, as corporate behavior in the Third World makes clear.[25]

But here gender, as implosive and explosive of conceptualizing nation, comes back to provide one anchor in a whirlpool that threatens to swallow the disenfranchised. In the United States the shrinking of the social safety net of unemployment benefits revolved around debates on the existence of pathological black women breeding for economic gain, just as women are at the center of the corporate strategies for worker super-exploitation in the export processing zones. Like Hopkins, Delany, and the BPP, West's analyses make it clear that black nationalist African-American men, like democratic government men in the Caribbean, find themselves exiled by the holders of armies and capital or else patronized, and so an unwinnable war sits on one side, with denationalization on the other. In the black ghettos of the New World, too many men take to war on each other and on women and children; in the Caribbean, as throughout the United States, elites of all colors hire armed private guards and fortify personal security systems.

In this return to chaos for the majority, new concepts of development, as the economic expression of a communal political agenda, lie in new collective leadership redefined after the debates on gender, sexuality, and nation. If for Delany and de Boissière the key to the solution was the power of the nation-state, and for Hopkins and Harris it was the rejection of an internalized historical violence, the Oakland Panthers and Sistren both found that war from all sides was always the result. Denationalization as a sign of gender comes to mean that what was once exiled to the province of women comes to occupy center stage and redefine the debates, unraveling the orderly march of the traditional epistemologies of nation and community.

Interestingly, as we forge into the twenty-first century, for West and Rodríguez the secret to the humane revitalization of gender, nation, and development in reconceptualizing power and identity and in writing culture is embracing community across borders. For West it is a function of moral courage; for Rodríguez it is a fact of functional necessity. Julian falters in having black gay men cross that bridge again—the persistence of the most hostile inversion of Black Power's internal politics makes the black community a dangerous place, another reason for retreating to the house and locking the door. Nevertheless, Julian's characters are only as safe as their environment, and safety here is a political concept.

Where Julian retreats, West and Rodríguez advance into the new horizon with precisely the central agenda of "a moral commitment to and engagement with causes beyond that of one's self and family" (West 37).

The will to collective empowerment and the determination to open up the system, once marshaled under the concept of nationalism, persists for them in the face of an inexorable interconnectedness that comes with globalization. The alternative is exile—Haiti, Ethiopia, denationalized corpses; or civil war—Ethiopia, the Los Angeles revolts, war in the world's inner cities, Bosnia/Kosovo, nationalized corpses. In these cases, genocide is seen as a sign of success.

By grappling with difference and disconnection as defining present-day geopolitics and geoculture and by writing from a house at the end of a dead-end street, Rodríguez and West replace the signs of war with the drive to connect, the dream of a common language. Democracy becomes the realization of human rights against the relentless escalation of profit margins for 2 percent of the world's population. In Rodríguez and West, the struggle for the inclusion of women as women, gay men as gay men, and people as people within (trans)nationalism rewrites courage in the vanguard as public and concrete political expressions of tenderness, insight, and love.

# NOTES

## Introduction

1   See, for example, Armstrong, which looks at the region now encompassing Europe and the Middle East; Akzin, whose chapter "Nationalism in Developing Areas" examines the European colonial system as a European colonialist system; Anthony D. Smith, *Theories of Nationalism,* which traverses the globe but mentions the West Indies only once (in a list documenting the spread of the British Empire); Deutsch, whose neoimperialist chapter "Nationalism in the Developing Countries" deserves no comment; Mellor, whose focus is almost exclusively Europe; and Colin H. Williams, who looks at current nationalist issues in Ireland, Wales, Scotland, northern Spain, Belgium, and Quebec. More useful works, although none deal with the Caribbean or African-America, are Gellner, which has become a standard in the field for its analysis of agrarian and industrial societies, as well as for its piercing analysis of the terms of the field; Watson, which is of interest because of its focus on the issue of minority rights qua minority rights; Snyder, which trots the globe but has a small section on U.S. black nationalism albeit none on the Caribbean, is useful for its focus on the "minination" into which both African-America and the West Indies would fall; Sathyamurthy, which is useful for its focus on Asia; Benedict Anderson, which treats nationalism as a discursive event causing harm more than anything else; and Anthony D. Smith, *The Ethnic Origins of Nations.* See also Bhabha, ed., *Nation and Narration,* which intentionally develops the same general approach as Anderson in reading nationalism through the lens of poststructuralism. The African-American and West Indian critics who have developed the field are referred to in the pertinent chapters.

2   Chatterjee's *The Nation and Its Fragments* follows the implications of that truth through India's nationalist histories in a study that has revealing parallels with my own.

3   See Premdas, "Public Policy and Ethnic Conflict." See also, for example, Ibrahim; Koenig; and LaGuerre.

4   Hobsbawm's marxist analysis, while embedded in European culture and history, is nevertheless extremely useful in debunking the mythology of nationalism (the post-structuralists' agenda) while reading behind the scenes for the power maneuvers that are at stake in nation formation. At the same time, I say "consolidate" because many of the ideas in Hobsbawm's theses have appeared in a more or less chaotic form in the work of other writers. The problem of defining "nation," for example, and the thesis that nationalism is at first primarily the province of the elite, appears in Anderson's *Imagined Communities*. In his clarity of perspective on the field and character of nationalisms and their corollaries, however, Hobsbawm provides a thought-provoking counternarrative to the work I have undertaken here. The division of the nationalist movement into three stages he takes from Hroch. The narratives of Hobsbawm's book, along with Ileana Rodríguez's studies on Latin American and Caribbean nationalisms, *House/Garden/Nation* and *Women, Guerrillas, and Love*, form the primary European and Latin American macrotheoretical interlocutors in this study.

5   Samir Amin argues that the conflicts and confusions around the meaning of "nation" stem from the different contexts in which the term takes on real political weight and from the role of bourgeois revolutions in nation formation. Thus in France and England "national reality" is not diverted "into the construction of some biological myth" (as in Germany) but was "formulated in a social (that is, not naturalistic) vision of society" (81). Germany's subsequent constitution of a state "could not base its legitimacy upon democratic values; it substituted 'nationalism' for them, a concept of the nation based not on the social contract [as in France and England] but on blood descent" (82). Thus we see the difference the absence of bourgeois revolutions makes in nationalism in Germany and in central, eastern, and southern Europe versus England, France, and Holland.

Hogan's *Colonialism and Cultural Identity* provides a provocative exploration of the tenets of postcolonial identity formation in literature from Africa, India, and the West Indies. Hogan ultimately finds that at the root of his analysis is the question of "the physical pain of colonialism and the extinction of rooted culture" as "the result of economic and political inequality" in which democratic socialism and political economics become central to social justice (314–15). My project begins with this assertion. My project also connects to Edmondson's in that she identifies the problematic relationship between the (re)presentation of the "folk" of nationalist discourse and the troubled figure of woman's (re)presentation within it, wrapped in a West Indian dialogue with Victorian Englishness on black national identity. These relationships are central to the Boom writers of the 1950s and 1960s, for example, Trinidad's Vidia Naipaul and Barbados's George Lamming. Both Hogan and Edmondson address critical moments in the writing of a black West Indian identity and address critical contexts in which West Indian conflicts and confusions around the emergent meanings of nation took place.

6 Bhabha is by no means the only theorist who dismisses nationalism as an evil leading to disaster perpetrated on the people. In his *In Theory*, Ahmad provides a critique of the debate on nationalism and the antisocialist impulse with which critiques of nationalism are often conflated.

7 That is, form an ethnic group and from there, with claims to state representation, constitute the nation. The relationship between ethnicity and nationalism is particularly complex, as the literature makes clear.

8 See, for example, Jacquith et al.

9 I use these concepts and the distinctions between them as laid out by Mohanty in her classic essay "Under Western Eyes": "The relationship between 'Woman'—a cultural and ideological composite Other constructed through diverse representational discourses (scientific, literary, juridical, linguistic, cinematic, etc.)—and 'women'—real, material subjects of collective histories—is one of the central questions the practices of feminist scholarship seeks to address" (173–74). Mohanty goes on to engage with the concepts of representation within feminist discourses that are also elaborated throughout this text in dialogue with Spivak and the Indian Subaltern Studies Group, particularly Guha.

10 See Mies; Hall; Rodríguez; Franco; Spivak; Mohanty; Alexander and Mohanty; and Sommer, among many other second-wave feminists from around the world who have contributed to this debate over the past two decades.

11 There is, of course, much debate surrounding the origins of black presence in the Americas. See, however, Van Sertima.

12 The literature on these issues is extensive. For two classic instances, however, see Lewis, *Main Currents*, and Jordan.

13 See, for example, Light; Glantz; Traub; and Arnold. Of those trying to provide a corrective, see Sowell's works; Allen and Farley; Steinberg; Farley; and Kasinitz.

14 Throughout this study, I refer to the English-speaking Caribbean as the West Indies. When I do use the term Caribbean I mean the West Indies together with the other islands in the Caribbean basin, Central America, and to the extent it shares a history with the others, South America as well.

15 See, among other texts, Chatterjee, *The Nation and Its Fragments;* also Wilson-Tagoe; and the debates that raged over Fredric Jameson's "Third World Literature in the Era of Multinational Capital," including Aijaz Ahmad's response, reprinted as chapter 3 in Ahmad's *In Theory*. See also Spivak's discussion of literature in chapter 2 of *A Critique of Postcolonial Reason*.

16 The politics of this project are in alliance with Randall Robinson's essay on his exemplary activism in *Black Genius*.

17 For a discussion of the global political implications of African-American empowerment, see Randall Robinson, "Perfecting Our Democracy."

18 For example, Nathaniel Mackey, editor of a special issue of *Callaloo* dedicated to Harris, in reviewing an earlier version of chapter 5 of this book, argues that it contains

"problematic assertions and characterizations (e.g., especially, reference to Harris's 'nationalist sentiments' and related suggestions, which are not only blatantly not borne out by Harris's writings, pronouncements, and general stance, but in conflict with the reading of *The Secret Ladder* the essay advances)" (personal communication). Later I will argue that *The Guyana Quartet* is explicitly a series of novels located in Guyana focusing on Guyanese historical experiences and land and social formations peculiar to Guyana—in the name of Guyana's, and the world's, greater good. Mackey's comments appear in his reader's evaluations to the author of April 1994. Criticisms of Pauline Hopkins's constant—even stubborn—use of the mulatta figure appeared in the letters to the editor sections of various issues of *The Colored American*.

19  See Adeleke, "Black Biography."

20  On nineteenth-century West Indian nationalism, see Lewis's "The Growth of Nationalist Thought to 1900" in his *Main Currents in Caribbean Thought*. I recognize that I am disagreeing with critics who claim a beginning in the likes of Marcus Garvey, C. L. R. James, and George Padmore, but it seems to me, as will become clear in the course of my readings, that much of the international thrust of black nationalism is in fact a projection of the national situation overseas as either a metonym of their own suffering, or the utopia in which their particular brand of suffering will cease to exist. In either case, the particulars of the political situation in the foreign territory onto which the utopia is projected are inevitably lost in the shuffle. If the novels I analyze by Delany and Hopkins fall into this trap (as do characters in de Boissière, Harris, and Sistren), they nevertheless spend the bulk of their time and attention on the U.S. situation.

21  See, specifically, his lecture on *The Secret Ladder* published in his *An Introduction to the Study of West Indian Literature*.

22  See Bolles, *We Paid Our Dues*.

## 1   F(o)unding Black Capital

1  The "Southernizing/New South position" refers to the belief that a racially democratic reconstructed South was a realistic possibility.

2  The argument that black labor built the United States has a long history predating Delany. See, for example, Walker's *Appeal to the Colored Citizens of the World*, which first appeared in 1829.

3  See also Tunde Adeleke's "Black Biography in the Service of Revolution" and "Race and Ethnicity in Martin R. Delany's Struggle."

4  See, for example, Delany's speech to the 1848 National Convention on Emigration, "The Political Destiny of the Colored People."

5  Moses, in *Golden Age*, a more moderate perspective than Painter's, has amply documented that the problem of class inducing this split is endemic to nineteenth-century

black nationalism and that, as Benedict Anderson and Eric Hobsbawm also argue, nationalism emerges from these writings as an inherently bourgeois movement.

6   See also Levine; and Genovese.

7   I invoke the concept of the "subaltern" as developed by the East Asian Subaltern Studies Group to rethink the political history of India, as well as that taken up for the New World by the Latin American Subaltern Studies Group in part as a response to the failure of marxist paradigms and revolutionary nation-states in Latin America to understand "the people" of Latin America. See Rodríguez, *Reader*. Following Guha's insights requires at least a double procedure. On one hand, given that the records of subaltern insurgency are written by and for the repressive forces, key nouns and adjectives must be coded with an opposite valence. Thus for every "terrible and wanton atrocity on the inhabitants" Guha writes, the subalternist must substitute a "resistance to oppression" ("Prose" 59), a strategy mirrored by antebellum black leadership across the board. On the other hand, such a substitution is only a beginning. For beyond the question of rescripting the documents of history lies the caesura in the place of subaltern agency, a caesura that can only be approached after a reading of the rescripted history through subaltern culture. In "Subaltern Studies in a U.S. Frame," Eve Cherniasky does a careful job of suggesting how subaltern studies might play out in the U.S. context by taking into account the question of translating to the United States a paradigm developed for South Asian postcolonial historiography. See also Pandey, "Voices from the Edge," Guha and Spivak, eds., *Selected Subaltern Studies*, Rabasa, Saujinés, and Carr, and Rodríguez, eds., *Reader*.

8   "Relative" to slaves, that is.

9   Douglass describes the circle in his 1849 *Narrative* and comes back to it in later versions.

10  This argument has been raised in terms of African culture in Africa as well. Two contributions to the debate are Davidson's *The Black Man's Burden* and Laitin's *Hegemony and Culture*.

11  See Urban; also Douglass's "Cuba and the United States," in *Life and Writings* 2:159–63.

12  Delany's epigraphs are quotes by Harriet Beecher Stowe; *Blake* is also a response to *Uncle Tom's Cabin*. For Delany's thinking on black/Anglo-feminist coalitions implicit in the nineteenth century protofeminist slogan of "the slavery of sex," see the "Cornelia Woodward" installment of *Blake* (chapter 5).

13  27,000 copies of *The Narrative of Solomon Northrup* were sold in 1853 and 1854, while William Wells Brown's *Narrative* sold out four editions in the first year. See Bontemps, "The Slave Narrative" xviii. For the narrative of a repentant trader, see Capt. Richard Drake, *Revelations of a Slave Smuggler*.

14  See Ollmann and Birnbaum, *The United States Constitution* 306–20.

15  See Sundquist, *To Wake the Nations* 190–91, 196–97, and 200–3, for an astute synopsis of the relationship between the novel and the debate over the reopening of the slave trade.

16    See Miller, *Blake* 315 n.5; and Sundquist, *To Wake the Nations* 190.

17    Hamilton estimated that post-Revolutionary foreign and domestic debt stood at over $76 million in January 1975 (cited in Ollmann and Birnbaum 43).

18    Relying on treasury records from the 1780s, Merrill Jensen notes an income ranging from a marked high of $1,557,179 in 1788 to a low of $422,897 in 1789.

19    Although somewhat awkward, the language used here to describe same-sex-identified men and women in the eighteenth and nineteenth centuries is important if we are to be historically accurate. The work done on this issue is extensive, but see, for some examples, Katz's groundbreaking *Gay American History* as well as his *Love Stories* and *Invention of Heterosexuality*; D'Emilio; D'Emilio and Freedman; and Greenberg.

20    This was the third of Douglass's three articles on slavery and the Constitution, reprinted in *Life and Writings*. For a broader sense of the debate, see his response to C. H. Chase's argument at the Anti-Slavery Convention that the U.S. Constitution was antislavery "in all its provisions" (*Life* 1:352–53) as well as his "Address to Southern Delegates of Congress to their Constituents" (*Life* 1:353–60). See also his speech "The Constitution of the United States: Is It Pro-Slavery or Anti-Slavery?" delivered in Glasgow, Scotland, on March 26, 1860 (*Life* 2:467–80), and his "The Meaning of the Fourth of July for the Negro" speech at Rochester, New York, on July 5, 1852 (*Life* 2:206–9).

21    MacKinnon defines a "negative state" as "the view that government best promotes freedom when it stays out of existing social arrangements" (164). Consider the implications of such a statement in nineteenth-century U.S. jurisprudence.

22    The increase in laws defining the position of blacks points to a crisis in the state's ability to control the habits and practices of the population. The Fugitive Slave Act thus explicitly criminalizes the aid to fugitive slaves that was spurred by the abolitionist movement and liberal sentiment. The Kansas-Nebraska Act tries to resolve the growing tensions between slaveholding and nonslaveholding planters. Dred Scott cements the exclusion of free blacks from the practices, policies, and privileges of free people in the United States, because the concept of free blacks confuses the relationship between race and political status, and so on. As Sundquist notes, elections and party politics increasingly incorporated abolition as a campaign issue.

23    See Brown, *Narrative*, as one example.

24    Lee and Passell do not mention if they corrected for inflation.

25    See Skinner, "The Impact of West Indian Emancipation."

26    Delany had gone to Pittsburgh to join the prosecution of a slave speculator who had abducted and sold a young Jamaican boy, Alexander Hendrickson (Ullman 152). Delany also later joined forces with Robert Campbell, a Jamaican emigrationist teaching in Philadelphia; see Blackett, "Martin R. Delany and Robert Campbell." Delany's (and, as we shall see, also Hopkins's) faith in the British government is belied by the experience of blacks in the Caribbean. The narrative of James Williams exposes the realities of the British moral debates as the discourse finds its material manifestation

in the lives of blacks in the periphery, rendered half-slave/half-worker by the abolitionists' apprenticeship compromise, in which British magistrates were to mediate labor disputes between the soon-to-be-freed "apprentices" and their angry masters: "Some of them magistrate don't care what them do to apprentices, as long as them can get good eating and drinking with the massa and busha, and sometimes them set the massa in to do worse than them want. All the apprentice say that Major Light make it a constant rule to do so, and myself see Mr. Rawlinson do so one time—it was the very morning them flog me with the lancewood switches" (24–25). The narrative of Archibald Monteith also questions the moral superiority of British abolitionism touted in the United States.

27 A brief consideration of Henry's difference from Turner, however, brings to a crisis the differential between Delany's hero and Turner as an agent of insurgent destruction in a way that opens onto Delany's ideological investments and the questions of political (re)presentation—Marx's *Vertretung* versus *Darstellung*. See Miller's introduction to *Blake*. On the difference between *Darstellung* and *Vertretung*, see Spivak, *Critique of Postcolonial Reason*, 258; also Carr, "Crossing the First World/Third World Divides."

28 Such moments, common in the narratives of ex-slaves, present an instance of the inextricability of the "'idealist' predication of the subject" (consciousness) and the "'materialist' predication of the subject" (labor power) speculated on in Spivak's "Scattered Speculations on the Question of Value."

29 As Miller notes in his introduction to *Blake*, Delany drew on strategies devised by runaway slaves and published in their autobiographies. See also Bibb; and Henson.

30 This dilemma also runs throughout Stuckey's narrative. Even as Stuckey's monumental work on *Slave Culture* attempts to ground the nineteenth-century black nationalist movement in slave culture, his study falters in actualizing that connection in proving that the black nationalist culture of men like Delany is genuinely founded in the world the slaves made. In fact, the complex blend of African and New World cultures he details in his long first chapter becomes increasingly reified as he moves through his studies of a range of black nationalist leaders, ideologies, and problematics. This reification, I would argue, points directly to the problem I am scrutinizing here, that of ethnicity in the new black nationalist cultural formations that Delany proposes.

31 Turner's difference from the role of conjure in slave culture is marked repeatedly in his *Confessions*. This difference from conjure is deferred in instances such as Brantley's attack "with a cutaneous eruption . . . [with] blood [that] oozed from the pores of his skin" because, assumedly, of Turner's words to him (103). Whereas such an event would have been proof of conjure for believers, Turner believes he later cures Brantley through the "Spirit" that moves within him (103). Such a comparison again speaks to the issues of (re)presentation (*Vertretung* versus *Darstellung*).

32 See Adeleke, "Race and Ethnicity."

33 Delany's scenario in fact concurs with Harriet Jacobs's exposé, which also was published in 1861.

34    Initially Blake asks the slaves he encounters if there is a man or woman who has been granted a leadership role by the community. Before long, however, the formula is reduced to men as leaders and women as sources of inspiration and helpmeets to their men. I disagree, then, with Tolagbe Ogunleye, who argues, using the example of women's election to office on the 1854 Ohio National Emigration Board, that Delany was in fact far ahead of his time by his gender inclusiveness. The dynamics of such an offering does not itself mean gender equality in the political imaginary, and the evidence within the novel and elsewhere provides ample examples to the contrary. As Ogunleye herself notes, the role of Delany's wife, Catherine, was to be "a strong woman who encouraged and urged Delany in the 'most doubtful moments' " and so on, in a replication of women's role as the "angel of the hearth" everywhere in evidence at the time. What does become "radical" for the times, to my mind, is Delany's determination, shared by others, to have black women occupy the same political economic strata as white women.

35    See, as examples, the debate over Douglass's narratives and the establishment of black masculinity in Olney; Gerber; Franchot; and Maurice Wallace.

36    See Spillers, "Mama's Baby, Papa's Maybe."

37    See Adeleke, *UnAfrican Americans*.

38    See the Enlightenment debates on the role of blood in blackness in Eze; Jordon; and Frederickson.

39    For an analysis of race, gender, and ethnicity in Latin American nation formation, see chapter 1 of Rodríguez, *House/Garden/Nation*, especially her discussion of Gallegos's *Doña Bárbara* and of the culture of the nation in the neoliberal horizon.

40    Rodríguez, *House/Garden/Nation* part 1, "Transitions: The Masculine."

## 2   *Of What Use Is History?*

1    See Marable's *Blackwater* and *Negro Thought in America*.

2    The most famous of her short stories is probably "Talma Gordon." Her second novel, *Hagar's Daughter*, written under the pseudonym Sarah Allen, was serialized in *Colored American Magazine* in 1902, and her third, *Winona*, was serialized there in 1902 as well.

3    See Meier, "Booker T. Washington."

4    Much of the attention paid to Hopkins has surrounded her interest in the mystical and occult, or in the idea of the "new woman" and the "fallen woman." See, for example, Gilman; Otten; Brooks; and McCann. Several critics have tried to overcome what they see as limitations in Hopkins's use of melodrama, limitations that have led them to assert that in fact her novel betrays her politics. Sean McCann's astute critique of such readings is worth citing:

> These responses to Hopkins' work run some evident theoretical risks, I believe— especially insofar as they claim to discover an intention in Hopkins' texts that also

contradicts those texts. But more importantly, they may be practically misleading. In their effort to dismiss much of Hopkins' writing as an aberration untrue to her legitimate thinking about race and gender, these readings pass over what I will suggest was the extraordinary usefulness of melodrama for Hopkins' political thought. By the same token, the ascription of a particular type of ambivalence to Hopkins' novels—one that promises to rescue them from their currently distasteful implications—actually threatens to simplify the novels and ignore the complicated ways that Hopkins deployed the gendered conventions of melodrama in the service of a racial politics. From this perspective, Hopkins's plots weren't merely an "effective" but limiting "literary vehicle" for an already formed "urgent message." Instead they embodied and produced Hopkins's account of race. (790−91)

The same bears saying for Delany's *Blake*.

5 For an excellent discussion of black nineteenth-century feminism in general, and, specifically, the work of Hopkins, Wells, and Harper at the turn of the century, see Hazel Carby, *Reconstructing Womanhood*.

6 There is a growing body of literature supporting this argument. See, as examples, Rodríguez, *House/Garden/Nation* and *Women, Guerrillas, and Love*; Sommer, *Foundational Fictions*; and Franco, *Plotting Women*.

7 See Harper, *Iola LeRoy*. For an analysis of the figure of the mulatta in fiction, see, for example, the first chapters of Christian's *Black Women Novelists*; and Spillers, "Notes on an Alternative Model—Neither/Nor."

8 See Bernal, *Black Athena*, and the controversy surrounding its publication. There is, of course, a broader heated debate surrounding who claims Egypt. For examples, see Poe, *Black Spark, White Fire*; or, on the other side of the debate, Howe, *Afrocentrism*. Moses has entered into the debate with his *Afrotopia*.

9 This reflects both a stereotype and a reality. The use of mulattas in U.S. brothels is well known, for example, in New Orleans. Beckles provides a more detailed historical analysis of Caribbean slave prostitution in *Centering Woman* 22−37. The fascination of black men with light-skinned black women in both the United States and the Caribbean is well known. For a West Indian analysis, see Mohammed, "But Most of All Mi Love Mi Browning."

10 See, for example, Carby's *Reconstructing Womanhood*; Hopkins's prospectus for *Contending Forces*; and Tate, "Pauline Hopkins."

11 See also Wilkinson, *Bermuda from Sail to Steam*.

12 Cf. Brown's 1853 *Clotel* and his *Narrative*, in which the narrator marvels at a beautiful white woman who was a slave herself.

13 See Carby, *Reconstructing Womanhood*.

14 See for example, Rhys's *Wide Sargasso Sea*; Athill's introduction to *Jean Rhys*; Shand's *The Orchid House*; and Bridges's *Child of the Tropics*.

15 See, for example, the function of skin color in the escapes of William Wells Brown's *Narrative*, and in Craft and Craft's *Running a Thousand Miles for Freedom*. Note that

James Williams's *Narrative* and Mary Prince's *History of Mary Prince* find both of them in England, and neither of them adopted into families.

16  See Drucker, "The New Pluralisms."

17  I therefore take some issue with Brooks's and McCann's arguments that Hopkins's Sappho falls into an irresolvable dichotomy between "an embodiment of history and a New Woman" (McCann 793) or a "New Woman" and a "Fallen Woman" (Brooks). Both of these readings miss the significance of the political dilemma Hopkins confronts in the figure of the mulatta.

18  Brooks points out that the "New Woman who worked outside the home" was "masculinized" in fiction (92).

19  We could trace this strategy back as early as the end of the eighteenth century to the narrative of Venture Smith. Smith was brought from Africa and sold into slavery but nevertheless managed to buy his freedom and start his own farm, owning slaves himself. At the end of his life, Smith owned several large farms and several houses. See Venture Smith, *A Narrative*. It is arguable that this is the defining thread through much of African-American literature. Certainly, the socialist work of, say, the commune Josiah Henson describes at the end of his *Life* (1848) stands in remarkable contradistinction to the ideology of a Delany.

20  Cf. Jed, *Chaste Thinking*.

21  Cf. Butler, *Bodies That Matter*.

22  See, for example, Nancy Prince's sister (12–17, 20), and Mary Seacole's shock at what she witnessed among women in Panama (59–61, 100). We can contrast both Mary Prince's denials of attacks on her virtue and the figure of Amelié in Rhys's *Wide Sargasso Sea*.

23  Otten and McCann each provide excellent analyses of these figures. For Otten, Hopkins brings African understandings to questions that stymie the psychological sciences of the day. For McCann, Madam Francis is "the spiritual force of the race" (808). My own reading foregrounds questions of power as a political idea.

24  This is linked to the debates over the dual role of black women as mothers of families and mothers of "the race." Berg summarizes this debate in "Reconstructing Motherhood," 137–39.

25  Otten makes this point.

26  It is telling, of course, that Dr. Peters guards the church, signaling his dethronement on the one hand and the place of conjure as the threshold of black religious culture on the other.

27  For Hopkins the occult powers out of Africa are wielded by the black community against its own, while the white power structure remains outside its sphere (see *Contending Forces* 199).

28  Politics, Hopkins editorialized in 1903, morally degrades women and their "honorable position as wife and mother." See *Colored American Magazine* 1903, 33, where Hopkins is not entirely supportive of the franchise for women.

29 See *Race Men* for Carby's reading of the politics of black masculinity in Du Bois and beyond. Compare the following: McLaren on the constitution of masculinity through deviance in *The Trials of Masculinity;* Rotundo on masculinity and individualism in *American Manhood;* the three categories of U.S. manhood (the Heroic Artisan, the Genteel Patriarch, and the Self-Made Man) discussed by Kimmel in *Manhood in America;* Brod and Kaufman, *Theorizing Masculinities;* and Chapman and Rutherford, *Male Order.*

30 See Rodríguez, *House/Garden/Nation,* and Doris Sommer, *Foundational Fictions.*

31 See Franco, "Killing Priests, Nuns, Women, and Children."

### 3 From Larva to Chrysalis

1 The question of the inclusion of Indo-Trinidadians in nationalist narratives is a complex one with its own history and struggles that are only now being properly examined. For a brief overview of Indo-Trinidadian political history, see LaGuerre. It is important to note that, despite cries to the contrary, the national movement led by Eric Williams in Trinidad did equate poverty with black poverty. The racialization of political parties and political thought down into the present day is one reflection of this split. Note that Tobago is similarly marginal to the novel.

2 See G. K. Lewis's *Main Currents in Caribbean Thought,* which points out that Caribbean nationalism is born when the disparity between the interests of the colonial elite and the imperial elite takes the form of policy. The first moment of Caribbean nationalism, then, is the proslavery movement emanating from the planter class. The later work of J. B. Philippe (1824) and J. J. Thomas (1869 and 1889) thus comes as a moment of transition to black nationalism because neither argues for Independence or the claims of the black majority, although they fight against the racist policies and statements flung back and forth in the debate over Caribbean self-rule. It is a mark of their transitional status that both Philippe and Thomas address themselves not to the local population but to the readership of the metropolis, in particular the elite among the policy makers. See Carl Campbell's introduction to Paria's reedition of Philippe's *Free Mulatto.*

3 *Froudacity* was written in direct response to James Anthony Froude's rearticulation of the need for colonial rule in the West Indies. A highly respected British historian, Froude, after a brief tour of the British West Indies, produced a racist tract typically transcendentalized in its title *The English in the West Indies; or The Bow of Ulysses* (1888). Froude undertook his tour to answer the question of the fitness of the local black population for self-rule. Predictably, Froude found blacks biologically—and thus politically—wanting. Note, too, that although Thomas and Philippe do address anticolonial concerns and call for the reconceptualization of the local population as people rather than talking apes, they address themselves to the English overlords. On the parameters of Philippe's highly questionable place in the nineteenth-century protonationalist pantheon, see Gerard Besson's pointed foreword to the Paria edition.

4 For a contemporary account, see Arthur Lewis, "The 1930s Social Revolution."

5 See Martin, 359–60.

6 See Basdeo, who argues that there was "no development of long-term policies for the British Caribbean within the Colonial Office" before 1919 (3).

7 For a history of the struggle over wages from Emancipation until the riots of 1938, including another element in the emergent tensions between Afro- and Indo-Trinidadians at the political level, see Millette. Although the tensions between Muslim Indo-Trinidadians and Hindu Indo-Trinidadians also persist (see Chatterjee for a genealogy of this historical animosity in India) there is a spate of new work being done by scholars such as Premdas, LaGuerre, Moore, Rhedock, Ryan (*Jhandi*), and Mohammed who work to analyze and understand the complexities of the creolization process of Indo-Trinidadians and Indo-Guyanese and the impact of this process on nation building and national cohesion. For a broader analysis of systems of domination after slavery, see Boland.

   After Emancipation most of the black population abandoned the estates (as a reminder of their enslavement) to farm their own plots. The East Indian population was indentured from colonial India with the promise of return passage or a plot of land of their own. Escaping from a caste society into the relative freedom of the colony, Indo-Trinidadians worked the plantations and then their own land. The large East Indian population of both Trinidad and Guyana was thus more or less divided into a majority of farmers and a small number of shopkeepers. At the end of the twentieth century, the political muscle the East Indian population musters is directly related to the financial bloc they represent and their importance in agro-industry. Nevertheless, the propensity of the black population to disparage Indo-Trinidadians as penurious and rude (for the managerial clique) and workhorses (for the laborers) and for the Indian population to label blacks as immoral, lazy, ignorant (where not stupid), corrupt, and bigoted has created ethnic tensions that often determine the path of elections and divide the society. In chapter 4, we will see Guyanese novelist Wilson Harris grapple with the problem of interethnic tensions, and see the power of the Indo-Guyanese rice farmer lobby in the competition for scarce development resources against the black communities in Guyana's jungle interior. Ethnic tensions permeate de Boissière's text as racial tensions endemic to colonial society stratified on the basis of race, a stratification to be superceded in the new nation fought for by the black workers' rebellion through alliances, race mixing, and the notion of mulatto culture. The novel is thus focused on the utopic implications and processes of the black workers' uprising and the promise of Le Maitre and Cassie. The novels written in the 1950s, when de Boissière's novel found a publisher, are more direct in addressing the role of race and ethnicity in power and social stratification: Edgar Mittelhölzer's *A Morning at the Office* is a perfect example. For excellent discussions of the role and functions of ethnicity and the tensions within and between ethnic groups in Trinidad, see Yelvington's work in *Producing Power* as well as the essays that in his edited volume, *Trinidad Ethnicity*.

8   Caulder-Marshall also noted the link between the West Indian experience of racial politics in World War I: "The betrayal of Abyssinia [Ethiopia] is nearly as much to blame for the riots in Trinidad and Tobago as is the high cost of living" (254).

9   This bifurcation is succinctly characterized in Howard Johnson's article "Oil, Imperial Policy, and the Trinidad Disturbances, 1937." See, for example, Governor Fletcher's proclamation, where he wrote that the "present state of unrest has been occasioned by an increase in cost of living" (Johnson 146), and his observation to William Ormsby-Gore, secretary of state for the colonies, that there was "a clear cut racial demarcation between employers and workers and there is a pressing need for establishing and maintaining Government contact with both sides" (148). The response of business interests is summed up well in a statement sent to Ormsby-Gore by Sir George Huggins, a wealthy Trinidadian businessman: "It would be a serious thing for the Colony if Capital were to be withdrawn from the Island and Business curtailed on account of labour unrest and insufficient protection of life and property" (150). The governor's nascent understanding that this was a protonationalist struggle, communicated in his observation to Ormsby-Gore on the role of race as an economic concept in the island, is mirrored in the remark of the representative of the Woodford Lodge Estate, that the labor riots were an act of "racial violence. It is extermination, not only against labourers but against white women and children" (157). On the resolution of the crisis through legalizing a negotiating structure, the telegraph of United British Oilfields of Trinidad to its London office, forwarded to Ormsby-Gore, commented that "throughout community those fully experienced with native labour strongly oppose Government continued pandering to labour at the expense of employers. While satisfied that improvement possible we feel local Government repeating mistakes United States administration namely pressing social reform far too rapidly by action and speech thereby increasing labour and racial unrest" (153). That is, they fear a New Deal for Trinidad.

10  Sander has noted the extent to which the *Beacon* writers were caught up in a worldwide shift to the Left by the intelligentsia in the wake of World War I (24). Although some U.S. writers expatriated to Paris, and many African-American writers cast their lot with the Socialist Party or the Harlem Renaissance, many West Indian writers emigrated to the colonial and new imperial metropolises of London and New York respectively. At the same time, with the incarceration of Butler and the suppression of the riots in the oilfields, members of the *Beacon* group who remained at home and stepped into local political office repeated the pattern of bureaucratic co-opting that they had criticized so vociferously in the pages of their magazines.

11  In the pages of the *Beacon* Sidney C. Harland takes up the "vexed question of 'race admixture' in its biological and sociological aspects" in order to prove the inferiority of black blood (25). Drawing on the latest scientific articles published in the United States, Harland proves that what will come to be called apartheid in South Africa provides a better basis for social stratification because what was "formerly based on family and now mostly on money, will have to give way to set of new standards, and a

scheme of social stratification based on biology" (29). C. L. R. James responds in his "The Intelligence of the Negro."

12 Like the Mafia, the ruling classes abhor publicity. See Fussell; also Domhoff.

13 See Rodríguez, *House/Garden/Nation.*

14 Alfred Mendes's *Pitch Lake* explores, from this perspective, the birth/death cries of national frontiers, in that the main character is split between his desire to succeed in elite colonial society through marriage to one of its own and the humanization he feels for the colored maid he impregnates. In this sense, Joe da Costa's story can be read as a failed attempt at creole nation formation. When da Costa goes mad and murders the Indian maid, Stella, he is simply acting out personally the political reality that once liberal ideas have crept into play, the old and new national orders are trapped in an either/or endgame. Da Costa's madness thus reflects the author's (proto)nationalist sympathies on the one hand, and the moral and psychological decrepitude of the old order on the other.

15 Reinhard Sander notes that de Boissière's stated investment in writing *Crown Jewel* and *Rum and Coca-Cola* as history presents a critical problem where *Rum and Coca-Cola* ends with William's capitalist Independence platform being embraced by the Trinidadian people (143). As a result, de Boissière resorts to a carnival instead of William's victory, and thus a Bakhtinian revolt, such as it is, instead of a socialist revolution. The dialogism and commitment to history of de Boissière's critical realism thus finds its limit. For a discussion of critical realism, see Lukács, *The Meaning of Contemporary Realism.*

16 The pages of the *Beacon* were filled with barrack yard stories in which women were featured whose hardships were wrapped up in their relationships to abusive men. Alfred Mendes's *Black Fauns* and C. L. R. James's *Minty Alley* spin the barrack yard stories into novel length. If the *Beacon* group had a tendency to romanticize barrack yard life, it is also true that they recognized the value of James Cummings's exposé because Cummings came from the yards: see his "Barrack Rooms" and "What the Planter Plants." The literarization of poor local reality, then, seems to equal its romanticization: to depict the poor as noble and constitute a defense of the underclasses against the bourgeoisie requires a view of the harsh realities through a rose-colored glass, even as those realities make the underclass the fulcrum of change and new national consciousness.

17 "Venezuelan-made slippers with tops of knitted twine" (de Boissière's note).

18 Cf. Pantin, *Black Power Day.*

19 The figure of La Roche appears in *Rum and Coca-Cola,* de Boissière's sequel to *Crown Jewel.*

## 4 The New Man in the Jungle

1 See Harris's remarks in his 1984 introduction to the *Quartet* on Guyana's "need to deepen its insights into the soil of place in which ancient masquerades exist to validate the risks a community may take if it is to come abreast of its hidden potential" (14).

2   See Fanon's argument that although Freud "insisted that the individual factor be taken into account through psychoanalysis," he himself insists that beside "phylogeny and ontogeny stands sociogeny," and "that the black man's alienation is not an individual question" (*Black Skin, White Masks* 11). For Fanon's elaboration of these ideas, see his *Studies in a Dying Colonialism; Toward the African Revolution;* and *The Wretched of the Earth.*

3   Alfred Lopez thus takes up concerns that are traditionally central to analyses of Harris's work. Lopez is one of a group of Harris analysts whose concern is with Harris's extensive use of myth and his rewriting of European texts. Lopez sums up much of these critics' view on Harris's writing of "Guyana" in the idea that "it is paradoxically . . . the extent to which Harris's fiction diverges from (European) conventions of realism that it succeeds in representing Guyana's otherness" (201). My own view is very different because I am interested in the ways in which Harris's work takes to task the ethnic factionalism that marks Guyanese sociopolitical history. From this perspective, Harris's work tackles the question of national identity and finds a "cross-cultural" answer. This is not to reduce Harris, as many would argue, but rather to recognize and respect the impact of the Guyanese (postcolonial, if you wish) reality on subject formation. For to constitute Harris as somehow not particularly Guyanese (or "beyond Guyanese") is to ignore the persistence of Guyana as a topos—even a center—in Harris work, concerns, and worldview. I recognize that this is a controversial stance. See Lopez for the traditional analyses of Harris's work in terms of myth and Guyanese folklore; the essays comprising the special issue of *Review of Contemporary Fiction* (17.2 [1997]) dedicated to Harris; the special issue of *Callaloo* (18.1 [1995]) on Harris, in which an earlier, less-controversial version of this chapter appeared; Schaefer; K. L. Johnson; Webb; Maes-Jelink; and Gilkes. Sandra Drake provides a provocative analysis examining the role of the unconscious in Harris's work using Lacan and Derrida, among others, in *Wilson Harris and the Modern Tradition.* But note that the novel that is the focus of this chapter, perhaps because it is more explicit in its political discussion of Guyana and much less interested in myth and folklore (except the function of rumor), is rarely discussed.

4   I have adopted the phrase "shamanic dialectics" from Gregory Shaw, "The Novelist as Shaman."

5   The Harris quotes are taken from Wilson Harris, *The Guyana Prize for Literature.* See also Harris's essays in *History, Fable, and Myth in the Caribbean and Guianas; Explorations;* and *Selected Essays of Wilson Harris.*

6   For a substantive discussion of ethnicity and national politics in Guyana, see Premdas, "Ethnic Conflict and Development: The Case of Guyana."

7   See Despres.

8   Harris endorses her view in his introduction. Compare the image of maroon communities in, for example, the work of Price and Price, *Equatoria* or *Alabi's World.* On Catalena's function, see McWatt.

1   See, among many examples, Stern; S. E. Anderson; Aldridge; Marable, *Race, Reform and Rebellion;* Karenga, "Which Road" and "Ideology and Struggle"; Cruse, *Rebellion or Revolution* and *The Crisis of the Negro Intellectual;* Baraka, *Raise, Race, Rays, Raze* and *Autobiography;* and Haines.

2   Because most readers may never have had the opportunity to see the BPP's powerful and, in many ways, still urgently relevant and radical founding document, I include it here. It is important to note how many of the BPP's points are, under different names, still sources of controversy today: for example, "racial profiling"; the racial inequities of mandatory sentencing; black suspicion of targeted ballot fraud in Florida in the 2000 presidential elections; higher than average unemployment rates and salaries for African-Americans; multiculturalism and honest history and cultural analysis of U.S. society not allowed and encouraged in the schools, particularly secondary schools and tertiary institutions; the conditions of inner city black-dominated schools; the high percentage of black men in the correctional system and the corresponding disregard of this fact by state and federal governments, and so on. The Black Panther Party platform and program is quoted as follows:

October 1966

BLACK PANTHER PARTY

PLATFORM AND PROGRAM

WHAT WE WANT

WHAT WE BELIEVE

1. *We want freedom. We want power to determine the destiny of our Black Community.* We believe that Black people will not be free until we are able to determine our destiny.

2. *We want full employment for our people.*

We believe that the federal government is responsible and obligated to give every man employment or a guaranteed income. We believe that if the white American businessmen will not give full employment, then the means of production should be taken from the business and placed in the community so that the people of the community can organize and employ all of its people and give a high standard of living.

3. *We want an end to the robbery by the capitalist of our Black community.*

We believe that this racist government has robbed us and now we are demanding the overdue debt of forty acres and two mules. Forty acres and two mules were promised 100 years ago as restitution for slave labor and mass murder of Black people. We will accept the payment in currency which will be distributed to our many communities. The Germans are now aiding the Jews in Israel for the genocide of the Jewish people. The Germans murdered six million Jews. The American racist has taken part in the slaughter of over fifty million Black people; therefore, we feel that this is a modest demand that we make.

4. *We want decent housing, fit for shelter of human beings.*

We believe that if the white landlords will not give decent housing to our Black community, then the housing and the land should be made into co-operatives so that our community, with government aid, can build and make decent housing for its people.

5. *We want education for our people that exposes the true nature of this decadent American society. We want education that teaches us our true history and our role in the present-day society.*

We believe in an educational system that will give to our people a knowledge of self. If a man does not have knowledge of himself and his position in society and the world, then he has little chance to relate to anything else.

6. *We want all black men exempt from military service.*

We believe that Black people should not be forced to fight in the military service to defend a racist government that does not protect us. We will not fight and kill other people of color in the world who, like black people, are being victimized by the white racist government of America. We will protect ourselves from the force and violence of the racist police and the racist military, by whatever means necessary.

7. *We want an immediate end to POLICE BRUTALITY and MURDER of Black people.*

We believe we can end police brutality in our Black community by organizing Black self-defense groups that are dedicated to defending our Black community from racist police oppression and brutality. The Second Amendment to the Constitution of the United States gives a right to bear arms. We therefore believe that all Black people should arm themselves for self-defense.

8. *We want freedom for all Black men held in federal, state, county and city prisons and jails.*

We believe that all Black people should be released from the many jails and prisons because they have not received a fair and impartial trial.

9. *We want all Black people when brought to trial to be tried in court by a jury of their peer group or people from their Black communities, as defined by the Constitution of the United States.*

We believe that the courts should follow the United States Constitution so that Black people will receive fair trials. The Fourteenth Amendment of the U.S. Constitution gives a man a right to be tried by his peer group. A peer is a person from a similar economic, social, religious, geographical, environmental, historical, and racial background. To do this the court will be forced to select a jury from the Black community from which the Black defendant came. We have been and are being tried by all-white juries that have no understanding of the "average reasoning man" of the Black community.

10. *We want land, bread, housing, education, clothing, justice, and peace. And as our major political objective, a United Nations-supervised plebiscite to be held throughout the Black colony in which only Black colonial subjects will be allowed to participate, for the purpose of determining the will of Black people as to their destiny.*

When, in the course of human events, it becomes necessary for one people to dissolve the political bands which have connected them with another, and to assume, among the powers of the earth, the separate and equal station to which the laws of nature and nature's God entitle them, a decent respect to the opinions of mankind requires that they should declare the causes which impel them to the separation.

We hold these truths to be self-evident, that all men are created equal; that they are endowed by their Creator with certain unalienable rights; that among these are life, liberty, and the pursuit of happiness. That, to secure these rights, governments are instituted among men, deriving their just powers from the consent of the governed; that, whenever any form of government becomes destructive of these ends, it is the right of the people to alter or to abolish it, and to institute a new government, laying its foundation on such principles, and organizing its powers in such form, as to them shall seem most likely to effect their safety and happiness. Prudence, indeed, will dictate that governments long established should not be changed for light and transient causes; and, accordingly, all experience hath shown, that mankind are more disposed to suffer, while evils are sufferable, than to right themselves by abolishing the forms to which they are accustomed. But, when a long train of abuses and usurpations, pursuing invariably the same object, evinces a design to reduce them under absolute despotism, it is their right, it is their duty, to throw off such government, and to provide new guards for their future security.

3 See, for example, such contemporary analyses in the social sciences as Caplan; Schulz; and Parker and Kleiner.

4 For two of the important counterpoints to Moynihan, see Collins; and Giddings.

5 As Judith Butler argues in *Bodies That Matter*, "sex" "is a regulatory idea whose materialization is compelled, and materialization takes place (or fails to take place) through certain highly regulated practices" (1). See also Butler, *The Psychic Life of Power*. Women and gay men thus become "abject beings." On theories of sex, gender, and the body, see, among others, Butler's work; Wienke; and Bordo.

6 See also Hampton and Fayer for oral histories of FBI involvement in undermining the Civil Rights movement.

7 See Carson; Ungar (esp. 387–88 on FBI alliances with the Klan); Fry (for an analysis and folk history of the Klan as social control); Toledano (a sympathetic biography of J. Edgar Hoover); and Churchill and Wall 58, 397, n.2.

8 Mercer and Julien also make and expand on this point in "Race, Sexual Politics, and Black Masculinity." See also Foucault, *Power/Knowledge*, and the work of Fanon.

9 See also Powell, "Black Macho and Black Feminism," for a critique of Wallace's book.

10 See Gallen; also Breitman, Porter, and Smith. For FBI involvement in Martin Luther King Jr.'s assassination, see Lane and Gregory; and D. Lewis. For FBI surveillance of Baldwin, see James Campbell, *Talking at the Gates*, esp. 164–78; also Churchill and Wall.

11 See the famous picture of Katherine Cleaver as a Panther guerrilla reproduced in Churchill and Wall, 89. See also the interview with Deborah Johnson in Hampton and Fayer.

12 Thus racializing Foucault, as a reading of Foucault through Franz Fanon suggests.

13 See Butler, *Bodies That Matter*.

14 Compare Forman's "The Black Panther Party" in his *The Making of Black Revolutionaries*.

15 For an old-school black marxist critique of the BPP, see Winston.

16 See S. E. Anderson, where, in a general attack on the Oakland Panthers, he argues that they "bogarted the Northern California Panther Party out of existence" and points out that both the San Francisco Panthers and the Harlem Panthers preceded the Oakland BPP (105). James Forman's account is somewhat different, in which the Black Panther Party of Southern California "dissolved itself in January, 1968, and [became] the SNCC chapter in Los Angeles. The one in northern California had basically disintegrated" (528).

17 See Kimmel, "Masculinity as Homophobia"; Rodríguez, "Tenderness"; and Mercer and Julien.

18 The literature on Baldwin is, of course, extensive, but nowhere could I find a review or essay that grappled directly with the nexus of race, sex, and politics in *Tell Me How Long the Train's Been Gone*. A sampling of essays that skirt the subject—by not mentioning politics, not mentioning homosexuality, or reacting by vilifying the novel without actually being explicit about the issue of sexuality—runs as follows: Sylvander; Pratt; Maceguh; E. S. Nelson; Irving Howe; Puzo; DeMott; and Cohen. Alexander's "The 'Stink' of Reality" is thought-provoking, but a certain homophobia that equates gayness with misogyny undermines some of the integrity of her argument. Standley and Standley's *James Baldwin: A Reference Guide* provides a complete bibliography through to 1979.

19 See Newton's bulletin to the BPP.

20 See Kimmel, "Masculinity as Homophobia."

21 This is, of course, elaborated by Carby in *Race Men*.

22 It is arguable, of course, that the lumpen ideology itself, especially under Cleaver's direction, is epistemically indebted to nineteenth-century pathological studies.

## 6   A Politics of Change

1 This is the case if we count the 1950 publication of W. A. Lewis's *Industrial Development in the Caribbean* as the beginning of "development theory" in the West Indian context.

2 See Girvan's "Notes on the Meaning and Significance of Development." Girvan outlines Arthur Lewis's economic strategy, which according to Ralph Henry has experienced a resurgence, and identifies a "subsistence" sector and a "capitalist" sector. The "subsistence" sector, empirical evidence shows repeatedly (see Momsen, *Women and*

*Development*), is peopled by women, while the "capitalist" sector is overwhelmingly male.

3 See Midgley for an overview of the debates.

4 See Momsen, *Women and Development*. For analyses of development theories of the 1970s, see Bolles, "Theories of Women in Development"; Buvinic; Antrobus, "Women in Development" and "Gender Implications"; Safa; Henry; Rivera; Beneria; and Sen. For more recent accounts and evaluations, see Leo-Rhynie, Bailey, and Bailey; Momsen, *Women and Change;* Hart; Scott; and Visvanathan, Duggan, and Nisonoff.

5 Over the course of the 1980s the impact of the feminist movement was felt by developmental agencies, primarily located in North America and Europe. For an excellent overview and critique of World Bank/United Nations gender planning and development by a senior urban social policy specialist at the World Bank, see Moser. See also Payer. For a critique from the Caribbean, see Catherine Williams.

6 See Bolles, "Theories of Women"; also Power.

7 For an overview of how this plays out to the failures of development policies, see Moser, chapter 6.

8 Another exception was Grenada under Maurice Bishop and the New Jewel Revolution. See Antrobus, "Women in Development."

9 Some of Ambursley's figures are from Girvan, *Foreign Capital*.

10 See Francis, as well as Stephens and Stephens and other leftist economic historians. Jamaica's inflow of foreign capital, in U.S. dollars, dropped from $254 million in 1973 to $115 million, and by 1978 there was a net outflow of $83 million, reaching $214 by 1986 (C. Thomas 235), suggesting that Reagan had his own agenda and so did the multinational corporations.

11 Edward Seaga's accession to power was heralded by President Reagan as a new beginning, and he declared that by the time he was finished Jamaica would be a model for the world. The failed Caribbean Basin Initiative was an attempt to follow through on this promise (see Phillips and Shaw). Seaga's government received a loan from the IMF of US$698 million over three years, without a schedule of devaluations, wage freezes, or price controls, and this U.S. stamp of approval opened the way for some US$400 million in loans from First World sources (Ambursley 93).

12 For a feminist critique of the status of women after almost one hundred years of U.S. colonialism in Puerto Rico and its promotion as the U.S.-backed model of development for the Caribbean, see Colón-Warren and Alegría-Ortega.

13 The total population then stood about two million.

14 According to many sources, the CIA moved in, made an alliance with the disaffected local capitalist contingency of twenty-one families and the JLP party (headed by Edward Seaga), and proceeded to incite, fund, and arm civil violence and unrest. The PNP, many Jamaicans of all classes say, responded in kind. Together, they imported large shipments of guns and distributed them to their cadres in the ghettos. The

result was the transformation of gangs into political terrorist groups with a sophistication of weaponry unheard of in Jamaican history. Among the many voices making this case, see Manley, *Jamaica;* Kaufman; and, from within the CIA, Agee's *A CIA Diary*. Predictably, many commentators shy away from this issue.

15 Since I first ventured this assertion, the truth of this statement has been repeatedly borne out by development analysts. See, for example, Antrobus, who states: "Both components of existing structural adjustment policies—those aimed at increasing export-oriented production (the emphasis on the promotion of export processing zones)—depend on assumptions about the roles into which most women have been socialised" ("Women and Planning" 39).

16 See also other works by Lynn Bolles, including "Economic Crisis and Female-Headed Households in Urban Jamaica," "Kitchens Hit by Priorities: Employed Working-Class Jamaican Women Confront the IMF," "Structural Adjustment and the Quest for Participation," and "Surviving Manley and Seaga."

17 See also Scott's chapter "Marxism, Masculinity and Dependency Theory" in her *Gender and Development*.

18 See LeFranc; also D. Powell et al.

19 See Moser, who states, first, "that the household consists of a nuclear family of husband, wife and two or three children"; second, "that the household functions as a socio-economic unit within which there is equal control over resources and power of decision-making between all adult members in matters influencing the household's livelihood"; and third, "that within the household there is a clear division of labour based on gender. The man of the family, as the 'breadwinner,' is primarily involved in productive work outside the home, while the woman as the housewife and 'homemaker' takes overall responsibility for the reproductive and domestic work involved in the organization of the household" (15–16). See also Barriteau.

20 Some of their work has been documented. See for example, Peake; also Di Cenzo and Bennet. Hart records the excitement and ferment that accompanied the publication of *Lionheart Gal* in his introduction to *Women and the Sexual Division of Labour*.

21 See *Women, Guerrillas, and Love,* chapter 14.

22 See Ambursely.

23 Kenneth Ramchand makes this point in his classic work *The West Indian Novel and Its Background*. See also Kamau Braithwaite, *History of the Voice*.

24 "I constructed each interview around three questions: How did you first become aware of the fact that you were oppressed as a woman? How did that experience affect your life? How have you tried to change it?" (Ford-Smith xxviii).

25 The question of this kind of (un)official language is also raised by Eduard Glissant for the French Caribbean. Glissant's analysis of political repression as linguistic silencing and the emergence of a (protonational?) written creole does not allow for the critical role of dialects in West Indian elections and daily society. See, for example, Michael Manley's use of dialect in Michael Manley and Jamaicans, *Not For Sale,* and

also Eric Williams's use of the slogan "Massa day done" in the elections that swept him to a lifelong career as Trinidad's prime minister, marking the difference between Independence and French departmental status.

26   For slave women's resistance in the Caribbean, see, for example, Mathurin; Brereton, "Family Strategies;" Beckles, "Sex and Gender" and *Centering Woman;* Castañeda; and Moitt.

27   For upper-class women's documentation of life in Jamaica, see, for example, Lady Maria Nugent's *Journal;* or for the local white elite of Trinidad, see Bridges, *Child of the Tropics.* For an analysis of these and other women's texts of the nineteenth century, see Brereton, "Text, Testimony, and Gender" and "Gendered Testimonies."

28   A U.S. comparison that comes immediately to mind is Harriet Wilson's sardonic *Our Nig,* which makes the same argument about subaltern black women in antebellum North America. The reinscription of the poor into slavery thus has a transnational history—remember sharecropping (U.S./West Indian) and the taxation strategies— that comes down into the present.

29   On the function of rumor among the Jamaican poor, see Besson.

30   See the article "Civilians Turn Out for Gay Bashing," in the *Gleaner,* June 10, 1993. It was rumored that there was to be a gay and lesbian rights march in Kingston, the capital city. "Many homophobes armed wth weapons such as pick-axe sticks, ma-chetes, and iron pipe, waited at the park" to kill them en masse right there on the street, the *Gleaner* reported (3).

31   The Spivak reference is to *A Critique of Postcolonial Reason.*

32   A thorny, phallic cactus.

33   "Yard" in Patwah refers to both that of an individual house and a "tenement yard."

34   Corrugated zinc replaced the pile of stones in the barrack/tenement yards.

35   The JLP gave out free cornmeal and flour rumored to be infested with weevils—hence "weevil" flour. Norman Manley, Michael Manley's father and then head of the PNP, responded in rallies with "look at how many mothers need food for their children and can't buy it. The people need employment and education. The children must go to school." Reported in "Veteran by Veteran," in Sistren 161.

36   A dangerous person; someone to be avoided.

37   Manley is here referring to a far-Left faction within the PNP that criticized Manley's policies as not going far enough, á la Fitzroy Ambursley. The split resulted in an attempt by several members of the PNP to set up the separate, far-Left Workers' Party.

38   See the group's founding statement and *The Latin American Subaltern Studies Reader,* ed. Rodríguez.


## 7   Geopolitics/Geoculture

1   Spivak is also on the mark when she writes, "It is now more than ever impossible for the new or developing states—the newly decolonizing or the old decolonizing—the

newly decolonizing or the old decolonized nations—to escape the orthodox constraints of a 'neo-liberal' world economic system that, in the name of Development, and now, 'sustainable development,' removes all barriers between itself and fragile national economies, so that any possibility of social redistribution is severely damaged" (*Critique* 357).

2   See Ohmae on the passing of the Coca-Cola model in *The Borderless World*. See also his *The End of the Nation-State*.

3   See Randall Robinson's appeal and a report on his own activism in Mosley, ed., *Black Genius*. See also Amnesty International's important work on police brutality in the ghettos of Jamaica.

4   President Clinton tried to address this in 1999 with his tour of underdeveloped pockets within the United States (Watts, Pine Ridge Reservation, Appalachia, rural black Mississippi) promoting corporate investment in impoverished areas.

5   See Chow, esp. chapter 1 and the introduction; see also Spivak, *Critique of Postcolonial Reason*.

6   For a discussion of the political economics of Third World texts in First World markets, see Carr, "Crossing the First World/Third World Divides."

7   Sommer, "Irresistible Romance"; and Rodríguez, *House/Garden/Nation* and *Understanding War*.

8   The ground on which this battle is being waged is, of course, gay civil rights. In several Caribbean countries, the dislocation of globality and the adoption of U.S. and European models of "democracy" is leading governments to consider bills granting equal rights to all citizens. The caveat "except homosexuals" is openly posed. In some cases, behind the scenes, such illogic stymies these bills.

9   As Spivak writes: "The predicament of the developing state, in spite of the fact that it negotiates with nationalism and is still the site of justice and redistribution . . . is plagued . . . from the inside by the forces of internal colonization and the local bourgeoisie and plagued from the outside by these increasingly orthodox economic contraints under global economic restructuring" (*Critique of Postcolonial Reason*, 381).

10   See Levy; Moser and Holland; and Gunst.

11   See Elaine Brown's *A Taste of Power*. Brown was the main lover of Huey Newton at the time of his arrest, and she describes the beatings that both she and other BPP members received at the hands of BPP members as a matter of policy. Her autobiography exemplifies the argument I have made about the Panthers' self-destruction.

12   Each group confronts this dilemma directly. For the Caribbean see, as one example, Nettleford's *Inward Stretch, Outward Reach*; for African-Americans, see Mosley, ed., *Black Genius*; and Gates and West.

13   From the perspective of the migrant postcolonial elite, Spivak puts it this way: "In this new transnationality, 'the new diaspora,' the new scattering of the seeds of 'developing' nations so that they can take root on developed ground, means: Eurocentric migration, labor export both male and female, border crossings, the seeking of politi-

cal asylum, and the haunting in-place uprooting of 'comfort women' in Asia and Africa" (*Critique* 357). Samir Amin, of course, phrases this phenomenon very differently in *Capitalism in the Age of Globalization*.

14  See Taylor.

15  See E. Robinson. The figures change, of course, but since the 1990s the discrepancy has remained the same.

16  On the absorption of individuals into capital under globalism, see Alliez and Feher; Rodríguez, "Rethinking the Subaltern"; Hardt and Negri; and Carr, "From *Glory* to *Menace II Society*."

17  I mean the logic behind, for example, the essays that make up the special issue of *Caribbean Affairs* 3.4 (1990) "The Caribbean in the Twenty-first Century." See also Hall; Hall and Benn; Meeks and Lindahl.

18  Note that the Americans United with the Congolese People changed State Department policy toward Zaire and formed part of a team guiding the expulsion of fascist dictator Mobutu Sese Seko, who was put in place by the United States as cold war strategy and made head—with control of the treasury and the military—by President George Bush.

19  See Doris Sommer's *Foundational Fictions*. Rodríguez's *Women, Guerrillas, and Love* was in fact triggered by Sommer's "Irresistible Romance."

20  I am grateful to Fred Pfeil for bringing this study to my attention.

21  See, for example, his provocative essay "Black Sexuality," in *Race Matters*. The real impact, however, of West's work on homophobia and sexism in the African-American community is felt throughout the book in essays that on the surface do not signal a crisis of gender and sexuality. See, as an example, his point in "The Pitfalls of Racial Reasoning" on the nature of black and white support for Clarence Thomas in the Hill/Thomas debacle:

> In white America, cultural conservatism takes the form of a chronic racism, sexism, and homophobia. Hence, only certain kinds of black people deserve high positions, that is, those who accept the rules of the game played by white America. In black America, cultural conservatism takes the form of a inchoate xenophobia (e.g., against whites, Jews, and Asians), systemic sexism and homophobia. . . . In this way, black nationalist and black male-centered claims to black authenticity reinforce black cultural conservatism. The support of Louis Farrakhan's Nation of Islam for Clarence Thomas—despite Farrakhan's critique of Republican Party racist and conservative policies—highlights this fact. It also shows how racial reasoning leads different and disparate view points in black America to the same dead end—with substantive ethical principles and savvy wise politics left out. (27–28)

22  See Sagar's analysis of the novel that follows the arguments that "the mothers assume an especial prominence when it comes to questions of memory and cultural history in the world of the novel, where homosexual men face a combination of denial and violence that allows little acknowledgement of their being in the world" (29).

23  The failure of black representation in the United States and in the Caribbean converges in the example of Haiti. Apart from the death toll of Haitians crossing to the United States, there is the accelerated slaughter of Haitians that off and on becomes the policy of military governments (see French). For a view of the Haitian crises from inside Washington, D.C.'s power politics, see Randall Robinson.

24  It is worth noting that 95 percent of HIV-positive persons currently live in the developing world where the majority have simply been unable to afford antiretrovirals, a situation that has exacerbated the AIDS crisis worldwide. The current arrangements to lower the cost of drugs, dragged out of the megapharmaceutical companies, need to be seen as an astute economic move. Without such a decrease, 95 percent of their market, globally, could not otherwise afford to be consumers of their product. The increasing need, however, has been giving rise to the erosion of the possibility of profits by creating a market for generic substitutes produced by Cuba and Brazil. Thus poor persons living with HIV/AIDS in the developing world find haven in becoming a market, as the logic of capitalism as a monstrous undertaking repeats itself inexorably.

25  See the 1998 U.N. *Human Development Report* which documents the stark inequalities in consumption: globally, 20 percent of the world's people in the highest-income countries account for 86 percent of total private consumption expenditures—the poorest 20 percent a minuscule 1.3 percent. More specifically, the richest fifth consume 45 percent of all meat and fish, 58 percent of total energy, and 84 percent of all paper; and have 74 percent of all telephone lines and 87 percent of the world's vehicle fleet. Also see Crossette: "Americans and Europeans spend $17 billion a year on pet food—$4 billion more that the estimated annual additional total needed to provide basic health care and nutrition for everyone in the world."

# BIBLIOGRAPHY

Abrahams, Roger D., and John F. Szwed, eds. *After Africa: Extracts from British Travel Accounts and Journals of the Seventeenth, Eighteenth, and Nineteenth Centuries Concerning the Slaves, Their Manners, and Customs in the British West Indies.* New Haven: Yale University Press, 1983.

Adams, E. C. L. "Churchyard." *Nigger to Nigger.* New York: Scribner's, 1928.

Adeleke, Tunde. "Black Biography in the Service of Revolution: Martin R. Delany in Afro-American Historiography." *Biography* 17.3 (1994): 248–67.

——. "Race and Ethnicity in Martin R. Delany's Struggle." *Journal of Thought* 29.1 (spring 1994): 19–49.

——. *UnAfrican Americans: Nineteenth-Century Black Nationalists and the Civilizing Mission.* Lexington: University of Kentucky Press, 1998.

Agee, Philip. *A CIA Diary.* New York: Stonehall Publishing, 1975.

Ahmad, Aijaz. "Jameson's Rhetoric of Otherness and the 'National Allegory.'" *In Theory: Classes, Nations, Literatures.* London: Verso, 1993.

Akzin, Benjamin *States and Nations.* New York: Anchor Books/Doubleday, 1966.

Aldridge, Danny. "Politics in Command of Economics." *Monthly Review* 21.6 (November 1969): 115–16.

Alexander, Charlotte. "The 'Stink' of Reality: Mothers and Whores in James Baldwin's Fiction." *Literature and Psychology* 18.1 (1968): 9–26.

Alexander, M. Jacqui, and Chandra Talpade Mohanty, eds. *Feminist Genealogies, Colonial Legacies, Democratic Futures.* New York: Routledge, 1997.

Allen, Walter, and Reynolds Farley. *The Color Line and the Quality of Life: The Problem of the Twentieth Century.* New York: Russell Sage Foundation, 1987.

Allfrey Shand, Phyllis. *The Orchid House.* Washington, D.C.: Three Continents Press, 1985.

Alliez, Eric, and Michel Feher. "The Luster of Capital." *Zone* 1/2 (1987): 314–59.

Ambursley, Fitzroy. "Jamaica: From Michael Manley to Edward Seaga." Ambursley and Cohen 72–104.

Ambursely, Fitzroy, and Robin Cohen, eds. *Crisis in the Caribbean.* New York: Monthly Review Press, 1983.

Amin, Samir. *Capitalism in the Age of Globalization.* London: Zed Books, 1997.

Anderson, Benedict. *Imagined Communities: Reflections on the Origin and Spread of Nationalism.* London: Verso, 1983.

Anderson, S. E. "Revolutionary Black Nationalism and the Pan-African Idea." Barbour 99–128.

Antrobus, Peggy. "Gender Implications of the Development Crisis." Girvan and Beckford 145–60.
——. "Women and Planning: The Need for an Alternative Analysis." Leo-Rhynie et al. 38–55.
——. "Women in Development Programmes: The Caribbean Experience (1975–1985)." Mohammed and Shepherd 35–50.
Armstrong, John A. *Nations before Nationalism.* Chapel Hill: University of North Carolina Press, 1982.
Arnold, Faye W. "West Indians and London's Hierarchy of Discrimination." *Ethnic Groups* 6 (1984): 47.
"At America's Door." *Economist* July 24, 1993: 11–12.
Athill, Diana. Introduction. *Jean Rhys: The Collected Short Stories.* Ed. Diana Athill. New York: Norton, 1987.
Balibar, Etienne, and Immanuel Wallerstein. *Race, Nation, Class: Ambiguous Identities.* London: Verso, 1991.
Baldwin, James. *Tell Me How Long the Train's Been Gone.* 1968. New York: Vintage, 1998.
Baraka, Imamu Amiri. *The Autobiography of LeRoi Jones/Amiri Baraka.* New York: Freund-lich Books, 1984.
——. *Raise, Race, Rays, Raze: Essays since 1965.* New York: Random House, 1971.
——. "The Toilet." 1964; Galloway and Sabisch 388–404.
Barbour, Floyd B., ed. *The Black Seventies.* Boston: Extending Horizon, 1970.
Barriteau, Eudine. "Theorizing Gender Systems and the Project of Modernity in the Twentieth-Century Caribbean." Mohammed, *Rethinking Caribbean Difference* 186–210.
Barrow, Christine. *Caribbean Portraits: Essays on Gender Ideologies and Identities.* Kingston: Ian Randle Publishers, 1998.
Basdeo, Sahadeo. *Labour Organization and Labour Reform in Trinidad, 1919–1939.* St. Augustine, Trinidad: ISER, 1983.
Beam, Joseph. "Brother to Brother: Words from the Heart." Beam and Hemphill 230–42.
Beam, Joseph, and Essex Hemphill, eds. *In the Life: A Black Gay Anthology.* Boston: Alyson Publications, 1986.
Beckles, Hilary M. *Centering Woman: Gender Discourse in Caribbean Slave Society.* Kingston, Jamaica: Ian Randle Publishers; Princeton, N.J.: Markus Weiner Publishers; Oxford: James Currey Publishers, 1999.
——. "Historicizing Slavery in West Indian Feminisms." Mohammed, *Rethinking Caribbean Difference* 34–56.
——. "Sex and Gender in the Historiography of Caribbean Slavery." Shepherd, Brereton, and Bailey 125–40.
Beckles, Hilary, and Verene Shepherd, eds. *Caribbean Freedom: Economy and Society from Emancipation to the Present.* Kingston, Jamaica: Ian Randle Publishers; London: James Currey Publishers; Princeton, N.J.: Markus Wiener Publishers, 1996.
Bell, Derrick. *And We Are Not Saved: The Elusive Quest for Racial Justice.* New York: Harper-Collins, 1987.
Benería, Lourdes, ed. *Women and Development: The Sexual Division of Labour in Rural Societies.* New York: Praeger, 1982.
Berg, Allison. "Reconstructing Motherhood: Pauline Hopkins' *Contending Forces.*" *Studies in American Fiction* 24.2 (1996): 131–50.
Berger, Martin A. *Man Made: Thomas Eakins and the Construction of Gilded-Age Manhood.* Berkeley: University of California Press, 2000.
Berger, Maurice, Brian Wallis, and Simon Watson, eds. *Constructing Masculinity.* New York: Routledge, 1996.
Bernal, Martin. *Black Athena: The Afro-Asiatic Roots of Classical Civilization.* 2 vols. New Brunswick: Rutgers University Press, 1987.

Besson, Jean. "Reputation and Respectability Reconsidered: A New Perspective on Afro-Caribbean Peasant Women." Momsen 15–37.

Beverley, John. "Writing in Reverse (on the Project of the Latin American Subaltern Studies Group)." *Dispositio/n* xix.46 (fall 1994): 271–88.

Bhabha, Homi. *The Location of Culture.* London: Routledge, 1994.

——, ed. *Nation and Narration.* London: Routledge, 1990.

Bibb, Henry. *Narrative of the Life and Adventures of Henry Bibb, An American Slave.* 3rd ed. 1850. Miami: Mnemosyne Publishing, 1969.

Black Panther Party. *Ten Point Platform,* available at http://www.etext.org/Politics/AlternativeOrange/1/v1n4_bppp.html.

Blackett, Richard. "Martin R. Delany and Robert Campbell: Black Americans in Search of an African Colony." *Journal of Negro History* 62.1 (January 1977): 1–25.

Blomström, Magnus, and Björn Hettne. *Development Theory in Transition. The Dependency Debate and Beyond: Third World Responses.* London: Zed Books, 1984.

Blonsky, Marshall, ed. *On Signs.* Baltimore: Johns Hopkins University Press, 1985.

Boland, O. Nigel. "Systems of Domination after Slavery: The Control of Land and Labour in the British West Indies after 1838." Beckles and Shepherd 107–23.

Bolles, Lynn. "Economic Crisis and Female-Headed Households in Urban Jamaica." Nash and Safa 65–82.

——. "Kitchens Hit by Priorities: Employed Working-Class Jamaican Women Confront the IMF." Nash and Fernández-Kelly 138–60.

——. "My Mother Who Fathered Me and Others: Gender and Kinship in the Caribbean." Working paper no. 175. Michigan State University, December 1988.

——. "Structural Adjustment and the Quest for Participation." Deere et al. 87–119.

——. "Surviving Manley and Seaga: Case Studies of Women's Responses to Structural Adjustment Policies." *Review of Radical Political Economics* 23.3–4 (1991): 20–36.

——. "Theories of Women in Development in the Caribbean: The Ongoing Debate." Mohammed and Shepherd 23–34.

——. *We Paid Our Dues: Women Trade Union Leaders of the Caribbean.* Washington, D.C.: Howard University Press, 1996.

Bontemps, Arna, ed. "The Slave Narrative: An American Genre." *Great Slave Narratives.* Boston: Beacon Press, 1969.

Boorstein, Daniel. *The Americans: The National Experience.* New York: Vintage Books, 1965.

Bordo, Susan. "Reading the Male Body." *Michigan Quarterly Review* 32.4 (fall 1993): 696–737.

Boserup, Ester. *Women's Role in Economic Development.* New York: St. Martin's Press, 1970.

Braithwaite, Edward. *The Arrivants: A New World Trilogy.* Oxford: Oxford University Press, 1973.

Braithwaite, Kamau. *History of the Voice: The Development of Nation Language in Anglophone Caribbean Poetry.* London: New Beacon Books, 1984.

Breitman, George, Herman Porter, and Baxter Smith. *The Assassination of Malcolm X.* New York: Pathfinder Press, 1976.

Brereton, Bridget. "Family Strategies, Gender, and the Shift to Wage Labour in the British Caribbean." Brereton and Yelvington 77–107.

——. "Text, Testimony, and Gender: An Examination of Some Texts by Women on the English-Speaking Caribbean, from the 1770s to the 1920s." Shepherd, Brereton, and Bailey 63–93.

Brereton, Bridget, and Kevin A. Yelvington, eds. *The Colonial Caribbean in Transition: Essays on Postemancipation Social and Cultural History.* Kingston, Jamaica: University Press of the West Indies; Gainesville: University Press of Florida, 1999.

Bridges, Yseult. *Child of the Tropics: Victorian Memoirs.* Ed. Nicholas Guppy. Port of Spain, Trinidad & Tobago: Aquarella Galleries, 1988.

Brod, Harry. "Some Thoughts on Some Histories of Some Masculinities: Jews and Others." Brod and Kaufman 82–96.

Brod, Harry, and Michael Kaufman, eds. *Theorizing Masculinities*. Thousand Oaks, Calif.: Sage Publications, 1994.

Brodber, Erna. *Yards in the City of Kingston*. Mona, Jamaica: Institute of Social and Economic Research, University of the West Indies, 1975.

Brooks, Kristina. "New Woman, Fallen Woman: The Crisis of Reputation in Turn-of-the-Century Novels by Pauline Hopkins and Edith Wharton." *Legacy* 13.2 (1996): 91–112.

Brown, Elaine. *A Taste of Power: A Black Woman's Story*. New York: Pantheon Books, 1992.

Brown, William Wells. *Clotel; or The President's Daughter*. 1853. New York: University Books/Carol Publishing Group, 1969.

——. *Narrative of William W. Brown, A Fugitive Slave, Written by Himself*. 1847. *Five Slave Narratives: A Compendium*. Ed. William Loren Katz. New York: Arno Press, 1968.

Butler, Judith. *Bodies That Matter: On the Discursive Limits of Sex*. London: Routledge, 1993.

——. *The Psychic Life of Power: Theories in Subjection*. Stanford: Stanford University Press, 1997.

Buvinic, Mayra. "Women's Issues in Third World Poverty: A Policy Analysis." Buvinic, Lycette, and McGreevey 14–31.

Buvinic, M., M. Lycette, and W. P. McGreevey, eds. *Women and Poverty in the Third World*. Baltimore: Johns Hopkins University Press, 1983.

Campbell, Carl. Introduction. *Free Mulatto*. By J. B. Philippe.

Campbell, James. *Talking at the Gates: A Life of James Baldwin*. New York: Viking, 1991.

Campbell Wilkinson, Henry. *Bermuda from Sail to Steam*. 2 vols. London: Oxford University Press, 1973.

Caplan, Nathan. "The New Ghetto Man: A Review of Recent Empirical Studies." *Journal of Social Issues* 26.1 (1970): 59–73.

Carby, Hazel. *Race Men*. Cambridge: Harvard University Press, 1998.

——. *Reconstructing Womanhood: The Emergence of the Afro-American Woman Novelist*. New York: Oxford University Press, 1987.

Carew, Jan. *Fulcrums of Change*. Washington, D.C.: African World Press, 1988.

Carmichael, Stokley, and Charles V. Hamilton. *Black Power: The Politics of Liberation in America*. New York: Random House, 1967.

Carr, Robert. "Crossing the First World/Third World Divides: Testimonial, Transnational Feminisms, and the Postmodern Condition." Grewal and Kaplan 153–72.

——. "From *Glory* to *Menace II Society*: African-American Subalternity and the Ungovernability of the Democratic Impulse under Super-Capitalist Orders." Rodríguez, *Reader* 227–40.

Carson, Clayborne. *In Struggle: SNCC and the Black Awakening of the 1960s*. Cambridge: Harvard University Press, 1981.

Casteñeda, Digna. "The Female Slave in Cuba during the First Half of the Nineteenth Century." Shepherd, Brereton, and Bailey 141–54.

Caulder-Marshall, Arthur. *Glory Dead*. London: M. Joseph, 1939.

Chapman, Rowena, and Jonathan Rutherford, eds. *Male Order: Unwrapping Masculinity*. London: Lawrence and Wishart, 1988.

Chatterjee, Partha. *Nationalist Thought and the Colonial World: A Derivative Discourse*. Minneapolis: University of Minnesota Press, 1993.

——. *The Nation and Its Fragments*. Princeton: Princeton University Press, 1993.

Chen, Xiaomei. "Occidentalism as Counterdiscourse: 'He Shang' in Post-Mao China." *Critical Inquiry* 18 (summer 1992): 686–712.

Cherniasky, Eve. "Subaltern Studies in a U.S. Frame." *boundary 2* 23.2 (1996): 85–110.

Chow, Rey. *Ethics after Idealism: Theory—Culture—Ethnicity—Reading*. Bloomington: Indiana University Press, 1998.

Christian, Barbara. *Black Women Novelists: The Development of a Tradition, 1892–1976.* Westport, Conn.: Greenwood Press, 1980.

Churchill, Ward, and Jim Vander Wall. *Agents of Repression: The FBI's Secret War against the Black Panther Party and the American Indian Movement.* Boston: South End Press, 1990.

Cixous, Hélène, and Catherine Clément. *The Newly Born Woman.* Minneapolis: University of Minnesota Press, 1986.

Clarke, Cheryl. "The Failure to Transform: Homophobia in the Black Community." B. Smith 197–208.

Clarke, John Henrik, ed. *William Styron's Nat Turner: Ten Black Writers Respond.* Boston: Beacon Press, 1968.

Cleaver, Eldridge. *Soul on Ice.* New York: McGraw-Hill, 1968.

Cobham, Rhonda. Introduction. *Pitch Lake.* By Alfred Mendes.

Cohen, William A. "Liberalism, Libido, Liberation: Baldwin's *Another Country.*" *Genders* 12 (winter 1991): 1–21.

Cole, Merrill. "Nat Turner's Thing." Lane 261–81.

Collins, Patricia Hill. *Black Feminist Thought: Knowledge, Consciousness, and the Politics of Empowerment.* Boston: Unwin Hyman, 1990.

Colón-Warren, Alice E., and Idsa Alegría-Ortega. "Shattering the Illusion of Development: The Changing Status of Women and Challenges for the Feminist Movement in Puerto Rico." Mohammed, *Rethinking Caribbean Difference* 101–17.

Cooper, Anna Julia. *A Voice from the South.* 1892. New York: Oxford University Press, 1988.

Coore, David. "Address to the Eighteenth Special Session of the General Assembly Relating to International Economic Cooperation." New York, April 1990.

Craft, Ellen, and William Craft. *Running a Thousand Miles for Freedom; or, The Escape of William and Ellen Craft from Slavery.* 1860. Bontemps 269–331.

Craig, Susan. *Smiles and Blood: The Ruling Class Response to the Workers' Rebellion of 1937 in Trinidad and Tobago.* London: New Beacon Books, 1988.

Crossette, Barbara. "Kofi Annan's Astonishing Facts!" *New York Times* September 27, 1998.

Cruse, Harold. *The Crisis of the Negro Intellectual.* 1967. New York: Quill, 1984.

——. *Rebellion or Revolution.* New York: William Morrow, 1968.

Cummings, James. "Barrack Rooms." *The Beacon* 1.7 (October 1931): 21–22.

——. "What the Planter Plants." *The Beacon* 1.8 (November 1931): 21.

Davidson, Basil. *The Black Man's Burden: Africa and the Curse of the Nation-State.* New York: Times Books/Random House, 1992.

de Boissière, Ralph. *Crown Jewel.* Melbourne: Australasian Book Society, 1952.

——. *Rum and Coca-Cola.* Melbourne: Australasian Book Society, 1956.

de Certeau, Michel. "On Montaigne's 'On Savages.'" *Heterologies: Discourses on the Other.* Trans. Brian Massumi. Minneapolis: University of Minnesota Press, 1986.

Deere, Carmen Diana (coordinator), Peggy Antrobus, Lynn Bolles, Edwin Melendez, Peter Phillips, Marcia Rivera, and Helen Safa. *In the Shadows of the Sun: Caribbean Development Alternatives and U.S. Policy.* Boulder: Westview Press, 1990.

Delany, Martin R. *Blake; or The Huts of America.* 1859–1862. Ed. Floyd J. Miller. Boston: Beacon Press, 1970.

——. *The Condition, Elevation, and Destiny of the Colored People of the United States.* 1852. Salem, N.H.: Ayers Publishing Company, 1988.

——. *Official Report of the Niger Valley Exploring Party.* 1861. Philadelphia: Historic Publications, 1969.

——. "The Political Destiny of the Colored Race." 1854. Stuckey 195–236.

Deleuze, Gilles, and Félix Guattari. *Capitalism and Schizophrenia: Anti-Oedipus.* Trans. Robert Hurley, Mark Seem, and Helen R. Lane. New York: Viking, 1977.

De Lisser, H. G. *The White Witch of Rosehall.* London: Macmillan, 1982.

D'Emilio, John. "Capitalism and Gay Identity." Snitow, Stansell, and Thompson 100–16.

D'Emilio, John, and Estelle B. Freedman. *Intimate Matters: A History of Sexuality in America*. 2nd ed. Chicago: University of Chicago Press, 1997.

DeMott, Benjamin. "James Baldwin on the Sixties: Acts and Revelations." Kinnamon.

Despres, Leo A. *Cultural Pluralism and Nationalist Politics in British Guiana*. Chicago: Rand McNally, 1967.

Deutsch, Karl W. *Nationalism and Its Alternatives*. New York: Knopf, 1969.

Di Cenzo, Maria, and Susan Bennet. "Women, Popular Theatre, and Social Action: Interviews with Cynthia Grant and the Sistren Theatre Collective." *Ariel: A Review of International English Literature* 23.1 (January 1992): 81–94.

Dolan, Edward F., and Margaret Scariano. *Cuba and the United States: Troubled Neighbours*. New York: F. Watts, 1987.

Domhoff, G. William. *The Power Elite and the State: How Policy Is Made in America*. New York: Gruyter, 1990.

Douglass, Frederick. *The Life and Writings of Frederick Douglass*. Comp. Philip S. Foner. 5 vols. New York: International Publishers, 1955.

——. *Narrative of the Life of Frederick Douglass, an American Slave*. 1845. New York: New American Library, 1968.

Drake, Capt. Richard. *Revelations of a Slave Smuggler: Being the Autobiography of Capt. Richard Drake, an African Trader for Fifty Years—from 1807 to 1857; during which period he was concerned in the transportation of a half million blacks from African coasts to America*. 1858. Northbrook, Ill.: Metro Books, 1972.

Drake, Sandra. "Language and Revolutionary Hope." Gilkes 65–81.

——. "Revolutionary Hope as Immanent Moment: The Writing of Wilson Harris." Rodríguez and Zimmerman 168–75.

——. *Wilson Harris and the Modern Tradition*. Westport, Conn.: Greenwood Press, 1986.

Drucker, Peter F. "The New Pluralisms." *Dialogue* 89 (March 1990): 5.

Du Bois, W. E. B. *The Negro American Family*. New York: Negro Universities Press, 1969.

Eco, Umberto. "Toward a New Middle Ages." Blonsky 488–504.

Edmondson, Belinda. *Making Men: Gender, Literary Authority, and Women's Writing in Caribbean Narrative*. Durham: Duke University Press, 1999.

Elkins, W. F. *Black Power in the Caribbean: The Beginnings of the Modern National Movements*. New York: Revisionist Press, 1977.

Eze, Emmanuel Chukwudi, ed. *Race and Enlightenment: A Reader*. Boston: Blackwell Publishers, 1997.

Fanon, Franz. *Black Skin, White Masks*. New York: Grove Press, 1982.

——. *Studies in a Dying Colonialism*. New York: Monthly Review Press, 1965.

——. *Toward the African Revolution*. New York: Grove Press, 1967.

——. *The Wretched of the Earth*. New York: Grove Press, 1965.

Farley, Reynolds. "The Myth of West Indian Success." National Academy of Sciences Report no. 6. Washington, D.C.: National Research Council, Commission on Behavioral and Social Sciences and Education, 1986.

Felman, Shoshana. *Writing and Madness: Literature/Philosophy/Psychoanalysis*. Trans. Martha Noel Evans, Shoshana Felman, and Brian Massumi. Ithaca: Cornell University Press, 1985.

Flax, Jane. "What Is Enlightenment? A Feminist Rereading." Postmodernism and Rereadings of Modernity Conference, University of Essex, July 9–11, 1990.

Ford-Smith, Honor. Introduction. *Lionheart Gal*. By Sistren.

——. "Sistren: Jamaica Woman's Theatre." Khan and Neumaier 84–91.

Forman, James. *The Making of Black Revolutionaries*. Seattle: Open Hand Publishing, 1985.

Foucault, Michel. *The Birth of the Clinic: An Archaeology of Knowledge*. Trans. A. M. Sheridan Smith. New York: Pantheon Books, 1972.

——. *Discipline and Punish: The Birth of the Prison*. Trans. Alan Sheridan. New York: Vintage Books, 1979.

——. *Power/Knowledge: Selected Interviews and Other Writings, 1972–1977.* New York: Pantheon Books, 1982.

——. *Madness and Civilization: A History of Insanity in the Age of Reason.* Trans. Richard Howard. New York: Vintage Books, 1973.

Franchot, Jenny. "The Punishment of Esther: Frederick Douglass and the Construction of the Feminine." Sundquist 141–65.

Francis, A. A. *Taxing the Transnationals in the Struggle over Bauxite.* The Hague: Institute for Social Studies; Kingston, Jamaica: Heinemann Educational Books, Caribbean Ltd., 1981.

Franco, Jean. "Killing Priests, Nuns, Women, and Children." Blonsky 414–20.

——. *Plotting Women: Gender and Representation in Mexico.* New York: Columbia University Press, 1989.

Frazier, E. Franklin. *The Negro Family in the United States.* New York: Dryden Press, 1948.

Frederickson, George M. *The Black Image in the White Mind: The Debate on Afro-American Character and Destiny, 1817–1914.* Hanover, N.H.: University Press of New England, 1990.

French, Howard W. "Months of Terror Leave Hundreds Dead across Haiti." *New York Times* April 2, 1994: A1, A2.

Froude, James Anthony. *The English in the West Indies; or The Bow of Ulysses.* 1888. New York: Negro Universities Press, 1969.

Fry, Gladys-Marie. *Night Riders in Black Folk History.* Athens: University of Georgia Press, 1991.

Fussell, Paul. *Class: A Guide through the American Status System.* New York: Summit Books, 1983.

Gallegos, Romulo. *Doña Bárbara.* Caracas: Ayacucho, 1977.

Gallen, David, ed. *Malcolm X: The FBI File.* New York: Carroll and Graff Publishers, 1991.

Galloway, David, and Christian Sabisch, eds. *Calamus: Male Homosexuality in Twentieth-Century Literature.* New York: William Morrow, 1982.

Gates, Henry Louis Jr. "Critical Fanonism." *Critical Inquiry* 17.3 (spring 1991): 457–70.

——, ed. *"Race," Writing, and Difference.* Chicago: University of Chicago Press, 1986.

——, ed. *Six Women's Slave Narratives.* New York: Oxford University Press, 1988.

——, ed. *Spiritual Narratives.* New York: Oxford University Press, 1988.

Gates, Henry Louis Jr., and Cornel West. *The Future of the Race.* New York: Vintage Books/Random House, 1997.

Gellner, Ernest. *Nations and Nationalism.* Ithaca: Cornell University Press, 1983.

Genovese, Eugene D. *Roll, Jordan, Roll: The World the Slaves Made.* New York: Random House/Vintage Books, 1976.

Gerber, Gwen. "Myths of Masculinity: The Oedipus Complex and Douglass's 1845 *Narrative.*" Lane 241–60.

Giddings, Paula. *When and Where I Enter: The Impact of Black Women on Race and Sex in America.* New York: William Morrow, 1984.

Gilkes, Michael, ed. *The Literate Imagination: Essays on the Novels of Wilson Harris.* London: Macmillan Caribbean, 1989.

——. *Wilson Harris and the Caribbean Novel.* Port of Spain, Trinidad: Longman Caribbean, 1975.

Gilman, Sander. "Pauline Hopkins and the Occult: African-American Revisions of Nineteenth-Century Sciences." *American Literary History* 8.1 (1996): 57–82.

Gilroy, Paul. *The Black Atlantic: Modernity and Double Consciousness.* Cambridge: Harvard University Press, 1993.

Girvan, Norman. *Foreign Capital and Economic Underdevelopment in Jamaica.* Kingston, Jamaica: ISER, 1971.

——. "Notes on the Meaning and Significance of Development." Mohammed and Shepherd 13–22.

Girvan, Norman, and George Beckford, eds. *Development in Suspense*. Kingston, Jamaica: Frederick Ebert Stifting and the Association of Caribbean Economists, 1989.

Glantz, Oscar. "Native Sons and Immigrants: Some Beliefs and Values of American Born and West Indian Blacks at Brooklyn College." *Ethnicity* 5 (1978): 189–202.

Glissant, Edouard. *Caribbean Discourse: Selected Essays*. Trans. Michael Dash. Charlottesville: University Press of Virginia, 1989.

Gomes, Albert. "Black Man." *Beacon* 1.4 (July 1931): 1–2.

Greenberg, David F. *The Construction of Homosexuality*. Chicago: University of Chicago Press, 1988.

Grewal, Inderpal, and Caren Kaplan, eds. *Scattered Hegemonies: Postmodernism and Transnational Feminist Practices*. Minneapolis: University of Minnesota Press, 1994.

Grossman, Rachel. "Women's Place in the Integrated Circuit." *Radical America* 14.1 (1980): 24–49.

Guevara, Che. *Guerilla Warfare*. New York: Random House, 1969.

Guha, Ranajit. "On Some Aspects of the Historiography of Colonial India." Guha and Spivak 37–44.

———. "The Prose of Counter-Insurgency." Guha and Spivak 45–86.

———, ed. *Subaltern Studies V: Writings on South Asian History and Society*. New Delhi: Oxford University Press, 1989.

Guha, Ranajit, and Gayatri Chakravorty Spivak, eds. *Selected Subaltern Studies*. New York: Oxford University Press, 1988.

Gunst, Laurie. *Born Fi' Dead: A Journey through the Jamaican Posse Underworld*. London: Payback Press, 1999.

Hacker, Louis M. *The Triumph of American Capitalism*. New York: Simon and Schuster, 1940.

Hage, Jerry, and Charles S. Powers. *Post-Industrial Lives: Roles and Relationships in the Twenty-First Century*. Newbury Park, Calif.: Sage Publications, 1992.

Haines, Herbert H. *Black Radicals and the Civil Rights Mainstream*. Knoxville: University of Tennessee Press, 1988.

Hall, Catherine. "Gender Politics and Imperial Politics: Rethinking the Histories of Empire." Shepherd, Brereton, and Bailey 48–59.

Hall, Kenneth O., ed. *The Caribbean Community: Beyond Survival*. Kingston, Jamaica: Ian Randle Publishers, 2001.

Hall, Kenneth, and Denis Benn, eds. *Contending with Destiny: The Caribbean in the 21st Century*. Kingston, Jamaica: Ian Randle Publishers, 2000.

Hampton, Henry, and Steve Fayer. *Voices of Freedom: An Oral History of the Civil Rights Movements from the 1950s through the 1980s*. New York: Bantam Books, 1990.

Hardt, Michael, and Antonio Negri. *Empire*. Cambridge, Mass.: Harvard University Press, 2000.

Harland, Sidney C. "Race Admixture." *Beacon* 1.4 (July 1931): 25–29.

Harper, Frances. *Iola LeRoy; or Shadows Uplifted*. 1893. New York: AMS Press, 1971.

———. "Woman's Political Future." *World's Congress of Representative Women*. Ed. May Wright Sewall. Chicago: Rand McNally, 1894.

Harris, Wilson. *Explorations: A Selection of Talks and Articles, 1966–1988*. Ed. Hena Maes-Jelinek. Mundelstrup, Denmark: Dangaroo Press, 1988.

———. *The Guyana Prize for Literature, 1987: Commemorative Issue*. Georgetown, Guyana: Demerara Publishers Ltd./Guyana National Printers Ltd., 1987.

———. *The Guyana Quartet*. 1960–64. London: Faber and Faber, 1985.

———. *History, Fable, and Myth in the Caribbean and Guianas*. Rev. ed. Wellesley, Mass.: Callaloux, 1995.

———. *Selected Essays of Wilson Harris: The Unfinished Genesis of the Imagination*. New York: Routledge, 1999.

Hart, Keith, ed. *Women and the Sexual Division of Labour in the Caribbean*. Kingston, Jamaica: Canoe Press, 1996.

Hemphill, Essex, ed. *Brother to Brother.* Boston: Alyson Publications, 1991.

Henry, Ralph. "Jobs, Gender, and Development Strategy in the Commonwealth Caribbean." Mohammed and Shepherd 176–96.

Henson, Josiah. *Truth Stranger than Fiction: Father Henson's Story of His Own Life.* 1858. New Jersey: Gregg Press, 1970.

Herskovists, Melville, and Frances Herskovists. *Suriname Folklore.* New York: Columbia University Press, 1936.

Hobbes, Thomas. *Leviathan: Authoritative Text, Backgrounds, Interpretations.* 1651. Ed. Richard E. Flathman and David Johnston. New York: Norton, 1997.

Hobsbawm, Eric. *Nations and Nationalism since 1780: Programme, Myth, Reality.* 2nd ed. Cambridge: Cambridge University Press, 1992.

Hogan, Patrick Colm. *Colonialism and Cultural Identity: Crises of Tradition in the Anglophone Literatures of India, Africa, and the Caribbean.* Albany, N.Y.: State University of New York Press, 2000.

hooks, bell. *Yearning: Race, Gender, and Cultural Politics.* Boston: South End Press, 1990.

Hopkins, Pauline. *Contending Forces: A Romance Illustrative of Negro Life North and South.* 1899. New York: Oxford University Press, 1988.

——. "Famous Women of the Negro Race." *Colored American Magazine* 4–5 (November 1901–October 1902).

——. "Hagar's Daughter: A Story of Southern Caste Prejudice." Hopkins, *Magazine Novels* 1–284.

——. *The Magazine Novels of Pauline Hopkins.* New York: Oxford University Press, 1988.

——. "Of One Blood, or, The Hidden Self." 1902. Hopkins, *Magazine Novels* 439–621.

——. Prospectus for *Contending Forces. Colored American Magazine* 1 (September 1900): 195–95.

——. "Some Literary Workers, Part 1." *Colored American Magazine* 4 (March 1902): 276–80, 277.

——. "Talma Gordon." *Colored American Magazine* 1 (October 1900): 271–90.

——. "Winona: A Tale of Negro Life in the South and Southwest." Hopkins, *Magazine Novels* 285–438.

Howe, Irving. "James Baldwin: At Ease in Apocalypse." *Harper's Magazine* September 1968: 92, 95–100.

Howe, Stephen. *Afrocentrism: Mythical Pasts and Imagined Homes.* New York: Verso Books, 1998.

Hroch, Miroslav. *Social Conditions of National Revival in Europe.* Cambridge: Cambridge University Press, 1985.

Ibrahim, Saad Eddin. "Management and Mismanagement of Diversity: The Case of Ethnic Conflict and State-Building in the Arab World." Management of Social Transformations Clearinghouse, Discussion Paper no. 10. New York: UNESCO, 1995.

Ifill, Max, ed. *Proceedings of a Sesquicentennial Conference on Human Development.* Port of Spain, Trinidad: Economic and Business Research, 1989.

Irigaray, Luce. *Speculum of the Other Woman.* New York: Columbia University Press, 1985.

——. *This Sex Which Is Not One.* Ithaca: Cornell University Press, 1985.

Jacobs, Harriet A. *Incidents in the Life of a Slave Girl, Written by Herself.* 1861. Ed. Lydia Maria Child (1861) and Jean Fagin Yellin (1987). New York: Harvard University Press, 1987.

James, C. L. R. "The Intelligence of the Negro: A Few Words in Response." *Beacon* 1.5 (August 1931): 6–10.

——. *Minty Alley.* 1936. London: New Beacon, 1981.

Jameson, Fredric. "Third World Literature in the Era of Multinational Capital." *Social Text* (fall 1986): 65–88.

JanMohammed, Abdul. "The Economy of Manichean Allegory: The Function of Racial Difference in Colonialist Literature." Gates, *"Race," Writing, and Difference* 78–106.

Jaquith, Cindy, Don Rojas, Nils Castro, and Fidel Castro. *Panama: The Truth about the U.S. Invasion.* New York: Pathfinder, 1990.

Jardine, Alice. *Gynesis: Configurations of Woman and Modernity.* Ithaca: Cornell University Press, 1985.

Jed, Stephanie. *Chaste Thinking: The Rape of Lucrecia and the Birth of Humanism.* Bloomington: Indiana University Press, 1989.

Jensen, Merrill. "The Roots of Recovery: Growth of Business Enterprise." Nash 126–35.

Johnson, Deborah. Interview. Hampton and Fayer 521, 526, 530, 533, 534–35.

Johnson, Howard. "Oil, Imperial Policy, and the Trinidad Disturbances, 1937." R. Thomas 141–81.

Johnson, K. L. "From Muse to Majesty: Rape, Landscape, and Agency in the Early Novels of Wilson Harris." *World Literature Written in English* 35.2 (1996): 71–89.

Jordan, Winthrop D. *White over Black: American Attitudes Towards the Negro, 1550–1812.* Baltimore: Penguin, 1969.

Jourdain, Silvester. *Plaine Description of the Barmudas.* 1610. New York: Da Capo Press, 1971.

Julian. *Just Being Guys Together.* Unpublished manuscript, 1992.

Karenga, Maulana Ron. "Ideology and Struggle: Some Preliminary Notes." *The Black Scholar* 6.5 (January–February 1975): 23–30.

———. "Which Road: Nationalism, Pan-Africanism, Socialism?" *The Black Scholar* 6.2 (October 1972): 21–30.

Kasinitz, Philip. *Caribbean New York: Black Immigrants and the Politics of Race.* Ithaca: Cornell University Press, 1992.

Katz, Jonathan Ned. *Gay American History: Lesbians and Gay Men in the U.S.A.: A Documentary History.* Rev. ed. New York: Meridian, 1992.

———. *The Invention of Heterosexuality.* New York: Dutton, 1995.

———. *Love Stories: Sex between Men before Homosexuality.* Chicago: University of Chicago Press, 2001.

Katz, William Loren, ed. *Five Slave Narratives: A Compendium.* New York: Arno Press, 1968.

Kaufman, Michael. *Jamaica under Manley: Dilemmas of Socialism and Democracy.* London: Zed Books; Westport, Conn.: Lawrence Hill, 1985.

Kerry, Robert. "Opening Statement of Senator Bob Kerry, Intelligence Committee Hearing on Cuba, July 29, 1993." Washington, D.C.: U.S. Senate, 1993.

Khan, Douglas, and Diane Neumaier, eds. *Cultures in Contention.* Seattle: Real Comet Press, 1985.

Kimmel, Michael. *Manhood in America: A Cultural History.* New York: Free Press, 1997.

———. "Masculinity as Homophobia: Fear, Shame, and Silence in the Construction of Gender Identity." Brod and Kaufman 119–41.

King, Bruce, ed. *West Indian Literature.* London: Macmillan Education, 1995.

King, Martin Luther Jr. "Walk for Freedom." *Fellowship* 22 (May 1956): 5–7.

Kinnamon, Kenneth, ed. *James Baldwin: A Collection of Critical Essays.* Englewood Cliffs, N.J.: Prentice-Hall, 1974.

Koenig, Matthias. "Democratic Governance in Multicultural Societies: Social Conditions for the Implementation of International Human Rights through Multicultural Policies." Management of Social Transformations Clearinghouse, Discussion Paper no. 30. New York: UNESCO, 1999.

Laclau, Ernesto, ed. *The Making of Political Identities.* London: Verso, 1994.

LaGuerre, John Gaffar. "Leadership in a Plural Society: The Case of the Indians in Trinidad and Tobago." Ryan 83–112.

Laitin, David D. *Hegemony and Culture: Politics and Religious Change among Yoruba.* Chicago: University of Chicago Press, 1986.

Lamming, George. "Bonds That Unite the Caribbean." *Trinidad and Tobago Review* 13.5 (March/April 1991): 16.

Lane, Christopher, ed. *The Psychoanalysis of Race.* New York: Columbia University Press, 1998.

Lane, Mark, and Dick Gregory. *Code Name "Zorro": The Murder of Martin Luther King, Jr.* Englewood Cliffs, N.J.: Prentice Hall, 1977.

Latin American Subaltern Studies Group. "Founding Statement." Rabassa, Sanjinés, and Carr 1–11.

Ledgister, F. S. J. *Class Alliances and the Liberal Authoritarian State: The Roots of Post-Colonial Democracy in Jamaica, Trinidad and Tobago, and Surinam.* Trenton, N.J.: African World Press, 1998.

Lee, Jarena. *Religious Experience and Journal of Mrs. Jarena Lee.* Philadelphia, PA: n.p. 1849.

Lee, Susan Previant, and Peter Passell. *A New Economic View of American History.* New York: Norton, 1979.

LeFranc, Elsie. "Petty Trading and Labour Mobility: Higglers in the Kingston Metropolitan Area of Jamaica." Hart 105–31.

Leo-Rhynie, Elsa, Barbara Bailey, and Christine Barrow, eds. *Gender: A Caribbean Multi-Disciplinary Perspective.* Kingston, Jamaica: Ian Randle Publishers, 1997.

Levine, Lawrence. *Black Culture and Black Consciousness: Afro-American Folk Thought from Slavery to Freedom.* New York: Oxford University Press, 1977.

Levy, Horace, comp. *They Cry 'Respect'! Urban Violence and Poverty in Jamaica.* Direction and Foreword by Barry Chevannes. Rev. ed. Mona, Jamaica: Centre for Population, Community, and Social Change, 2000.

Lewis, David. *King: A Biography.* Urbana: University of Illinois Press, 1978.

Lewis, Gordon K. *Main Currents in Caribbean Thought.* Baltimore: Johns Hopkins University Press, 1983.

Lewis W. Arthur. *Industrial Development in the Caribbean.* Port of Spain, Trinidad: Caribbean Commission, 1950.

—. "The 1930s Social Revolution." *Labour in the West Indies: The Birth of a Workers Movement.* London: Fabian Society, 1938. Rpt. in Beckles and Shepherd 376–92.

Light, Ivan. *Ethnic Enterprise in America.* Berkeley: University of California Press, 1972.

Lima, Maria Helena. "Revolutionary Developments: Michelle Cliff's *No Telephone to Heaven* and Merle Collins' *Angel*." *Ariel: A Review of International English Literature* 24.1 (January 1993): 35–56.

Litwack, Leon, and August Meier, eds. *Black Leaders of the Nineteenth Century.* Urbana: University of Illinois Press, 1988.

Lopez, Alfred. "Meaningful Paradox: The 'Strange Genius' of Wilson Harris." *Conradiana* 28.3 (1996): 190–205.

López, Maria Milagros. "Hegemonic Regulation and the Text of Fear in Puerto Rico: Toward a Restructuring of Common Sense." Rabasa, Sanjinés, and Carr 95–112.

Lubiano, Wahneema. "Black Nationalism: Literary Critical Production and the Creation of a Non-State Romanticized Subject." Unpublished manuscript 1996.

Lukács, Georg. *The Meaning of Contemporary Realism.* Trans. John and Necke Mander. London: Merlin Press, 1963.

—. *Political Writings, 1919–1929.* London: NLB, 1972.

Maceguh, Stanley. *James Baldwin: A Critical Study.* New York: Third Press, 1973.

Mackey, Nathaniel, ed. *Wilson Harris. Callaloo* 18.1 (1995): 1–218.

MacKinnon, Catherine A. *Toward a Feminist Theory of the State.* Cambridge: Harvard University Press, 1989.

Madden, R. R. *A Twelvemonth's Residence in the West Indies, During the Transition from Slavery to Apprenticeship.* 2 vols. 1835. Westport, Conn.: Negro Universities Press, 1970.

Maes-Jelink, Hena. "Wilson Harris." King 139–51.

—. *Wilson Harris.* Boston: Twayne Publishers, 1982.

Manley, Michael. *Jamaica: Struggle in the Periphery.* Oxford: Third World Media Ltd./Writers and Readers Publishing Cooperative Society Ltd., 1982.

—. *The Politics of Change: A Jamaican Testament.* Rev. ed. Washington, D.C.: Howard University Press, 1990.

——. *The Poverty of Nations: Reflections on Underdevelopment and the World Economy*. New York: Pluto Press, 1991.

——. *Up the Down Escalator: Development and the International Economy: A Jamaican Case Study*. Washington, D.C.: Howard University Press, 1987.

——. *A Voice at the Workplace: Reflections on Colonialism and the Jamaican Worker*. Washington, D.C.: Howard University Press, 1991.

Manley, Michael, and Jamaicans. *Not for Sale; with a Relevant Supplement by C. L. R. James*. San Francisco: Editorial Consultants, n.d.

Marable, Manning. *Blackwater*. New York: Vantage, 1982.

——. *Negro Thought in America, 1880–1915: Racial Ideologies in the Age of Booker T. Washington*. Ann Arbor: University of Michigan Press, 1966.

——. *Race, Reform, and Rebellion: The Second Reconstruction in Black America, 1945–1990*. Jackson: University Press of Mississippi, 1991.

Martin, Tony. "Marcus Garvey, the Caribbean, and the Struggle for Black Jamaican Nationhood." Beckles and Shepherd 359–69.

Marx, Karl. *On Colonialism*. Moscow: Progressive Publishers, 1959.

Mathurin, Lucille. *The Rebel Woman in the British West Indies during Slavery*. Kingston, Jamaica: African-Caribbean Publications, 1990.

McCann, Sean. " 'Bonds of Brotherhood': Pauline Hopkins and the Work of Melodrama." *ELH* 64.3 (1997): 789–822.

McDowell, Deborah, and Arnold Rampersad, eds. *Slavery and the Literary Imagination*. Baltimore: Johns Hopkins University Press, 1989.

McIntyre, Charsee C. L. *Criminalizing a Race: Free Blacks during Slavery*. Queens, N.Y.: Kayode Publications, 1993.

McLaren, Angus. *The Trials of Masculinity: Policing Sexual Boundaries, 1870–1930*. Chicago: University of Chicago Press, 1999.

McWatt, Mark. "The Madonna/Whore: Womb of Possibilities (the Early Novels)." Gilkes 31–44.

Meeks, Brian, and Folke Lindahl, eds. *New Caribbean Thought: A Reader*. Mona, Jamaica: University of the West Indies, 2001.

Meese, Elizabeth, and Alice Parker, eds. *The Difference Within: Feminism and Critical Theory*. Amsterdam: John Benjamins Publishing Company, 1989.

Meier, August. "Booker T. Washington and the Negro Press." *Journal of Negro History* 38 (January 1953): 67–90.

Meier, August, Eliott Rudwick, and John Bracey Jr., eds. *Black Protest in the Sixties: Articles from the* New York Times. New York: Markus Wiener Publishing, 1991.

Mellor, Roy E. H. *Nation, State, and Territory: A Political Geography*. London: Routledge, 1989.

Mendes, Alfred. *Black Fauns*. 1935. London: New Beacon Books, 1984.

——. *Pitch Lake*. 1934. London: New Beacon Books, 1980.

Mercer, Kobena, and Isaac Julien. "Race, Sexual Politics, and Black Masculinity: A Dossier." Chapman and Rutherford 97–164.

Midgley, James. *Social Development: The Development Perspective in Social Welfare*. London: Sage Publications, 1995.

Mies, Maria. *Patriarchy and Accumulation on a World Scale: Women in the International Division of Labour*. London: Zed Books, 1986.

Mies, Maria, Veronika Bennholdt-Thomsen, and Claudia von Werlhof. *Women: The Last Colony*. London: Zed Books, 1988.

Miller, Floyd J. Introduction. *Blake*. By Martin R. Delany.

——. *The Search for a Black Nationality: Black Emigration and Colonization, 1787–1863*. Urbana: University of Illinois Press, 1975.

Millette, James. "The Wage Problem in Trinidad and Tobago 1838–1938." Brereton and Yelvington 55–76.

Mittelhölzer, Edgar. *A Morning at the Office, a Novel*. London: Hogarth Press, 1950.

Mongia, Padmini, ed. *Contemporary Postcolonial Theory: A Reader.* London: Arnold, 1997.

Mohammed, Patricia. "'But Most of All Mi Love Mi Browning': The Emergence of the Mulatto Woman as the Desired in Eighteenth and Nineteenth Century Jamaica." Stevens 18–37.

———. "Rethinking Caribbean Difference." *Feminist Review* 59 (summer 1998): 1–254.

Mohammed, Patricia, and Catherine Shepherd, eds. *Gender in Caribbean Development.* Mona, Jamaica: University of the West Indies Women and Development Studies Project, 1988.

Mohanty, Chandra Talpade. "Under Western Eyes: Feminist Scholarship and Colonial Discourses." Mongia 172–97.

Mohanty, Chandra Talpade, Ann Russo, and Lourdes Torres, eds. *Third World Women and the Politics of Feminism.* Bloomington: Indiana University Press, 1991.

Moitt, Bernard. "Women, Work, and Resistance in the French Caribbean during Slavery, 1700–1848." Shepherd, Brereton, and Bailey 155–75.

Momsen, Janet, ed. *Women and Change in the Caribbean.* Kingston, Jamaica: Ian Randle; Bloomington: Indiana University Press; London: James Currey, 1993.

———. *Women and Development in the Third World.* London: Routledge, 1991.

Monteith, Archibald John. "Archibald John Monteith: Native Helper and Assistant in the Jamaica Mission at New Carmel, 1853." *Callaloo* 13.1 (winter 1990): 102–14.

Moore, Dennison. *Origins and Development of Racial Ideology in Trinidad: The Black View of the East Indian.* Ontario, Canada: NYCAN International, 1995.

Moser, Caroline O. N. *Gender Planning and Development: Theory, Practice, and Training.* New York: Routledge, 1993.

Moser, Caroline, and Jeremy Holland. *Urban Poverty and Violence in Jamaica.* Washington, D.C.: World Bank, 1997.

Moses, Wilson Jeremiah. *Afrotopia: The Roots of African American Popular History.* Cambridge: Cambridge University Press, 1998.

———. *Classical Black Nationalism: From the American Revolution to Marcus Garvey.* New York: New York University Press, 1996.

———. *The Golden Age of Black Nationalism, 1850–1925.* New York: Oxford University Press, 1978.

———. *The Wings of Ethiopia: Studies in African-American Life and Letters.* Ames: Iowa State University Press, 1990.

Mosley, Walter, Manthia Diawara, Clyde Taylor, and Regina Austin, eds. *Black Genius: African American Solutions to African American Problems.* New York: W. W. Norton, 1999.

Moynihan, Patrick. *The Negro Family: The Case for National Action.* Washington, D.C.: Government Printing Office, 1965.

Munro, Ian, and Reinhard Sander, eds. *Kas-Kas: Interviews with Three Caribbean Writers in Texas: George Lamming, C. L. R. James, Wilson Harris.* Austin: African and Afro-American Research Institute, University of Texas at Austin, 1972.

Nash, Gerlad D., ed. *Issues in American Economic History.* 2nd ed. Boston: D. C. Heath, 1972.

Nash, June, and María Patricia Fernández-Kelly, eds. *Women, Men, and the International Division of Labor.* Albany: State University of New York Press, 1983.

Nash, June, and Helen Safa, eds. *Women and Change in Latin America.* Boston: Bergin and Garvey Publishers, 1985.

Nelson, Cary, and Lawrence Grossberg, eds. *Marxism and the Interpretation of Culture.* Urbana: University of Illinois Press, 1988.

Nelson, Emmanuel S. "James Baldwin's Vision of Otherness and Community." *MELUS* 10.2 (1983): 27–31. Rpt. in Standley and Burt 121–25.

Nettleford, Rex. *Inward Stretch, Outward Reach: A Voice from the Caribbean.* London: Macmillan Caribbean, 1993.

Newton, Huey P., with the assistance of J. Herman Blake. *Revolutionary Suicide.* New York: Harcourt Brace Jovanovich, 1973.

Newton, Michael. *Bitter Grain: Huey Newton and the Black Panther Party.* Los Angeles: Holloway House Publishing Company, 1991.

Northrup, Solomon. *The Narrative of Solomon Northrup.* 1853. Baton Rouge: Louisiana State University Press, 1968.

Norwood, Richard. *The Journal of Richard Norwood, Surveyor of Bermuda.* New York: Scholars Facsimile and Reprints, 1945.

Nugent, Lady Maria. *Lady Nugent's Journal of her Residence in Jamaica from 1810 to 1805.* Rev. ed. Ed. Philip Wright. Kingston, Jamaica: Institute of Jamaica, 1966.

Ogunleye, Tolagbe. "Dr. Martin Robinson Delany, Nineteenth-Century Africana Womanist. Reflections on His Avant-Garde Politics Concerning Gender, Colorism, and Nation-Building." *Journal of Black Studies* 28.5 (May 1998): 628–49.

Ohmae, Kenichi. *The Borderless World: Power and Strategy in the Interlinked Economy.* New York: HarperPerennial, 1991.

——. *The End of the Nation-State: The Rise of Global Economies.* New York: Free Press, 1996.

Okpaluba, Chuks. *The Evolution of Labour Relations Legislation in Trinidad and Tobago.* St. Augustine, Trinidad: ISER, 1980.

Ollmann, Bertell, and Jonathan Birnbaum. *The United States Constitution: Two Hundred Years of Anti-Federalist, Abolitionist, Feminist, Muckraking, Progressive, and Especially Socialist Criticism.* New York: New York University Press, 1990.

Olney, James. "The Founding Fathers—Frederick Douglass and Booker T. Washington." McDowell and Rampersad 1–24.

Otten, Thomas J. "Pauline Hopkins and the Hidden Self of Race." *ELH* 59 (1992): 227–56.

Painter, Nell Irvin. "Martin Delany: Elitism and Black Nationalism." Litwack and Meier 149–71.

Pandey, Gyanendra. "Voices from the Edge: The Struggle to Write Subaltern Studies." *Ethnos* 60.3–4 (1995): 223–42.

Pantin, Raoul. *Black Power Day: The 1970 February Revolution, a Reporter's Story.* Santa Cruz, Trinidad: Hatuey Productions, 1990.

Parker, Seymor, and Robert J. Kleiner. "Social and Psychological Dimensions of the Family Role Performance of the Negro Male." *Journal of Marriage and Family* (August 1969): 500–6.

Patterson, Orlando. *Slavery and Social Death.* Cambridge: Harvard University Press, 1982.

Payer, Cheryl. *The World Bank: A Critical Analysis.* New York: Monthly Review Press, 1982.

Peake, Linda. "The Development and Role of Women's Political Organizations in Guyana." Momsen 109–31.

Pearse, Andrew. "Carnival in Nineteenth-Century Trinidad." *Caribbean Quarterly* 4.3–4 (1956): 175–93.

Pennington, J. W. C. *The Fugitive Blacksmith; or, Events in the History of James W. C. Pennington.* Bontemps 193–267.

Peterson, Carla. *Doers of the Word: African-American Women Reformers in the North, 1830–1879.* New York: Oxford University Press, 1995.

Philippe, J. B. *Free Mulatto.* 1824. Port of Spain, Trinidad: Paria Publishing, 1987.

Phillips, Glenn O., and Talbert O. Shaw, eds. *The Caribbean Basin Initiative: Genuine or Deceptive? An Early Assessment.* Baltimore: Morgan State University Press, 1987.

Poe, Richard. *Black Spark, White Fire: Did African Explorers Civilize Ancient Europe?* New York: Prima Publishing, 1998.

Powell, Dorian, Eleanor Wint, Erna Brodber, and Versada Campbell. *Street Foods of Kingston.* Kingston, Jamaica: Institute of Social and Economic Research, University of the West Indies, 1990.

Powell, Linda C. "Black Macho and Black Feminism." B. Smith 283–92.

Powell, Patricia. *A Small Gathering of Bones.* London: Heinemann, 1994.

Power, Sarah. "Freezone Women Assess the Freezone Report." *Sistren* 12.1 (1990): 8–12.

Pratt, Louis H. *James Baldwin.* Boston: Twayne Publishers, 1978.

Premdas, Ralph. "Ethnic Conflict and Development: The Case of Guyana." Geneva: United Nations Research Institute for Social Development, 1992.

———. "Public Policy and Ethnic Conflict." Management of Social Transformations Clearing-house, Discussion Paper no. 12. New York: UNESCO, 1997.

Price, Richard, and Sally Price. *Alabi's World*. Baltimore: Johns Hopkins University Press, 1990.

———. *Equatoria*. New York: Routledge, 1992.

Prince, Mary. *History of Mary Prince, a West Indian Slave*. 1831. Gates, *Six Women's Slave Narratives* 1–40.

Prince, Nancy. *The Life and Travels of Nancy Prince*. 2nd ed. New York: Oxford University Press, 1988.

Pryse, Marjorie, and Hortense Spillers, eds. *Conjuring: Black Women, Fiction, and Literary Tradition*. Bloomington: Indiana University Press, 1985.

Puzo, Mario. "His Cardboard Lovers." *New York Times Book Review* 23 (June 1968): 5, 34. Rpt. in Standley and Burt 155–58.

Quarles, Benjamin. Introduction. *Condition, Elevation, and Destiny*. By Martin R. Delany.

Ramchand, Kenneth. *An Introduction to the Study of West Indian Literature*. Hong Kong: Nelson Caribbean, 1980.

———. *The West Indian Novel and Its Background*. London: Heinemann, 1983.

Rabassa, José, Javier Sanjinés, and Robert Carr, eds. *Subaltern Studies in the Americas*. Special issue of *dispositio/n* 19.46 (1994): iii–296.

Rhedock, Rhoda. "Contestations over National Culture in Trinidad and Tobago: Consider-ations of Ethnicity, Class and Gender." Barrow 414–35.

———. "Women's Organizations and the Movements in the Commonwealth Caribbean: The Response to Global Economic Crisis in the 1980s." Mohammed, *Rethinking Caribbean Difference* 57–73.

Rhys, Jean. *Wide Sargasso Sea*. New York: Norton, 1966.

Rivera, Marcia. "Women in the Caribbean Underground Economy." Girvan and Beckford 161–70.

Robinson, Eugene. "Worldwide Migration Nears Crisis: Politics, Economics Cited in U.N. Study." *Washington Post* July 7, 1993: A1, A24.

Robinson, Randall. "Perfecting Our Democracy for the Benefit of the Black World." Mosley et al. 294–311.

Rodríguez, Ileana. *House/Garden/Nation: Representations of Space, Ethnicity, and Gender in Transitional Post-Colonial Literatures by Women*. Durham: Duke University Press, 1994.

———, ed. *The Latin American Subaltern Studies Reader*. Durham: Duke University Press, 2001.

———. "Rethinking the Subaltern: Patterns and Places of Subalternity in the New Millen-nium." *dispositio/n* 19.46 (1996): 13–25.

———. "Tenderness: A Mediator of Identity and Gender Construction in Politics." *Modern Fiction Studies* 44.1 (spring 1998): 240–49.

———. *Women, Guerrillas, and Love: Understanding War in Central America*. Minneapolis: University of Minnesota Press, 1996.

Rodríguez, Ileana, and Marc Zimmerman, eds. *Process of Unity in Caribbean Society: Ide-ologies and Literature*. Minneapolis: Institute for the Study of Ideologies and Litera-tures, 1983.

Rotundo, E. Anthony. *American Manhood: Transformations in Masculinity from the Revolu-tion to the Modern Era*. New York: Basic Books, 1994.

Ryan, Selwyn. "The Caribbean State in the Twenty-first Century." *Caribbean Affairs* 3.4 (1990): 4–12.

———. *The Jhandi and the Cross: The Clash of Cultures in Post-Creole Trinidad and Tobago*. Trinidad: ISES, 1999.

—. *Race and Nationalism in Trinidad and Tobago: A Study of Decolonization in a Multiracial Society*. Kingston, Jamaica: Institute of Social and Economic Research, University of the West Indies, 1972.

—, ed. *Social and Occupational Stratification in Contemporary Trinidad and Tobago*. St. Augustine, Trinidad: ISER, 1991.

Safa, Helen. "Runaway Shops and Female Employment: The Search for Cheap Labor." *Signs* 7 (winter 1981): 418–33.

Sagar, Aparajita. "AIDS and the Question of Memory: Patricia Powell's *A Small Gathering of Bones*." *Small Axe* (March 2000): 28–43.

Samaroo, Brinsley. "The Trinidad Disturbances of 1917–20: Precursor to 1937." R. Thomas 21–56.

Sander, Reinhard. *The Trinidad Awakening: West Indian Literature of the Nineteen Thirties*. Westport, Conn.: Greenwood Press, 1988.

Sanjínes, Javier. "Entre la cruz y la tribuna del pueblo: 'Relocalización' y nuevos movimientos populare en Bolivia." Paper presented at the First Latin American Subaltern Studies Conference, George Mason University, April 23–26, 1992.

Sathyamurthy, T. V. *Nationalism in the Contemporary World: Political and Sociological Perspectives*. London: Frances Pinter/Allaheld, Osmun Publishers, 1983.

Schaefer, U. "'Both/And' and/or 'Either/Or': Syncretism and Imagination in the Novels of Wilson Harris and Bessie Head." *Cross Cultures* 26 (1996): 41–48.

Schulz, David A. *Coming Up Black: Patterns of Ghetto Socialization*. Englewood Cliffs, N.J.: Prentice Hall, 1969.

Schwarz, Henry. "Provocations Towards a Theory of Third World Literature." *Mississippi Review* 49/50 17.1–2 (1989): 177–201.

Scott, Catherine V. *Gender and Development: Rethinking Modernization and Dependency Theory*. Boulder: Lynn Rienner Publishers, 1995.

Seacole, Mary. *Wonderful Adventures of Mrs. Seacole in Many Lands*. Ed. Ziggi Alexander and Audrey Dewjee. Bristol: Falling Wall Press, 1984.

Seale, Bobby. *Seize the Time: The Story of the Black Panther Party and Huey P. Newton*. 1970. Baltimore: Black Classic Press, 1991.

Sealy, Clifford. "*Crown Jewel*: A Note on Ralph de Boissière." *Voices* 2–3 (March 1973): 1–3.

Searwar, L. *Co-Op Republic: Guyana 1970. A Study of Aspects of Our Way of Life*. Georgetown, Guyana: n.p., 1970.

Sen, Gita. "Women Workers and the Green Revolution." Benería 29–64.

Shand, Phyllis Allfrey. *The Orchid House*. Washington, D.C.: Three Continents Press, 1985.

Shaw, Gregory. "The Novelist as Shaman: Art and Dialectic in the Work of Wilson Harris." Gilkes 141–51.

Shepherd, Verene, Bridget Brereton, and Barbara Bailey, eds. *Engendering History: Caribbean Women in Historical Perspective*. London: James Currey Publishers; Kingston: Ian Randle Publishers, 1995.

Simmons, Ron. "Some Thoughts on the Challenges Facing Black Gay Intellectuals." Hemphill 211–28.

Sistren, with Honor Ford-Smith. *Lionheart Gal: Life Stories of Jamaican Women*. London: Women's Press, 1986.

Skinner, Elliott P. "The Impact of West Indian Emancipation on Afro-Americans: Emigrate or Struggle for Liberty in the USA." Ifill 64–88.

Smith, Anna Deveare. "Public Lives, Private Selves: Toward an Open Conversation." Mosley et al. 272–90.

Smith, Anthony D. *The Ethnic Origins of Nations*. Oxford: Basil Blackwell, 1987.

—. *Theories of Nationalism*. New York: Harper and Row, 1972.

Smith, Barbara, ed. *Home Girls: A Black Feminist Anthology*. New York: Kitchen Table Press, 1983.

Smith, Venture. *A Narrative of the Life and Adventures of Venture, a Native of Africa; but*

*Resident about Sixty Years in the United States of America. Related by Himself.* New London, Conn.: C. Holt, 1798.

Snitow, Ann, Christine Stansell, and Sharon Thompson, eds. *Powers of Desire: The Politics of Sexuality.* New York: Monthly Review Press, 1983.

Snyder, Louis L. *Global Mini-Nationalisms: Autonomy or Independence?* Westport, Conn.: Greenwood Press, 1982.

Sommer, Doris. *Foundational Fictions: The National Romances of Latin America.* Berkeley: University of California Press, 1991.

——. "Irresistible Romance: The Foundational Fictions of Latin America." Bhabha 71–98.

Sowell, Thomas. *The Economics and Politics of Race: An International Perspective.* New York: Morrow, 1983.

——, ed. *Essays and Data on American Ethnic Groups.* Washington, D.C.: Urban Institute, 1978.

——. *Ethnic America.* New York: Basic Books, 1981.

Spillers, Hortense, ed. *Comparative American Identities: Race, Sex, and Nationality in the Modern Text.* New York: Routledge, 1991.

——. "Introduction: Who Cuts the Border? Some Readings on 'America.' " Spillers 1–25.

——. "Mama's Baby, Papa's Maybe." *Diacritics* (summer 1987): 65–81.

——. "Notes on an Alternative Model–Neither / Nor." Meese and Parker 165–87.

Spivak, Gayatri Chakravorty. *A Critique of Postcolonial Reason: Toward a History of the Vanishing Present.* Cambridge: Harvard University Press, 1999.

——. "Scattered Speculations on the Question of Value." *In Other Worlds: Essays in Cultural Politics.* New York: Methuen, 1987.

Standley, Fred, and Nancy Standley. *James Baldwin: A Reference Guide.* Boston: G. K. Hall, 1980.

Standley, Fred, and Nancy V. Burt. *Critical Essays on James Baldwin.* Boston: G. K. Hall, 1988.

Steinberg, Stephen. *The Ethnic Myth.* Boston: Beacon Press, 1981.

Stephens, Evelyn Huber, and John D. Stephens. *Democratic Socialism in Jamaica: The Political Movement and the Social Transformation in Dependent Capitalism.* Princeton: Princeton University Press, 1986.

Stern, Sol. "The Call of the Black Panthers." *New York Times Magazine* August 6, 1967. Rpt. in Meier, Rudwick, and Bracey Jr. 230.

Stevens, Jacquelin, ed. *Differentiating Caribbean Womanhood.* Kingston, Jamaica: Centre for Gender and Development Studies, 2000.

Stewart, Maria. *Productions of Mrs. Maria Stewart, presented to the First African Baptist Church and Society of the City of Boston.* 1835. Rpt. in Gates, *Spiritual Narratives.*

Stowe, Harriet Beecher. *Uncle Tom's Cabin; or, Life among the Lowly.* 1852. New York: Viking Press, 1982.

Stuckey, Sterling, ed. *The Ideological Origins of Black Nationalism.* Boston: Beacon Press, 1972.

——. *Slave Culture: Nationalist Theory and the Foundations of Black America.* New York: Oxford University Press, 1987.

Sundquist, Eric J., ed. *New Literary and Historical Essays on Frederick Douglass.* New York: Cambridge University Press, 1990.

——. *To Wake the Nations: Race in the Making of American Literature.* Cambridge: Harvard University Press, 1993.

Sylvander, Carolyn Wedin. *James Baldwin.* New York: Frederick Ungar Publishing, 1980.

Tate, Claudia. "Pauline Hopkins: Our Literary Foremother." Pryse and Spillers 53–66.

Taylor, Paul. "Getting Back to Business in South Africa: After a Decade of Disinvestment, Digital Equipment and Others Cautiously Test the Waters." *Washington Post* July 4, 1993: H1, H5.

Thomas, Clive Y. *The Poor and the Powerless: Economic Policy and Change in the Caribbean.* New York: Monthly Review Press, 1988.

Thomas, Elean. "Lionhearted Women: The Sistren Theatre Collective." *Race and Class* 28.3 (winter 1987): 66–72.

Thomas, J. J. *Froudacity: West Indian Fables by James Anthony Froude, Explained by J. J. Thomas, Author of "Creole Grammar."* 1889. London: New Beacon Books, 1969.

——. *The Theory and Practice of Creole Grammar (Patois).* 1869. London: New Beacon Books, 1969.

Thomas, Roy, ed. *The Trinidad Labour Riots of 1937: Perspectives Fifty Years Later.* St. Augustine, Trinidad: University of the West Indies Extra-Mural Studies Unit, 1987.

Toledano, Ralph de. *J. Edgar Hoover: The Man in His Time.* New Rochelle, N.Y.: Arlington House, 1973.

Traub, James. "You Can Get It If You Really Want." *Harpers* 264 (1981): 27–31.

Turner, Nat. *The Confessions of Nat Turner, the Leader of the Late Insurrection in Southhampton, VA., as fully and voluntarily made to Thomas R. Gray.* 1831. Rpt. in John Clarke 93–117.

Ullman, Victor. *Martin R. Delany: The Beginnings of Black Nationalism.* Boston: Beacon Press, 1971.

Ungar, Sanford. *FBI.* Boston: Little, Brown, 1976.

United Nations. *Human Development Report 1998. Consumption for Human Development.* New York: Human Development Report Office, 1998.

Urban, C. Stanley. "The Africanization of Cuba Scare." *Hispanic American Historical Review* 37.1 (February 1957): 29–45.

Van Sertina. *They Came before Columbus.* New York: Random House, 1976.

Visvanathan, Nalini, Lynn Duggan, and Laurie Nisonoff, eds. *The Women, Gender, and Development Reader.* London: Zed Books, 1997.

Walker, David. *Appeal to the Colored Citizens of World.* 1829. New York: Hill and Wang, 1965.

Wallace, Maurice. " 'Are We Men?': Prince Hall, Martin Delany, and the Masculine Ideal of Black Freemasonry, 1775–1865." *American Literary History* 9.3 (fall 1997) 396–424.

Wallace, Michelle. "Introduction: How I Saw It Then, How I See It Now." *Black Macho and the Myth of the Superwoman.* London: Verso, 1990.

Wallerstein, Immanuel. *Geopolitics and Geoculture: Essays on the Changing World-System.* Cambridge: Cambridge University Press, 1991.

Washington, Booker T. *Up from Slavery.* New York: Viking Penguin, 1986.

Watson, Michael, ed. *Contemporary Minority Nationalism.* London: Routledge, Chapman and Hall, 1990.

Webb, Barbara J. *Myth and History in Caribbean Fiction: Alejo Carpentier, Wilson Harris, and Edouard Glissant.* Amherst: University of Massachusetts Press, 1992.

Wedin Sylvander, Carolyn. *James Baldwin.* New York: Frederick Ungar, 1980.

West, Cornel. *Prophesy Deliverance! An Afro-American Revolutionary Christianity.* Louisville, Ky.: Westminster/John Knox, 1982.

——. *Race Matters.* Boston: Beacon Press, 1993.

Wienke, Chris. "Negotiating the Male Body: Men, Masculinity, and Cultural Ideals." *Journal of Men's Studies* 6.3 (spring 1998): 225–82.

Wilkins, Roy, and Ramsey Clarke. *Commission of Enquiry into the Black Panthers and the Police. Search and Destroy: A Report.* New York: Metropolitan Applied Research Center, 1973.

Wilkinson, Henry Campbell. *Bermuda from Sail to Steam.* 2 vols. London: Oxford University Press, 1973.

Williams, Catherine. "Mainstreaming Gender Analysis in the Development Planning Process." Leo-Rhynie et al. 56–75.

Williams, Colin H., ed. *National Separatism.* Vancouver: University of British Columbia Press, 1982.

Williams, James. *A Narrative of Events since the First of August, 1834 by James Williams, An Apprenticed Laborer in Jamaica.* 3rd ed. London: Aldine Chambers, 1837.

Williams, Robert F. *Negroes with Guns.* Ed. Marc Schleifer. 1962. Chicago: Third World Press, 1973.

Wilson, Harriet. *Our Nig; or Sketches from the Life of a Free Black, In a Two-Story White House, North. Showing the Slavery's Shadows Fall Even There.* 1859. New York: Vintage Books, 1983.

Wilson-Tagoe, Nana. *Historical Thought and Literary Representation in West Indian Literature.* Gainesville: University Press of Florida; Kingston: Jamaica: University Press of the West Indies; Oxford: James Currey, 1998.

Wiltshire-Brodber, Rosina. "Gender, Race and Class in the Caribbean." Mohammed and Shepherd 136–48.

Winston, Henry. *Strategy for a Black Agenda: A Critique of New Theories of Liberation in the United States and Africa.* New York: International Publishers, 1973.

X, Malcolm. *The Autobiography of Malcolm X.* As told to Alex Haley. New York: Random House, 1964.

Yelvington, Kevin A. *Producing Power: Ethnicity, Gender, and Class in a Caribbean Workplace.* Philadelphia: Temple University Press, 1995.

——, ed. *Trinidad Ethnicity.* Knoxville: University of Tennessee Press, 1993.

# INDEX

Sandanistas, 281, 286, 303; Somoza regime, 281

Sander, Reinhard, 21, 112

Seaga, Edward, 232, 239

Seale, Bobby, 9, 186, 190–198, 205, 210–216, 224, 265, 294; *Seize the Time*, 192, 193, 215, 265; "Who I Am," 215. *See also* Black Panthers

*Secret Ladder, The*, 151–158, 168, 176; Bryant, 158, 163, 165, 182–185, 304; Canje River, 158–160, 163, 167, 175; Carroll, 151; Catalena Perez, 152, 158, 162, 163, 166, 171–173, 177, 181–185, 304; Chiung, 171, 177, 178; Fenwick, 153, 157–184, 268; Jordan, 170–174, 178–182, 265, 268; Poseidon, 163–185, 281; Stoll, 172, 177; "The Day Readers," 166, 176; "The Night Readers," 166, 176, 177; "The Reading," 177; Weng, 170, 171, 177–180, 184. See also *Guyana Quartet*

September 11, 2001, 5

Shango, 141

Simmons, Roy, 191

Sistren Collective, 10, 15, 18–23, 225, 226, 229, 230, 234–247, 251, 262, 263, 270, 274–283, 289–294, 300, 304–307, 310–312; Orange Street fire, 239; *QPH*, 240; Queenie, 240

Smith, Adam, 274

Smith, Anna Deavere, 18

Sommer, Doris, 13

South America, 63, 65, 66

South Asia Subaltern Studies Group, 43, 44

South Carolina, 40

Soviet Union, 4, 225

Spain, 34

Spanish American War, 68

Spillers, Hortense, 17, 20, 58, 58, 190

Spivak, Gayatri, 272, 287, 302, 310

Stowe, Harriet Beecher, 32, 61

Stuckey, Sterling, 27–31, 50

Subaltern/subalternity 30–31, 41, 43–52, 63, 65, 112, 117, 121, 123, 124, 142–143, 144, 145, 149, 153–154, 158, 163, 166, 168–171, 180, 185, 225–269, 273, 274, 276, 277, 281, 283, 285, 290, 291, 293, 301, 303, 308, 309, 310

Sundquist, Eric, 27

Tenement yard, 239, 240, 261

Thomas, Elean, 236

Thomas, J.J., 107

Thompson, E.P., 5

TransAfrica, 274

Trinidad, 9, 19, 21, 106–133, 227, 269, 288, 308

*Trinidad* (magazine), 106, 256

Turner, Nat, 44–51

UNESCO, 156, 287

UN Human Development Report, 1998, 285

U.S. Congress, 285

U.S. Constitution, 13, 35–38, 40, 84, 157, 190, 202, 205, 206, 213, 214; Fourteenth Amendment, 84

Vesey, Denmark, 46, 47

Virginia, 39

Walker, David, 55, 63

Wallace, Michelle, 22, 191

Wallerstein, Immanuel, 6, 273, 308

War of Independence (U.S.), 44

Washington, Booker T., 69, 89, 100, 301

Washington, D.C., 32, 40, 41, 46, 73

Wells, Ida B., 69

West, Cornel, 10, 23, 270, 272, 278, 288, 297, 299, 301, 307–313; *Race Matters*, 278, 297, 307, 311

Whipper, William, 26

Williams, Eric, 111, 134, 145, 149

Williams, Robert F., 200

Witness for Peace, 302, 303

Women and Development Unit (UWI), 228

Woodson, Lewis, 26

Robert Carr is an HIV/AIDS management consultant
in the Caribbean.

Library of Congress Cataloging-in-Publication Data
Carr, Robert.
Black nationalism in the New world : reading the african-
american and west indian experience / by Robert Carr.
p. cm. — (Latin America otherwise)
Includes bibliographical references and index.
ISBN 0-8223-2982-4 (cloth : alk. paper)
ISBN 0-8223-2973-5 (pbk. : alk. paper)
1. Black nationalism—United States. 2. African Americans—
Race identity. 3. Black nationalism—West Indies. 4. Blacks—
Race identity—West Indies. 1. Title. 11. Series.
E185.625 .C357 2002   305.896'073—dc21   2002005497